REFRAMING PAQUIMÉ

Reframing Paquimé

Community Formation in Northwest Chihuahua

MICHAEL E. WHALEN *and*
PAUL E. MINNIS

THE UNIVERSITY OF
ARIZONA PRESS
TUCSON

The University of Arizona Press
www.uapress.arizona.edu

We respectfully acknowledge the University of Arizona is on the land and territories of Indigenous peoples. Today, Arizona is home to twenty-two federally recognized tribes, with Tucson being home to the O'odham and the Yaqui. Committed to diversity and inclusion, the University strives to build sustainable relationships with sovereign Native Nations and Indigenous communities through education offerings, partnerships, and community service.

© 2025 by The Arizona Board of Regents
All rights reserved. Published 2025

ISBN-13: 978-0-8165-5466-9 (hardcover)
ISBN-13: 978-0-8165-5467-6 (ebook)

Cover photo by Adriel Heisey
Typeset by Sara Thaxton in 10.5/14.5 Minion Pro with Baskerville Com

Publication of this book was made possible in part with funds from the George H. Odell Memorial Foundation, Department of Anthropology, The University of Tulsa.

Library of Congress Cataloging-in-Publication Data
Names: Whalen, Michael E., author. | Minnis, Paul E., author.
Title: Reframing Paquimé : community formation in northwest Chihuahua / Michael E. Whalen and Paul E. Minnis.
Description: Tucson : University of Arizona Press, 2025. | Includes bibliographical references and index.
Identifiers: LCCN 2024025377 (print) | LCCN 2024025378 (ebook) | ISBN 9780816554669 (hardcover) | ISBN 9780816554676 (ebook)
Subjects: LCSH: Casas Grandes culture. | Indians of Mexico—Mexico—Chihuahua (State)—Antiquities. | Land settlement patterns, Prehistoric—Mexico—Chihuahua (State) | Casas Grandes Site (Mexico) | Chihuahua (Mexico : State)—Antiquities.
Classification: LCC F1219.1.C3 W536 2025 (print) | LCC F1219.1.C3 (ebook) | DDC 972/.16—dc23/eng/20241216
LC record available at https://lccn.loc.gov/2024025377
LC ebook record available at https://lccn.loc.gov/2024025378

Printed in the United States of America
♾ This paper meets the requirements of ANSI/NISO Z39.48-1992 (Permanence of Paper).

Respectfully dedicated to Dr. Charles C. Di Peso
and his colleagues of the Joint Casas Grandes Expedition,
who got so much of this started

Contents

List of Illustrations	*xi*
Acknowledgments	*xvii*

1. Understanding Paquimé and Its Neighbors: Concepts, Progress, and Concerns — **3**

Terms and Concepts	4
The Site and the Region	*4*
When Was Paquimé?	*5*
What Was the Medio Period?	*6*
Estimating Settlement Occupational Histories	9
Evaluating Settlement Complexity and Function	9
The Small Site Problem	10

2. Settlement Patterns Reexamined — **12**

The Viejo Period	12
The Medio Period	14
Mound Height and Room Block Size	*18*
Mound Area and Room Block Size	*22*
Room Count	*26*
Artifact Density	*28*
Mound Grouping	*30*
Settlement Population Estimates	*33*
Regional Settlement Distribution	*36*
Post-Paquimé Occupations	36

3 The Inner Core Zone Excavation Project: Sites and Chronology — **38**

Site Selection: The Large Sites	38
Site 315	*40*
Site 565	*41*

Site Selection: The Small Sites	41
Site 290	46
Site 299A	46
Site 321	49
Site 355	49
Chronologies of the Inner Core Sites	52
Site 315	54
Site 565	56
Site 290	56
Site 299A	59
Site 321	59
Site 355	60
Occupational Histories of the Core Zone Sites	61

4	**The Architecture of the Core Zone**	**63**
	Viejo Period Pit Structures	63
	Early Surface Room Blocks	67
	Convento	68
	Paquimé	69
	Los Reyes No. 2	70
	Area Z, Site 565	72
	ROOM 30	74
	ROOM 31	75
	ROOM 32	78
	ROOM 33	78
	ROOM 34	78
	ROOM 35	79
	The Area Z Chronology	79
	The Casas Grandes Architectural Tradition	82
	Wall Thickness	82
	Room Size	85
	Room Shape	87
	Intramural Human Burials	88
	Intramural Architectural Elements	91
	DOORWAYS	91
	WALL NICHES	93
	ADOBE CONSTRUCTIONS	94
	POST COLLARS	96
	FIRE FEATURES	98
	Room Function at Paquimé	106
	Room Function at Neighboring Sites	108

The End of the Casas Grandes Architectural Tradition | 113
   Site 315 | *113*
   Site 355 | *118*
   Site 321 | *121*
   Site 290 | *121*
Concluding Thoughts | 125

5. **Medio Period Ceramics of the Core Zone** | **126**

The Distribution of Ceramic Wares in the Core Zone | 126
Ceramic Type Distributions in the Core Zone | 128
Medio Period Ceramics and Chronology | 131
The Post-Paquimé Ceramic Assemblage | 136
Analyzing Ceramic Vessels for Form and Function | 137
   Determination of Vessel Form from Sherds | *138*
   Vessel Volume Calculated from Rim Diameters | *141*
   Vessel Diameter Estimated from Body Sherds | *148*
   Vessel Function | *151*
      EXTERIOR SOOT | 152
      INTERIOR RESIDUES | 156
      INTERIOR SURFACE EROSION | 156
Concluding Thoughts | 159

6. **Medio Period Lithics of the Core Zone** | **162**

Raw Materials for Flaking and Grinding | 162
Previous Outer Core Chipped Stone Studies | 164
New Inner Core Chipped Stone Studies | 165
   Chipped Stone Frequencies | *165*
   Raw Materials | *166*
   Assemblage Composition | *166*
   Cores | *168*
   Flakes | *170*
      RAW MATERIALS | 171
      FLAKE SIZES | 173
      OTHER FLAKE ATTRIBUTES | 175
Chipped Stone Tool Analyses | 180
Ground Stone Implements on Core Zone Sites | 183
   Raw Materials | *186*
   Manos | *188*
   Metates | *190*
   Other Ground Stone Implements | *191*
Stone Tool Use in Core Zone Settlements | 193

Contents

7. Exotic and Ritual Items and Facilities in the Core Zone 193
- Shell 197
- Macaws 202
- Copper 204
- Turquoise, Crystal, and Other Minerals 207
- Concluding Thoughts 208

8. Floral and Faunal Remains: Domestic and Community Food Economy and Ecology 210
- Plant Remains 211
  - *Propagules for Food* 212
    - LITTLE BARLEY 216
    - CHILE 217
    - CACAO OR YAUPON HOLLY 218
  - *Differential Plant Use in the Core Zone* 219
  - *Wood* 221
  - *Anthropogenic Ecology of Plant Populations* 224
    - A REGIONAL COMPARISON 225
- Faunal Remains 225
  - *Animals in Domestic and Community Food Economies* 225
  - *Turkeys* 229
    - TURKEY BREEDING AND TRADING AT PAQUIMÉ 230
    - USES OF TURKEYS IN THE CASAS GRANDES AREA 233
  - *Anthropogenic Ecology of Animal Populations* 234
- Concluding Thoughts 235

9. Paquimé and Its Neighbors: Community Formation and Fragmentation 238
- Site Occupational Histories 239
- The Organization of the Core Zone 245
  - *The Relative Richness of Core Zone Settlements* 246
- The Medio Period, Reconsidered 251
  - *An Early Medio Developmental Scenario* 254
  - *A Late Medio Developmental Scenario* 255
- The Paquimé Community 257
  - *Relations Between Paquimé and Its Neighbors* 259
- The End of Paquimé and the Medio Period 262
- Concluding Thoughts 268

References Cited 271
Index 287

Illustrations

Figures

2.1	Histograms of mound height, by zone	20
2.2	Mound area histograms, by zone	23
2.3	Small mound area histograms, by zone	24
2.4	Regression of room count on excavated area for the Inner and Outer Core Zones	27
2.5	Single room block size histograms, by zone	32
3.1	The Site 315 mound and excavation areas	40
3.2	Excavated rooms at Site 315	42
3.3	The Site 565 mound and excavation areas	43
3.4	Excavated rooms at Site 565	44
3.5	The Inner Core Zone and Middle Zone small site size histograms	45
3.6	The Site 290 mound on the heavily eroded piedmont slope	47
3.7	Excavated rooms at Site 290	47
3.8	The Site 299A mound and test trenches	48
3.9	The oven at Site 299A	49
3.10	The Site 321 mound and excavation area	50
3.11	Excavated rooms at Site 321	50
3.12	The Site 355 mound and the stone arc built upslope from it	51
3.13	Excavated rooms at Site 355	52
3.14	Probability distribution for sub-subfloor radiocarbon dates from Site 315	56
3.15	Summed probability distribution for floor-level radiocarbon dates from Site 315	56
3.16	Summed probability distribution for subfloor dates from Area Z, Site 565	57
3.17	Summed probability distribution for floor-level radiocarbon dates from Area Z, Site 565	57
3.18	Summed probability distribution for floor dates, Site 290	58
3.19	Summed probability distribution for radiocarbon dates from Site 321	59

3.20	Summed probability distribution for radiocarbon dates from Site 355	60
3.21	Estimated occupation spans of the Core Zone sites	61
3.22	Summed probability distribution for Outer Core Zone small Sites 231 and 317	62
4.1	Large pit structures from Core Zone Sites 204, 315, and 317	64
4.2	A large pit house and associated activity area on Site 315	65
4.3	Small pit structures on Core Zone Sites 204 and 565	66
4.4	Viejo period jacal surface structures from the Convento site of the Inner Core Zone	69
4.5	Examples of jacal surface structures from Paquimé	70
4.6	Jacal surface structures at Los Reyes No. 2 site	71
4.7	The Site 565 mound and the location of the excavation areas	73
4.8	Excavated rooms in Area Z, Site 565	73
4.9	Jacal structures from Area Z, Site 565	76
4.10	Architectural succession at Site 565	80
4.11	Histogram of jacal room floor areas	82
4.12	Adobe wall construction in the Casas Grandes Architectural Tradition at Sites 204 and 315	83
4.13	Wall thickness histograms for Core Zone Sites 315, 565, and 204	84
4.14	Alcoves at Inner Core Zone Sites 565 and 315	89
4.15	Doorways at Core Zone Site 315	92
4.16	Wall niches at Inner Core Site 315	94
4.17	Adobe steps and platforms from Inner Core Site 565	95
4.18	Adobe columns and their remodeling at Site 315	96
4.19	Post collars in Room 70 and Room 5 at Site 315	97
4.20	Intramural fire pits from Site 565	99
4.21	Platform hearths from neighboring sites	100
4.22	Special purpose Rooms 7/8 at Site 315	109
4.23	Special purpose Room 70 at Site 315	111
4.24	Subterranean Room 1 at Site 290	112
4.25	Small shallow hemispherical fire pits in Rooms 7 and 8	114
4.26	Pit oven in Room 7 at Site 315	115
4.27	Ritual assemblage from the floor of Room 7, Site 315	116
4.28	Remodeling at Inner Core Zone small Site 355	119
4.29	Original adobe walls and stones later piled atop them at Site 321	120
4.30	Walls and floors of CGAT Type 1 in Rooms 7 and 12 at Site 290	122
4.31	Hemispherical floor hearths of CGAT Type 1 in Room 10 at Site 290	122
4.32	Walls of PCGAT Type 2 construction in Rooms 5 and 8 at Site 290	123
4.33	Fire feature succession in Room 7 at Site 290	124
5.1	Polychrome painting styles	130
5.2	Early and Late Medio ceramic assemblages	132
5.3	Brown jar and bowl volumes on Core Zone sites	143
5.4	Brown jar volumes on small Inner Core sites	144

5.5	Textured jar volumes, by Inner Core site size class	145
5.6	Red-slipped jar volumes, by Inner Core site size class	146
5.7	Black jar volumes on large Core Zone sites	147
5.8	Polychrome jar volumes on Inner Core sites	147
5.9	Diameter estimates from vessels of known sizes	149
5.10	Estimated diameters of Brown body sherds on Core Zone sites, by size class	150
5.11	Estimated diameters of sooted vessels on Core Zone sites	155
6.1	Chert projectile points from Inner Core sites	181
6.2	Obsidian projectile points from Inner Core sites	181
6.3	Curated early points found on Inner Core Sites 315 and 565	182
6.4	Effigies and birdcage door stones from Inner Core Site 315	187
6.5	A vesicular basalt mano blank from Inner Core Site 315	189
6.6	Small manos from Inner Core Sites 315 and 565	189
6.7	Shaped and unshaped metates from Inner Core Site 315	190
6.8	Stone bowls and pestles from Inner Core Sites 315, 355, and 565	192
7.1	Shell ornaments from Core Zone Sites 315 and 565	198
7.2	Freshwater shell from Inner Core Site 565	201
7.3	Macaw cage door stones from Inner Core Site 315	205
7.4	Copper pendant and ore fragments from Inner Core Site 315	206
7.5	Minerals from Core Zone Sites 315 and 355	208
8.1	Burned maize cobbs in a hearth on Site 315	215
9.1	Calibrated date frequency histograms for large Core Zone sites	240
9.2	Date frequency histograms for small Core Zone sites	242
9.3	Bar chart of Core Zone richness scores	251

Maps

1.1	The Casas Grandes area and Paquimé	4
2.1	Sites of the Casas Grandes area, as published in 1974	16
2.2	The Inner, Middle, and Outer survey zones	17
3.1	Large and small sites of the Inner Core Zone	39

Tables

2.1	Mound height class frequencies in the Core and Middle Zones	21
2.2	Room block mound areas, by zone	24
2.3	Mound size class frequencies, by zone	24
2.4	Mound size class densities, by survey zone	25
2.5	Mound size class descriptive statistics	25
2.6	Ceramic densities on mounds, by size class and zone	28
2.7	Percentage of mounds with imported sherds in surface collections, by mound size class	29
2.8	Room blocks per settlement, by zone	30
2.9	Densities of settlements per square kilometer, by zone	31

2.10	Descriptive statistics for single room block mounds, by zone	33
3.1	Radiocarbon dates from Inner Core sites	53
3.2	Radiocarbon dates from Site 315	55
3.3	Radiocarbon dates from Areas A and Z, Site 565	55
3.4	Radiocarbon dates from Site 290	58
3.5	Radiocarbon dates from Site 321	59
3.6	Radiocarbon dates from Site 355	60
4.1	Area Z exterior wall dimensions	75
4.2	The ceramic inventory of Area Z, Site 565	81
4.3	Room floor area statistics for Core Zone sites	86
4.4	Doorway characteristics in the Core Zone	93
4.5	Fire feature type frequencies at Inner Core sites	101
4.6	Hemispherical hearth mean sizes, in liters	101
4.7	Platform hearth types and frequencies at Core Zone sites	103
4.8	Ratios of platform to basin hearths at Core Zone sites	103
4.9	Platform hearth descriptive statistics for Paquimé and its Core Zone neighbors	103
5.1	Ceramic ware frequencies on large and small Core Zone sites	127
5.2	Small site ceramic type diversity scores	129
5.3	Polychrome frequencies in Room 50, Area B, Site 315	134
5.4	Jar and bowl rim sherd characteristics in the Core Zone, by ware group	140
5.5	Frequencies of utilitarian jar and bowl rims by site size class and Core Zone position	141
5.6	Frequencies of body sherd diameter groups on large sites, by Core Zone location	151
5.7	Frequencies of exterior soot on Core Zone body sherds	153
5.8	Distributions of diameter estimates for body sherds with and without soot	154
5.9	Interior surface pitting frequency in Medio ware groups	157
5.10	Interior surface erosion by site size and location	158
6.1	Raw materials on large and small Core Zone sites	167
6.2	Composition of Core Zone lithic assemblages	167
6.3	Whole and fragmentary core frequencies on Core Zone sites	169
6.4	Frequencies of core types, by site size and location	169
6.5	Flake and debris counts on Core Zone sites	171
6.6	Flake raw materials on Core Zone sites, by size class	172
6.7	Flake dimensions on Core Zone sites, by raw material group	174
6.8	Striking platform characteristics on Inner Core sites	176
6.9	Lips and bulbs on Core Zone flakes	177
6.10	Dorsal surface characteristics in the Core Zone	178
6.11	Flake terminations on Core Zone sites	179
6.12	Frequencies of ground stone implements on Core Zone sites	184
7.1	Shell items at Paquimé and its neighbors	198

7.2	Genera of shell found on Core Zone sites	200
7.3	Minerals from large Core Zone sites	207
8.1	Summary of flotation samples from Inner Core Sites 315 and 565	213
8.2	Comparison of propagule ubiquity scores from Inner Core large Sites 315 and 565	214
8.3	Chile seeds from Sites 315 and 565	218
8.4	Comparison of propagule ubiquity scores from lowland Site 315 and Upland Site 204	220
8.5	Summary of wood identifications from Inner Core Sites 315 and 565	221
8.6	Rank order comparison of wood remains in flotation samples from lowland Sites 315 and 565	222
8.7	Rank order comparison of wood remains in flotation samples from lowland Site 315 and upland Site 204	222
8.8	Faunal remains from Inner Core Sites 315 and 355	228
9.1	Richness scores for Core Zone sites	250

Acknowledgments

The work reported in this volume took place between 2008 and 2014 in the Casas Grandes River valley, ultimately involving five seasons of fieldwork at five of the nearest large and small neighbors of Paquimé. One full season was devoted to lab work as well. Like every such endeavor, this one resulted from the support, cooperation, and hard work of many institutions and people. Financial support for the two-season (2008–9) dig at Site 315 came from National Science Foundation Grant SBR-0810057. Work at Site 565 took place over a partial season in 2009, followed by a full season's excavation in 2010, supported by the James W. Whalen Memorial Fund. Three small sites in the study area were excavated and their materials analyzed in the 2012–13 field seasons, followed by a 2014 season of lab work. The small site project was funded by National Science Foundation Grant SBR-1259010. Extra expenses were covered by grants from the University of Tulsa's Office of Research. Our thanks go to all these institutions for their generosity.

In Mexico, authorizations to conduct the work were issued by the Instituto Nacional de Antropología e Historia. The Consejo de Arqueología reviewed our proposals and reports at the beginning and end of each field season. At the state level, the Centro INAH Chihuahua monitored the projects, gave us official letters of introduction to local officials, and facilitated the work in many other ways. The director of the Chihuahua center during our work, Elsa Rodríguez García, deserves special thanks for her unfailingly enthusiastic assistance with all aspects of the projects. In Casas Grandes, two successive directors of INAH's Museo de las Culturas del Norte, Mercedes Jiménez del Arco and Mauricio Salgado Servín, most generously opened their institution to us, providing work areas, fax machine access, and a setting for a series of pleasant and productive research conferences. There were many stimulating discussions with archaeologists from INAH Chihuahua, including Eduardo Gamboa, Rafael Cruz, Francisco Mendiola, and Arturo Guevara. We are greatly indebted to all our Mexican colleagues for their friendship, collegiality, and unstinting assistance.

At home, the Universities of Tulsa and Oklahoma provided us with the many facilities needed for proposal and report writing, data analysis, and manuscript preparation and publication subvention. A field vehicle was provided free of charge for all seasons by the

University of Tulsa. Two grants from the University of Tulsa's Office of Research helped to pay for a few extra radiocarbon dates.

The U.S. base for our work was El Paso, Texas, where we assembled crews, organized equipment, and transacted all kinds of business before and after each field season. As they have done since the beginning of our work in Chihuahua in 1989, Bonnie and Bill Whalen provided an invaluable local support network. The Whalen guesthouse was always available for transient archaeologists, and heavy use was made of it. The constant availability of this base of operations enormously facilitated the projects.

No analysis can be better than the underlying field and laboratory work, and the highest standards of professional performance were consistently maintained by our crews. A list follows of the archaeology students and professionals from the United States, Canada, and Mexico who worked in the field and laboratories: José Alvarez, Shelby Bartlett, Emma Britton, Chris Casserino, Dee Culver, Dolores Dávalos N., María Delgadillo S., Andrew Fernández, Randee Fladeboe, Mike Franz, Lauren Kingston, M. Galloway, Jennifer Gutzeit, Abby Holeman, Jeremy Loven, Marco Antonio Martínez G., Yasmín Medina R., Keith Mendez, Elizabeth Mills, Joelle Morgan, Matthew Pailes, Elizabeth Peterson, Todd Pitezel, Katy Putsavage, Patrick Rivera, Thomas Robinson, Thatcher Rogers, Victor Salazar S., Chris Salinas, Adam Searcy, Mike Searcy, J. Sealey, Jacob Sedig, Alana Shockley, Fabiola Silva, Mike Storozum, Elizabeth Toney, Antonio Vásquez M., Kristina Wykoff, Caitlyn Wichlacz, and Arturo Závala S.

The five sites we report on in this volume lay on lands with diverse ownership patterns. All five lie on lands in and around the municipios of Casas Grandes and Nuevo Casas Grandes. We are most appreciative of the cooperation of municipal officials and citizens of these localities. The research could not have been conducted without these generous permissions and cooperations, and we owe these landholders a great debt of gratitude.

Professor Julián Alejandro Hernández Chávez, now-retired director of the Escuela Preparatoria Francisco Villa in the city of Nuevo Casas Grandes, continued to be the rock of our local support, as he has been since the inception of our work in 1989. He was instrumental in securing permission for us to work on sites 315 and 565, he provided secure storage at his home for a mountain of project equipment, and his other assistances and kindnesses have been too numerous to list here. It would be impossible to overstate the value of Professor Hernández's contributions to all our work in Chihuahua.

Finally, we most respectfully acknowledge the work of the late Dr. Charles C. Di Peso and all his Mexican and North American colleagues of the Joint Casas Grandes Project, to whom this volume is dedicated. Although we have disagreed with their interpretations at many points, we salute their painstaking fieldwork, accurate data recording, extensive and detailed analyses, and prompt and thorough reporting of the vast body of data from Paquimé and neighboring sites. This is the essential base for all subsequent work.

REFRAMING PAQUIMÉ

 **Chapter 1**

Understanding Paquimé and Its Neighbors

Concepts, Progress, and Concerns

The large center of Paquimé, also known as Casas Grandes, lies in northwest Chihuahua, Mexico (map 1.1). It dominates the archaeological record because of its size, elaborate construction, ritual facilities, and concentration of exotic goods. Consequently, it has long been famous among archaeologists on both sides of the international border. Paquimé, although known and written about since the sixteenth century, was not intensively investigated until 1959. This was the beginning of what would be a massive three-year excavation by the Joint Casas Grandes Expedition (JCGE). That work is too well known to require discussion here, but an illustrated introduction to the project and the site may be found in the first volume of the Casas Grandes series (Di Peso 1974:1:1–44). The second volume of the series contains Di Peso's detailed narrative of the center's rise and fall (Di Peso 1974:2:289–319). For more than 40 years this remained the most extensive and widely accepted interpretation of the rise, reign, and ruin of Paquimé.

The last several decades have seen an explosion of survey, excavation, and analytical work in the Casas Grandes area (e.g., Minnis and Whalen 2015; Newell and Gallaga 2004; Pailes 2017; Pailes and Searcy 2022; Rakita 2006; C. VanPool and VanPool 2007). Nevertheless, considerable uncertainty remains about many fundamental questions. When and from what antecedents did Paquimé originate? How big was it? How did it operate? How widespread was its influence? When, how, and why did it collapse? What happened in the Casas Grandes region after the decline of Paquimé? We still have far to go toward adequate understanding of these issues, and clearly no single study could provide answers to all of them. Rather, we must build and refine understandings piece by piece over generations of researchers. As part of this process, our work since 2001 has focused on one broad question: How and to what extent did Paquimé affect its near and distant neighbors? We first approached this problem through a regional survey that recorded some 400 sites of many sizes and types. These data were used to reconstruct settlement patterns from the immediate environs of Paquimé to a distance of about 100 km (Whalen and Minnis 2001a). The second stage was excavation of nine of the near neighbors of Paquimé. These communities ranged from small to large (Whalen and Minnis 2009, 2012, and this volume).

MAP 1.1 The Casas Grandes area and Paquimé.

Each of these studies used what was then known to interpret aspects of the operation of Paquimé and its interaction with its neighbors. Naturally, as research continued, each interpretation was subject to modification in light of emerging data and fresh ideas. We intend this third volume to continue the trend, reaching back to previous projects and their ideas in light of the understandings and ideas that we currently possess. Previous studies necessarily looked from the outside inward, or from more distant neighbors toward the center of Paquimé. The present volume alters this situation with a new set of excavation data from the nearest neighbors of Paquimé, some of which lie less than 1 km from the center. With these data, we will be able for the first time to look from the center outward, first at nearer neighbors, and then to more distant ones. Before beginning this process, however, several terms and concepts used throughout our discussion require clarification.

Terms and Concepts

The Site and the Region

Two names are in current use in the literature: Casas Grandes and Paquimé. The former is the name under which Charles C. Di Peso and his JCGE colleagues published the influential site report that continues to be a mainstay of all scholars interested in the area. In recent years, however, there has been a tendency to use the name Paquimé to refer to the site. The name Casas Grandes also has for centuries been applied to the region of northwestern

Chihuahua, Mexico, wherein lies Paquimé, as well as to the eponymous river on which the site is located. The present volume follows this usage: the site is Paquimé, and the region and its major river are Casas Grandes.

Beyond the Casas Grandes region, the present study is concerned with a large area including the northern parts of the current Mexican states of Chihuahua and Sonora, as well as the Southwest region of the United States. North American archaeologists often have simply used the term Southwest or the Greater Southwest to refer to this large international area. Naturally, this terminology does not sit well with our Mexican colleagues, to whom the area is the Northwest. Other terms like the Gran Chichimeca (Di Peso 1974:1:1) and Aztlán (Riley 2005) have been applied to the region without becoming very popular. Both are broad, general terms with specific meanings in Mesoamerican and Mexican ethnohistory. See Riley (2005:5–7) for a discussion of these. In the present study, we prefer to avoid these associations, simply referring to northwestern Chihuahua, northern Sonora, and the U.S. Southwest as Northwest Mexico and the Southwest United States. This is a cumbersome term, so we abbreviate it in subsequent discussion as NW/SW.

When Was Paquimé?

The beginnings of Paquimé are still unclear. Di Peso reported pit houses beneath Unit 6 and surface jacal structures beneath Unit 8 (Di Peso et al. 1974:4:317–22 and 331–37), but their extent is unknown. Their stratigraphic positions clearly place them before the construction of the heavy adobe architecture that characterized the site. These antecedent occupations may not have been large. In fact, Lekson (2000, 2008) has argued that there were relatively few Viejo settlements in the Casas Grandes area. We see more, although the situation is still unclear. It is noteworthy, however, that Mimbres Black-on-white, a Late Viejo period trade ware, is rare in Paquimé assemblages, as is Early Medio period Dublán Polychrome. Lekson (2008:316–17) provides an excellent discussion of the timing of the end of the Viejo period and the beginning of the Early Medio in and around the Casas Grandes area.

The question of when Paquimé ended has several parts. We might ask (1) when the community ceased to function as a regional power center; and (2) when the settlement was finally abandoned. An often-cited end date for construction at Paquimé is AD 1450, with some construction possibly as late as the early 1470s (Dean and Ravesloot 1993:93). This is based on reanalysis of 46 original tree-ring samples from Paquimé, which is discussed in the source just cited. This 1470 end date has been criticized by others (e.g., Phillips and Gamboa 2015; Schaafsma and Riley 1999). These authors argue that an end-of-construction date after 1450 is based on a single tree-ring sample's estimated felling date. These dates are established through a complex statistical process that yields a probability distribution, expressible at 1σ or 2σ, within which the true date likely is contained. The young end of the 2σ probability distribution of the sample in question is 1473 (Dean and Ravesloot 1993:95, table 6.2). None of the other 2σ probability distributions for estimated felling dates at Paquimé extend so far forward in time, and we agree with Phillips and Gamboa (2015:150), who consider this date a statistical outlier that should be dropped from the dataset. Schaafsma and Riley (1999:244), in their review of the revised tree-ring dates, raised a similar point: "We are quite dubious about extending Casas Grandes (Paquimé) itself beyond about 1425." In pursuit of this question, Phillips and Gamboa (2015) consider the small body of other chronometric information from Paquimé. The following discussion is abstracted from that source. There are four radiocarbon dates from Di Peso's work at the site. These were originally used without correction, but new calibration with modern methods yields 2σ probability ranges ending in the early 1420s. There are also four AMS dates on bone collagen from Paquimé human remains (Casserino 2009:85, table 9 and fig. 25). One of the 2σ date ranges extends to the early 1430s, and the other three extend into the mid-1200s (one date) and the late 1300s (two dates). These dates roughly define the occupation span of the community, and it is noteworthy that none of *maximum* ages, determined by the upper ends of their 2σ ranges, extend far into the 1400s. There seems to be general agreement in the literature that Paquimé rose rapidly to its peak in the late 1200s and 1300s, and that it held this apogee during the 1300s and perhaps a decade or two into the 1400s. This period of roughly 150 years is considered here to be the time of the community's maximum regional prominence.

What Was the Medio Period?

Based on work at Paquimé, Di Peso and colleagues defined the Medio period as the time of the rise, reign, and ruin of the center. This was the first large-scale excavation done in the region, however, so Paquimé was necessarily studied nearly in isolation, and all interpretations were Paquimé focused. Also at issue was Di Peso's well-known conviction that Paquimé had nonlocal antecedents, owing its existence to stimuli from Mesoamerica. Paquimé was thus the founder of a new tradition of economics, religion, social organization, external contacts, architecture, and material culture, all of which represented so extreme a departure from the old ways that they formed a "cultural hiatus" (Di Peso 1974:1:100, fig. 82-1). Moreover, it was argued that the exogenic transition to the new culture pattern took only five to ten years, leaving neither time nor necessity for much Indigenous development (Di Peso 1974:2:292 and 653, note 7).

Since the Medio period was originally defined as the time of Paquimé, its beginning, ending, and material characteristics were necessarily those of the center. Chief among these was architecture of both domestic and ceremonial sorts. The Paquimé building style included adobe room blocks, some of them multistoried. The walls of these rooms were very thick, and they were built using "a very sophisticated cluster of architectural traits which appeared to have been introduced into the (Casas Grandes) valley from Mesoamerica" (Di Peso et al. 1974:4:198). The rooms of Paquimé were much larger than those found among the pueblos of the U.S. Southwest. Some of these rooms were of intricate shapes, and many of them contained such elaborate intramural features as colonnades, posts with thick adobe collars, and platform hearths in various zoomorphic and geometric forms. The ritual architecture of Paquimé consisted of platform mounds and at least one large I-shaped ball court. There is also a water control system, the reservoirs of which have been interpreted as water shrines (Walker and McGahee 2006). This complex defined the Medio period. In addition, stratigraphy and perceived differences in building styles were used to establish three subdivisions, or phases, within the period (Di Peso et al. 1974:6:80). There is a difficulty here, as building styles are likely to change slowly. Moreover, once built, large edifices are more likely to be remodeled than replaced, leading to subtle combinations of traits and thus to ambiguous series of stylistic change. Most archaeologists are inclined toward time markers that change more rapidly and less ambiguously for good reason.

Chief among these are decorated ceramics. Both archaeological and ethnohistoric studies demonstrate that ceramic decorative styles can be counted on to fluctuate over relatively short time intervals. This variation provides sensitive and easily recognizable chronological markers. This strategy, however, was not followed at Paquimé. Found with all the community's construction from beginning to end, and thus in all three proposed phases, was a ceramic assemblage containing more than 20 locally produced types of plain, textured, slipped, and painted wares. Because of their association with the architecture just described, these ceramics were considered to characterize the Medio period throughout its existence. That is, the same pottery types in almost the same frequencies were found with building styles assigned to all three phases. These architecture-based intervals have since fallen out of use, as the Buena Fe and Paquimé phases appear to be more contemporary than successive (e.g., Frost 2000; Whalen et al. 2010). The exception to this is the final Diablo phase, which might still be a useful marker of the degeneration of the community's architecture at the end of its occupation.

The question, then, is on what grounds is the Medio period best defined? If architecture is the salient trait, then the period exists in its complete form only at Paquimé. Di Peso argued that the same was true of the associated ceramic assemblage, which occurred in its entirety only at Paquimé and its immediate vicinity in the Casas Grandes River valley. Outside this small area, there was "a gradation in decreasing degree of use" of the full assemblage (Di Peso 1974:2:84). The Medio period was Paquimé, and Paquimé was the Medio period's pure form. Di Peso also wrote of a "Casas Grandes Culture Complex," marked by architectural and material culture traits, including simplified versions of the architecture and the ceramic assemblage of the primate center, although these material culture traits were defined only in the most ambiguous terms. The Medio period culture was spread from Paquimé, first throughout the Casas Grandes River valley and then outward as a means "to manipulate the Indigenous recipient society to its advantage" (Di Peso 1974:2:334).

Recent work, however, shows that most ceramic types that we use to define the Medio period existed long before the ascendency of Paquimé. Site 204 is a large Medio period community of the outer part of the Core Zone, and it is the only known site with deep, extensive midden deposits. A series of pits dug into these produced a radiocarbon-dated seriation of Medio period ceramics. These data are discussed in detail elsewhere (Whalen and Minnis 2009:115–25). Briefly, this work defined and dated Early and Late Medio ceramic assemblages, which were used to define the eponymous periods. The Early Medio period dates from the mid- to late AD 1100s to about 1300, and the Late Medio period begins after 1300. When it ends is one of the subjects of the present volume.

The Early/Late Medio division is based largely on the presence of Ramos Polychrome in the upper levels of test pits that radiocarbon date after AD 1300. Ramos is the most elaborate of the finely painted Chihuahuan polychromes. It is widespread in the Casas Grandes area and at Paquimé. Lower test pit levels at Site 204 date before 1300, and they contain no Ramos Polychrome or any of its finely painted variants. Instead, early polychromes are of the simple, coarse-lined variety, which also continues into Late Medio times. The fine-line varieties like Ramos are Late Medio add-ons to the existing assemblage. It should be emphasized that polychromes of any type are relatively rare, so Early and Late Medio assemblages from the Site 204 test pits are overwhelmingly dominated by utilitarian ceramics of Plain Brown, Textured Brown, Red-slipped, and Black types.

Our contention is that a recognizable Medio period ceramic assemblage containing all of the utilitarian and coarse-lined painted types existed at least a century before the rise of Paquimé (Whalen and Minnis 2009, 2012). Instead of originating most of the Medio period assemblage, the rise of Paquimé saw the addition of a fine-lined painting technique that used some anthropomorphic and zoomorphic images in addition to the still-dominant geometric designs. These new images are thought to have been connected to religion, status, and social integration in the Late Medio world in general and at Paquimé in particular (e.g., Cunningham 2017; Kelley and Phillips 2017; Pailes and Searcy 2022; C. VanPool and VanPool 2007; Whalen and Minnis 2009, 2012). These highly visible painted ceramics did not replace local utilitarian wares, which continued to dominate Late Medio assemblages.

Architecture at Paquimé seems to follow a similar trend of augmentation of an existing style. Through excavation at Site 204, a large segment of the main mound provided floor-contact dates that were exclusively Early Medio, or ca. AD 1180–1300 (Whalen and Minnis 2009:48 and 53), while other excavation areas gave Late Medio floor-contact dates of ca. AD 1300–1425. The architecture of the Early Medio rooms seems antecedent to the Late Medio building of Paquimé. The Early Medio adobe walls were built in broad horizontal layers (Whalen and Minnis 2009:73, fig. 3.1, upper frame). Di Peso termed this technique "puddled adobe," and he recognized it as the principal construction technique for Medio Paquimé. Early Medio floors and walls were coated with a hard grayish-white plaster (Whalen and Minnis 2009:73, fig. 3.1, lower frame), which continued to characterize all of the area's Late Medio building, including that of Paquimé. Early Medio rooms were of simple quadrilateral shapes, and these were also most common at Paquimé and at all of its Late Medio neighbors. The common floor feature of the Early Medio construction at Site 204 was the simple hemispherical fire pit that Di Peso classed as Type 1A at Paquimé. It was the most common type of fire feature at the principal center and in all other Late Medio construction. Wall features of the Early Medio at Site 204 included T-shaped and rectangular doorways, a wall niche, and an adobe stairway, all of them much like their Late Medio successors at Paquimé and elsewhere.

Despite these commonalities, the Early Medio rooms at Site 204 were not identical to those of Late Medio communities in general and of Paquimé in particular. Rooms at Early and Late Medio neighbors were not nearly as large as those of the principal center, nor are they known to occur in the elaborate shapes of some Paquimé rooms. Early Medio walls (and those of Late Medio neighbors) were only 25–35 cm thick, in marked contrast to the massive walls of Paquimé. The inventory of door shapes and intramural feature types found at Paquimé was much greater than that of the 204 Early Medio rooms, although we note that the number and variety of room features at Site 204 increased in the Late Medio occupation. The Early Medio architecture at Site 204 clearly was simpler and of smaller scale than that of Paquimé. Yet, it predates the principal center by about one hundred years. Much of what Di Peso described at Paquimé thus had smaller, simpler antecedents in the Casas Grandes area. We emphasize that our Early Medio designation does not include Di Peso's earliest part of the Medio period: the Buena Fe phase. Both this and his subsequent Paquimé and Diablo phases are contained in our Late Medio period.

In sum, the present volume makes use of the Medio period, its ceramic types, and the Casas Grandes Culture concept, although we do not see them exactly as Di Peso did. Instead of phenomena originating with Paquimé and emanating outward from it, we contend that Paquimé represents an elaborate, short-lived version of the preexisting Casas Grandes Culture. The rapid rise of the center, then, involved amplification of many extant patterns, rather than an inventory of new characteristics imported from Mesoamerica. We do not deny the presence of Mesoamerican symbols and concepts in the community, but we assign them a less central role than did Di Peso. With these understandings, we turn now to two areas of inquiry that are fundamental to our understanding of the relationship of Paquimé to its nearest neighbors: how long were they occupied, and what functions did they discharge?

Estimating Settlement Occupational Histories

These analyses must of necessity be based on radiocarbon dates, of which we currently have 268 from a range of large and small neighbors of the inner and outer parts of the Core Zone. Outer Core Zone dates were presented earlier (Whalen and Minnis 2009:45–67), and those from the Inner Core are discussed in the third chapter of this volume. It is most unfortunate that we have not been able to develop a dendrochronology apart from the one at Paquimé, which is critically discussed in a later chapter. More than 60 carbonized wood specimens from our Core Zone excavations were submitted for analysis, but none yielded dates. There has been a little archaeomagnetic dating done on sites excavated by us and others, and these results are discussed in a later chapter. Subsequent discussion will address the question of site occupational histories as thoroughly as possible, with the caveat that we do not have the precise chronological control that is commonplace in the adjacent U.S. Southwest.

Evaluating Settlement Complexity and Function

Data from Paquimé and its neighbors were used to tailor a list of specific observations for use in our Outer Core settlement analyses (Whalen and Minnis 2009); the succeeding chapters provide data to address these specific areas of inquiry for our new set of Inner Core Zone sites. The complexity of community function in northwest Chihuahua is indicated by the presence of the characteristics listed below, and the parenthetical expression following each is its specific manifestation in the Casas Grandes area. Specific indicators include:

An architecture of power (thick-walled, elaborate architecture)

Formal, ritual architecture and feasting facilities (ball courts and large ovens)

Conspicuous exotic and imported items (marine shells, macaws, pottery, minerals)

Ritual paraphernalia (altars, icons, designs, and effigies)

Materials of controlled or limited distribution (marine shells, some types of grinding implements of vesicular basalt, obsidian)

High frequencies of polychrome ceramics (especially Ramos Polychrome)

Large storage capacity (dedicated rooms, large unsooted ceramic vessels)

Large cooking and serving vessels

High-quality meat (bison, deer, and antelope versus rabbits and rats)

High-quality fuel (imported pine versus local oak and mesquite)

Elaborate human burials

Note that the last criterion—elaborate burials—has little practical significance in the Casas Grandes area, as extensive looting at all sites has effectively removed this component of the archaeological record. Our six months of excavation at the 200-room Tinaja site recovered no intact interments, for instance, although empty burial pits and scattered human bone fragments were common. Large Inner Core sites lacked some of these traits, for example, ball courts, large ovens, and visible remains of macaw cages. Most indicators of complexity of community function, however, are not visible on site surfaces. Only excavation will determine their presence or absence on Inner Core sites. Before turning to the excavation program, we have one remaining issue to investigate: the neglected small sites of the Casas Grandes area.

The Small Site Problem

As of 2012, little attention had been paid to the small residential sites that are the most common and least understood type of community in the area. The small sites of the Casas Grandes area contain a substantial percentage of the region's total room count, and they could have accommodated a significant segment of the regional population at some point(s) in the Medio period. This statement is necessarily vague because most small residential sites are dateable from surface ceramics only to Medio times. As a result, the most abundant site type plays almost no role in current interpretations of the rise, operation, and fall of Paquimé.

An argument familiar to every modern archaeologist is that settlement systems are the sum of all their parts, so that they cannot be adequately investigated by study of some components and omission of others. Unfortunately, there is a tendency to dismiss small residential sites as unproductive candidates for excavation. A benefit of cultural resource management work in the southwestern United States, however, is the investigation of many small residential sites that would have otherwise been ignored. These projects have yielded results that are often useful and sometimes surprising. It can also be easier to track demographic shifts at small residential sites than at their large counterparts. This is because small sites are always more thoroughly excavated than are large ones, leaving unexplored less of the total occupation. A large site might decline in population while a considerable percentage of the original area remains occupied, while a small residential site is more likely to be entirely abandoned. Both situations are traceable through the archaeological record, but the latter is the more straightforward. In short, the occupational histories of a region's small residential sites may be sensitive and efficient monitors of various growth and dissolution processes. For example, scattered populations may be displaced or absorbed by a rising center, resulting in large-scale abandonment of small residential settlements. Pauketat (2003) illustrates this process in the rise of the Mississippian center of Cahokia. Small communities may also increase in number in a settlement system as a result of factors such as demographic dispersals from aggregated communities, or inmigrations of other populations. Nelson (1999) examines such a situation in the Mimbres area, and Varien (2010) does the same for the Mesa Verde region, both of the U.S. Southwest.

Small residential sites were found in every surveyed area in the Casas Grandes region. They occur in the same river valley and piedmont locations as do larger residential sites, so that they clearly were not relegated to poor, low-productivity segments of the environment. The small sites reported on in the present volume are all located in the Casas Grandes River valley, as is Paquimé itself. It is the best-watered portion of the regional environment, with the highest potential for agricultural production. It should, therefore, have been a very attractive zone for Medio period populations and for such post-Paquimé populations as might have existed in the region. Such sites have not been identified before the present study.

There are a few excavated small sites outside the Casas Grandes River valley, including Outer Core Zone Sites 317, 231, and Casa Chica (Cruz Antillón et al., 2004). They seem to be small, simple residential loci, with evidence for a wide range of domestic activities, but with few or no luxuries. Outer Core Zone small Site 242, however, presents a very different picture. It evidently functioned as an administrative center for Paquimé, differing in every aspect from its small neighbors. From so small a sample, we cannot form an adequate concept of the range of variability of small residential site characteristics. We have gained all we could from study of these sites' sparse surface remains, and only their excavation will improve our current picture of their natures and their occupational histories. Our survey results provided a set of sites from which to select a sample of large and small sites for excavation. Before doing so, however, in chapter 2 we reevaluate the survey data in light of our current ideas on regional settlement patterns.

 *Chapter 2*

Settlement Patterns Reexamined

Our first work in the Casas Grandes area was a series of intensive site surveys (Whalen and Minnis 2001a). The results of these projects were used to characterize the settlement patterns of two of the region's major developmental episodes: the Medio (pueblo) period and, to a lesser extent, the preceding Viejo (late pit house and transitional) period. The remains of Medio pueblo room blocks were conspicuous all over the survey areas, while the remnants of Viejo period pit houses or jacal (mud-and-stick) structures left surface traces of much lower visibility. The Medio period dataset was much larger than that of the preceding Viejo. This paucity of Viejo period occupation has led some (e.g., Di Peso 1974:2:292; Lekson 2000:286, 2008:176, 2015:137) to the conclusion that the Casas Grandes area was sparsely occupied prior to its Medio period fluorescence. More has been learned about the settlement patterns of both periods in the past quarter-century, and the ensuing discussion uses these data to revise and expand on earlier ideas.

The Viejo Period

The period's definition was based on JCGE excavations at the Convento and Los Reyes No. 2 sites in the upper Casas Grandes River valley, only a few kilometers north of Paquimé. A few Viejo remains were also found beneath Medio buildings in a part of Paquimé, demonstrating the former period's stratigraphic priority. Accordingly, Di Peso defined the Viejo period as the area's pre-Paquimé occupation, a visible aspect of which were small percentages of Red-on-brown pottery in the predominantly Brown contemporary assemblage. Viejo architectural forms, usually invisible on the surface, consisted of pit houses, or structures built just below ground level. Domed superstructures were built of jacal. Toward the end of the period, these single structures began to be replaced by surface structures, the walls of which continued to be made of poles and mud plaster, otherwise known as jacal construction

The same developmental sequence of circular houses followed by jacal surface structures and, eventually, contiguous stone and adobe surface room blocks characterizes the adjacent U.S. Southwest. Di Peso saw Viejo populations as living in small scattered communities and practicing an early form of maize farming. The Viejo way of life, as seen in the 1960s, appeared very much smaller and simpler in every way than the Medio period situation defined at Paquimé, leading to the concept of a "cultural hiatus" between the two periods. The apparent paucity of Viejo remains led to the idea of the Casas Grandes area as an essentially empty niche into which Mesoamerican-based Paquimé exploded.

Our survey data appeared to confirm this idea, as we recorded only a handful of purely Viejo surface artifact scatters everywhere, from the vicinity of Paquimé to about 80 km away. Yet, we also recorded 48 sites where Viejo Red-on-brown pottery sherds formed minor components of ceramic collections made around room blocks of the Medio period, which were characterized by the distinctive pottery of that time. It was thought likely that Viejo occupations were overlain and concealed by those of the larger Medio period, as was known to be the case at Paquimé and the Los Reyes No. 2 sites. Both of these localities lay on terraces overlooking the prime agricultural land of the Casas Grandes River valley, as did some of the 48 sites with suspected multicomponent histories. Unfortunately, we could form no estimation of how many Viejo sites lay undetected beneath larger Medio occupations.

The low frequencies of diagnostic Red-on-brown sherds recovered from these multi-component sites led us to suspect that the underlying Viejo components were considerably smaller than what overlay them, but we could form no estimation of how large these occupations might have been. In the 2001 volume's necessarily brief discussion of the Viejo settlement pattern, we suggested that there were more Viejo sites in the Casas Grandes area than previously suspected. Although they formed a settlement system a good deal smaller than in the succeeding period, Viejo sites were found in all the environmental zones so heavily occupied in Medio times. Still, we recorded more of them in secondary drainages and in upland areas. They appeared to be less common on the terraces of the Casas Grandes River valley, which is the region's best agricultural land. Viejo occupations might lie hidden beneath the many Medio sites that fill the area's prime agricultural niches, but we could not further develop this idea in 2001.

Our subsequent excavations on large Medio period Site 204, overlooking a major secondary drainage (Whalen and Minnis 2009:12–17), and two sites of the Casas Grandes River valley (315 and 565, this volume) discovered Viejo period structures and features in every case. The same is true of the JCGE work at Paquimé and the Reyes No. 2 sites. In short, 100 percent of excavations on Medio period sites of the upper Casas Grandes River valley, from 1963 to the present, revealed underlying Viejo occupations. We remain unable to estimate the sizes of these hidden occupations, but discovery of them under every large Medio site dug in the area suggests that they are not rare. All large Medio sites of the middle Casas Grandes River valley have been destroyed by mechanized agriculture and associated land-leveling machinery, so we know nothing of underlying Viejo components there.

We did survey work in the lower Casas Grandes River valley, at its confluence with the San Pedro River and near the modern town of Janos, and recorded the same pattern. Large Medio sites in prime farming positions in the Casas Grandes drainage and in the confluent San Pedro drainage showed small components of Red-on-brown and Mimbres Black-on-white pottery in their surface ceramic assemblages. One of the largest of these sites has been nearly destroyed by backhoe looting, and local residents told us that it yielded many Mimbres Black-on-white vessels. Our surface collections confirmed this, recovering unusual numbers of Red-on-brown and imported Mimbres Black-on-white sherds as components of the predominantly Medio assemblage. There is almost certainly a Viejo component beneath this site.

These major Medio sites occupy prime farming locations, as many Viejo sites appear to have done. We continue to assert, therefore, that the Casas Grandes region was far from an empty niche into which Medio populations expanded in unprecedented ways. Instead, the Viejo period settlement pattern appears to represent a smaller version of what we found in the succeeding Medio period. Unfortunately, we cannot now say more about Viejo period settlement patterns, although we are pleased to note that work continues on the Viejo sites of the upper Casas Grandes and Palanganas drainages (e.g., Searcy and Pitezel 2017).

The Medio Period

Sites of the Medio period were recognized by surface scatters of the ceramic assemblage described at Paquimé. That classification system was found to be as applicable to the near and distant neighbors of Paquimé as it was to the center itself. Frequently associated with these ceramics were low mounds representing decomposed abode room blocks. The primary recognition criterion of a Medio period site, however, was its ceramic assemblage. For nearly a century we have had a modicum of knowledge about the settlement pattern of the succeeding Medio period. Early reconnaissance in the Casas Grandes area (e.g., Brand 1933; Sayles 1936a) produced a picture of Paquimé and a few large settlements located in major drainages and surrounded by many small sites. Like their Viejo predecessors, Medio occupations clearly were attracted to the region's drainages, and their frequency seemed to be in proportion to the sizes of the drainages and the amount of arable land they contained. Room block size data were not often recorded, but the sparse extant measurements suggested that the largest sites were much smaller than Paquimé. The combined surveys of Brand and Sayles recorded some 200 sites in the Casas Grandes area. They were identified by what we now recognize as the Medio period ceramic assemblage, initially described by Sayles (1936b) and later elaborated by Di Peso and colleagues at Paquimé.

Brand (1933) used the term Casas Grandes sites, for which we here use the more current term Medio period. He briefly described these sites, sometimes giving estimates of room block mound area. It is evident, however, that he divided Medio sites into two classes: (a) the larger and more conspicuous sites that he visited and briefly described, and (b) smaller sites whose presence he noted but did not individually describe. He usually gave rough mound size estimates (e.g., "50 by 60 yards") only when dealing with sites he considered significant. In addition, Brand frequently described a larger site and noted that several smaller ones were in its vicinity. A picture thus emerges of a few larger sites surrounded by many smaller ones. Even his large sites were not enormous, however. These ranged from 900 to 2,850 m^2 of mound area, with a mean size of 1,400 m^2 (σ = 634). It was also clear that all significant drainages contained these sites near their watercourses. Brand did not examine upland areas.

A similar impression comes from Sayles's reconnaissance (1936a), and he examined areas outside the lowland drainage channels. His descriptions of Medio period sites are as brief as Brand's, and mound size information is lacking. Sayles notes, however, that almost none of the mound sites he visited seemed to have had more than one story (Sayles 1936a:30). Like Brand, he described a pattern of large sites surrounded by more numerous small ones. All of this early reconnaissance thus showed a Medio period settlement system headed by the very large center of Paquimé and consisting elsewhere of a few large communities and many small ones. The sparse mound size data suggested that the largest sites were of modest size, single storied, and much smaller than Paquimé. They were clearly drawn strongly to the region's drainages, and their presence seemed to be in direct proportion to the available water and arable land. Our surveys support this picture.

Decades later, a regional survey was done in the Casas Grandes area in the summer of 1959 as part of the JCGE (Di Peso et al. 1974:4:38). Site data from this project were combined with those of Brand and Sayles to yield a figure of more than 1,000 sites of the Medio period. The combined surveys of Brand and Sayles recorded some 200 sites in the Casas Grandes area, so most of the localities (over 800 of them) must have come from the 1959 survey. This is an astounding number of sites to have recorded in a single summer. We note that our intensive surveys of small portions of the Casas Grandes region recorded on the order of 300 sites using three survey crews in 20 weeks of work. No records are known for the 800 sites from the 1959 survey. A regional map showing these sites, without identifying numbers, was published as an appended figure in a later Casas Grandes volume (Di Peso et al. 1974:5:fig. 284-5). It is reproduced here as map 2.1. Despite lack of any site data beyond location, the Di Peso map echoes the findings of earlier work by showing river and drainage valleys full of sites. After evaluation of these data, Lekson and coauthors (Lekson et al. 2004) argued that the site densities shown on the Di Peso map are probably accurate. We agree with this conclusion in that the region's drainages contain a few large Medio settlements surrounded by many small ones.

We now turn to understandings and ideas generated by our intensive surveys in the Casas Grandes area. Primary site identification criteria were the ceramic types described at Paquimé for the Medio period and at the Convento site for the Viejo period. We found this ceramic typology to be entirely applicable to sites all over our northwest Chihuahua survey areas. Most of the 400 recorded sites belonged to the Medio period, so its settlement pattern was examined in the greatest detail in the 2001 volume. Our objective was to define differences among Medio period communities at a range of distances around Paquimé. Survey zones were accordingly designated at increasing distances from the major center.

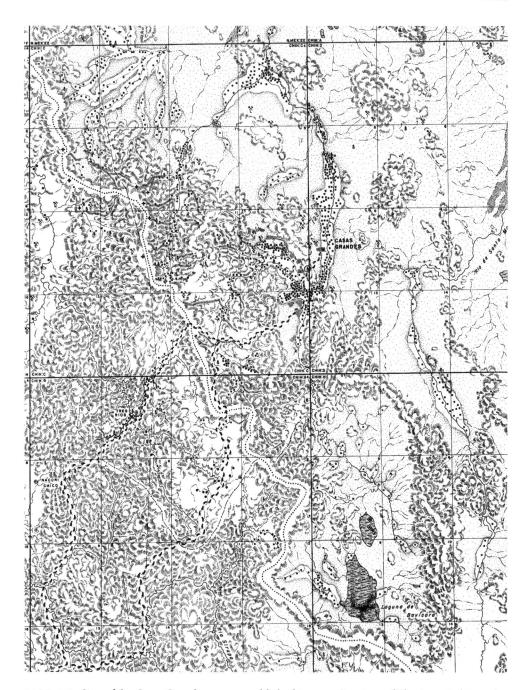

MAP 2.1 Sites of the Casas Grandes area, as published in 1974. Courtesy of The Amerind Foundation, Inc., Dragoon, Arizona. Alice Wesche, Illustrator.

To provide a context for the present research, it is necessary to review and reconsider the structures of these zones. The surveyed units were grouped under the headings of Inner and Middle Zones (map 2.2). All Inner Zone survey areas lay within about 30 km around Paquimé, while the surveyed areas of the Middle Zone were located from 50 to 80 km from the primate center. Based on a brief 1989 reconnaissance, we defined an Outer Zone,

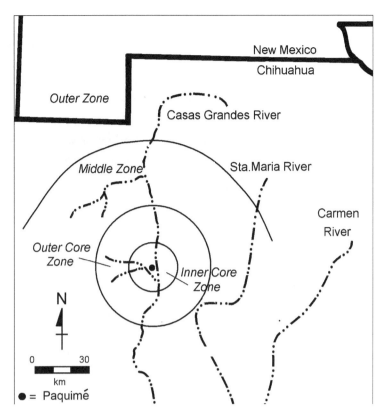

MAP 2.2 The Inner, Middle, and Outer survey zones.

examined areas of which were 100 to 150 km to the north and northwest of Paquimé. No intensive survey was done in the Outer Zone, however.

Most of the 2001 study was devoted to comparison and contrast of the site characteristics and settlement patterns of the Inner and Middle Zones. Compared to their Inner Zone contemporaries, the communities of the Middle Zone were found to be smaller, simpler, and lacking in the ball courts, large ovens, and birdcages presumed to have served in social, economic, political, and ceremonial organization and integration. All of these features and facilities were conspicuously present in the Inner Zone as well as at Paquimé itself. Accordingly, the Inner Zone was postulated to have been more formally organized than the Middle Zone. Both zones were clearly affected by Paquimé, but we saw no indication of a simple, uniform hegemony over the entire area. Instead, data from each zone suggested different intensities of interaction and variable levels of integration into the regional system. Control by Paquimé was postulated to have been uneven in a fragmented political landscape.

In addition to these broad patterns, the 2001 study noted some potentially significant variability within the Inner Zone, and this was again based on frequencies of recorded ball courts, large ovens, and birdcages. These facilities were concentrated in the Inner Zone, but they were not evenly distributed over all of its area. The largest ball courts and ovens, plus the most numerous birdcages, were found by Di Peso and colleagues at Paquimé. Few large ovens and no ball courts or birdcages were recorded on Medio period communities within a radius of about 15 km from the center. From about 15 km to about 30 km from Paquimé, however, surveys recorded all the rest of the Inner Zone's total of courts, cages, and ovens. This suggests that Paquimé absorbed from its nearest neighbors many of the organizational and integrative functions ascribed to these facilities. The monopoly does not appear to have extended to Inner Zone communities beyond 15 km. This distance has been termed the "limit of daily interaction," as it is as far as a person on foot can go and return in a single day (Wilcox 1995:289). To be able to refer to this division without using cumbersome terms like the Outer Inner Zone, the 2009 study replaced the term Inner Zone with Core Zone, which was divided into inner and outer parts using the 15 km range described above. The present study contrasts the Medio period settlement patterns and community characteristics of the inner and outer parts of the Core Zone, seeking to define additional variability among them. This will provide a finer picture of regional organization than was achieved in earlier studies.

The basic unit of analysis for Medio period residential sites is the room block mound. These elemental residential units ranged in size from very small to very large, but in all cases, they were formed by the melted adobe roofs and walls of contiguous room blocks. They looked very much alike in every survey zone. Using a spatial rule of association, to be discussed shortly, we defined settlements as one or more of these room blocks. We already know that Inner and Outer Core Zones showed different frequencies of ritual architecture and integrative facilities. Accordingly, there is the suggestion that the inner and outer parts of the Core Zone were not organized in the same way or to the same extent. In pursuit of this idea, the following analyses seek corresponding differences in room blocks and their combination into settlements.

Mound Height and Room Block Size

There are two ways to characterize room blocks: (1) mound height, possibly reflecting the number of stories in the original room block, and (2) a mound's "footprint," or the area in square meters covered by the structure. If the first measure is found to be variable, then the second is of questionable reliability. If mound heights are broadly similar, however, footprint is a handy comparative measure. Paquimé has long been famous for its multistory construction, although a restudy (Whalen et al. 2010) considers the problem of correlating mound height to the number of floors. The ensuing discussion is abstracted from the source just cited. All agree that there was multistory construction in the central room block at Paquimé, but the number of stories has been the subject of much and variable speculation for many years. The Casas Grandes site report combined all of this early discussion to give a broad estimate of three to seven stories (Di Peso 1974:2:675, note 377.18). In recent years, opinion seems to be settling on five stories (e.g., Contreras Sánchez 1986; Guevara Sánchez 1991; Lekson 1999). None of these estimates, however, provided supporting measurements of the site's architecture.

The question of how many stories there were at Paquimé can be pursued by using Di Peso's data on ceiling heights and floor-roof thicknesses in the rooms he dug. In all excavated rooms there was an average of 2.16 m from floor to ceiling, or upper story, and mean ceiling or floor thickness was 0.66 m. Standard deviations were not given (Di Peso et al. 1974:4:251, fig. 178-4). Combining these figures, a five-story building would have required original walls about 14 m high. After considering the remnant wall height, wall thickness, and likely rates of erosion, we concluded that the original maximum wall height was about 8.5 m, enclosing three stories. Nonetheless, only a small fraction of Casas Grandes likely reached this postulated three-story height. The Sanchez Blanco map is a topographic rendering of the site of Paquimé, produced by a surveyor just before the excavations began. It shows three peaks in the main room block mound, one each in units 8, 16, and 14. These are surrounded and connected by lower remains. This pattern is clear at the site today, and it was evident to earlier visitors as well. American traveler John Bartlett wrote (1854:350) that the outer portions of the room block were only one story high, while the multistory rooms were located in the center of the ruin. Mexican archaeologist Eduardo Noguera (1930) also observed that the ruins' highest walls were interior ones, while those of the exterior were of lower, single-story construction. He used the metaphor of a stair step to describe the main ruin, observing that only a small central part had the maximum number of stories. We note that this terraced, or stepped, construction is commonly seen on pueblos of all ages in the adjacent U.S. Southwest. In sum, it was argued in the reanalysis that only about 10 percent of the excavated part of Casas Grandes reached three stories, while about half of the main room block's construction was only one story. Two-story rooms composed the remainder.

But what was the situation among the center's neighbors? It is our contention that single-story rooms would have required original wall heights of about 2.8 m. This figure comes from data just cited for Paquimé room heights and ceiling thicknesses. Two stories and a roof would have required some 5.6 m of original wall height. Preceding discussion of wall erosion suggests that 30 percent is a reasonable figure. For details of this argument, see Whalen et al. (2010). Thus, an eroded room block that was originally two stories tall should have standing walls about 3.9 m high. Even if we assume 50 percent wall height erosion for thinner-walled structures, a two-story room block should have standing walls about 2.8 m high.

Our regional surveys (Whalen and Minnis 2001a:107) recorded 449 Medio period room block mounds. Among these, only 11 mounds (about 2.4%) were at least 2 m in maximum height, and only one reached 2.6 meters. Exposure by excavation or looting of walls in these tallest sites showed that none were anywhere near as thick as those of Paquimé. Instead, their basal thicknesses were 30 to 50 cm. From all these data, we argued in the 2001 volume that single-story construction was the norm in the Core and Middle Zones, but mound height was not compared for the inner and outer parts of the Core. We do so below, adding Middle Zone data for additional contrast.

In the Inner Core, 64 mounds showed heights ranging from 10 to 250 cm, and mean height was 86.7 cm (SD = 61.1). For 137 mounds from the Outer Core, height ranged from 20 to 260 cm, with a mean of 93.6 cm (SD = 52.1). The 141 room block mounds of the Middle Zone ranged in height from 10 to 250 cm, with a mean of 73.2 cm (SD = 48.1). These data are represented in figure 2.1.

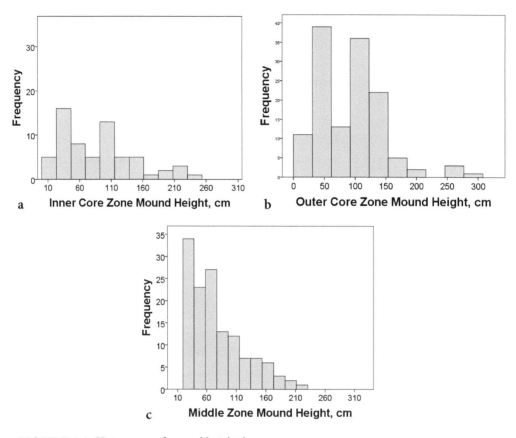

FIGURE 2.1 Histograms of mound height, by zone.

The means of these three height distributions were compared among the three zones using one-way analysis of variance, and significant difference was detected (F = 5.418, df = 337, p = .0001). Fisher's LSD (least significant difference) post hoc test was used to identify the location(s) of the difference among the three zones. It found that the inner and outer parts of the Core Zone did not differ significantly in the mean mound heights given above (p = .391). Rather, the difference lay between the Middle Zone and both parts of the Core Zone. For the Inner and Outer Core Zones versus the Middle Zone, p = >.001 in both comparisons. The mound height means given above show that the room block mounds of the Middle Zone were, on average, less tall than those of both parts of the Core Zone. Wall construction techniques seemed broadly similar in all survey zones, so the pattern just observed might reflect slightly thicker walls in the Core Zone. The 2001 study went on to divide mound heights into six classes (table 2.1). Shown there are counts and percentages of these height classes in the Inner and Outer Core Zones and the Middle Zone. These data emphasize that mounds up to 100 cm in height were by far the region's most common type of Medio period construction.

The tallest mound recorded in the entire survey sample is at Outer Core Zone Site 242 and is not typical of the area in which it is located. As this site is mentioned often in the present volume, its characteristics are reiterated here from the original publication

TABLE 2.1 Mound height class frequencies in the Core and Middle Zones

Class	Height (cm)	Inner Core		Outer Core		Middle Zone	
		Count	%	Count	%	Count	%
1	Up to 50	45	57.0	123	56.7	74	48.3
2	51–100	17	21.4	56	25.8	49	32.0
3	101–150	9	11.4	27	12.4	18	11.8
4	151–200	4	5.1	7	3.2	9	5.9
5	201–250	4	5.1	3	1.4	3	2.0
6	251–300	0	0	1[a]	0.5	0	0
Total		79	100.0	217	100.0	153	100.0

[a] This mound was 2.6 meters high.

(Whalen and Minnis 2001b). With a mound area of about 1,500 m², Site 242 falls into our small settlement category. The mound is unusually tall at 2.6 m, although we found no indication of more than one story. Excavation showed a well-preserved block of 15–20 rooms, some of which exceeded 20 m² in floor area, while others were of elaborate shapes. Wall thickness averaged over 50 cm, or within the lower end of the range of variation of the single-story Paquimé wall thicknesses. Site 242 thus shows the Paquimé tradition of large, thick-walled, irregularly shaped rooms. Several of the excavated rooms contained platform hearths complete with vent, fire pit, and ash pit, and the presence of a number of these fire features sets Site 242 apart from its excavated neighbors. Last, neatly plastered T-shaped doorways provided the investigated rooms with a high degree of interconnection. In short, the interior feature assemblage of Site 242 contains elements that are well known from Paquimé.

Outside the mound area, a vast system of agricultural terraces lies in a major arroyo about 500 m from the room block mound and ball court. Construction and use of these terraces would have been far beyond the capacity of the few dozen permanent residents of Site 242, and the system's production would have been vastly greater than their subsistence requirements. We postulated assemblies of people to work the system, to participate in rituals, and to feast. There are indications of temporary quarters at Site 242. Scattered around the room block mound are several large arc-shaped foundations of heavy stones. The arcs measure 4–6 m in diameter, and they are defined by one course of upright stones and by sufficient tumbled stone to have formed walls about 1 m high. Concentrations of Medio period pottery and chipped stone refuse were found in the arcs. Finally, there is strong evidence of commensal activity at Site 242, which contained many very large jars together with copious evidence of the interior surface erosion in ceramic vessels that we associate with preparation of fermented drink, such as corn beer.

All of these data demonstrate that thick-walled Site 242, although small, was a very elaborate community. The site shows, at small scale and in simplified form, many of the characteristics of Paquimé: thick-walled architecture, a large I-shaped ball court with a platform mound, and strong evidence of commensal activity, all in association with a huge system of agricultural terraces. We argued that this settlement was an outpost of Paquimé, organizing food production in a part of the uplands and imitating the primate center's architecture of power and ceremonialism to enhance its legitimacy (Whalen and Minnis 2001b).

None of the recorded room block mounds provided convincing evidence of more than one story, as table 2.1 shows. In fact, room block mounds with maximum present-day heights of 150 cm or less, which is certainly indicative of single-story construction, make up more than 90 percent of the observed cases all over the Core and Middle Zones. We may safely conclude that the overwhelming majority of the Core and Middle Zone neighbors of Paquimé were of single-story construction. This allows us to use area, or footprint, as a simple measure of mound size.

Mound Area and Room Block Size.

The 2001 study measured 79 cases in the Inner Core and 217 of their Outer Core counterparts. These figures are contrasted with 153 measurements from mounds in the Middle Zone. Figure 2.2 shows histograms of mound areas by zone. It is clear from the strongly right-skewed distributions of all three that most room block mounds were small. It is also apparent that mounds of the Inner Core Zone were, on average, considerably larger than those of the Outer Core or Middle Zone. This is reflected in the mound area means shown in table 2.2.

These means were compared using one-way analysis of variance, which detected a significant difference (F = 11.042, df = 2,392, p = .0001). The exact points of difference were highlighted by Fisher's LSD post hoc test. The mounds of the Inner Core Zone were significantly larger, on average, than those of the Outer Core or of the Middle Zone (p = .0001 in each comparison). The mean sizes of the mounds of the Outer Core and Middle Zone did not differ significantly (p = .591). The high level of variability in room block mound size all over the three zones, as shown by the standard deviations in table 2.2, raises doubt about the suitability of the mean as an effective measure of central tendency. Median room block mound areas of table 2.2 show a similar pattern, however. The Inner Core Zone still stands out, while the Outer Core and the Middle Zone are similar.

The coefficients of variation shown in the table are a simple comparative measure of datasets with different means and standard deviations. The coefficient is calculated as the standard deviation times 100 divided by the mean (Thomas 1986:83). Although coefficients of variation cannot be compared statistically, they show that Middle Zone mounds were more variable in area than were their Core Zone contemporaries. Nevertheless, it is not appropriate to use these data to argue that all Inner Core room block mounds are significantly larger than their Outer Core and Middle Zone counterparts.

To see where differences lay, the mounds of all three zones were divided into size classes, as in the 2001 study. There, small mounds are less than 1,000 m² in area. Medium-sized mounds ranged from 1,000 m² to 4,999 m². Large mounds measured from 5,000 m² to 9,999 m², and very large mounds exceeded 10,000 m². These divisions were adequate for

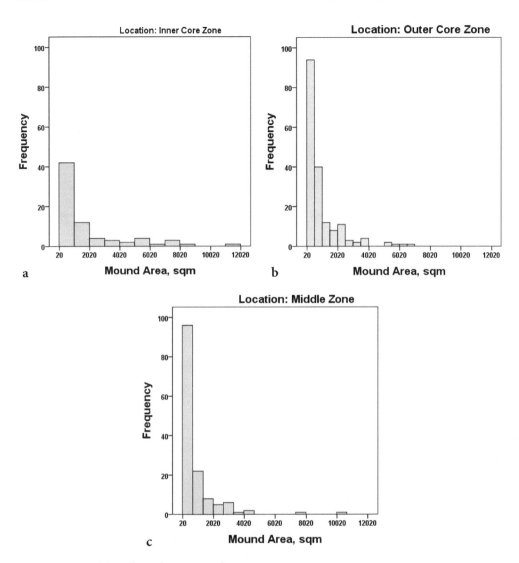

FIGURE 2.2 Mound area histograms, by zone.

the coarse-grained survey analysis, but the present study seeks a finer perspective on the small mounds that make up most of the recorded Medio period occurrences in all zones. Histograms of small mound areas (figure 2.3) show a bimodal distribution, justifying a further division into "very small" and "small" categories.

Using this new division, counts and frequencies of these mound size classes in the Core and Middle Zones are compared in table 2.3. It is interesting to observe that most of the smallest mounds fall into the "very small" category, covering less than 500 m^2 in area.

A chi-squared test was performed using the Inner Core, Outer Core, and Middle Zone counts of very small, small, and medium mounds shown in table 2.3. Large sites were not included, as one of their expected frequencies was too low for the chi-squared test. In any case, large sites are clearly much more common in the Inner Core Zone (12.7% of the total)

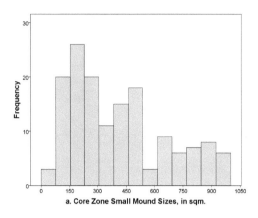
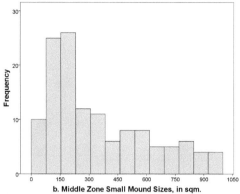

a. Core Zone Small Mound Sizes, in sqm.
b. Middle Zone Small Mound Sizes, in sqm.

FIGURE 2.3 Small mound histograms, by zone.

TABLE 2.2 Room block mound areas, by zone

Zone	n	Mean (m²)	Std. dev.	CV[a]	Median (m²)
Inner Core	79	1,882.2	2,538.8	139	2,481.2
Outer Core	217	918.9	1,148.7	128	445.0
Middle	153	835.2	1,340.9	159	400.0

[a]CV = coefficients of variation

TABLE 2.3 Mound size class frequencies, by zone

	Inner Core		Outer Core		Middle Zone	
Size class	Count	%	Count	%	Count	%
Very small	36	45.6	131	60.4	94	61.4
Small	15	19.0	38	17.5	30	19.6
Medium	18	22.8	43	19.8	27	17.6
Large	10	12.7	5	2.3	2	1.4
Total	79	100.0	217	100.0	153	100.0

than in the Outer Core Zone (2.3%) or the Middle Zone (1.4%). Table 2.4 shows the chi-squared result for the first three size categories. The test indicates no significant difference in size class frequencies by zone (x^2 = 2.94, df = 4, two-tailed p = .568).

In this sample, very small, small, and medium room block mounds are about equally common in each zone. Large sites, as just noted, are much more common in the Inner Core Zone. These data are suggestive, but the three survey zones are of unequal size, the Inner and Outer Core Zones each covering about 50 km², while the Middle Zone surveyed area was about 125 km². To obtain a more accurate picture of size class frequencies, we should consider the density in mounds per square kilometer. The mound size class densities for each zone are shown in table 2.5. These data again emphasize that very small and small mounds were more common in the Outer Core than in its inner part.

TABLE 2.4 Mound size class densities, by survey zone, in mounds per square kilometer

Size class	Inner Core	Outer Core	Middle Zone
Very small	0.60	1.98	0.80
Small	0.26	0.64	0.26
Medium	0.44	0.58	0.25
Large	0.12	0.06	0.48
Very large	0.02	0.0	0.01

TABLE 2.5 Mound size class descriptive statistics

Location	Size class	n	Mean	Std. dev.
	Very small	36	288.6	144.5
	Small	15	743.1	153.1
Inner Core Zone	Medium	18	2,205.4	1,152.9
	Large	9	8,159.5	2,448.8
	Very large	1	—	—
	Very small	97	254.7	121.0
	Small	38	727.8	141.1
Outer Core Zone	Medium	43	2,046.5	793.7
	Large	5	5,693.8	654.1
	Very large	0	—	—
	Very small	94	247.3	145.8
	Small	30	698.8	223.7
Middle Zone	Medium	27	2,249.5	869.5
	Large	1	7,167.9	1,906.5

The size class means and standard deviations of the three zones are shown in table 2.5. Large and very large mounds were combined into a single class for the analysis of variance used to compare the mean areas of mounds in the small, medium, and large classes across the three zones. A significant difference was detected ($F = 3.187$, df = 2,286, $p = .043$). Fisher's LSD post hoc test indicates that the significant difference among the small mound mean sizes is between the Inner Core and the means of the Outer Core and Middle Zones ($p = .014$ and .042, respectively). The small mounds of the Inner Core are larger than those of the other two zones (table 2.5). Medium-sized mound mean areas do not differ significantly among the three zones ($F = .496$, df = 2,85, $p = .611$). The large mound averages, however, contain a significant difference ($F = 2.334$, df = 2,15, $p = .031$). Fisher's LSD post hoc test shows that the difference lies in the Outer Core Zone, which differs from the Inner Core ($p = .038$) and from the Middle Zone ($p = .015$). The large mounds of the Outer Core Zone are smaller than those of either the Inner Core or the Middle Zone (table 2.5). This difference is attributable to the absence of very large mounds in the Outer Core Zone, while this size class is present in both the Inner Core and Middle Zones.

All of these analyses can be summed up as follows. Mounds are tallest in the Inner Core Zone, which might argue for somewhat thicker walls there. The complete range of mound areas, from small to very large, is present in the Inner Core. There are no very large mounds in the Outer Core Zone, and the single Middle Zone example barely reaches minimum size for inclusion in the "very large" category. Said another way, the largest mound sizes and frequencies drop from the Inner Core outward. Medium-sized mounds also appear to follow this trend, but at a lower, nonsignificant, level, as shown in table 2.5. Small mounds, on the other hand, are numerous in every zone, but they are at their largest in the Inner Core, while they decline in average size through the Outer Core and Middle Zones.

Room Count

To this point, we have not considered the number of contiguous rooms represented by mounds of each size class. To do this, we require counts of excavated rooms from contiguous areas on mounds of a range of sizes. The 2001 study had data from Paquimé, but these rooms were so much larger than any from neighboring sites that they were poor candidates for the task at hand. Site 298 of the Inner Core is fully uncovered by looting, exposing 22 rooms in an area of about 600 m^2 (Whalen and Minnis 2001a:111, fig. 4.6). A sample of one was not a reliable basis for room count projection, so the question remained unresolved. A later effort (Whalen and Pitezel 2015) produced a regression-based estimation of room count from excavated areas on sites up to about 500 m^2 in area. Here, room count could be read from the least-squares line for small sites. The fit of the least-squares line was good (R^2 linear = 0.89), but data points were few, and such estimators could not be projected beyond the upper limit of the dataset (mounds of ca. 500 m^2). Now, years later, data are available from more sites of a range of sizes in the inner and outer parts of the Core Zone, as shown in figure 2.4.

Regressions were done separately for the two parts of the core. For the Inner Core, R^2 = 0.992, and it was an almost identical 0.998 for the Outer Core. This means that we can predict room count from mound area on core sites with a very high level of precision. As the R^2 values were almost equal for the Inner and Outer Core, we use a single predictive formula, which is $Y = 1.81 + 0.05x$, where Y is estimated room count and x is room block area. Small mounds of 500 to 1,000 m^2 in area make up about 70 percent of all room block mounds in the core, and for the first time, we are in a strong position to estimate the number of rooms contained in these units.

Application of this predictive formula to 186 very small and small Core Zone mounds of up to 750 m^2 in area produces a total of 3,259 rooms in the surveyed areas. About 900 of these rooms are located in the Inner Core, while about 2,300 lie in the Outer Core. A considerable fraction of all Medio period rooms thus occurs in the small and very small room block mounds of the core. We do not have data to produce a regression-based room count estimator in the Middle Zone, but we have already noted that very small and small room block mounds make up about 80 percent of the recorded Medio total. Without being

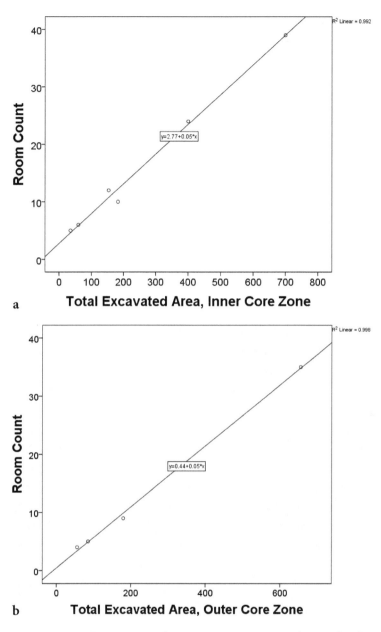

FIGURE 2.4 Regressions of room count on excavated areas for the Inner and Outer Core Zones.

able to estimate their number, we can assume that a considerable percentage of all Medio period rooms were in the smallest room block mounds of the Middle Zone. It thus appears that these small room blocks increase in frequency with movement outward from Paquimé and the Inner Core.

Unfortunately, the regression-based room estimation formula cannot be used on large sites, as the original dataset extends to only 700 m² of mound area. Our rough field estimate for Inner Core large Site 315 is about 170 rooms, while Inner Core large Site 565 had on the order of 200 rooms. Outer Core large Site 204 is estimated to have had roughly 250 rooms in its main mound.

Artifact Density

The next step in characterizing the room block mounds is considering the density of surface material. Two categories of artifacts are of particular significance here: sherds of imported ceramics and the stone doors of birdcages. The 2001 study (Whalen and Minnis 2001a:115–17), from which the following discussion is abstracted, described how ceramic collections were made from measured areas around each recorded mound. Mean and median ceramic densities of the Inner and Middle Zones were contrasted, and they were not found to differ at a statistically significant level. It was, however, noted that mounds with very low surface ceramic densities (up to five sherds per square meter) were present in both zones. There were, however, many more of them in the Inner Zone (95 mounds) than in the Middle Zone (38 mounds). It was further observed that about 95 percent of these low-density mounds fell into the small size category. The presence of many small mounds with very low ceramic densities suggested the existence of a class of small room blocks that were briefly occupied. These were found in both survey zones, but they were most common in the Inner (now Core) Zone. To these 2001 conclusions, we now add this volume's Inner and Outer Core distinction. Ceramic density data by zone and site size class are shown in table 2.6.

These data show that the lowest ceramic densities were found on the smallest mounds of the Inner Core Zone. In more specific terms, 31 of the 35 very small and small Inner Core mounds (ca. 89%) have ceramic densities of fewer than five sherds per square meter. The comparable figures in the Outer Core Zone are 68 of 111 mounds (ca. 61%) with fewer than five sherds per square meter. To our 2001 observation that the smallest Medio period room blocks were most numerous in the Core Zone, we add the understanding that those small sites with very low ceramic densities were most numerous in the Inner Core Zone.

TABLE 2.6 Ceramic densities on mounds by size class and zone, in sherds per square meter

Zone	Very small and small	Medium	Very large and large
Inner Core	$\bar{x} = 4.2$ $\sigma = 10.6$ $n = 35$	$\bar{x} = 21.9$ $\sigma = 29.5$ $n = 18$	$\bar{x} = 34.3$ $\sigma = 21.6$ $n = 8$
Outer Core	$\bar{x} = 8.1$ $\sigma = 12.3$ $n = 111$	$\bar{x} = 11.2$ $\sigma = 10.3$ $n = 31$	$\bar{x} = 21.7$ $\sigma = 17.1$ $n = 4$
Middle	$\bar{x} = 10.7$ $\sigma = 47.8$ $n = 118$	$\bar{x} = 13.4$ $\sigma = 19.4$ $n = 25$	$\bar{x} = 21.7$ $\sigma = 17.1$ $n = 4$

TABLE 2.7 Percentages of mounds with imported sherds in surface collections, by size class

Zone	Very small mounds (%)	Small mounds (%)	Medium mounds (%)	Large mounds (%)	Very large mounds (%)
Inner Core	26.7	44.8	50.0	100.0	100.0
Outer Core	5.8	10.8	11.1	40.0	—
Middle	9.4	37.5	46.2	100.0	100.0

The ceramics discussed to this point fit into the Medio period typologies, so they are presumed to be locally made. We should also consider the distributions of sherds from vessels presumed to have been imported. As at Paquimé, these are types known from the adjacent U.S. Southwest, including El Paso Polychrome, Chupadero Black-on-white, Salado Polychromes, and Mimbres Black-on-white. From the 2001 study, imported sherds were known to be slightly more common in the Inner (now Core) Zone than in the Middle Zone. It also was noted that much of the Middle Zone's imported pottery was Mimbres Black-on-white. Unlike the other imported types mentioned above, Mimbres Black-on-white is not contemporary with the Medio assemblages, in which it sometimes forms small components. Instead, it reflects underlying Viejo period occupations, as discussed earlier in this chapter. Percentages of mounds with imported sherds in the Core and Middle Zones are shown in table 2.7.

The Inner Core Zone clearly stands out across all mound size categories as having high frequencies of imported sherds in its surface collections. This is predictable, as Paquimé lies in the Inner Core, and that community contained the region's highest frequencies of imported ceramics. More surprising is the high frequency of imported sherds on very small Inner Core Zone mounds. This figure greatly exceeds the Outer Core and Middle Zone frequencies. Also surprising is the low frequency of imported sherds across all Outer Core Zone mound size categories. (Recall that there were no very large mounds in the Outer Core Zone survey area.)

Other artifacts found on the surfaces of survey sites are perforated stone disks and heavy plugs that closed them. These appear to have formed the lower doors of birdcages (see Di Peso 1974:2:598, fig. 385-2, for examples from Paquimé). We have argued that bird keeping, especially macaw husbandry, was an important part of ritual and social integration at Paquimé and among its neighbors. These cages were concentrated at Paquimé, although they were rare among adjacent communities of the Inner Core Zone, where their fragments were noted on just 3 of 74 mounds (4.1%). In the Outer Core, in contrast, cage door fragments were present on 27 of 181 mounds (14.9%). They were entirely absent on the mounds of the Middle Zone. In sum, while the Inner Core Zone mounds showed a much higher frequency of imported sherds, the mounds of the Outer Core contained a higher frequency of birdcage door stones. Ball courts show a similar pattern: concentrated at Paquimé, absent among its Inner Core neighbors, present in the Outer Core, and nearly absent in the Middle Zone. These differences likely have organizational implications, considered later in this volume.

Mound Grouping

How were these room block mounds distributed with respect to one another? How many occur alone, and how many in association with other room blocks? Of critical importance is room block contemporaneity. All of them show a Medio period ceramic assemblage. We have made a ceramic-based division of the period into early and late parts. This is not a useful basis for seriation of Medio period mounds, however, as most of the common wares are present all through the period. Further discussion of this problem is found in the original study (Whalen and Minnis 2009:115–34). Because we cannot use surface ceramic collections to separate Early from Late Medio occupation components on the area's room blocks, we are forced to consider all room block mounds simply as Medio period.

Preceding discussion contrasted room block mound spacing within the Inner and Outer Core Zones and the Middle Zone. We now turn to combination of these room blocks into settlements. In the 2001 study, we used a maximum intermound spacing of 160 m to define proximate room blocks, which were combined into settlements. It is noteworthy that this practice coincided closely with in-the-field decisions by survey crews on which room block mounds were close enough to justify grouping into settlements. Settlements, thus defined, contained from one to eight room block mounds. Settlement composition in the Inner and Outer Core Zones and in the adjacent Middle Zone is shown in table 2.8.

These data show that single room block settlements were most numerous in all zones. Two-mound settlements are the next most common, although these frequencies never approach those of their single room block counterparts. Settlements with larger numbers of component room block mounds are much rarer. Simple frequencies of room block numbers, however, do not tell the full story for each zone. Four-room block settlements, for example, were recorded twice in the Inner Core Zone and the same number of times in the Middle Zone, suggesting that such settlements were equally common in the two zones. Densities, in occurrences per square kilometer of surveyed land, of settlements with four room blocks provide a more accurate measure of their rarity, as shown in table 2.9.

TABLE 2.8 Room blocks per settlement, by zone

| | # Room blocks | | | | | | | | |
	1	2	3	4	5	6	7	8	Total
Inner Core	37	8	2	2	0	0	0	2	51
	72.5%	15.4%	3.9%	3.9%	0	0	0	3.9%	100.0%
Outer Core	67	18	12	3	4	0	0	0	104
	64.4%	17.3%	11.5%	2.9%	3.8%	0	0	0	100.0%
Middle Zone	77	18	6	2	0	1	0	0	104
	73.3%	17.1%	5.7%	1.9%	0	1.0%	0	0	100.0%

TABLE 2.9 Densities of settlements per square kilometer, by zone

	# Room blocks				
	1	2	3	4	5 to 8
Inner Core (45 km^2)	0.82 (37/45)[a]	0.18 (8/45)	0.04 (2/45)	0.04 (2/45)	0.04 (2/45)
Outer Core (55 km^2)	1.22 (67/55)	0.33 (18/55)	0.34 (12/55)	0.05 (3/55)	0.07 (4/55)
Middle Zone (125 km^2)	0.62 (77/125)	0.05 (6/125)	0.05 (6/125)	>.02 (2/125)	>.01 (1/125)

[a] Number of recorded settlements divided by that zone's total surveyed area in square kilometers.

It is interesting to note that the Outer Core Zone shows higher counts and densities of multiple-room block sites than either the Inner Core or Middle Zones. This could reflect a different occupational history in the Outer Core, or a different pattern of site destruction in the past. This leads to consideration of the sizes of room blocks that make up the settlements of each zone. We begin this comparison with the most common category of Medio period settlement: those with only one room block. Histograms of single room block sizes by zone, as measured by mound area, are shown in figure 2.5. All three histograms are strongly skewed toward small room block mound areas. In fact, most of these are in the "very small" category, up to 500 square meters. It is also clear, however, that single room block settlements show a wide range of mound sizes. Descriptive statistics on room block mounds that occur alone are provided in table 2.10.

The data show that the single room block settlements of the Inner Core Zone differ in several ways from those of the Outer Core and Middle Zones. First, the very small room blocks of the Inner Core are the largest, on average. An analysis of variance and a least significant difference post hoc test show that the very small Inner Core mounds are significantly larger than those of the Outer Core or Middle Zone ($p = .012$). They are also less common, composing 36.6 percent of Inner Core Zone room blocks, while the comparable figures for the Outer Core and Middle Zones are both about 54 percent. Second, room block mounds of the small and medium size classes are somewhat larger in the Inner Core Zone, although these differences do not reach statistically significant levels, and their frequencies are about the same in all three zones.

A third observation concerns the large and very large room block mounds. These occur in all three zones, but they were found at the highest frequency in the Inner Core Zone (16.7%), while the Outer Core figure is 2.8 percent, and that of the Middle Zone is 6.1 percent. Not only are the largest room blocks the least common in the Outer Core Zone, but they are also smallest in the Outer Core Zone. The largest blocks of the Inner Core and Middle Zones exceed 10,000 m^2 in area, but their largest counterpart in the Outer Core is substantially smaller, at only 6,500 m^2. The largest single room block settlement of the Outer Core, then, is much smaller than the same sorts of settlements in the other two zones. There is not, in other words, a distance decline in the frequency and size of the largest room blocks from the Inner Core outward. Rather, there is a substantial drop in

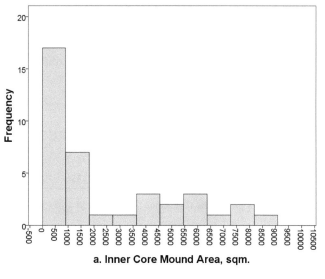

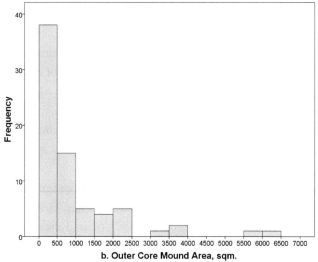

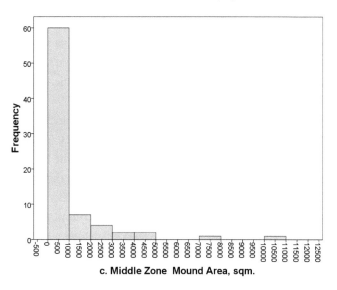

FIGURE 2.5 Single room block mound size histograms, by zone.

TABLE 2.10 Descriptive statistics for single room block mounds, by zone

	Very small	Small	Medium	Large and very large
Inner Core	$\bar{x} = 360.1$[a] a = 144.5 $n = 11$ rg:57–500[b] 36.6%[c]	$\bar{x} = 763.3$ a = 150.6 $n = 7$ rg:519–950 23.4%	$\bar{x} = 2,493.4$ a = 1,398.2 $n = 7$ rg:1,075–4,200 23.3%	$\bar{x} = 2,493.4$ a = 1,763.6 $n = 5$ rg:5,300–10,400 16.7%
Outer Core	$\bar{x} = 265.8$ a = 104.9 $n = 39$ rg:114–500 54.2%	$\bar{x} = 682.6$ a = 136.9 $n = 14$ rg:520–930 19.4%	$\bar{x} = 2,081.8$ a = 812.2 $n = 17$ rg:1,050–3,825 23.6%	$\bar{x} = 5,777.5$ a = 314.7 $n = 2$ rg:5,555–6,500 2.8%
Middle Zone	$\bar{x} = 230.1$ a = 125.3 $n = 44$ rg:50–499 53.7%	$\bar{x} = 717.1$ a = 166.0 $n = 16$ rg:502–980 19.5%	$\bar{x} = 2,234.9$ a = 918.5 $n = 17$ rg:1,210–4,050 20.7%	$\bar{x} = 7,930.0$ a = 1,696.1 $n = 5$ rg:5,875–10,675 6.1%

[a] Mound area in square meters.
[b] Range of observed room block mound sizes, in square meters.
[c] Percentage of each room block size class within its zone.

frequency and size of the largest single room blocks of the adjacent Outer Core. These figures rise again from the Outer Core to the Middle Zone.

Settlement Population Estimates

The preceding consideration of settlement sizes based on room block mound areas leaves an open question: How many people resided in these settlements? This is a notoriously difficult question to answer with any sort of settlement pattern data (for example, see the discussion in Drennan et al. 2015). To date, there has been only one large-scale attempt to assign population numbers to Medio period settlements using the 1959 survey map discussed earlier in this chapter and partially reproduced as map 2.1. It shows more than 1,000 Casas Grandes sites that are presumably Medio period.

Serious points of difference, however, are the population estimates assigned to these sites. In addition to locations, the Di Peso map shows two categories of sites: those with assumed populations of 100 to 500 people and a few with 500 to 1,000 residents. Di Peso's estimates have been correctly termed "arbitrary" (Lekson et al. 2004:60). There is no published discussion to justify the map's figures. Almost all of the more than 1,000 sites on the Di Peso map belong to the smaller of these two population size categories. This is more than 1,000 sites, each with 100 to 500 people. The Di Peso map thus argues for a population of 100,000 to 500,000 people within about 60 km of Paquimé, assuming that all Medio period occupations were contemporary. This is an incredible population density for anywhere in the arid NW/SW, and Di Peso further argued that Paquimé itself could have had as many as 5,000 residents (Di Peso et al. 1974:4:207). Clearly, he saw an enormous center surrounded by a vast regional population.

For more than two decades, the Di Peso map was the only published presentation of settlement pattern, site density, and population size in northwest Chihuahua. Comparative data ultimately were provided by an intensive regional survey in 1994–95 (Whalen and Minnis 2001a). This work recorded more than 300 Medio period mound sites at a range of distances to the north and west of Paquimé. A number of these sites are identifiable on the Di Peso map, so the first point of comparison is site density in particular drainages. The 1994–95 survey units cannot be presumed to be exactly congruent with earlier ones. Even so, site counts in major drainages do not differ greatly between the Di Peso map and the 1994–95 survey.

The estimated sizes of these sites is another matter. The 1994–95 survey recorded mound area as a measure of site size. Brand (1933) did the same to a limited extent. The 1994–95 survey sites were divided into very small, small, medium, large, and very large categories based on room block mound area (Whalen and Minnis 2001a:108–10 and this chapter). The smallest categories of sites overwhelmingly dominated the settlement array in every part of the survey area, and the median size of all mounds was less than 500 m². This suggests a relatively small population, even assuming that many of the smallest sites were occupied at the same time as their larger counterparts.

Discussion earlier in this chapter (refer to figure 2.4) uses old and new data to produce a regression-based formula to estimate room count from excavated area. Estimated room count can either be read directly from the least-squares line, or it can be calculated using the values of constants provided by the regression formula. In either case, these data show that a mound of 200 m² should have about 10 rooms, while one of 500 m² should contain on the order of 25. These estimates are obviously not very precise because of the small number of data points. Even if the estimated room count is doubled, however, we still have a situation in which half of all Medio period room block mounds recorded by the 1994–95 survey have fewer than 25 rooms. Preceding discussion also showed that most settlements consisted of single room blocks. Using the regression formula of figure 2.4, we can estimate the numbers of rooms in these smallest settlements in the surveyed portions of each of the three zones discussed here. For the Inner Core Zone, we estimate a total of 460 rooms; for the Outer Core Zone, the estimate is 1,120 rooms; and for the Middle Zone, 1,430 rooms. The estimated total for the smallest settlements, then, is just over 3,000 rooms. This is substantial housing capacity.

There is no precise way to translate pueblo room count into a population estimate. The problems are well known, including abandoned rooms, changes in room function, cultural ideas of proper space allocation, and variable family sizes. Further discussion is provided elsewhere (e.g., Drennan et al. 2015). A literature search shows that the number of people estimated by archaeologists per pueblo room varies from 0.5 to 2.0. These are useful estimators for the present study only if the Casas Grandes area rooms are about the same size as those of the U.S. Southwest. We discussed this issue in an earlier study (Whalen and Minnis 2009:74–75). Apart from Paquimé itself, the Casas Grandes area rooms fall into the middle of the size distribution for nearly 3,000 rooms on 27 prehistoric pueblos in the U.S. Southwest. The neighbors of Paquimé thus had rooms of about the same sizes as those of the Southwest, and it is valid to use that area's population estimator figures. If we take the highest of these figures, or an average of two residents per room, and multiply it by double our estimated room counts, we still have fewer than 30 people at half of the Medio period sites recorded by the intensive survey. These are many of the same sites to which the Di Peso map assigned populations of 100 to 500 residents.

We cannot use the regression of figure 2.4 for larger sites, as the analysis is only valid within the specified range of simulated mound areas (i.e., up to 700 m^2). We can, however, calculate the percentage of room block mound area excavated in the main mound at large Site 204 and extrapolate the number of rooms dug to the whole room block mound. The area covered by the main mound at Site 204 is about 9,250 m^2. We dug about 800 m^2, or about 8.6 percent of the mound (Whalen and Minnis 2009). The excavated areas that total 800 m^2 come from all parts of the main mound, and together they contain 31 rooms of various shapes and sizes. If 800 m^2 contained 31 rooms, then 100 percent of the mound should contain about 360 rooms. We reduce this total by 20 percent to compensate for outward "smearing" of the room block perimeter, arriving at a total of about 250 rooms for the main mound of Outer Core Zone large Site 204.

Applying the estimates of 0.5 to 2.0 people per room gives a population estimate at the site's peak of about 150–580 residents. The 20 percent figure is arbitrary, but whether the room count is reduced by 10 percent, 15 percent, or 20 percent, the estimated population of the site remains between the mid-100s and the mid-600s, which we summarize as a few hundred people. We emphasize that Site 204 is one of the region's largest according to the 1994–95 survey. The Di Peso map's *smallest* sites were estimated to have had 100 to 500 people, while we estimate about that population to have been present at one of the 1994–95 survey's *largest* communities. Our contention, then, is that the Di Peso map vastly overestimates the Medio period population of northwest Chihuahua in general and of the Casas Grandes region in particular. We do not attribute this difference to change in site sizes (e.g., by erosion) between the times of Di Peso's work and the 1994–95 survey some 35 years later. In the few cases where the 1994–95 survey and Brand's survey (1933) recorded what appears to be the same site, size estimates are comparable. We have recently argued (Whalen et al. 2010) that the center of Paquimé itself was much smaller than Di Peso esti-mated, with a correspondingly smaller population. We now extend the same argument to the population of the center's hinterland. We see a Medio period settlement system that was described fairly accurately by early reconnaissance in the region. It contained many settle-ments, most of which were small places with populations of about 30 people. The region's few larger communities had, by our estimation, populations of a few hundred people. This argues that the size of the region's Medio period population has been much overestimated. Reduction of population estimates significantly reduces the scale of regional organization needed to form and operate any sort of polity.

Regional Settlement Distribution

Also to be considered in the Inner Core Zone is the distribution of settlements with regard to the region's central place. Our survey showed that a range of large, medium, and small Medio sites lie within two to seven kilometers of Paquimé. Map 2.1 shows this settlement pattern. It is noteworthy that this concentration of large and very large Medio period communities is unmatched anywhere else in the region. That is, the Inner Core Zone's Casas Grandes River valley contains more sizable Medio communities than any other part of the region, and they are closer together than in any other surveyed area. Some are less than 1 km apart, and two of the large Inner Core sites are less than 2 km to the south and east from Paquimé itself. A third large settlement lies about 5 km south of the center. The archaeological record immediately north of Paquimé has been all but expunged by the modern town of Old Casas Grandes, so the situation that we observe south of Paquimé may have been replicated to the north.

Di Peso observed the same phenomenon, and he considered the Casas Grandes Culture to be at its maximum size in the eponymous river valley, or what we now term the Inner Core Zone. We see several possible explanations for the proximity of large communities. In the first of these, the peaks of the larger communities of the Inner Core Zone are not contemporary with the Late Medio fluorescence of Paquimé. Instead, most of their occupations date to the early part of the Medio, before the apogee of the primate center. In this scenario, the populations of the nearest neighbors diminish as that of Paquimé rises. In an alternative chronological scenario, large, medium, and small communities of the Inner Core Zone are contemporary with Paquimé, all existing at their peaks in the Late Medio period. We emphasize that all the larger sites of the Inner Core have substantial amounts of Ramos Polychrome in their surface ceramic assemblages, showing at least some site use in the Late Medio. The crucial question, of course, is how much Late Medio occupation is present, and this cannot be determined reliably from surface observations.

Post-Paquimé Occupations

In the long-dominant Di Peso model, there was no occupation in the upper Casas Grandes River valley after the abandonment of Paquimé. In this model, the last occupations of Paquimé were characterized by a crude form of architectural remodeling that he termed the Diablo phase of the Medio period (Di Peso 1974:2:316–25). We now date Diablo times to the early decades of the 1400s. The complete Medio period ceramic assemblage continued to be used. The end of the Diablo phase, of the Medio period, of Paquimé, and of occupation of the upper Casas Grandes River valley were all synchronous. The waning center was sacked and burned, and much of its population were massacred by outside invaders from the east. The survivors of this attack fled from the Casas Grandes area and into the adjacent Sierra Madre, resulting in the abandonment of the valley. This interpretation was strongly Paquimé centered, and little consideration was given to the fates of the many satellite villages in the area.

In the remnant population's mountain occupation, Di Peso saw great simplification of the ceramic assemblage and architectural style. This complex differed so much from the old Medio period way of life that he termed it the Robles phase of the Tardío (Late) period. Robles occupations were confined to the mountains, and none was recognized in the now-empty upper Casas Grandes River valley. This classification has since been criticized by others, who assert that the so-called Robles phase ceramics should still be classed as Late Medio, thereby rejecting the need for new phase and period designations (Phillips and Carpenter 1999).

It will not be possible to decide among these scenarios in the Casas Grandes area until we know a good deal more about the occupational chronologies and levels of functional diversity of sites closest to the center. The succeeding chapter first describes the sites selected for excavation in the Inner Core project, and then discusses their chronologies.

# Chapter 3

The Inner Core Zone Excavation Project

Sites and Chronology

Inner Core communities were dependent on Paquimé for at least some of their public ritual activities, but the nature and extent of this dependency were not clear from surface data alone. Knowledge of how the center's nearest neighbors were integrated into the regional system is crucial to the developing picture of how, when, and to what extent Paquimé organized its immediate surroundings. Accordingly, the Inner Core Zone Excavation Program was begun in 2008 to investigate a set of the nearest large and small neighbors of Paquimé. This strategy was intended to produce data comparable to those of the Outer Core Zone Excavation Project (Whalen and Minnis 2009). To the new Inner Core data, whenever possible, we add the published data from Paquimé (Di Peso et al. 1974).

Site Selection: The Large Sites

Surveys from Brand's in 1933 to ours in 1994 show many Medio period communities in the Inner Core Zone, which is today and always has been the regional center of population growth and intensive agriculture. Accordingly, destruction of sites there is extensive. Surveys early in the twentieth century, made when modern populations were much smaller, recorded many sites that have since been destroyed. Likewise, a number of the Inner Core sites recorded by us in 1989 and 1994 are gone today, lost to housing, field leveling, and road construction. The second site destruction factor is looting to satisfy the high demand for Casas Grandes Polychrome vessels on the international antiquities market. The situation in Chihuahua is much like that of the Classic Mimbres area in nearby New Mexico. Sites near population centers are the most severely looted, and the larger and more conspicuous sites have suffered the most extensively.

As a result, surviving large sites in the Inner Core Zone are few and heavily damaged, but they are the only sources of the critical organizational information discussed in the preceding chapter. These are far from ideal conditions under which to select sites for excavation, as decisions must be based more on what is left than on what would be best. There

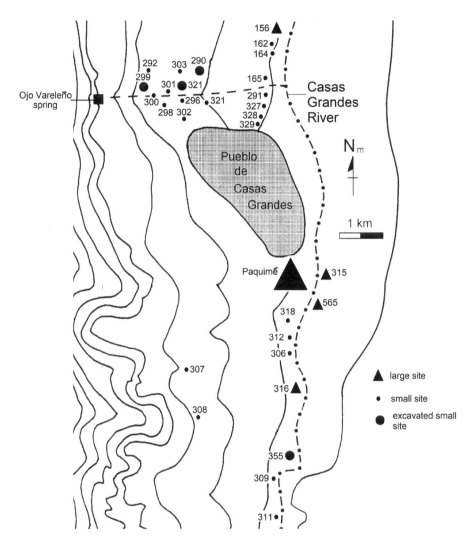

MAP 3.1 Large and small sites of the Inner Core Zone.

are four larger sites remaining in the Inner Core Zone (map 3.1). Site 316 lies about 3 km south of Casas Grandes, and Site 156 is about 6.5 km north of Paquimé. Both large sites and the center lie in the valley of the Casas Grandes River. Both large sites have room block mound areas, placing them at the lower end of our "large" community size category. The third and fourth sites, numbers 315 and 565, are situated somewhat differently, lying on the floodplain of the Casas Grandes River, some 2 km east of the primate center. Site 315 falls at the high end of our "medium" community size category, and it is the last surviving example of a larger floodplain community in the Inner Core Zone. Site 565 also lies on the east side of the Río Casas Grandes on a low terrace. It is slightly less than two kilometers from Paquimé. The 565 mound falls well within our "large" site category.

All of these sites have dense surface assemblages of Medio period pottery. Ramos Polychrome is prominent on all four large sites, proving that at least some of their occupations are Late Medio, or after AD 1300. Also present, however, is Dublán Polychrome, which occurs most commonly in the Early Medio. All four sites thus have surface indications of extensive Medio period occupation. The extent of looting was a critical point of difference among the three sites. Damage at large Site 156 was so severe as to remove it from consideration, as much of its mound has been destroyed by machine excavation. The three mounds of large Site 316 are very heavily looted by hand digging and by a little Historic construction. A dense mesquite thicket covered all three mounds, making for very difficult access. Site 565 consists of a single long room block mound, which was free of mesquite but severely damaged by extensive Historic construction as well as by modern farming activity. Intact deposits were expected to have survived in both cases, however, and either Site 316 or 565 could have been investigated in pursuit of this project's goals. Site 565 was selected for this round of excavation because of its relative ease of access. Medium to large Site 315 presents a much better picture. About 20 percent of the mound area was dug away by machine at some point in the past, and the remaining part of the mound was looted at a typical moderate level by hand digging. This site was selected for investigation because of its condition and its close proximity to Paquimé. The two selected sites are described below.

Site 315

This community lies on the east side of the Río Casas Grandes valley floor (refer to map 3.1). The site's single room block mound rises about 1.5 m above the level of the surrounding fields. Local people informed us that on rare occasions, the river has flooded all these low-lying fields without reaching the mound itself. The site consists of a single-storied block of contiguous adobe-walled rooms covering about 6,500 m² (figure 3.1). The mound is compact in shape, although several small plazas were visible on the undamaged sides. Extensive plowing of the surrounding area has removed any traces of the exterior features

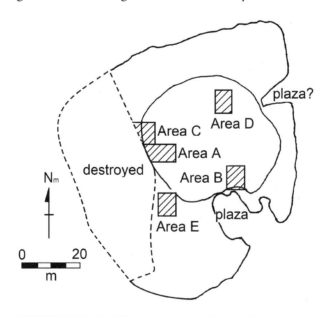

FIGURE 3.1 The Site 315 mound and excavation areas.

and facilities that might have surrounded the community. Ceramics collected before excavation from the surface of the mound indicated an occupation across the entire Medio period, making the site ideal for the project goals expressed earlier in this chapter.

The western side of the mound was dug away by machine for use as road fill, as shown in figure 3.1. Although unfortunate, this illicit excavation provided a profile that passed near the center of the mound. Visible in this cut were adobe walls and floors, and some of the excavation areas worked inward from these architectural features. Other excavation areas were spread over the central part of the site. In two seasons of work, 21 complete rooms were dug, as were surviving fragments of five badly damaged rooms. These rooms are shown by excavation area in figure 3.2.

Subfloor work in Rooms 5 and 10 of Area A revealed a pit house of the preceding Viejo period. The structure was extensively cut up, but it appears to have been circular, with a diameter of about 3 m and an area of roughly 7 m². No intramural features were found, but at least some of the undated extramural features found beneath the Medio period floors of nearby Room 2 likely belonged to this pit house occupation. This structure is illustrated and discussed under the Viejo period heading in chapter 4.

Site 565

This community is located on the east side of the Río Casas Grandes, almost directly opposite the ruins of Paquimé and about 1 km south of Site 315 (refer to map 3.1). Site 565 consists of a single elongated room block measuring about 230 m north–south by about 50 m east–west. The northern half of the mound was leveled by machine, and the loosened earth was pushed into a large water reservoir, as shown in figure 3.3. Despite this destruction, wall segments were visible, and relatively intact deposits were expected. The western edge of the mound was less disturbed than the eastern side, which had been heavily plowed for years, but disturbance on all sides of the mound was so extensive as to remove traces of the extramural features and facilities that must have existed around the community.

Nearly ten weeks of excavations were carried out in the four areas marked in figure 3.3. Sixteen surface rooms were completely excavated, as shown in figure 3.4. In addition, a segment of a rectangular room with low adobe walls was found beneath the room block remains in Area Z. This structure most closely resembles the pit house-to-pueblo transition dwellings of the Late Viejo period located by Di Peso and colleagues at the nearby Convento site. A nearby roasting pit, also beneath the pueblo floor level, contained sherds of the Red-on-brown pottery that characterizes Viejo times. Both the structure and the feature are illustrated and discussed in more detail in the next chapter.

Site Selection: The Small Sites

Small residential sites are the region's most common and least understood type of community. In the preceding chapter, we estimate that these small occupations accommodated a

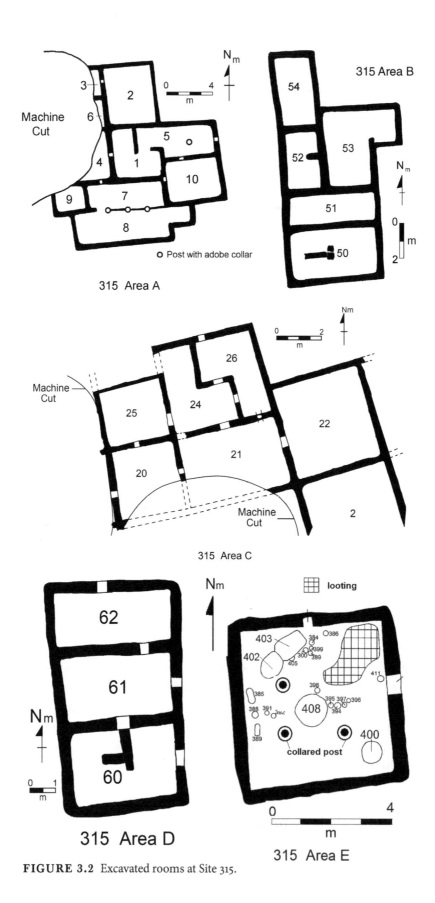
FIGURE 3.2 Excavated rooms at Site 315.

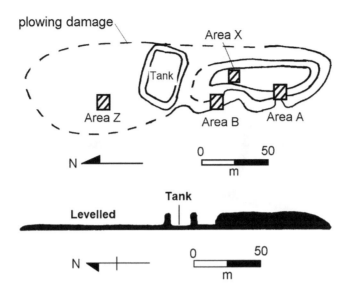

FIGURE 3.3 The Site 565 mound and excavation areas.

significant part of the regional population during some or all of the Medio period. They contribute about three-quarters of Medio period room block mounds recorded in our survey areas. In the Inner Core, the figure is 76 percent (26/34). All consist of a single low mound less than 1 m high, and half of these are less than 60 cm in height. The presence of a visible mound suggests architecture more substantial than jacal, or mud-and-stick construction, but their low mound heights argue for thin-walled adobe construction, of which a number of examples were visible in looters' excavations. Small residential site sizes are measured as the number of square meters covered by the room block mound. Histograms of these mound sizes for the Inner Core Zone, most of which are less than 500 m², are shown in figure 3.5. The distribution, however, is bimodal, with a second group of small sites measuring more than 500 m² but less than 1,000 m². In both groups, surface artifact assemblages are relatively sparse and simple. On many small residential sites, utility wares make up large percentages of surface collections, and no polychromes at all are found on the surfaces of some of these sites. In contrast, polychrome ceramics comprise 10 to 15 percent of large site assemblages and are always well represented in those surface collections.

Small Medio period residential sites were found in every surveyed area in the Casas Grandes region. They occur in the same river valley and piedmont locations as do larger residential sites, so they were clearly not restricted to poor, low-productivity segments of the environment. The small sites reported on in the present volume are all located in or around the Casas Grandes River valley, as is Paquimé itself. It is the best-watered portion of the regional environment, with the highest potential for agricultural production. It should, therefore, have been the most attractive zone for Medio period populations.

Small sites are also plentiful in the Outer Core Zone, where a few have been excavated. Sites 231, 242, and 317 were dug in the early days of our project. These were selected based on the unpublished results of a discriminant analysis of ceramics, which suggested that 231

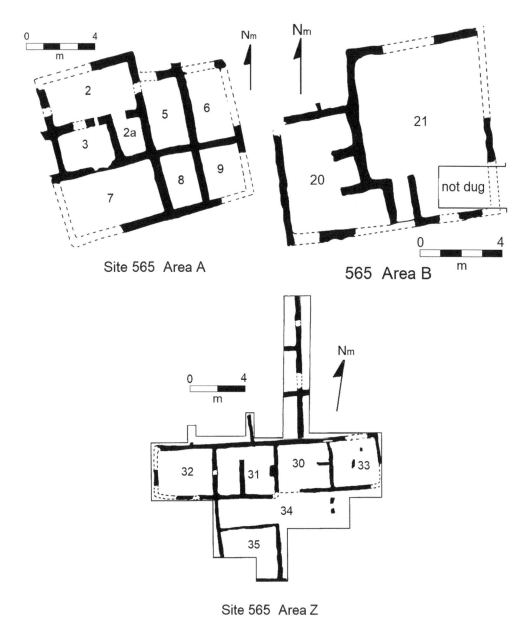

FIGURE 3.4 Excavated Rooms at Site 565.

was early in the Medio period, while the others were late. Subsequent dating showed that all were Late Medio. The Casa Chica site was investigated by INAH archaeologists based on the high frequency of El Paso Polychrome on its surface (Cruz Antillón et al. 2004). With the exception of Site 242, the others seem to be small, simple residential loci, with evidence for agriculture and the usual range of domestic activities, but with few or no luxuries. From so small a sample we cannot say whether this is an accurate characterization of the site type as a whole. Neither do we have any adequate concept of the range of variability of small residential site characteristics. We had gained all we could from study of these sites'

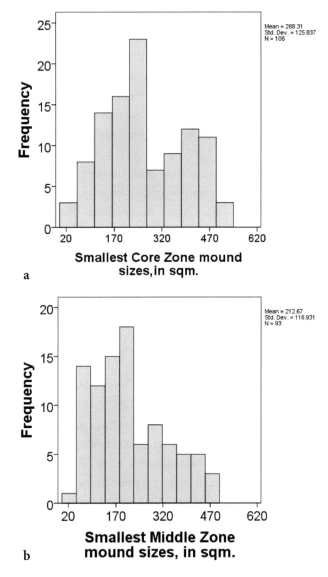

FIGURE 3.5 Inner Core Zone and Middle Zone smallest site size histograms.

sparse surface remains, and only their excavation would improve our current picture of their natures and their occupational histories.

The small Inner Core sites excavated in the 2013–14 seasons were chosen from 26 candidates to produce a sample of settlements north and south of Paquimé. All are shown on map 3.1. Permission to excavate on Sites 306, 312, and 318 was refused by the landowner, removing these from consideration. Sites 327, 328, and 329 had been completely destroyed since we recorded them in 1994. Site 291 was found to be a Historic occupation associated with the nearby Convento of San Antonio de Padua. Sites 310 and 311 were found to be in poor condition. Other small sites in the rocky uplands were omitted. Sites 355, 321, 299A, and 290 were better preserved, and excavation permission was secured.

Of the selected sites, 290, 299A, and 321 are located about 5 km north of Paquimé on the broad piedmont slope overlooking the drainage of the Ojo Vareleño (see map 3.1). This is a productive spring that rises from the foot of the hills along the west side of the Casas Grandes River valley. Below it is a broad piedmont slope that extends down to the edge of the river valley. This piedmont slope appears to have been the scene of extensive agave cultivation, as roasting pits and great quantities of burned stone were observed on the eroded ground surfaces. Also sometimes present were the small stone piles that were used as a moisture-conserving mulch around the bases of agave plants. This is a practice observed elsewhere in the Casas Grandes area, as well as in southern Arizona (S. Fish et al. 1992; Minnis and Whalen 2020). The lower portion of this piedmont slope forms the first terrace of the western side of the valley of the Casas Grandes River. The fourth selected site, 355, is the only exception to this locational pattern. It is located some 3.5 km south of Paquimé on the edge of a terrace overlooking the Casas Grandes valley. Excavation was planned at other nearby sites in similar locations, but as noted above, difficulties with a landowner prevented their investigation. Each of the four selected small sites is described below.

Site 290

This is a single low room block mound, probably originally C-shaped, on the lower part of the Ojo Vareleño piedmont slope. Surface collections yielded small quantities of sherds belonging to characteristic Medio period Brown, Red, and corrugated utilitarian types, plus a little Ramos Polychrome. The mound covers about 200 m², and its height above ground surface was about 40 cm. Its center portion had been dug out with power machinery (figure 3.6), leaving a few visible wall segments. Nine complete rooms and surviving fragments of four others were excavated in the 2014 season, as shown in figure 3.7, and they are typical of small residential communities. What was unusual, however, was the paucity of intramural floor features, especially the hemispherical hearths with plastered sides that are found on Medio sites of all sizes. Some were present in a few of the rooms, but other large interior spaces had none. In addition, the construction technique of Site 290's rooms was markedly different than we had previously encountered on large or small Medio period sites. It is described in chapter 4 under the heading "The End of the Casas Grandes Architectural Tradition." What appeared to be a small midden area lay at the southwest corner of the mound, but it was extensively eroded and deflated.

Site 299A

This small mound lies near the highest part of the piedmont slope, less than 1 km from Ojo Vareleño. The single mound of Site 299A was as small and simple as that of Site 291, measuring 80 m² and rising less than 50 cm above ground level (figure 3.8). The soil was darkly stained, and what appeared to be small fire features were visible in several places around the perimeter of the mound. Surface collection produced the normal range of Medio period pottery sherds plus a large assemblage of chipped stone. The site was

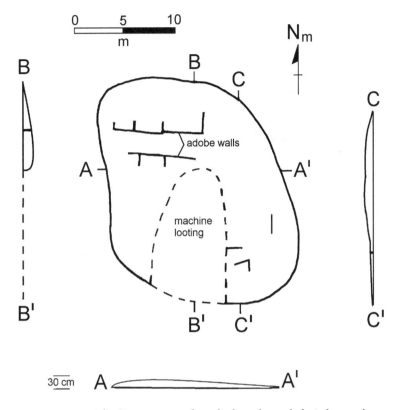

FIGURE 3.6 The Site 290 mound on the heavily eroded piedmont slope.

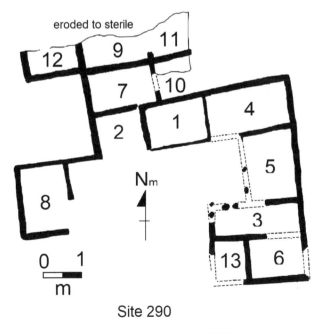

FIGURE 3.7 Excavated rooms at small Site 290.

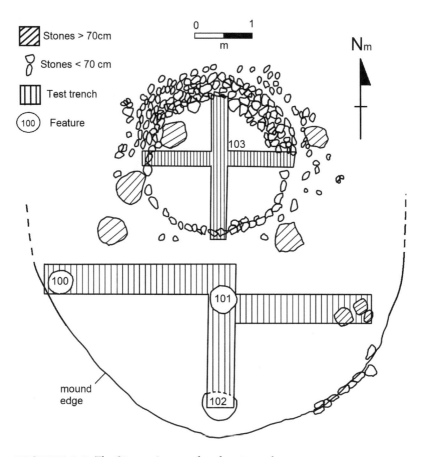

FIGURE 3.8 The Site 299A mound and test trenches.

thought to be a small residential room block, although it did not look exactly like the others studied by this project. It was chosen for excavation to capture a broad range of variability in this site type.

The southern edge of the mound was best defined, as the northern edge intersected the land's slope. Test Trenches 1, 2, and 3 were placed across the southern side of the mound, encountering no walls, but several small fire pits were filled with burned rock. As these did not appear to be residential deposits, Test Trench 4 was extended to the north. The nature of the mound soon became clear. At its center was an enormous roasting oven, and a vast quantity of debris from the oven appears to have formed much of the mound (figure 3.9).

Work at Paquimé by Di Peso and colleagues revealed five of these large facilities, which are presumed to have been used for large-scale baking of agave in public feasting contexts. We investigated five more of these ovens in the Casas Grandes area (Minnis and Whalen 2005, 2020:52–57; Whalen and Minnis 2009:23). The ovens of Paquimé stood out as by far the largest. The smallest four of them ranged from 12.6 to 19.2 m^3, with an average of 16.3 m^3 ($\sigma = 2.7$). The fifth and largest oven measured 42.4 m^3. The five ovens we excavated in the hinterlands of Paquimé, although built in an identical manner to those at the center, were uniformly much smaller. Their mean volume was only 8.4 m^3 ($\sigma = 1.6$). The newly excavated

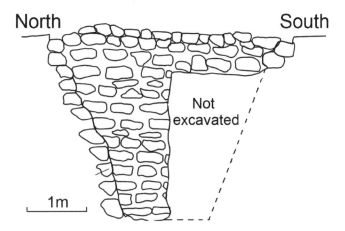

FIGURE 3.9 The oven at Site 299A.

oven from Site 299A alters this picture. It is by far the largest ever dug outside Paquimé, with a volume of some 20.3 m³. In fact, the Site 299A oven is exceeded in size only by the largest one at Paquimé. The excavation at Site 299A, then, did not expand our sample of small residential sites, but the oven is a welcome addition to the large oven dataset.

Site 321

This small Medio period mound lies on the north side of the piedmont slope overlooking the Arroyo Vareleño (refer to map 2.1). The area around the site was the scene of extensive lime (or caliche) mining in recent times. Power equipment had made large cuts in the landscape, wholly or partially obliterating a number of sites. The center of the single mound forming Site 321 was cut away by this activity, and the site has also been extensively looted by hand and machine digging (figure 3.10).

Despite its condition, our attention was drawn to the site because of the extensive and unusual stone construction on the east side of the room block (figure 3.11). Rough stone building like this is not a Medio period technique, and it clearly was done atop the Medio wall remains. The original Medio floors were reused by the stone builders. This stone construction was not a ubiquitous feature of this community but was confined to a small portion of the room block's periphery. Late Medio period pottery sherds were lightly scattered all over and around the mound, including the area of stone construction. Careful examination revealed no Historic artifacts in or around these stones. We believe that this stone building was completed after the collapse of Paquimé, a topic discussed in more detail in subsequent chapters.

Site 355

Only one of our Casas Grandes valley small site samples is not located around the drainage of the spring north of Paquimé. Site 355 lies about 3.5 km south of Paquimé (refer

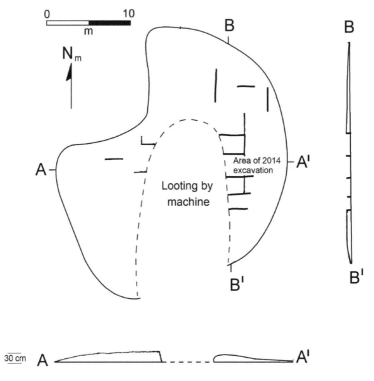

FIGURE 3.10 The Site 321 mound and excavation area.

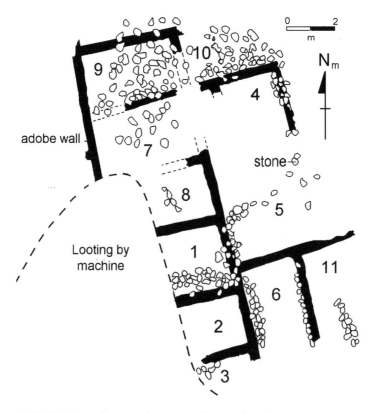

FIGURE 3.11 Excavated rooms at Site 321, showing stone construction that was later added over the original adobe walls.

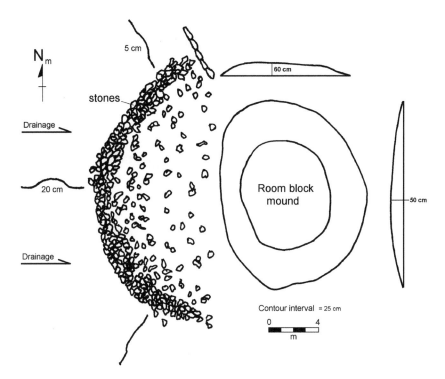

FIGURE 3.12 The Site 355 mound and the stone arc built upslope from it.

to map 3.1) and in the same topographic situation: on the edge of the western terrace overlooking the fertile Casas Grandes valley. Immediately behind the 355 community, to the west, is a steep, rugged piedmont zone leading to high hills. The oval room block mound measures about 15 m north–south and 12 m east–west. It covers some 155 m^2 and rises to a maximum of 60 cm above ground level. An unusual feature of Site 355 is the stone arc to the west of the mound and upslope of it. Small stones of 10–15 cm in maximum dimension have been piled together into an arc surrounding the room block mound. The arc measured about 20 m long by 3 m wide. The stones are piled about 20 cm above ground level in the center and about 5 cm high at the ends of the arc, but the original height of the feature is unknown. Its purpose was apparently to divert runoff water from the adjacent piedmont slope (figure 3.12). There is no indication of the date of construction of the arc. It could belong to the Medio period, which is the site's major occupation component. The 1994 survey, however, recorded several other small Medio period sites in comparable locations along the lower edge of piedmont slopes, but none has similar stone arcs.

Like Site 321, many large, rough stones are jumbled along one portion of the 355 mound's perimeter (figure 3.13). In both cases this represents coarse construction not done in the Medio period style but added later in the occupations of both sites. Site 355 was less disturbed and eroded than 321 so that we were able to observe more evidence of the added construction. These observations and their implications are discussed in chapter 4.

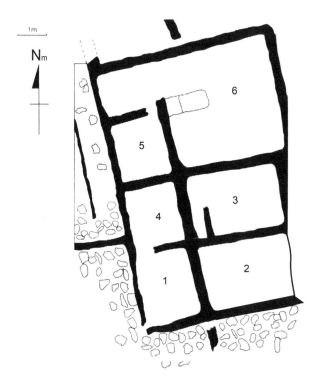

FIGURE 3.13 Excavated rooms at Site 355, showing stone construction later added over the adobe walls.

Chronologies of the Inner Core Sites

There are 45 new radiocarbon dates from the six Inner Core sites analyzed in this volume. All were standard dates, corrected for isotopic fractionation, and all were processed with extended counting. Normal counting time is about 2,000 minutes, while extended counts are done for 4,000 minutes to reduce the standard deviation of each date. No samples were processed for AMS dating. The number of dates at each site are listed in table 3.1.

Site 565 has a small number of dates given its large size. The Late Medio age of most of the site's excavated provenances was clear from the ceramic assemblages and architectural characteristics, so that dating resources were concentrated in Area Z, where unusual architecture was discovered. This area contained much less carbonized material than did ordinary Medio period deposits, severely reducing the charcoal sample. Likewise, the small sites (290, 321, and 355) were found to contain lighter densities of everything, including charcoal, than their larger counterparts.

Despite this limitation, each of the sites has multiple radiocarbon dates. Each date in each set covers a time span, as reflected by their standard deviations of each date, or the ± factor. A radiocarbon "date" is thus actually a probability statement about where the true sample age falls. It does not, therefore, identify a specific point in time. Rather, it establishes a time interval that contains the sample's true age at a given probability. There is a complication with part of the time interval of interest to this study. Some of our radiocarbon

TABLE 3.1 Radiocarbon dates from Inner Core sites

Site	Number of radiocarbon dates
565	8
315	17
290	7
291	4
321	5
355	4

dates fall on a major "wiggle," or what Taylor (1997) terms a "short-term variation" in the calibration curve. A time interval, therefore, may intersect the calibration curve at several points, producing several dates, each with an associated probability of occurrence. This situation is discussed and illustrated in an earlier volume (Whalen and Minnis 2009:48–49). In accordance with standard practice, both date intervals produced by wiggles, and their associated probabilities, are given in the tables that follow. If the probabilities are very different, the most probable date is used. In the case of probabilities that are about the same, we use the entire interval encompassed by both dates. Only one time interval is given when dates do not fall on a "wiggle."

Another complication is that any set of radiocarbon dates is likely to contain *outliers*, or dates that strongly diverge from the rest. These present a large problem in the analysis of radiocarbon date series (e.g., Aitken 1990; Long and Rippeteau 1974; Schott 1986:212; Ward and Wilson 1978; Wilson and Ward 1981). Of the approaches to identifying outliers, we use here the statistical analysis developed by Ward and Wilson (1978), which tests the null hypothesis that the individual dates are all dating the same event within the limits of radiocarbon precision. The alternative hypothesis is that the dates are not coeval, and thus do not all measure the same event. The statistic used for this test is T′, calculated as:

$$T' = \sum_{i=1}^{n} (Ai - Ap)^2 / S_i^2$$

Here, A_i is a radiocarbon date in years BP, A_p is the weighted or pooled average of the entire series of dates, and S_i is the sum of several error terms. Refer to Schott (1992) or Ward and Wilson (1978) for a fuller explanation. The T′ statistic has a chi-squared distribution with $n - 1$ degrees of freedom, so the table of critical values of chi-squared provides the associated probabilities to use in deciding whether to accept or reject the null hypothesis. Acceptance of the null hypothesis means that no dates are identified as outliers and that no date rejection is required. In addition, since all dates have been shown to be measuring the same event, they can meaningfully be averaged into a single figure (Ward and Wilson 1978). This is the weighted mean and its standard deviation, which can then be calibrated to produce a calendar date (Ottaway 1987). Rejection of the null hypothesis calls for removal of the date that contributed most to the value of the T′ statistic leading to that rejection.

The weighted mean is then recalculated, and the null hypothesis is retested. This process is repeated until the null hypothesis is accepted.

Even with this trimming, series of dates with different midpoints and spreads are difficult to interpret visually. Several methods have been devised to summarize a series of dates in graphic form, including the summed probability approach, as exemplified by Kintigh (2002:99–101). The dates used in this analysis are uncalibrated radiocarbon years before present. Each radiocarbon date in a series is treated as a normal probability distribution, with a mean and a standard deviation supplied by the laboratory, for example, 550 BP + 50. This means that there is about a 68 percent probability that the true date falls within one standard deviation of the mean, here 500–600 years BP. There is about a 95 percent probability that the true date falls within two standard deviations of the mean, here 450–650 years BP. This can be expressed as the familiar standard normal curve. A number of date distributions plotted on the same time axis would show some degree of overlap, so that any given time interval would have portions of multiple date distributions above it. Each date distribution can be expressed as a normal curve, and the area under each curve at any point represents that date's probability of falling into that time interval. The analysis sums these probabilities for all dates at each time interval, presenting these data as percentages in a single histogram that shows which time intervals contain the highest probability sums for the date series. The arrows in the figure enclose 68 percent of the combined date distribution, and the horizontal dash shows the center of the distribution. The shape of this cumulative probability histogram provides additional information about the occupation span. A compact, unimodal histogram will be produced when the date ranges have a high degree of overlap. This suggests a single continuous occupation. A multimodal histogram indicates discrete groups of dates, as when several parts of a site have different occupational histories. Strong multimodality could also indicate gaps in the occupation sequence.

We turn now to site-specific chronologies. All dated samples were wood charcoal, and all were processed with extended counting of 4,000 minutes. Dates prefaced with A are from the Radiocarbon Laboratory at the University of Arizona. Those marked B were done by Beta Analytic, Inc. Dates were calibrated using the OxCal v4.4.4 program (Bronk Ramsey 2021), with atmospheric data from Reimer et al. (2020).

Site 315

This single-mound community at the upper end of our medium-sized category had complex deposits and abundant charcoal for dating. Its 17 radiocarbon dates from floor and subfloor contexts are shown in table 3.2.

We focus first on the eight samples from subfloor contexts. As indicated in the table, one of the subfloor samples (A-14987) was small, and the resulting date has a larger than normal standard deviation. In addition, the date is considerably outside the range of the other subfloor contexts, and it was identified by the processing laboratory as questionable. The test for consistency rejected the null hypothesis that all seven are coeval (T′ = 20.82,

TABLE 3.2 Radiocarbon dates from Site 315

Sample*	Context	Years BP	$\delta^{13}C$ (%)	Years AD, cal., 2σ
A-14981	Area A, Rm. 51, subfloor	930 ± 30	−24.0	1025–1169
A-14985	Area A, Rm. 7, subfloor	895 ± 30	−24.0	1040–1110 (39.1%)
				1116–1215 (56.3%)
A-14982	Area A, Rm. 2, subfloor	895 ± 35	−24.9	1039–1215
B-15296	Area D, Rm. 60, subfloor	830 ± 30	−22.8	1060–1190
A-14986	Area A, Rm. 2, subfloor	810 ± 30	−24.6	1175–1271
B-15293	Area D, Rm. 62, subfloor	800 ± 35	−23.9	1200–1280
A-14980	Area B, Rm. 50, subfloor	760 ± 55	−19.7	1160–1305 (92.1%)
				1364–1385 (3.3%)
A-14987	Area B, Rm. 53, subfloor (small sample)	595 ± 50	−13.1	1290–1420
A-14983	Area A, Rm. 5, floor contact	755 ± 30	−23.2	1220–1285
B-15294	Area C, Rm. 24, floor hearth	745 ± 30	−24.4	1225–1295
A-14978	Area A, Rm. 1, floor contact	755 ± 30	−24.4	1222–1289
B-15291	Area C, Rm. 20, floor hearth	660 ± 30	−19.5	1293–1398
A-14977	Area B, Rm. 50, floor feature	640 ± 30	−27.0	1283–1329 (41.2%)
				1340–1396 (54.2%)
A-14984	Area A, Rm. 2, floor feature	625 ± 30	−25.4	1290–1399
B-15295	Area C, Rm. 24, floor contact	610 ± 30	−22.0	1299–1404
A-14979	Area A, Rm. 5, floor feature	605 ± 30	−24.2	1296–1406
B-15292	Area C, Rm. 21, floor hearth (small sample)	570 ± 35	−15.9	1305–1366 (57.3%)
				1383–1425 (38.2%)

$\chi^2_{.05} = 11.07$). Removal of A-14987 allows acceptance of the null hypothesis of coeval dates for the remaining seven (T′ = 9.29, $\chi^2_{.05} = 9.49$). Their summed probability distribution is shown in figure 3.14. Occupation in the late part of the Viejo period is indicated.

It is clear from the table that dates from floor contexts are later than those from subfloor contexts. The test for consistency among these floor dates rejected the null hypothesis of no significant difference (T′ = 24.24, $\chi^2_{.05} = 14.07$). The cause of this result is that sample A-15292 was smaller than the recommended minimum sample size. Its date is at odds with the other floor-context dates, and so it is omitted from further consideration. This satisfies the coeval test requirement. The remaining eight dates can reliably be considered to date the same event. Their probability histogram is unimodal (figure 3.15). We interpret this as reflecting site occupation in the Early and Late Medio in discrete parts of the room block mound. Sixty-eight percent of the area under the curve encloses a span of 760–610 BP. The calendar equivalent is calibrated 2σ AD 1219–1411, which includes much of the Early Medio period and all of the Late Medio. The date range of figure 3.14 shows that Site 315 had a significant Viejo, or pit house, period occupation, while the result shown in figure 3.15 indicates that pueblo architecture began to be built in the Early Medio period and was expanded through the Late Medio, or after 1300. The figure also suggests little activity in the excavated portions of the site by the early 1400s. This closely mirrors the occupational sequence of Paquimé.

```
Years    Rel     Cum%                          Years   Rel     Cum%
B.P.     AD1950  Dates                         B.P.    AD1950  Dates
1000     950     0.44   |                      
980      970     1.80   |*                     820     1130    0.38   |
960      990     5.18   |***                   800     1150    1.68   |*
940      1010    11.00  |****                  780     1170    5.06   |**
920      1030    18.10 >|*****                 760     1190    10.85  |***
900      1050    24.73  |******                740     1210    17.44 >|****
880      1070    30.14  |******                720     1230    22.71  |*****
860      1090    35.28  |*******               700     1250    27.02  |*******
840      1110    42.06  |*********             680     1270    32.78  |********
820      1130    51.58 -|**********            660     1290    42.13  |*********
800      1150    62.90  |***********           640     1310    55.04 -|************
780      1170    74.13  |**********            620     1330    69.32  |*************
760      1190    83.99  |**********            600     1350    81.79  |***********
740      1210    91.31 >|*******               580     1370    90.52 >|*********
720      1230    95.76  |****                  560     1390    95.66  |*****
700      1250    98.03  |**                    540     1410    98.28  |***
680      1270    99.11  |*                     520     1430    99.44  |*
660      1290    99.61  |*                     500     1450    99.86  |
640      1310    99.85  |
620      1330    99.95  |
600      1350    99.98  |
```

FIGURE 3.15 Summed probability distribution for floor-level radiocarbon dates, Site 315.

FIGURE 3.14 Probability distribution for subfloor radiocarbon dates from Site 315.

Site 565

This is the largest of the four sites, although relatively few radiocarbon samples were processed. The single radiocarbon date processed from the site's typical Medio period architecture and the radiocarbon dates from the area of unusual architecture in Area Z are shown in table 3.3. All dated samples were wood charcoal, and all were processed with extended counting. These two areas are separated here, as they will be discussed under separate headings in the architecture chapter.

These dates present a complex picture. Figure 3.16 shows the summed probability distribution for subfloor dates from Area Z, Site 565, and figure 3.17 shows the summed probability distribution for floor-level dates from Area Z. Table 3.3, Area A, shows a calibrated 2σ date of 1250–1390, or the end of the Early Medio and most of the Late Medio period. This is puzzling, as the architecture of Area Z is not what we regard as typical of the Medio period. The contemporary Area A date is associated with typical Medio period construction, as are all the other excavated but undated areas on the site. This issue is discussed in more detail in chapter 4.

Site 290

The seven radiocarbon dates from this small site are shown in table 3.4. Charcoal was surprisingly sparse here, and the dating opportunities were accordingly limited. All dated material is wood charcoal, and all samples were processed with extended counting.

TABLE 3.3 Radiocarbon dates from Areas A and Z, Site 565

Sample	Context	Years BP	δ13C (%)	Years AD, cal., 2σ
	Area A			
A-16383	Area A rm., floor	705 ± 30	−23.8	1250–1310 (76.2%)
				1350–1390 (19.2%)
	Area Z			
A-15522	Rm. 32, subfloor, feat. 115	895 ± 35	−24.6	1030–1220
A-15521	Rm. 32, subfloor, feat. 122	850 ± 30	−26.0	1040–1140 (10.3%)
				1150–1270 (85.0%)
A-15523	Rm. 32, floor feat. 121	670 ± 30	−25.2	1280–1330 (45.9%)
				1340–1400 (49.5%)
A-15524	Rm. 34, floor feat. 128	630 ± 35	−27.6	1320–1350 (13.3%)
				1390–1450 (82.1%)
A-16384	Rm. 2, floor feat. 21	615 ± 30	−26.7	1290–1410
A-16385	Rm. 34, floor feat. 140	605 ± 30	−27.0	1300–1410
A-15520	Rm. 34, floor feat. 29	525 ± 30	−27.5	1320–1350 (13.3%)
				1390–1450 (82.1%)

```
Years   Rel     Cum% of
B.P.    AD1950  Dates

1000    950     0.52   |
 980    970     2.16   |**
 960    990     6.22   |****
 940   1010    13.20   |*******
 920   1030    21.70  >|*********
 900   1050    29.57   |*******
 880   1070    35.71   |******
 860   1090    40.80   |*****
 840   1110    46.56   |******
 820   1130    54.15  -|********
 800   1150    63.21   |*********
 780   1170    72.87   |**********
 760   1190    82.33   |*********
 740   1210    90.03  >|********
 720   1230    95.01   |*****
 700   1250    97.66   |***
 680   1270    98.93   |*
 660   1290    99.54   |*
 640   1310    99.82   |
 620   1330    99.94   |
 600   1350    99.98   |
```

FIGURE 3.16 Summed probability distribution for subfloor dates from Area Z, Site 565.

```
Years   Cum%
B.P.    Dates
 800    0.04   |
 780    0.26   |
 760    1.19   |*
 740    3.79   |***
 720    8.95   |****
 700   16.60  >|********
 680   25.89   |*********
 660   36.45   |***********
 640   48.55   |*************
 620   61.59  -|**************
 600   72.90   |***********
 580   80.57   |********
 560   85.71  >|*****
 540   90.38   |*****
 520   94.84   |****
 500   97.96   |***
 480   99.44   |*
 460   99.90   |
 440   99.99   |
```

FIGURE 3.17 Summed probability distribution for floor-level dates from Area Z, Site 565.

TABLE 3.4 Radiocarbon dates from Site 290

Sample	Context	Years BP	δ^{13}C (%)	Years AD cal., 2σ
B-390728	Room 6, floor contact	910 ± 30	–24.1	1040–1214
B-390725	Room 10, hearth, upper floor	850 ± 30	–23.8	1157–1267
B-390726	Room 9, ash pit, upper floor	600 ± 30	–25.6	1301–1371 (71.0%)
				1377–1408 (24.5%)
B-390729	Room 9, hearth on floor 2	570 ± 30	–26.1	1306–1364 (57.7%)
				1385–1424 (37.7%)
B-390730	Room 7, hearth on floor 2	570 ± 30	–27.0	1306–1364 (57.7%)
				385–1424 (37.7%)
B-390724	Room 11, ash pit, upper floor	550 ± 30	–23.5	1318–1360 (37.4%)
				1388–1434 (58.0%)
B-390727	Room 4, hearth on upper floor	550 ± 30	–22.6	1318–1360 (37.4%)
				1388–1434 (58.0%)

```
Years   Rel     Cum%
B.P.    AD1950  Dates
 700    1250    0.02    |
 690    1260    0.05    |
 680    1270    0.13    |
 670    1280    0.34    |
 660    1290    0.77    |
 650    1300    1.62    |*
 640    1310    3.14    |**
 630    1320    5.64    |**
 620    1330    9.45    |****
 610    1340   14.89    |*****
 600    1350   22.11   >|*******
 590    1360   31.04    |********
 580    1370   41.38    |*********
 570    1380   52.55   -|**********
 560    1390   63.67    |**********
 550    1400   73.90    |*********
 540    1410   82.50    |********
 530    1420   89.10   >|*******
 520    1430   93.73    |*****
 510    1440   96.69    |***
 500    1450   98.40    |**
 490    1460   99.30    |*
 480    1470   99.72    |
 470    1480   99.90    |
 460    1490   99.97    |
 450    1500   99.99    |
 440    1510  100.00    |
```

FIGURE 3.18 Summed probability distribution for floor dates, Site 290.

The first two dates are at considerable variance with the remaining five. There is no obvious reason for this, as Rooms 6 and 10 were not distinctive from the rest of the site in stratigraphy, architecture, features, or artifacts. Application of the test for coeval dates rejects the null hypothesis that all seven are dating the same event (T' = 41.92, $\chi^2_{.05}$ = 12.59). Removing the top two dates from the table leaves five dates that satisfy the coeval test by accepting the null hypothesis (T' = 8.13, $\chi^2_{.05}$ = 9.49).

The summed probability histogram for the trimmed group of five floor dates from Site 290 is shown in figure 3.18. The smooth unimodal structure of the histogram reflects the tight clustering of the site's floor-context dates. The 68 percent spread is 600–530 radiocarbon years BP. The situation is complicated, however, by a "wiggle," or a short-term variation (Taylor 1997), in the calibration curve. This causes the radiocarbon date determination to cross the calibration two or more times. It is thus possible to read several dates from the plot. In this case, the 600–530 years BP spread of Site 290 has two calendar dates with nearly equal probabilities of occurrence: 1302–1367 (52.1%) and 1382–1429 (47.9%). There is no statistical way to decide between the two date ranges, and they are often combined into a single range, here 1302–1429. In any case, the occupation of Site 290 clearly falls into the Late Medio period. The site's architecture is crude compared with the usual Medio period building style, which argues that the later calendar date range (AD 1382–1429) might be more nearly correct. In any case, the occupation of Site 290 appears to have extended a few decades into the fifteenth century.

Site 299A

A single radiocarbon sample was processed from a charcoal-rich context near the bottom of the oven's fill, and it consisted entirely of carbonized wood. It was processed with extended counting. The BP date was 755 ± 30. Calibration at 2σ yields a range of 1220–1295. This is the Early Medio period, and it is the earliest date yet secured from a large roasting oven. Other known examples from Paquimé and from Outer Core Zone sites have been dated to Late Medio times (e.g., Whalen and Minnis 2009:22–23).

Site 321

Four radiocarbon samples were processed from this small settlement, as shown in table 3.5. All samples were wood charcoal.

These dates are so tightly clustered that no coeval test was required. All are assumed to be dating the same event, within the limits of radiocarbon precision. The summed probability histogram for the group of four dates from Site 321 is shown in figure 3.19.

```
Years    Cum%
B.P.    Dates
700     0.40   |
690     0.92   |*
680     1.89   |*
670     3.59   |**
660     6.30   |***
650    10.28   |****
640    15.72   |*****
630    22.65  >|*******
620    30.90   |********
610    40.16   |*********
600    50.00   |**********
590    59.84  -|***********
580    69.10   |*********
570    77.35   |********
560    84.28  >|*******
550    89.72   |*****
540    93.70   |****
530    96.41   |***
520    98.11   |**
510    99.08   |*
500    99.60   |*
```

FIGURE 3.19 Summed probability distribution for radiocarbon dates from Site 321.

TABLE 3.5 Radiocarbon dates from Site 321

Sample	Context	Years BP	$\delta^{13}C$ (%)	Years AD, cal., 2σ
B-390732	Room 5, floor hearth 1	630 ± 30	−23.6	1293–1398
B-390733	Room 4, floor hearth 1	600 ± 30	−24.3	1301–1371 (71.0%)
				1377–1408 (24.5%)
B-390731	Room 5, floor contact	590 ± 30	−26.3	1302–1369 (69.1%)
				1380–1421 (26.4%)
B-390734	Room 5, floor hearth 2	560 ± 30	−27.1	1312–1362 (48.6%)
				1387–1428 (46.9%)

TABLE 3.6 Radiocarbon dates from Site 355

Sample	Context	Years BP	$\delta^{13}C$ (%)	Years AD, cal., 2σ
A-16381	Room 1, rebuilding	570 ± 30	−23.8	1306–1364 (57.7%)
				1385–1424 (37.7%)
A-16380	Room 8, floor level 1	610 ± 30	−24.7	1295–1404
A-16382	Room 8, floor level 2	625 ± 30	−26.9	1300–1420
A-16388	Room 8, floor level 3	685 ± 30	−24.0	1270–1330 (56.9%)
				1340–1400 (38.5%)
A-16386	Room 2, floor contact 1	825 ± 30	−23.2	1160–1280
A-16387	Room 2, floor contact 2	725 ± 30	−23.0	1240–1310 (90.7%)
				1360–1390 (4.7%)
A-16389	Room 6, floor hearth	775 ± 30	−26.2	1215–1290

The smooth unimodal structure of the histogram reflects the tight clustering of the site's dates. The 68 percent spread is 630–560 radiocarbon years BP, which equates to a calendar date range of AD 1297–1412. The dated occupation of Site 321 is thus contemporary with the peak years of Paquimé in the Late Medio period.

Site 355

Abundant charcoal was recovered from this small room block, as was the typical Medio period ceramic assemblage. Seven radiocarbon samples were processed, as shown in table 3.6. All samples were wood charcoal.

The test for consistency among these dates accepts the null hypothesis of no significant difference (T' = 4.04, $\chi^2_{.05}$ = 12.07). Even so, the cumulative probability histogram of the dates (figure 3.20) is irregular in shape and suggestive of a complex occupational history. The last three dates in the

```
Years    Cum%
B.P.     Dates
900      0.00   |
880      0.01   |
860      0.10   |
840      0.56   |
820      2.07   |**
800      5.39   |***
780     10.60   |*****
760     16.92  >|******
740     23.89   |*******
720     31.36   |*******
700     38.80   |*******
680     45.81   |*******
660     52.82  -|*******
640     61.23   |********
620     71.29   |*********
600     81.29   |**********
580     89.58  >|********
560     95.31   |******
540     98.40   |***
520     99.61   |*
500     99.94   |
```

FIGURE 3.20 Summed probability distribution for radiocarbon dates from Site 355.

table are Early Medio, while the first four are solidly Late Medio. The Early Medio dates all come from rooms of unmistakable Medio period style, including well-built walls, smoothly plastered floors, a platform hearth, and hemispherical hearths of the common sort. The four Late Medio dates, in contrast, come from two adjacent rooms that appear to have been modified in a crude style after the main occupation of the room block. This situation is discussed in more detail in the architecture chapter.

Occupational Histories of the Core Zone Sites

The radiocarbon chronologies of the Inner Core Zone sites selected for excavation in the present study are presented in the preceding pages. Four Outer Core Zone sites are frequently referred to in the succeeding chapters, and their dates and occupational histories have been discussed elsewhere (Whalen and Minnis 2009:47–67). The estimated occupation spans of all Inner Core Zone and Outer Core Zone sites are summarized in figure 3.21. Paquimé is included in the figure, although its earliest components have not been dated. We know that there is a Viejo (or pit house) period occupation beneath some of the Late Medio buildings, so in figure 3.21, we presume that the occupational history of Paquimé was at least equal to those of its two nearest large neighbors, Sites 315 and 565.

The end dates for Paquimé have been discussed in detail elsewhere (Phillips and Gamboa 2015). They conclude that the settlement was primarily a phenomenon of the mid-thirteenth through the fourteenth centuries AD. The single tree-ring date in the mid-fifteenth century they dismiss as an outlier that does not define the major occupation of the site. They also show that "when newly calibrated and eliminating a humus fraction sample, Di Peso's four radiocarbon dates from Paquimé have 2-sigma spikes no later than 1423" (Phillips and Gamboa 2015:150). Schaafsma and Riley (1999:244) take a similar position, arguing that Paquimé had no more than minor occupation after about AD 1425. The Paquimé occupation span shown in figure 3.21 reflects this thinking. In fact, it is clear that large sites all over the Core Zone had similar occupation spans, extending from the Viejo period to their Late Medio ends in the late fourteenth and early fifteenth centuries. At this point in our understanding, we are left with the idea that the large settlements of the Core Zone had about the same occupational histories.

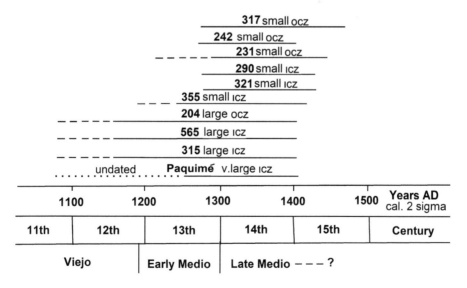

FIGURE 3.21 Estimated occupation spans of the Core Zone sites. Solid lines indicate major occupations. Dashed lines show minor components.

```
Middle   Rel to   Cum
  Date   AD1950   % Dates
  1000     950    0.00  |
   970     980    0.00  |
   940    1010    0.00  |
   910    1040    0.01  |
   880    1070    0.04  |
   850    1100    0.24  |
   820    1130    1.03  |*
   790    1160    3.35  |**
   760    1190    8.26  |*****
   730    1220    6.13  >|********
   700    1250    6.29  |**********
   670    1280    7.70  |***********
   640    1310    9.24  |*************
   610    1340   59.86  -|***********
   580    1370   69.20  |*********
   550    1400   77.25  |********
   520    1430   83.97  |*******
   490    1460   89.24  >|*****
   460    1490   93.14  |****
   430    1520   95.96  |***
   400    1550    7.93  |**
   370    1580   99.12  |*
   340    1610   99.70  |*
   310    1640   99.92  |
   280    1670   99.98  |
   250    1700  100.00  |
   220    1730  100.00  |
   190    1760  100.00  |
```

FIGURE 3.22 Summed probability distribution for Outer Core small Sites 231 and 317. Dates with very large standard errors are omitted.

Small sites show more variable occupation spans, although most of their occupations are Late Medio. Two of them, Site 355 of the Inner Core Zone and Outer Core Zone Site 231, had minor Early Medio components. Several small sites of the Core Zone have date ranges extending further into the 1400s than seems to be the case at the large sites. This raises the possibility that small sites continued to be occupied after the demise of Paquimé and its large Core Zone neighbors. How long these post-Paquimé occupations lasted is a more difficult problem. The 2009 volume (Whalen and Minnis 2009:60–67) contains critical discussion of the radiocarbon dates from Outer Core Zone small Sites 231 and 317. These were the first radiocarbon samples processed from our work in the Casas Grandes area. The dates were derived by several different laboratories and without the extended counting later used on all samples. Seven of these dates had standard errors greater than 100 years, extending occupation unrealistically far backward and forward. For the present study, we discard these seven dates, although we are still left with a body of dates suggesting that occupations of Outer Core Zone small Sites 231 and 317 extended into the mid- to late fourteenth century. The summed probability distribution of these 22 dates is shown in figure 3.22. The arrows mark 68 percent of the date range, denoting a time interval of ca. AD 1120–1460.

The exception to this pattern is Outer Core Zone small Site 242, the occupation span of which is closely congruent with that of Paquimé. This small but very elaborate site is interpreted as an agent community of Paquimé established to organize upland agricultural production using the vast system of surrounding terraces (Minnis et al. 2006; Whalen and Minnis 2001a, 2001b). Because of this special role, its close fit with the growth and end of Paquimé is expected. After this introduction to sites and chronologies, succeeding chapters turn to consideration of architecture and artifact assemblages.

# Chapter 4

The Architecture of the Core Zone

The ensuing discussion considers several types of Indigenous building in the Core Zone. First are the Viejo period pit structures. Second are the successors of pit structures: surface rooms with thin, irregular lower walls of adobe. These presumably supported light upper walls of wattle-and-daub, and the Spanish term *jacal* construction is used to identify them. They began to appear in Late Viejo times, marking the pit-house-to-pueblo transition. We argue that jacal structures continued to be in use in parts of the Medio period. Third are the adobe-walled blocks of contiguous rooms that characterize the Medio period. We see Paquimé as the apogee and most elaborate example of what we term the Casas Grandes Architectural Tradition (CGAT). It is the successor of the jacal-walled room blocks of the pit-house-to-pueblo transition, and it replaces these structures early in the Medio period. At the end of the Medio period, we see rough modifications within the CGAT, which we term the Terminal CGAT (TCGAT). Di Peso recognized a good deal of TCGAT (his Diablo phase) construction in the waning days of Paquimé, marking the decline and dissolution of the center. The present chapter shows that this phenomenon was not confined to Paquimé. Fourth is a group of crude, simple additions to CGAT structures (hereafter Post-CGAT, or PCGAT).

Viejo Period Pit Structures

This discussion of Viejo period architecture of the Core Zone is necessarily brief, as extant data are relatively sparse. In chapter 1, we argue that we have relatively few Viejo period data because so much of it is overlain by later Medio period pueblos, although new survey work is locating more Viejo sites in the Inner Core Zone (Pailes and Searcy 2022; Searcy and Pitezel 2017, 2018). We contend that Viejo period farming populations had expanded throughout the prime quality agricultural niches, which are the area's permanent watercourses. The best of these is the Casas Grandes River valley, which is the context for much of our Core Zone pit structure data.

Variety in this dataset is still poorly understood, but the pit structures that we excavated fall into two classes. The first consists of round, medium-sized structures about 3 to 4 m in diameter and with floor areas ranging from 7 m² to 12 m². These structures had hard, smooth plastered floors with low plastered curbs around their perimeters. They were not excavated far into sterile soil. Examples were found at Outer Core Zone Site 204 and at Inner Core large Sites 315 and 565. Di Peso reports similar structures from the Convento and Los Reyes No. 2 sites of the Casas Grandes River valley. The second type of pit structure consists of smaller quadrilateral constructions. Both kinds of structure date to the Viejo period, or the tenth through twelfth centuries AD. Hereafter, they are referred to as large and small pit structures. The large pit structures are illustrated in figure 4.1.

The first example of a large pit structure is 204-2 (figure 4.1a). It was damaged by looters' holes dug into the overlying pueblo rooms, but some of the perimeter and much of the floor survived. The perimeter of the 204-2 structure was formed of a solid adobe curb, remnants

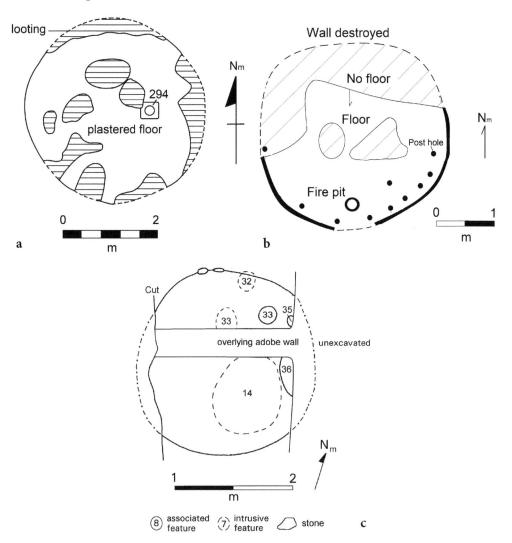

FIGURE 4.1 Large pit structures from Core Zone Sites 204, 315, and 317.

of which were about 12 cm high. Its original height is unknown. The floor of the structure covered about 11 m², and it consisted of several hard layers of fine grayish-white plaster. Its only floor feature was a small deep cylindrical fire pit surrounded by a low quadrilateral adobe platform. The platform enclosed the fire pit and elevated its mouth 6 cm above floor level. The fine floor and the elaborate hearth suggest a special status for Pit Structure 204-2, but we do not know whether it reflects familial prosperity or some ceremonial function. A good charcoal sample was secured from the bottom of the enclosed hearth, and it dated to 990 ± 30 BP, or calibrated AD 980–1160 (2σ).

A second example of a large pit structure comes from subpueblo deposits at Inner Core large Site 315 (figure 4.1b). Pit Structure 1 lay beneath Rooms 5 and 10 of Area A. It measured about 3.1 m in diameter, and its floor was enclosed by an adobe curb about 10 cm high. The floor and the curb were smoothly covered with a hard gray-white plaster. There were a few small post molds around undisturbed portions of the perimeter. Much of the floor was destroyed by intrusions from the overlying pueblo rooms. The only floor feature was a small hemispherical plaster-lined fire pit near the south edge of the structure.

The third large pit house underlay Medio period rooms on Outer Core small Site 317 (figure 4.1c). This was the first pit structure encountered by our project. It was round, measuring about 3.1 m in diameter. Its floor was covered by hard, smooth grayish-white plaster, and its area was about 7 m². The floor did not appear to have been dug into the sterile substrate. There were no unambiguous floor features or associated ceramics. Radiocarbon dates from the structure fell across the Medio period (Whalen and Minnis 2009:67, table 2.14). We note, however, that the structure had been extensively damaged by intrusive features of Early and Late Medio times. The original discussion concluded that the pit house resembled others of the Viejo period, but that it was inadequately dated. This is the only large pit house that we found outside the Casas Grandes River valley. It lies on an upland slope and thus in an environmental situation different from the others discussed here and in the Casas Grandes report. Finally, there is some indication that these structures did not occur alone, but were built in association with nearby areas containing various utilitarian features. One such complex, found at Inner Core Site 315, is illustrated in figure 4.2. The features were unlined small to medium pits, some of which were burned while others were not. This is a functional complex of house and work area, and it was likely a common arrangement. Pit structures in the nearby Jornada area near El Paso, Texas, for instance, usually had attached and heavily used activity areas (Whalen 1994:48), and we expect the same for those of the Casas Grandes area.

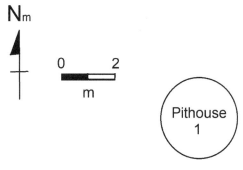

FIGURE 4.2 A large pit house and associated activity area on Site 315.

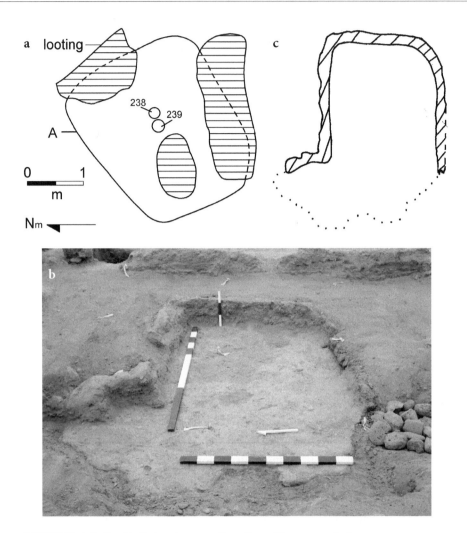

FIGURE 4.3 Small pit structures on Core Zone Sites 204 and 565.

The second type of Viejo period construction found in our Core Zone excavations is the small pit structure, found at sites 204 and 565, as illustrated in figure 4.3. Structure 204-1 (figure 4.3a) lay between sterile and Medio period construction on Outer Core large Site 204. The structure was roughly quadrilateral, with rounded corners. It was a single unit, without other contiguous rooms attached to it. The floor was covered by several layers of fine plaster, and two small Type 1A hemispherical hearths lay near the center of the structure. A radiocarbon sample from one of these gave a date of calibrated AD 1030–1120 (2σ).

Feature 116 of Inner Core Zone Site 565 was something like pit structure 204-1. It was the remnant of a small, apparently rectangular pit structure with rounded corners (figures 4.3b and 4.3c). It was dug some 25 cm into sterile soil, and its walls and floor were covered with a thin, coarse coating of adobe. At least half of the original floor area was destroyed by later intrusion. There were no floor features or associated artifacts, but there may have been an associated activity area. About 8 m southeast, on the same stratigraphic level and excavated 34 cm into sterile soil, was a small roasting pit. It was 59 cm in diameter, and it was filled with burned stone, lithics, and ceramics. Among the latter were a few of the Red-on-brown sherds that are diagnostic of the Viejo period. The pit may have been associated with the small pit structure just described, similar to the house-and-activity-area combination postulated for Pit Structure 1 at Site 315.

Overlaying the missing eastern part of the 565 small pit house was a fire feature likely associated with the first floor of jacal Room 32. From this fire feature came a Late Viejo/Early Medio radiocarbon date of calibrated AD 1030–1220 (2σ). Adjacent to it was a small fire pit, charcoal from which produced an Early Medio date of calibrated AD 1150–1270 (2σ). (Refer to chapter 3 for full data on these dates.) The floor of the pit structure thus appears to have been disturbed by other fire pits dating to the very end of the Viejo period or the Early Medio. Accordingly, we place the Site 565 pit structure at the end of Viejo times, or contemporary with the nearby roasting pit. We may be beginning to perceive a sequence visible in other, better-dated areas: large circular pit houses giving way to smaller, quadrilateral ones, although this is still unclear in the Casas Grandes area.

A striking feature of these Casas Grandes area pit structures is their simplicity when compared to reported Viejo structures from nearby south-central Chihuahua. Not only were many of these southern houses larger than those of the Casas Grandes area, but included among them were structures with low adobe wall bases around their perimeters. Examples of these adobe-walled pit structures come from the Quevedo and Calderón sites, representing the first known use of structural adobe in the region (Kelley 2017:35–45). It is also interesting to note that surface jacal structures, discussed below, are clearly the successors of Viejo pit structures in the Casas Grandes area, although they do not appear to be present on the south-central Chihuahuan sites. Pit structures in south-central Chihuahua may have been used longer or more heavily than those in the Casas Grandes area, resulting in larger and more substantial structures. We hesitate to speculate further, given our present state of ignorance about the Viejo period. Clearly, much remains to be learned.

Early Surface Room Blocks

The final category of architecture with roots in the Viejo period consists of quadrilateral surface structures with narrow, irregular adobe lower walls that supported light upper walls, likely built of jacal. At the Convento site, they closely overlie sterile soil and the pit structures that were excavated into the sterile stratum. Di Peso saw these Late Viejo surface room blocks as the successors of pit structures, or the first surface architecture in what is often termed the pit-house-to-pueblo transition.

This transition, however, was not explained in much detail for the Casas Grandes area. The problem is that the very elaborate architecture of Paquimé is far removed from the jacal structures of the Convento site. Di Peso coped with this difficulty by postulating a cultural hiatus, or a break, with earlier traditions at the beginning of the Medio period. As is well known, he ascribed the imposing architecture of Paquimé to Mesoamerican pochteca, or traveling merchants, who arrived in northwestern Chihuahua and organized the local populace to build on an unprecedented scale and in a new style.

Excavation at Outer Core Zone large Site 204 (Whalen and Minnis 2009) provided data to begin to fill the gap between Viejo jacal structures and CGAT adobe room blocks. The Early Medio period, dating from the mid- to late 1100s through the 1200s AD, was defined based on radiocarbon dates and associated ceramics from deep midden deposits. The Early Medio ceramic assemblage contains all the utility wares described by Di Peso and colleagues at Paquimé, plus a much smaller and simpler assemblage of the polychromes that are so conspicuous later at the central place. For further details, see Whalen and Minnis (2009:110–50). This Early Medio ceramic assemblage clearly predates Paquimé, and the architecture associated with it was a smaller-scale, thinner-walled antecedent from which we contend that the building style of Paquimé was elaborated in the Late Medio period, or after AD 1300. For the present, we leave aside the question of the roles of local or distant stimuli for this elaboration. In any event, recognition of this simpler antecedent style allows us to envision the transition more easily from jacal surface structures to substantial adobe-walled room blocks. We turn now to the data for this transition in the Inner Core. Twenty-five jacal rooms were previously reported from three Inner Core sites: Convento, Paquimé, and Los Reyes No. 2. Recent excavation at large Inner Core Site 565 adds 6 more, for a total of 31 rooms. In succeeding pages, we argue that jacal surface structures were not confined to the Late Viejo, as Di Peso originally argued. Instead, they are associated with ceramics from the Late Viejo into the Early Medio period.

Convento

Eight surface rooms were bounded by low, thin, irregular adobe lower walls. Posts were sometimes built into these lower walls to support light upper wall construction, and roofs were likely some sort of lightweight material. Floors were plastered with thin layers of adobe, and small hemispherical fire pits were in these floors. The structures are illustrated in figure 4.4, and they are described in detail elsewhere (Di Peso et al. 1974:4:179–97).

The chronological placement of these surface rooms seems clear from stratigraphy. They sit either on or only a few centimeters above sterile soil, and they closely overlie pit structures that were dug into this sterile stratum. Di Peso processed two radiocarbon samples from Convento contexts, but subsequent discussion (e.g., Douglas 2000:204, note 1; Stewart et al. 2005:174, table 2) shows that the resulting dates are fraught with technical and interpretive deficiencies and are many years too young. Reanalysis and calibration of the original radiocarbon ages gives calibrated 2σ age ranges of AD 460–890 and AD 773–1414. The authors just cited rightly concluded that these dates are not of much help in dating the Convento structures.

More useful are associated ceramics of local and nonlocal types. In the former category are Red-on-brown sherds, which are diagnostic of the Viejo period. Imported sherds are rare in Convento contexts, but John Douglas (2000:204, note 1) observes that sherds of Mimbres Classic Black-on-white vessels make up 75 percent of the painted sherds that are not Red-on-brown in the Convento surface structures and associated features. Mimbres Classic Black-on-white is well dated to AD 1000–1150 in adjacent southwestern New Mexico. Accepting this approximate age range for the Convento surface structures fits them neatly into the end of Viejo times, immediately before the AD 1150–1200 opening of the Medio period in the Casas Grandes area, when heavier CGAT adobe construction came into use. Jane Kelley (2017:32) reaches a similar conclusion in her consideration of the Viejo period as seen at the Convento site. A starting date for the Medio period in the mid-twelfth century to early thirteenth century has frequently been proposed in recent years (e.g., Pailes and Searcy 2022:86; Stewart et al. 2005; Whalen and Minnis 2009:115, 2012:411).

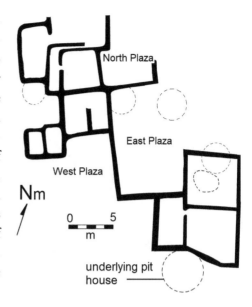

FIGURE 4.4 Viejo period jacal surface structures from the Convento site of the Inner Core Zone.

Di Peso took the Convento surface structures to mark the pit-house-to-pueblo transition at the end of the Viejo period, although these lightly built transitional structures do not now appear to have been solely a phenomenon of Viejo times. Similar surface structures appear at Medio period sites in the Inner Core Zone of the Casas Grandes valley. These sites include Paquimé (11 structures), Los Reyes No. 2 (6 structures), and newly excavated Site 565 (6 structures). All of these sites produced blocks of surface rooms with thin, irregular lower walls of adobe, much like those of the Convento site's structures.

Paquimé

This is a group of 11 jacal-walled structures discovered beneath a plaza of Unit 6 (Di Peso et al. 1974:4:331–37). They lay on top of the sterile stratum, or only a few centimeters above it. In the Casas Grandes River valley, this is an easily recognizable red gravelly stratum. Pit structures were dug into this sterile layer, and the first surface structures lay on or just above it. All Paquimé jacal structures were roughly quadrilateral surface rooms (figure 4.5). Floors were bounded by rough, irregular adobe walls, measuring about 12 to 25 cm thick and standing 8 to 15 cm above room floors. It is unclear how tall these walls originally were. Vertical posts ranging from 4 to 10 cm in diameter were sometimes encased in the narrow lower walls, especially at room corners. These posts presumably reinforced lightweight upper walls of unknown height. Roofs were presumably made of some light material like thatch, as the load-bearing capacity of the walls could not have been great.

The following discussion is abstracted from the original source (Di Peso et al. 1974:4:331–37). Room floors were 6 to 8 cm thick layers of adobe. In some cases, this coating could

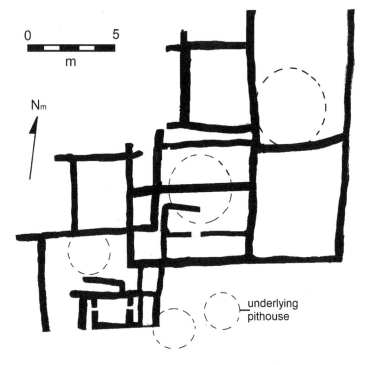

FIGURE 4.5 Examples of jacal surface structures from Paquimé.

be seen extending up the lower adobe walls where they contacted the floors. These floors contained various fire features. Hearths were usually of the simple hemispherical variety (Di Peso's Type 1A). Interior surfaces were plastered, and hearth openings were level with floor surfaces. There were a few rectangular fire pits of unlined and stone-lined varieties. Also present was a number of large (ca. 30 to 50 cm in diameter) floor pits of uncertain function. The jacal structures beneath Unit 6 showed no ceramic evidence that they were built before the beginning of the Medio period; that is, nothing but Medio ceramics were found in association with them.

Los Reyes No. 2

Another set of narrow-walled surface structures comes from the Los Reyes No. 2 site (D:9:14), which lies on an old terrace of the Río Casas Grandes about 500 m downstream from the Convento site. The stratigraphic situation is the same as that of Paquimé Unit 6 and the Convento site: narrow-walled surface rooms closely overlie sterile stratum, some of which contains Viejo period pit structures and features. The narrow-walled architecture from Los Reyes No. 2 has been described in more detail elsewhere (Di Peso et al. 1974:5:856–66). In brief, there is a group of roughly quadrilateral rooms with the usual low adobe footing walls and irregular adobe floors. The structures sit on or near the sterile stratum. Also present is a large circular structure (House 1), which Di Peso argued was a communal facility (figure 4.6).

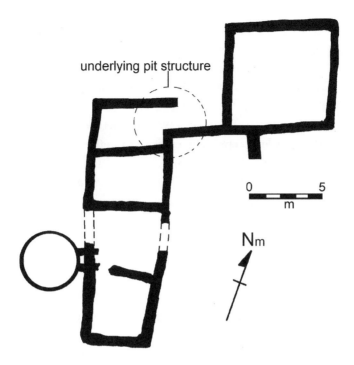

FIGURE 4.6 Jacal surface structures at the Los Reyes No. 2 site.

Two radiocarbon ages were reported from House 1: CG/185(A-609) at 740 +115 years BP and CG/189(A-411) at 710 +40 years BP (Di Peso et al. 1974:5:863). These ages have a number of problems. They were uncalibrated and uncorrected for fractionation, and Di Peso translated them directly into dates in years AD, simply by using the midpoint of the interval as the date of the structure. As others have concluded for Convento site radiocarbon dates with similar methodological and interpretive problems, we find these dates to be of little use in determining the age of the Reyes No. 2 structures.

The Reyes No. 2 site was described originally as "a small ruin" (Di Peso et al. 1974:5:856). This may have been so when compared to Paquimé, but our resurvey of the site in 1989 showed it to consist of a mound some 70 m by 70 m. At about 4,000 m² of mound area, the Reyes No. 2 site lies at the upper end of the medium-sized mound category in the classification discussed in chapter 1. The mound was extensively damaged by looting, and we could not determine where the JCGP excavations had taken place. The extensive artifact scatter around the mound, according to the original report, was a mixture of sherds from Viejo through Late Medio times. The site thus represents a sizable community with a long and heavy occupation.

The JCGP excavation reported that the fill overlying the jacal structures contained all kinds of polychromes. The floor levels, however, had Brown, Red, and Black types, with trace quantities of Villa Ahumada, Dublán, and Ramos Polychromes. As in our reconsideration of the age of the Paquimé Unit 6 jacal structures, we are unwilling to make too much of traces of Ramos Polychrome in floor levels underlying a stratum in which it was much more common. One other point to note is that our survey crews observed the presence of "crude Ramos Polychrome" in the surface assemblage. We suspect that this might have been what we now term White-Paste Babícora, a type we have argued elsewhere to be the Early Medio predecessor of Ramos Polychrome of the Late Medio period (Whalen and Minnis 2009:121–22). We do not know to what extent White-Paste Babícora might have been reported as Ramos Polychrome in the jacal structures' fill and floor levels. In jacal floor levels, we note the presence of Dublán Polychrome, a type most common in the Early Medio. The rest of the floor-level ceramic assemblage from these structures could be Early Medio. Di Peso placed the Reyes No. 2 structures in his Paquimé phase, or the Late Medio time of architecture done in the CGAT. We offer an alternative dating on stratigraphic and ceramic grounds: the Reyes No. 2 jacal structures belong to the Early Medio and are contemporaries of the Unit 6 jacal-walled room block under the later CGAT period building at Paquimé.

Area Z, Site 565

With the background of the published data from Convento, Paquimé, and Los Reyes No. 2, we now turn to a new set of narrow-walled surface rooms from Site 565, Area Z. These were located near the northern end of the CGAT room block mound. As described in chapter 3, much of this part of the mound had been scraped away by machinery, the earth being used to construct a large water reservoir closer to the center of the mound. This action allowed us an extensive look at the lowest levels of the mound, and it was here that a group of narrow-walled rooms was found.

The position of Area Z and the other excavation areas are shown in figure 4.7. The dotted line marks the approximate limit of the Medio period mound. These edges have been obscured by plowing and by bulldozing earth in Area Z and beyond to form the earthen embankments of the water tank. Area Z lies in what apparently was a plaza in the Medio period mound, and its structures were only revealed when much of the surface was bulldozed away to make a stock tank, as described in chapter 3.

All that remained of the Area Z structures were the lower walls and floors (figure 4.8). The middle and upper walls, plus whatever later constructions covered them, were completely destroyed. The surviving walls stood about 30 cm above floor surfaces, and they were narrow and uneven, measuring 15 to 32 cm at their bases, averaging 22.9 cm thick ($\sigma = 2.3$, $n = 22$, range: 12–31 cm). In contrast, the CGAT architecture of that part of the mound that had not been bladed had walls averaging 39.9 cm thick ($\sigma = 2.3$, $n = 26$, range: 30–51 cm). Predictably, a t-test showed that the Area Z wall thickness differs from those of the rest of the site at a statistically significant level ($t = -6.823$, df $= 44$, $p = <.001$).

Not only did the Area Z rooms differ as a group in wall thickness from the rest of the site's rooms, but they are divisible into two groups. The first is what we take to be the original construction. At 12 to 19 cm thick, these walls represent the lower part of the narrow-wall range just given. In addition, their surfaces were rough and irregular. The second group of Area Z walls occupy the upper end of the range: 24 to 32 cm in thickness. These thicker walls were also smooth faced and of more regular surface than their thinner counterparts.

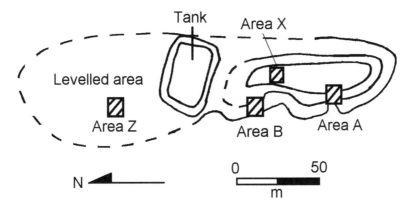

FIGURE 4.7 The Site 565 mound and the locations of the excavation areas.

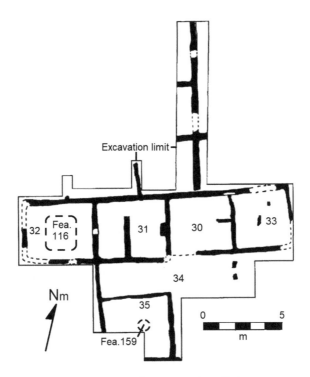

FIGURE 4.8 Excavated rooms in Area Z, Site 565.

Moreover, the adobe used to build the thicker walls was of a lighter shade than the narrow-wall adobe. We argue that these narrow, rough-surfaced walls represent the original surface room block construction in Area Z. Later in their occupational histories, the thin walls were strengthened, supplemented, or in some cases covered by thicker walls. Several rooms had interior partitions made in the same thick smooth-faced style as the supplementary walls, while others were narrow and irregular. This scenario agrees with the Late Medio radiocarbon dates from Area Z floor and feature contexts (refer to chapter 3).

It is clear from the preceding discussion that none of these walls was very thick, as compared to the usual CGAT construction found at this site and at all others excavated by this project. The implication is that middle and upper walls might have been made of some light material like jacal. Similar structures excavated by Di Peso at Los Reyes No. 2 and Paquimé Unit 6 had traces of molds where wooden posts had been set into the adobe footing walls, and molds for corner posts sometimes were in evidence. No post molds were seen in the wall segments of Area Z, although several corner post molds were detected. Di Peso termed this jacal, or mud-and-stick, construction, envisioning adobe footing walls topped by light upper walls. Unfortunately, the middle and upper parts of the Area Z walls were destroyed. This truncation likely removed those parts where doorways might have been, so room access or interconnection remains unknown. It is also noteworthy that the walls of Area Z were not truncated at a common level, which might be expected if their upper parts had been cut away by machine blading when the modern water tank was constructed. Instead, surviving walls varied from 12 to 32 cm. We suggest that the Area Z structures were leveled in antiquity to make way for later construction in the CGAT, which was subsequently bulldozed away to form the water tank.

The excavated Area Z rooms were heavily used, as there were multiple floors and many floor features, especially Type 1A hemispherical hearths. Some were open, and others were sealed by new adobe floors. Most hearths were flush with their floors, but there were also examples of hearths with adobe collars, or rims, forming a ring a few centimeters high. Also present were a few hearths enclosed by low adobe platforms. In their floor-feature assemblages, the Area Z rooms foreshadow those found in the CGAT construction. The Area Z structures contained another category of facility as well. These were large cylindrical pits, always in northwestern or southwestern corners of rooms. The pits were dug into the sterile substrate to depths of 50 to 90 cm ($\bar{x} = 47.0$ cm, $\sigma = 5.6$, $n = 5$), and their maximum diameters were 47 to 77 cm ($\bar{x} = 65.8$ cm, $\sigma = 11.4$, $n = 5$). Their functions remain unclear. They might originally have been storage pits, and most had been reused as pits for human burials. We note that human interments in cylindrical pits in room corners is characteristic of the CGAT architecture, although we do not see the Area Z preference for northwestern or southwestern corners. Wall dimensions for each of the excavated rooms are summarized in table 4.1. As descriptions of the Area Z structures have to date been published only in Spanish, succeeding pages provide a description of each room and its floor features. Plans and photographs of each room are shown in figure 4.9.

ROOM 30

This space (figures 4.9a and b) was roughly rectangular, with dimensions of 3.9 m north–south by 4.1 m east–west. The floor area was 15.8 m^2, about 35 percent of which was intact. The room's adobe footing walls varied in thickness between 15 and 23 cm, and they stood 25 to 30 cm above floor level. There were no traces of plaster on the rough wall surfaces. The room was constructed over about 20 cm of fill devoid of artifacts. Beneath this fill layer was the red sterile stratum. Room 30 had two thin, irregular adobe floors, and the many features they contained attest to the intensity of use of the space. Sixteen of these were Type 1A hemispherical hearths, averaging 19.1 cm in diameter ($\sigma = 3.4$ cm) by 14.6 cm deep ($\sigma = 4.4$ cm).

TABLE 4.1 Area Z exterior wall dimensions

Room	North	South	East	West
30	3.8/15–25[a]	3.9/12–23	4.0/16	4.1/25
31	3.6/18–28	3.7/12–25	4.1/25	4.0/15–25
32	3.7/20	3.8/18	4.0/15–25	~4.0/19[b]
33	~3.3/25	~3.3/22	~4.0/34	4.0/16
34	7.6/12–25	~7.5/12–23	destroyed	2.2/15–25
35	4.3/13–25	~4/12–23	3.9/15–25	~4/16–26

[a] The first number is the length of the wall in meters. After the / is the wall thickness in cm. When a thin wall was seen to have been overbuilt by a thick one, the thin measurement is given first, followed by the thick.
[b] The ~ is used when the exact wall length is unknown.

Feature 66 hearth had a low adobe ring, or collar, that rose about 3 cm above floor level, but its fire pit dimensions were the same as the other Type 1A hearths. There were two low adobe blocks, or steps, built onto the floor, the largest of which was some 25 cm on a side. Floor plaster was observed to extend up its sides. A mostly destroyed partition wall extended into the room. Finally, there were two large pits (Feature 110 and Feature 118) located in the northwest and southwest corners of the room. Feature 110 measured 65 cm in diameter and was 40 cm deep. Feature 118 was 68 cm in diameter and 51 cm deep. Feature 110 clearly originated from the floor surface. The floor around the mouth of Feature 118 was destroyed, but we presume that it, too, originated at the room floor.

ROOM 31

This approximately square room (figures 4.9c and d) was 3.6 m north–south by 4.5 m east–west. Its original floor area was about 16 m², roughly half of which was preserved. There were two thin, closely spaced floors of adobe. These lay over about 10 cm of fill that contained no artifacts. Immediately below this was the sterile stratum. The adobe footing walls were quite variable in thickness. The north wall was from 15 to 25 cm thick at the base, while the south wall varied from 12 to 23 cm. Both north and south walls had additional layers of adobe laid over them to reach their rebuilt thickness of 23 and 25 cm. The new adobe was of a slightly different color than the original. The east wall might have been thickened by additional adobe, but no traces of the original wall were visible. The west wall remained in what we believe to have been its original thin, irregular surface condition. The walls were truncated about 25–35 cm above the floor level, so their original construction technique and height are unknown. There were no traces of support poles built into the walls. There were no entryways in any of the surviving walls, although the adobe block built into the east wall might have served as a step for a now-destroyed door.

A partition wall extended across about 80 percent of the room's width from the south wall, to which it was abutted. It might have reached the north wall, dividing the room into two rectangular spaces, but this was unclear. The area where the partition wall would have

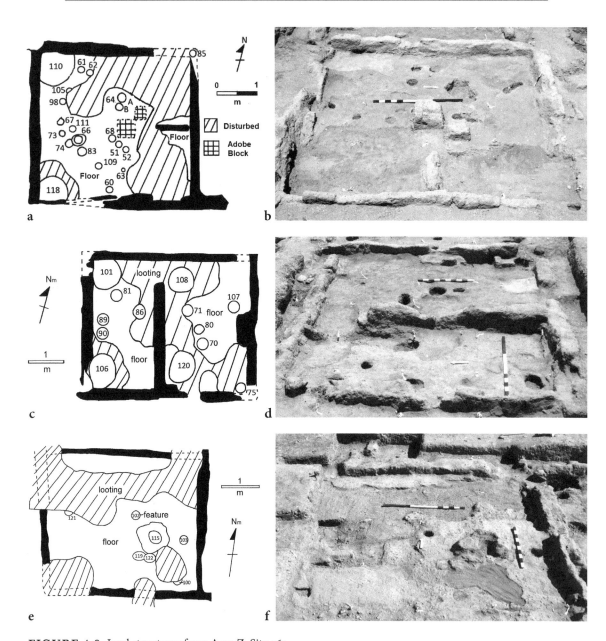

FIGURE 4.9 Jacal structures from Area Z, Site 565.

met the north wall was heavily damaged by later intrusive digging. That Room 31 might have functioned later in its history as two separate rooms is suggested by the presence of four large circular pits. Features 101 and 106 were dug in the northwest and southwest corners of the room. The former was 72 cm in diameter and 54 cm deep, while the latter was 78 cm in diameter and 52 cm deep. Features 108 (77 cm diameter by 50 cm deep) and 120 (97 cm diameter and 76 cm deep) lay in the northwest and southwest corners of the space defined by the partition wall. The floors contained seven hemispherical hearths with round or oval mouths. Their mean diameter was 22.9 cm ($\sigma = 8.7$). In addition to

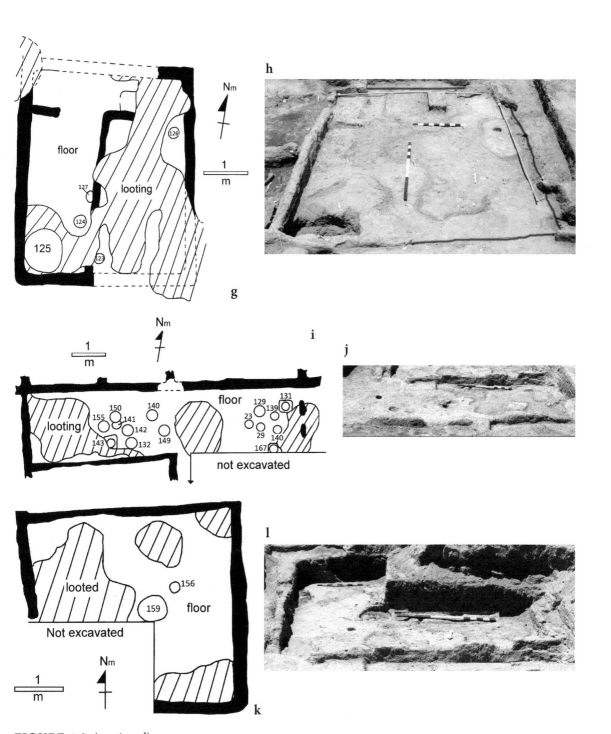

FIGURE 4.9 (*continued*)

hemispherical hearths, Feature 75, built into the southeast corner of the room, was possibly a platform hearth. There were remnants of adobe extending a few centimeters into the room from the fire pit. The fire pit was 21 cm in diameter by 17 cm deep, about the same as the others from this room.

ROOM 32

This might be an example of a space with minimal remodeling (figures 4.9e and f). All four of its walls were thin, at 15 to 25 cm, with rough, irregular surfaces. The north–south walls were 3.7 m in length, while the east–west walls were 4 m long. About half of the 14.8 m² floor area survived intact. The exterior walls stood 18 to 21 cm above the floor, without discernible entryways. Two floor surfaces were so closely spaced that they could not always be separated. The Room 32 floors lay over 10 cm of fill without artifacts. Immediately below this was the sterile stratum, into which a pit structure had been excavated to a depth of about 25 cm. This pit structure (Feature 116) was described earlier in this chapter.

The floors of Room 32 contained only a few fire pits, the paucity of which suggests a shorter occupation history than that of adjacent Room 31. Although there were fewer of them, the Room 32 fire pits contained much more carbonized wood than was found in other Area Z room features. It may be that Room 32 fell out of use after a short time, so its walls were not reinforced with more adobe, and its floor features received a protective covering of trash from nearby activity. Radiocarbon dates were obtained from two features in the central part of the room. Feature 115 is a large fire pit dating to 895 ± 35 BP, or calibrated AD 1030–1220 (2σ). This is the Late Viejo through the Early Medio period. The second date, from a smaller fire pit (Feature 122), was 850 ± 30 BP, or calibrated AD 1150–1270 (2σ). This falls entirely into the Early Medio period.

ROOM 33

This space measured about 3.3 m north–south by about 4.1 m east–west (figures 4.9g and h). Its walls stood about 35 cm above the floor surface, which was heavily damaged by later intrusive digging. About 35 percent of its 13.5 m² floor area remained intact, although it was in poor condition. The floor was laid over 19 cm of fill without artifacts. The east wall was clearly of the thin, irregular-surfaced variety, while its west and south walls were the thicker, smooth-faced reconstruction. The north wall was mostly destroyed. Later in its history, the room was partitioned by adobe walls built on the existing floor surface. Four Type 1A fire pits in the floor averaged 17.5 cm in diameter (σ = 2.6). Their mean depth was 10.8 cm (σ = 3.4). One of the large cylindrical pits lay in the southwestern corner of the room. It was 47 cm in diameter and 42 cm deep. An adobe block of unknown function was placed over the existing floor in the northwestern quadrant of the room.

ROOM 34

This is an odd-shaped space compared to the other rooms, and it appears to owe its final form to subdivision of a preexisting long rectangular space. What remained of a now-destroyed north–south wall appears to have divided the original space into two rectangular rooms of about equal size (figures 4.9i and j). This wall was cut down to floor level during a later use of the space, forming what might have been an open area adjoining Rooms 30 and 31. The space was about 7.5 m east–west by 2.2 m north–south, and its total floor area was about 16 m², of which less than half survived intact. There was clearly extensive reconstruction of the walls, as all of them showed the thick-over-thin construction characteristic of Area Z. There were at least three floors, spaced over about 15 cm of vertical distance. The lowest floor was laid over 18 cm of fill without artifacts.

There were two distinct clusters of features, one in the eastern part of Room 34 and the other at the western end. Most appeared to have been associated with the upper floors of the rooms. If the space functioned as a plaza late in its occupational history, then the eastern feature cluster might have been associated with Room 31, while the western one lay outside Room 30. The eastern feature cluster contained two severely damaged platform hearths, two hemispherical hearths averaging 18.5 cm in diameter and 12 cm deep, a small pit of uncertain function, and a small roasting pit (Feature 29) filled with cracked rock, ash, charcoal, and a few corncobs. From this feature came a radiocarbon age of 525 ± 30 years BP, or calibrated AD 1390–1450 (2σ). This is late in the Medio period. Charcoal from a nearby fire pit (Feature 129) provided another radiocarbon age of 630 ± 35 years BP, or calibrated AD 1290–1410 (2 σ). This also is a Late Medio period date. The western feature cluster of Room 34 contained eight features. One was a severely damaged platform hearth, the original size and shape of which could not be determined. The adobe platform was probably rectangular, and the enclosed fire pit was about 14 cm in diameter. Four features were hemispherical hearths averaging 19.0 cm in diameter (σ = 2.2). Their depths averaged 11.5 cm (σ = 3.0). The other three features were small pits of uncertain function.

ROOM 35

This space was incompletely excavated (figures 4.9k and l). Its four walls were defined, but only about 75 percent of its 16.4 m² floor area was exposed. All of its walls were combinations of narrow and wide remodeling. Despite this extensive rebuilding, few floor features were found. These were shallow depressions of unclear function. Like all of the Area Z rooms, this one was built over about 10 cm of fill containing no artifacts. Immediately below this fill layer was the red gravelly stratum, into which was dug a Viejo period roasting pit (Feature 159), described earlier in this chapter.

The Area Z Chronology

The occupational history of this area is complicated. Based on the radiocarbon dates presented here and in chapter 3, we posit three occupation episodes. The first dates to the Late Viejo period, represented by the pit structure under Room 32. A radiocarbon sample from this structure fell mostly into Late Viejo times. The roasting pit under Room 35 was not radiocarbon dated, but it contained sherds of Red-on-brown pottery, which is diagnostic

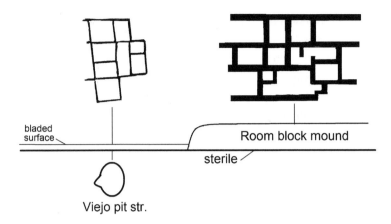

FIGURE 4.10 Architectural succession at Site 565.

of the Viejo period. From the lowest levels of surface Room 32 came another early Medio radiocarbon date. Charcoal samples from features in reconstructed Room 34 consistently gave Late Medio dates. Accordingly, we date the initial building of the narrow-walled surface structures of Area Z to the beginning of the Medio period, or the late 1100s to the mid-1200s AD. The rooms continued in use with the addition of thicker walls, new floors, interior partition walls, and more features in the initial part of the Late Medio, approximately the mid-1200s to the early 1300s. All of this precedes CGAT building, which characterized the majority of the architecture of Site 565 and of all other Late Medio communities in the area (figure 4.10).

These interpretations are consistent with the ceramics of Area Z. Although there were trace quantities of Viejo period Red-on-brown sherds, the types found over and around the surface structures are almost exclusively of the Medio period. The scraped ground surface and the uppermost levels, which together are only about 30 cm thick, contained nearly the entire inventory of Early Medio and Late Medio local types. In addition, there were a few sherds of imported El Paso Polychrome and Gila Polychrome. The next 10 cm were room floor levels, which contained all the Medio period Brown and Red utility wares, plus a set of polychromes dominated by Villa Ahumada and Ramos. The deposits were shallow and heavily disturbed, but this is consistent with the chronological sequence just postulated: the rooms were built in the late 1100s or early 1200s and remodeled in the mid- to late 1200s, when Ramos Polychrome began (table 4.2).

Every indication is that the narrow-walled structures of Area Z were the predecessors of the CGAT. Nevertheless, there still remains the question of what kind of occupation these rooms represent. Di Peso found similar rooms immediately under a CGAT plaza at Paquimé and explained them as quarters occupied by Medio period people while the heavy CGAT construction was under way. Later, the narrow-walled accommodations were built over by plazas or other CGAT buildings (Di Peso et al. 1974:4:331–37). This is plausible for all the narrow-walled structures at Paquimé, Los Reyes No. 2, and Site 565,

TABLE 4.2 The ceramic inventory of Area Z, Site 565

Period	Expected types	Surface	Upper fill	Floor feat.
Viejo	Red-on-brown	t[a]	o	t
	Plain Brown	+	+	+
	Incised Brown	+	+	+
	Scored Brown	+	+	+
	Corrugated Brown	+	+	+
Early Medio	Tool punched	+	+	+
	Playas Red	+	+	+
	Ramos Black	+	+	+
	Babícora Poly.	+	+	+
	Dublin Poly.	+	t	+
	Villa Ahumada Poly.	+	+	+
	White-Paste Babícora	+	+	o
Late Medio	Black-on-red	+	t	o
	Babícora, Ramos var.	o	o	o
	Carretas Poly.	+	t	t
	Corralitos Poly.	o	o	o
	Escondida Poly.	t	o	o
	Huérigos Poly.	+	t	t
	Ramos Poly.	+	+	+
	El Paso Poly.	+	t	t
	Gila Poly.	+	t	o

[a]Quantities of pottery are indicated by + for a moderate number, t for one or two sherds, and o for absent.

given the stratigraphic, chronometric, and ceramic data just discussed. In addition to the five rooms excavated in Area Z, other footing walls were observed extending more than 15 m into unexcavated areas to the north, south, and west (refer to figure 4.7). All of the rooms lay directly on, or just over, a red gravelly sterile stratum. Viejo period pit house fragments and a roasting pit were excavated into sterile soil beneath two of the rooms. The Area Z rooms were at the smaller end of the narrow-walled surface structures at the other sites discussed here. Nevertheless, as shown earlier, they were not statistically distinguishable from those of the other sites just discussed, all of which had some rooms of comparable size.

A last point of consideration is variation in the areas of these jacal-walled surface structures. Viejo period pit structures show a considerable range of floor areas, as do the later adobe rooms of the CGAT. Interestingly, there was much less variety in room area among the jacal surface structures. An analysis of variance test of mean room area showed no statistically significant difference among any of the four sites, that is, Convento, Paquimé, Los Reyes No. 2 and Site 565 (F = .530, p = .666). Multiple comparison p values for each of the four sites with every other site ranged from .239 to .925, meaning

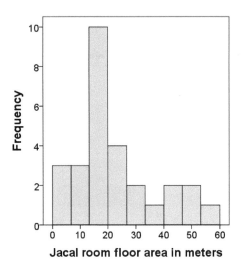

FIGURE 4.11 Histogram of jacal room floor areas.

that none of the four sites could be distinguished from any of the other three on the basis of mean room area.

Accordingly, a single histogram of the jacal room areas from all four sites (figure 4.11) shows the group mean (22.7 m^2) and standard deviation (14.3). A few rooms were above 40 m^2, but most floors at all four sites were in the 10 m^2 to 25 m^2 range. The significance of the larger rooms is not clear, as they had no other distinctive characteristics. Doors or entryways were not clearly defined. All these structures were distinctly different from the later, heavier architecture in the CGAT, although all were built of the same adobe using the coursed adobe technique.

The Casas Grandes Architectural Tradition

Excavations in the Inner Core Zone revealed the typical coursed adobe architecture that is characteristic of the Casas Grandes culture, which we have termed the Casas Grandes Architectural Tradition. Most of the rooms dug by our work in the Inner Core Zone, whether on large or small sites, were of typical CGAT construction. That is to say that they had coursed adobe walls formed of roughly horizontal sections of variable lengths (figure 4.12). Texture and color variations were observed in these horizontal wall sections. None of the excavated walls had stone footings. Instead, the first course of adobe was simply placed in a shallow trench in an existing ground surface. This kind of construction appears to have been used on large as well as small residential sites.

Wall Thickness

Wall thickness is highly variable among the sites of the CGAT. A constant characteristic of the architecture of Paquimé is very thick walls. The mean wall thickness for 230 excavated rooms in that community is 78 cm (σ = 15.2). Although other contemporary CGAT communities in the Casas Grandes area have walls built in the same way as those of Paquimé, no other known community equals the wall thickness figures of the principal center. What we have termed "thick-walled" architecture among the neighbors of Paquimé shows average thicknesses of 40–45 cm, while the walls of Outer Core Zone sites with thin-walled architecture average 25–35 cm in width. All investigated parts of these sites were fairly consistent in wall thickness. These data led to the supposition that all Medio period sites not directly connected to Paquimé had thin-walled architecture.

FIGURE 4.12 Adobe wall construction in the Casas Grandes Architectural Tradition at Sites 204 and 315.

The situation seems less clear-cut in the Inner Core Zone, where large Site 565 and medium-sized Site 315 show a broader range of wall thicknesses. The Site 565 range is 30 to 54 cm (mean = 39.3 cm, σ = 6.0, n = 41), while that of Site 315 is 27 to 48 cm (mean = 37.0 cm, σ = 4.3, n = 78). A t-test of means shows that a significant difference between these two sites in average wall thickness (t = -2.829, df = 61.7, 2-tailed p = .006). CGAT walls, on average, were slightly thicker at Site 565 than at 315. More meaningful, however, is the bimodal distribution for both sites (figure 4.13).

The histograms of figure 4.13 show that each of the two large sites has two modes of wall thicknesses. One group contains walls from about 28 to 40 cm thick, while the other is around 40 to 55 cm. We thus have thin-walled architecture and its thick-walled counterpart in the same sites. This pattern was not observed in other sites in the Outer Core Zone. Figure 4.13c shows a histogram of 127 wall thickness measurements from all parts of large Outer Core Zone Site 204. The distribution is unimodal, centering around 33 cm. Unimodality of wall thicknesses characterizes all the other investigated Outer Core sites as

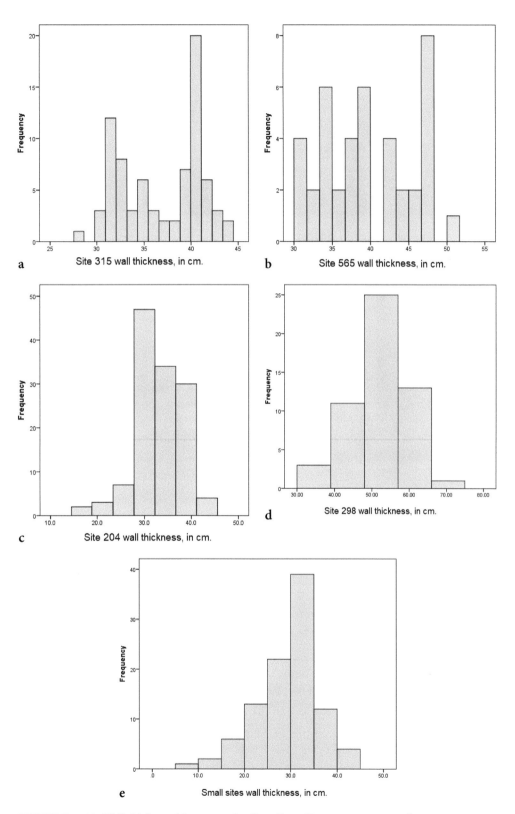

FIGURE 4.13 Wall thickness histograms for Core Zone Sites 315, 565, 204, and 298.

well. Wall thickness at ordinary large sites of the Outer Core Zone thus appears to be less variable than that of the Inner Core.

The proximity of Inner Core Sites 565 and 315 to Paquimé, with their thick and thin-walled construction, suggests that there may be more to thick-walled architecture than a symbolic projection of the authority of Paquimé among neighboring communities. There may be a chronological aspect as well, with the thin-walled construction dating earlier than the thick-walled rooms. It also may be that the more closely integrated with Paquimé was the community, or community segment, the thicker walled was its construction. Thick walls thus would still be a symbolic statement of importance, and the massively thick walls of Paquimé certainly would have distinguished it from its neighbors.

Several thick-walled settlements are thought to have been administrative satellites of Paquimé. Site 298 (figure 4.13d) is a small thick-walled community of the Inner Core Zone that was almost completely excavated by looters in the 1970s. The site is discussed and illustrated in an earlier source (Whalen and Minnis 2001b). As a result, thickness data were available from more than 50 walls, ranging from 38 cm to a massive 72 cm, with a mean value of 51 cm ($\sigma = 7.8$). The source just cited argued that Site 298 was the same sort of satellite community as Outer Core Zone Site 242, which was described in chapter 3 of this volume. Both sites presented the "architecture of power" in miniature, and both were thought to be control nodes of the Paquimé regional system. Site 242 lay next to the region's largest known system of trincheras (or terraces to control rainfall runoff), which facilitate upland agriculture. Site 298 sat near the head of a broad piedmont slope on which we believe agave was intensively cultivated.

There is a clear distinction between the wall thicknesses of the larger Inner Core Zone Sites 315 and 565, of the administrative satellite sites 242 and 298, and of small Inner Core pueblos 290, 321, and 355. The mean thickness for 79 walls at these three small sites is 28.6 cm ($\sigma = 6.8$). The distribution of these data is shown in figure 4.13e. The small site wall thickness histogram is clearly unimodal, with a small spread. This dataset includes none of the thicker category of walls recorded on large Site 565 and on medium Site 315. These data are consistent with those from small Sites 231 and 317 of the Outer Core Zone (Whalen and Minnis 2009:76). In short, all small residential sites excavated to date in the Casas Grandes area have mean wall thickness of 28–30 cm, consistently placing them in our thin-walled architecture category.

Room Size

The large rooms of Paquimé are another of the most prominent characteristics of its architecture. Neighboring Outer Core Zone communities were not found to contain such large spaces. All extant room size data from the Inner and Outer Core Zones are combined in table 4.3. In an earlier discussion of room size at neighboring communities (Whalen and Minnis 2009:74– 75), it was observed that a postulated control node of Paquimé in the Outer Core Zone (Site 242) had the largest known rooms and the largest mean room size in the region, apart from Paquimé itself. We now can amend this statement. The larger

TABLE 4.3 Room floor area statistics for Core Zone sites

Site	Zone[a]	Type	n	$\bar{x}$ (m²)	Σ (m²)	range (m²)
Paquimé	IC	Central	235	25.0	19.1	1.4–120.0
242	OC	Control node	5	19.4	7.9	9.9–28.8
298	IC	Control node	13	13.3	7.6	2.9–28.7
565	IC	Large residential	11	15.1	8.6	5.6–39.0
315	IC	Large	20	16.5	6.0	5.1–41.2
204	OC	Large	35	9.0	5.3	2.4–24.1
290	IC	Small residential	9	7.4	2.4	4.3–11.5
321	IC	Small residential	2	7.2	0.8	6.6–7.7
355	IC	Small residential	6	6.4	4.9	3.1–16.2
231	OC	Small residential	3	10.5	5.2	6.7–16.0
317	OC	Small residential	5	8.9	3.0	5.1–12.0

[a] IC = Inner Core; OC = Outer Core.

communities closest to Paquimé (sites 565 and 315) are now known to have at least one room each of Paquimé scale, and their mean room sizes are close to that of the central place.

The mean room size of the Inner Zone's postulated Paquimé control node (Site 298) is somewhat less than that of its Outer Core counterpart (Site 242), although both are thick-walled communities. Application of a t-test to the room size data of the preceding table shows that neither room size means nor the variation in these sizes is significantly different ($t = 1.521$, df = 16, $p = .148$; F=.043, $p = .838$). Despite this similarity of room sizes, the wall thickness of Site 298 ranges up to 72 cm, with many walls around 50 cm thick. These figures far exceed those of Site 242. All parts of the architecture of power thus do not seem to have been expressed with equal intensity in all the area's construction, except for at Paquimé itself.

For the analyses that follow, excavated sites are divided into large and small categories. The large sites are 204 (Outer Core), 315 (Inner Core), and 565 (Inner Core). This sample includes only one large site (204) of the Outer Core Zone, but the 35 rooms excavated there make a sample size comparable to the 31 rooms dug at the two large Inner Core sites (315 and 565). The small sites include Sites 290, 321, and 355 of the Inner Core Zone, the excavated room total of which is 17. Small Outer Core Zone Sites 231 and 317 contribute a total of 8 rooms to the sample. Note that postulated control node sites 242 (Outer Core) and 298 (Inner Core) are both small sites, but they are omitted from the present sample. This is because both sites are of a qualitatively different type than the small residential sites. Moreover, both control nodes were apparently built in imitation of the "architecture of power" at Paquimé. They therefore depart considerably from the architecture of the ordinary small residential sites that compose most of the Medio period settlement system.

We begin by noting that large sites contain all the sample's rooms above 20 m² in floor area. Rooms below 20 m² in floor area, which we consider to be small, are in the majority at all large sites, and they make up the entirety of small site rooms. The realization that small sites contain only small rooms leads to the question whether these small spaces differ between large and small Core Zone sites. In fact, small rooms are very much the same in size at large and small sites. The mean size of 28 Core Zone small rooms is 8.6 m^2 (σ = 4.6). An earlier study (Whalen and Minnis 2009:74) combined floor area data on 2,975 rooms from 27 prehistoric pueblos in the adjacent U.S. Southwest. The mean floor area of this dataset was 8.1 m^2 (σ = 2.6). This is similar to the Core Zone small room mean. We can thus conclude that the great majority of rooms at large and small pueblos in the Casas Grandes area were about the same size as those of the pueblos of the southwestern United States.

Preceding discussion has shown that large sites in the Casas Grandes area contain some rooms with areas greater than 20 m^2, and the question arises as to whether these large rooms are of comparable sizes in the inner and outer parts of the Core Zone. In fact, they are not. Large sites of the Inner Core contain five known rooms ranging between about 20 m^2 and 40 m^2. In contrast, the Outer Core's large site has only one known room of a little over 20 m^2. It will be recalled that about the same number of rooms were excavated in the Inner and Outer Core Zone. The organizational implications of this pattern are discussed later in this volume.

Room Shape

The irregular, or compound, room shapes of Paquimé are a part of the distinctive complex of traits that we have termed the "architecture of power" in northwestern Chihuahua. Preceding discussion (Whalen and Minnis 2009:75) defined simple rooms as those that were either quadrilateral, with four walls, or L-shaped, with six walls. Compound room shapes show at least eight walls, forming S, T, or X shapes, and some of the famous "butterfly rooms" at Paquimé have 16 walls (Di Peso 1974:2:395, fig. 91-2). Our previous analysis showed that compound rooms were, on average, significantly larger than the simple ones. Nevertheless, these conspicuous, elaborately shaped rooms are not the norm at Paquimé. More than 80 percent of the spaces dug by Di Peso and his colleagues were quadrilateral or L-shapes.

Among the neighbors of Paquimé, our excavations have found only two sites with compound room shapes. These are thick-walled sites 298 and 242, small communities that we presume to have been control nodes or administrative satellites, projecting the authority of Paquimé into its hinterland. In both cases, as at Paquimé itself, the majority of excavated rooms were of simple shapes, with only a few compound examples. Moreover, most of these compound rooms were of the simpler sorts. Site 298 had two S-shaped rooms, while Site 242 showed a single room with 14 walls in a modified butterfly shape. This is a total of only 3 rooms out of the entire Inner Core Zone sample of 48, or 6.3 percent, which is only a fraction of the figure of about 20 percent compound rooms at Paquimé.

Also to be considered under the heading of room shape are alcoves. These are quadrilateral spaces attached to rooms. They are about 2 m by 2 m, extending upward to the full height of the room. They are characteristic of the architecture of Paquimé. Also common is a box built inside the alcove using three of its walls, closing the front with a fourth wall about 1 m high, and capping the whole space with an adobe "roof." An adobe box enclosing about 5 m^3 was thus formed inside the alcove. Di Peso termed the upper surfaces of these boxes "bed platforms" (Di Peso et al. 1974:4:328, fig. 159-4). Discussion elsewhere by Whalen and Minnis (2009:82) argues that these enclosed alcoves were actually intramural storage facilities. It should be emphasized that although many room alcoves contained storage boxes, not all did.

Whether open or enclosed, room alcoves are common elements of the architecture of Paquimé, and they add to the elaborate shapes of many rooms. A few room alcoves were found at Site 242, the postulated Outer Core control node that imitated some of the architecture of power of Paquimé. A few alcoves also occurred at Outer Core Zone large community 204, which showed little of the architecture of power. Likewise, a few alcoves were found at Inner Core Zone large and medium Sites 565 and 315 (figure 4.14), as well as at Site 298, the supposed Paquimé control node. There is no indication in any of these cases of the construction of storage boxes inside the alcoves at sites 565 or 315, although the eroded condition of the walls of Site 298 prevent such a conclusion.

Rooms excavated among the large and small Inner Core Zone communities reported in this volume were of simple shapes. Even the most sizable rooms of large Site 565 and medium-sized Site 315 were four sided. It appears, therefore, that the full set of thick walls, large rooms, and compound shapes is found only at Paquimé and at its few administrative satellites, like Outer Core Site 242 and Inner Core Site 298. Other large communities in the Casas Grandes area show a more variable and less standardized pattern of simply shaped large and small rooms with thick and thin walls. The smallest residential sites are more uniform in their thin-walled architecture, forming small rooms of quadrilateral or L shapes. This is the uniformity of simplicity, however, and it is not to be equated with the uniformity that appears to have emanated from Paquimé. This is discussed in more detail in the concluding section of the present chapter.

Intramural Human Burials

Early and Late Medio period dead were commonly interred in cylindrical pits inside rooms, frequently in their corners. This sort of intramural burial appears to have been the common method of disposal of the dead, as many such interments were found in the excavations at Paquimé (Di Peso et al. 1974:8:355–411). These have been studied by many subsequent researchers (e.g., Benfer 1968; Butler 1972; Casserino 2009; Corruccini 1983; McConnan Borstad 2021; Offenbecker 2018; Rakita 2006; Ravesloot 1988; Turner 1999; Waller 2017; Weaver 1981). The remains and their contexts document not only the physical characteristics of the population but also its social structure. They are also relevant to the question of the origin of at least a portion of the population. Some have argued that the Medio period population around Paquimé was heavily augmented by nonlocal immigrants (most notably Di Peso 1974; and Lekson 2000, 2008) whereas others suggest the large Late Medio period population was mostly a local phenomenon. Recent research in bone chemistry has shed light on this topic, concluding that the proportion of immigrants was around 30 percent during the Medio period. The figure was about the same for the

FIGURE 4.14 Alcoves at Inner Core Zone Sites 565 and 315.

preceding Viejo period (Offenbecker 2018). While the current data are suggestive, we look forward to publication of ongoing research on the DNA of the Paquimé remains, which should be more definitive about the origin and composition of the Late Medio period population. As noted in chapter 1, the record of human burials from neighboring Medio sites is almost completely expunged by the extensive looting to which all ruins in the Casas Grandes area have been subjected. In all our excavations at Core Zone sites, for example, we did not recover a single intact interment. At Outer Core Site 204, empty burial pits were found in some room corners, and fragments of human bone were scattered over the site surface, doubtless the result of modern-day looting in search of the whole vessels that accompanied burials.

The record of human remains consists of more than burials, however. Isolated human remains are disarticulated, fragmented portions of human skeletons. They are mostly non diagnostic pieces of long bones or individual teeth. Both of these represent some of the hardest and most durable parts of the skeleton, although other bones are at least occasionally found as isolated remains. As many have noted, isolated human remains are commonly found on archaeological sites all over the world (e.g., Kunsel and Outram 2004; Margolis 2007; Nilsson Stutz and Larson 2016; Tucker 2010). Closer to the concerns of the present study is the U.S. Southwest, where isolated human remains are routinely found in various mortuary and nonmortuary contexts. At the Grasshopper Pueblo, for example, isolated human remains numbered about 1,800 in the excavated portions of the site, and more than 9,000 scattered remains are projected to exist in the whole site (Margolis 2007:57). Although they are plentiful, isolated human remains usually receive little analytical attention. One problem, note Kunsel and Outram (2004:85), is that scattered human remains fall outside the recording systems used for human burials, which are based on more-or-less complete individuals in discrete contexts. Moreover, isolated bone is considered of little analytical value in traditional mortuary studies.

How did fragmentary human bones come to be distributed among many contexts in prehistoric sites? Looting explains the bone on site surfaces, but what of remains found in archaeological contexts such as on room floors? The following discussion is abstracted from Rodrigues and Schaafsma (2008). A routine assumption has been that human bone arrived in its archaeological context as part of a mortuary event such as a burial, and that the only means of distribution after the event is later nonhuman postdepositional processes. Some bone doubtless was so scattered, but dismissing all scattered human remains as results of rodent disturbance, bioturbation, erosion, or other taphonomic processes masks potentially important patterning in the archaeological record.

It is, therefore, important to evaluate whether isolated human remains came to be through natural processes or through purposeful behavior. In the U.S. Southwest, both archaeological and ethnographic research indicate that living people interacted with the dead in various ways, so that human body parts were commonly used in rituals of various sorts (Rodrigues and Schaafsma 2008:40). Others have taken the same position, noting that only the final deposition of isolated human remains is visible to archaeologists, although bones may have experienced a series of treatments before deposition (Tucker 2010:187). Isolated human remains, then, are not necessarily simply disturbed bits of previous burials. They may be so, but they might have had greater symbolic value to those who placed them. It is argued that disturbed and scattered human remains can be parts of practices tied to permanence of place within the landscape (Nilsson Stutz and Larson 2016:715), or to closing offerings ensuring that the structure was abandoned symbolically as well as practically (Tucker 2010:147). In the U.S. Southwest, "there is a long history of human remains used in closure practices, not to sever connection with space, community, or landscape, but to continue material connections with these places" (E. C. Adams 1983:49). Interpretations are varied, but there is wide agreement that isolated human remains may not simply be casual discards.

This is of particular relevance to the present study, as most of the human bone recovered from Inner Core Site 315 was found highly fragmented and scattered over the floors of several rooms in different parts of the pueblo. These are Room 2 of Area A, Room 26 of Area C, and Room 70 of Area E. Age and sex for these remains were determined in the laboratory (Casserino and Mills 2009). All remains are those of adults. They were clearly scattered shortly after the rooms' abandonments, as they lay in direct contact with the floor surface. Bones and floor subsequently became covered with heavy layers of infill. Room 70 had several large burial pits, each containing fragmentary adult human remains, possibly males, shell beads, and several ceramic vessels. This seems to be a case where intramural burials were disturbed and some of the bones scattered over the floor, while a few long bone fragments were placed in an empty wall niche. Rooms 2 and 26 present a different picture, as there were many scattered and disarticulated adult human bones of undetermined sex in floor contact, although neither room had large pits that might once have contained burials. The scattering of these isolated human remains was certainly deliberate and might be interpreted as symbolic action. "The history of the kin group was read in the history of the house, and its very fabric remembered these changes and alterations" (Tucker 2010:22).

Intramural Architectural Elements

Architectural embellishments such as T-shaped doorways, niches, platforms, platform hearths, posthole collars, and columns were frequently found at Paquimé, and they are another component of the elaboration of its architecture. Previous discussion (Whalen and Minnis 2009:77–88) enumerated and illustrated these architectural elements at Paquimé and at neighboring sites in the Outer Core Zone. The following discussion is abstracted from the source just cited. Predictably, Paquimé had the largest and most variable array of architectural elements, distantly followed by Site 242, the presumed control node built in Paquimé style. The largest of the residential communities investigated in the Outer Core Zone (Site 204) had T-shaped doorways, but so did the small residential sites (231 and 317). In fact, large and small Outer Core Zone residential sites had not only T-shaped doors, but also a few wall niches and small adobe platforms. All of the investigated Outer Core Zone residential sites, whether large or small, thus had at least a few elements of architectural elaboration. The situation in the Inner Core Zone was found to have both similarities to and differences from the Outer Core Zone case just described, as noted below.

DOORWAYS

The presumed Inner Core Zone control node, Site 298, had a total of 15 observable doors. Eleven (73%) were T-shaped, and four (27%) were rectangular. Of the 15 doors, 10 (67%) were found open while 5 (33%) were sealed. Unfortunately, the walls of large residential Site 565 were worn down below door level by extensive erosion and looting, depriving us of any information on intramural passageways. At medium-sized Site 315, however, data were obtained for 31 doors. Of these, 15 (48%) were T-shaped, and the remaining 16 (52%) were rectangular. Of these 31 doors, 16 (52%) were found open, while 15 (48%) had been sealed shut with large stones and adobe mortar. The other Inner Core Zone site from which door data were recovered is small residential Site 355. Here, nine doors were found,

FIGURE 4.15 Doorways at Core Zone Site 315. Some were found sealed, while others were open.

only two of which (22%) were T-shaped. The remaining seven doors (78%) were simple rectangular openings. Three of the nine doors (33%) were found sealed, while the other six (67%) were open. Some of these entryways are illustrated in figure 4.15, and these doorway data for Inner and Outer Core Zone sites are summarized in table 4.4. The Outer Core Zone data were presented elsewhere (Whalen and Minnis 2009:77–78). Large Inner Core Zone Site 565 and small Outer Core Site 317 could not be included here, as their walls were eroded below door levels.

Several observations may be made from the following table. First, the postulated control node sites (242 and 298) are distinguished not only by their thick walls and compound room shapes, but also by high percentages of T-shaped doors. All of these are traits that the postulated control nodes shared with Paquimé. It is also interesting to note that the two larger Inner Core Zone residential sites investigated here (Sites 315 and 355) have lower percentages of T-shaped doors than do their Outer Core Zone counterparts.

Some of the doors of every shape were found open, while others were sealed by filling their openings with large stones and adobe mortar. The sealed opening was then covered with a coat of adobe plaster. At Casas Grandes, most doorways (402, or 74.7%) were found open, while 136 (25.3%) were sealed as just described (Di Peso et al. 1974:4:234–35). Interestingly, the neighboring sites all showed much higher percentages of sealed doors. The only exception is Site 298, the postulated control node that was entirely excavated by looters. Here, it is not clear whether the low frequency of sealed doors is accurate, or whether previously sealed doors were unblocked by the looters.

Sealed doors are commonly found at pueblo sites in the U.S. Southwest (e.g., Lekson 1986:28; Riggs 2001:77). Charles Riggs (2001:68) argues that many blocked doorways at the large Grasshopper Pueblo were sealed off before or during room use rather than after the abandonment of the space. The same author cites Victor Mindeleff's (1891:190) classic study

TABLE 4.4 Doorway characteristics in the Core Zone

Site	Zone	Type	T (%)	Sealed (%)
Paquimé[a]	IC[b]	Central place	59	25
298	IC	Control node	73	25
242	OC	Control node	72	78
204	OC	Large residential	62	64
315	IC	Medium residential	48	48
355	IC	Small residential	22	33
231	OC	Small residential	62	58

[a]Di Peso et al. 1974:4:235–37.
[b]IC = Inner Core; OC = Outer Core.

of Pueblo architecture, which showed that many doorways were used as temporary openings during room construction and were sealed at the room's completion. In alternative explanations the presence of many sealed doors has been taken to imply renovation and shifting room-use patterns throughout the site's occupational history. A third explanation for high frequencies of sealed doorways is planned abandonment of a pueblo, or at least parts of it, during a declining occupation. Thomas Windes (1987) traces such a situation at Chaco Canyon's Pueblo Bonito. He shows that door sealing was a noticeable feature of site-use behavior at Bonito in the early 1100s, or during the contraction of occupation just prior to the final abandonment of the community. We conclude, then, that door sealing in pueblo architecture results from a range of factors, from renovation to abandonment. The curious situation in northwestern Chihuahua is that Casas Grandes contained so few sealed doors (ca. 25%), while most of the neighboring communities had so many (58% to 78%). This raises the question whether the neighboring communities had the same occupational histories as Paquimé. In the final chapter of this volume, we argue that they did not.

WALL NICHES

There were 188 niches found in the upper parts of the walls of Paquimé. They occurred in various shapes, including square, stepped, rectangular, T-shaped, and arch topped. Nearly all of them were empty when excavated, but they were suggested to have served as repositories for religious objects (Di Peso et al. 1974:4:229). Our earlier study of Medio architecture (Whalen and Minnis 2009) showed that niches at Paquimé were distributed unevenly among rooms of different shapes. Quadrilateral and L-shaped rooms averaged 1.3 niches per room ($\sigma = 1.7$, $n = 195$), while rooms of compound shapes contained an average of 2.5 wall niches ($\sigma = 1.9$, $n = 40$). This mean difference is statistically significant ($t = -3.94$, df = 233, $p < .0001$). Rooms of compound shapes have, on average, more wall niches than do rooms of simple shapes.

Wall niches were present but rare at excavated Outer Core Zone sites (Whalen and Minnis 2009:78). One was found at large residential Site 204, and a second is from small residential Site 231. Both were of simple rectangular shapes and were empty on excavation. The Inner Core Zone sites investigated here yielded a greater number of wall niches. Two came from large Site 565, and four were found at medium Site 315. All six niches were rectangular. There were two oddities of construction among these niches. First, one of the niches passed completely through the wall separating two rooms (21 and 26) at Site 315. The niche was clearly built this way, as it was neatly finished on both wall faces. It contained a ground stone axe and another stone (figure 4.16a) that had been set in adobe plaster. The second oddity of niche construction came from Room 53 at Site 315, where a disused doorway had been remodeled into a wall niche that was found to be empty on excavation (figure 4.16b). A simple rectangular wall niche from the unusually large Room 70 on Site 315 contained several human limb bones. Human bone was scattered over the floor of this and another Site 315 room (Room 2). No wall niches were found at any of the small residential sites that we investigated.

ADOBE CONSTRUCTIONS

This last category of architectural elements includes small platforms, stairways, columns, and post collars. All of these are present at Paquimé, and most of them occur in low frequencies at the Outer Core Zone sites. One small adobe platform appears at Outer Core Zone small Site 231, and an adobe stair of three steps was found at Outer Core Zone large Site 204. Site 204's largest room also contained the bottom parts of two adobe columns (for illustrations, see Whalen and Minnis 2009:83–87). The same elements were found on Inner Core Zone sites, although they were a little more common than in the Outer Core. From Site 565 came two small low platforms of solid adobe (figure 4.17a). These were constructed against the walls of their rooms (2 and 5). They have no distinguishing features, and their function is unknown. They might have served as steps for features in the higher parts of

FIGURE 4.16 Wall niches at Inner Core Site 315.

walls that are now eroded away. Small adobe platforms, or steps, were found in the early surface structures of Area Z, Site 565 (figure 4.17b). No such platforms were found at any other Inner Core Zone sites.

Small stairways of adobe are known from two neighbors of Paquimé. One was recorded at large Outer Core Zone Site 204, and the other comes from Inner Core Zone Site 315. The example from Site 204 is three steps about 90 cm high, and its length, or run, is about 1.5 m (see Whalen and Minnis 2009:85 for a photo). The top of the stair is destroyed, but there is space there for several more steps. The stair from Site 315 is similar but smaller. It has only two steps, rising about 40 cm above floor level, and its run is only about 80 cm (figure 4.17c). Similar stairways are known from Paquimé. Of the 40 examples recorded there, 18 (45%) were of adobe construction. These ranged from 2 to 20 steps high (mean = 11 steps), and their runs were from 60 to 18 m (mean = 9.3 m) (Di Peso et al. 1974:4:247). It is thus apparent that the adobe stairways found at the neighbors of Paquimé were on the low end of their size range both in steps and in length. Stairways at Paquimé were interpreted

FIGURE 4.17 Adobe steps and platforms from Inner Core Site 565.

FIGURE 4.18 Adobe columns and their remodeling at Site 315.

as means of "vertical transport," or movement from one story to another (Di Peso et al. 1974:4:247). Neither Site 204 nor Site 315, however, had any indication of having been more than one story high. Their stairways might have served as roof access. In any case, stairways do not appear to have been common architectural elements among the neighbors of Paquimé. This is not necessarily a simple reflection of the preponderance of single-story architecture among these communities, as we believe the rooftops of Medio period rooms to have been used as activity spaces. This is a well-known pattern in the puebloan world of the U.S. Southwest.

Square columns of adobe are well-known elements of the architecture of Paquimé, where they served to support the roofs of open-sided rooms that opened onto plazas. They were spaced about 2 m apart and were quadrilateral in shape. Most measured 1 to 1.5 m on a side. In all cases, later walls were built between the existing columns to create enclosed rooms. A pair of columns closely fitting this description was found at Outer Core Zone large Site 204 (Whalen and Minnis 2009:86–87). A second pair occurred at Inner Core Zone Site 315, although they were considerably smaller, at about 50 cm on a side (figure 4.18). As at Paquimé, the columns at Site 204 (Whalen and Minnis 2009:86–87) originally opened onto a plaza, and they had a wall constructed directly in front of them to enclose the room space. The situation is less clear at Site 315, although the room with the columns was on the southern edge of the site and may once have overlooked a plaza.

POST COLLARS

Post collars are surroundings for large roof-support posts of 18–20 cm in diameter. Adobe rings some 10 to 15 cm wide and high encircled post bases and were built on room floors.

FIGURE 4.19 Post collars in Room 70 and Room 5 at Site 315.

These are well-known features at Paquimé, but none was found at any of the Outer Core Zone sites. In contrast, eight post collars were recorded at Inner Core Zone Site 315, all in the largest rooms. Room 7/8 measured almost 41 m², making it both Paquimé sized and the largest room excavated by our Core Zone projects. Three collared posts, each about 18 cm in diameter, extended in a row across the longest dimension of the room. The total span of the roof that they supported was about 5 m. A thin wall with a door opening had been built between the posts late in the room's history, dividing the space into north and south halves. The north half showed evidence of heavy reoccupation and reuse.

Room 70 at Site 315 was unusually large at 26 m². This is about an average-sized room at Paquimé. In Room 70, four large collared posts were arranged in a square inside the square room (figure 4.19a). The roof span in this case was a little over 5 m. Finally, Room 5, Site 315, contained a single large collared post (figure 4.19b), again supporting a roof span of some 5 m. This post is illustrated here, as it was found to have a deep posthole, the base of which was a large flat stone (figure 4.19c). Collared posts thus seem to be features of large rooms. No large rooms were found at any of the small sites excavated in the region, so it is not surprising that no collared posts came from these sites.

FIRE FEATURES

Fire pits and hearths are basic domestic facilities, and similar assemblages of them have been found in all excavated rooms of the Outer and Inner Core Zones. Almost all rooms contained at least one small fire pit, usually with a round or oval mouth and a simple hemispherical profile. These are by far the most common category of floor features on sites of every size. The discovery of multiple examples of these facilities inside many rooms shows that they were frequently filled and replaced with new ones. Di Peso and colleagues distinguished between fire features that were excavated into floors and those that were elevated above the floors, and this continues to be a useful division. Excavated fire features were almost always simple hemispherical or oval depressions measuring 10 to 25 cm in diameter and about the same in depth. The inner surfaces of about half of these facilities were coated with clay or adobe plaster that fired hard and red during use. These fire pits characteristically contained only ash, and it is surmised that charcoal was burned in them. This would provide nearly smokeless heat for the room, which appears to have been their primary purpose. Other hemispherical fire pits were ringed by low adobe collars, standing about 5 cm above floor surfaces. One type of fire pit that to date has been found only at Paquimé, at large Inner Core sites 315 and 565, and at large Outer Core Site 204 is the vented hearth. Vented hearths are simple hemispherical basins with one side dug down a few centimeters to provide the pit with an air vent. The pit's internal plastering extends up onto the surface of the vent. In fact, vented hearths look much like the vented fire pits found atop platform hearths. It is not clear whether the functions of these vented hearths differed from the simple hemispherical or platform types, as all of them were frequently found in the same rooms. Vented hearths do not correlate with room size or with any other measure of architectural elaboration, although they are known from all of the largest communities that we have investigated. Vented hearths were found at Paquimé and at large Sites 315 and 565, although they were not recorded at any small site in the Inner or Outer Core Zone. An example is shown in figure 4.20. The basin hearth typology developed for Paquimé was found to be adequate for classification of these features at all Core Zone neighbors.

The elevated fire features recognized by Di Peso at Paquimé were termed "platform hearths" (Di Peso et al. 1974:4:255–56). These consist of an adobe platform raised some 10 cm above floor surface (Figure 4.21a). The platform frequently has the form of a capital letter H with a thick crossbar. The open, lower part of the H is an air vent leading into the small fire pit, located in the center of the thick crossbar. The open upper end of the H is an ash pit (figure 4.21b). The hearth platform is characteristically found abutted to one of the room walls. Some of the elaborate platform hearths of Paquimé had decorative patterns of steps, swirls, or scrolls molded into the upper surfaces on either side of the vent. The following figure shows the relative simplicity of the platform hearths found at neighboring sites. The classes and frequencies of excavated and elevated fire features at Paquimé and at its Inner Core neighbors are listed in table 4.5.

This table makes clear how many different types of fire features were recognized only at Paquimé, and the table does not list all of the variety from that site. The neighboring sites consistently have more limited assemblages. It is also clear from the table that the large

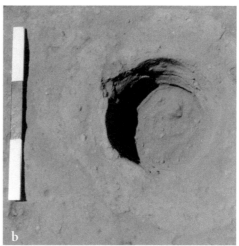
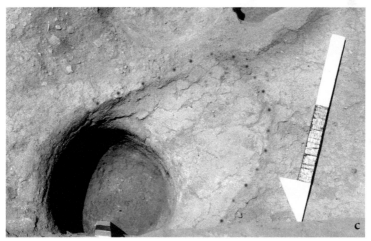

FIGURE 4.20 Intramural fire pits from Site 565. Dots show vent in figure c.

neighbors of Paquimé (Sites 565 and 315) had slightly more elaborate fire feature assemblages than did small Sites 290 and 355. At most of the other Inner Core sites, about half of the fire feature assemblage is composed of hemispherical adobe-lined hearths, which we consider to be the more formal variety of in-floor fire feature. This pattern is more than reversed at small Site 290, however, where only about one-quarter of recorded fire features were of the formal type, while about three-quarters were the unlined pits that we class as informal hearths. The preceding table, together with earlier discussions of architecture, allows us to postulate that the frequency of formal lined versus informal unlined basin fire pits correlates well with other measures of architectural elaboration. The architecture of small Site 290 is the least elaborate discussed here, and that site also stands out for the informal quality of its fire feature assemblage.

Platform hearths were common at Paquimé, where they composed about one-quarter of all recorded fire facilities. Lekson (1999:106) notes that platform hearths apparently are unique to Casas Grandes and related communities as far north as southwestern New

FIGURE 4.21 Platform hearths from neighboring sites.

Mexico, while they are apparently absent in the Chaco, Aztec, Mimbres, and El Paso areas. Platform hearths were much less common among the neighboring communities of the Casas Grandes area, but a few were found at both large sites of the Inner Core (565 and 315) and at one of the small ones (355). In the Outer Core, platform hearths were present at large Site 204, but not at small Sites 231 and 317. Platform hearths were present at Outer Core small Site 242, the settlement that was built in the style of Paquimé. They may have been present at another Paquimé lookalike, Site 298 (for a description, see Whalen and Minnis 2001b). Unfortunately, looting and heavy erosion at Site 298 destroyed all room floors and their features. In any case, all platform hearths found among the neighbors were simple, without the decorative patterns molded onto the horizontal surfaces of the platform hearths at Paquimé. Even so, the pattern of occurrence of platform hearths suggests that they are a piece of architectural elaboration seldom found in the simplest communities.

The three most common types of fire features are clay-lined fire pits, unlined fire pits, and platform hearths. Their dimensions are expressed in table 4.6 as hearth area at the floor or platform surface and hearth depth below that surface. Both lined and unlined fire pits represent approximate spherical segments, and the volumetric formula for that class of geometric solid (vol. = $\frac{1}{6}\pi h(h^2 - 3a^2)$), where a is the basal radius of the segment and h is its height, was used to approximate hemispherical hearth volumes. The means of these volumes were compared between Inner and Outer Core Zone sites and between large and small sites, regardless of zone. The data used in these analyses are shown in table 4.6. Inner

TABLE 4.5 Fire feature type frequencies at Inner Core sites

	Type[a]	Paquimé	565	315	355	290
Basin, lined	1a	57.2% (263)	41.2% (19)	52.5% (71)	53.3% (8)	28.6% (2)
Basin, lined, adobe collar	1b	0.2% (1)	2.2% (1)	3.0% (4)	0	0
Basin, lined, + ash pit	1c	12.1% (56)	0	0	0	0
Basin, lined, + air vent	1d	0.2% (1)	4.4% (2)	3.0% (4)	0	0
Basin, lined, stone collar	1f	0.2% (1)	0	0	0	0
Basin, ceramic liner	1h	1.3% (6)	0	0	0	0
Platform hearth	2	26.2% (121)	2.2% (1)	2.2% (3)	6.7% (1)	0
Basin, unlined	3	2.6% (12)	50.0% (23)	39.1% (52)	40.0% (6)	71.4% (5)
Totals		100% (461)	100% (46)	100% (24)	100% (15)	100% (7)

Note: Small sites 298 and 321 have no recorded floor features.
[a] Types assigned at Casas Grandes (Di Peso et al. 1974:4:252–53).

TABLE 4.6 Hemispherical hearth mean sizes, in liters

Context	n	$\bar{x}$	σ
Inner Core	229	1.24	2.01
Outer Core	166	1.67	5.92
Large sites	337	1.28	4.14
Small sites	58	2.23	4.02
Paquimé	275	9.79	No data

Core sites are 290, 315, 355, and 565. Outer Core sites are 204, 231, 242, and 317. Sites 204, 315, and 565 are grouped as "large," and sites 290, 231, 242, and 317 are "small."

Application of t-tests to these data show no statistically significant differences in mean hemispherical hearth size between Inner and Outer Core Zone sites. The same is true for large and small sites, even though their means differ considerably. This is because the t-test is strongly affected by standard deviations. The table also shows that all hemispherical hearths are highly variable in size, as indicated by the large standard deviations of every mean. Moreover, the standard deviation of the Outer Core Zone hemispherical hearth size mean is very large compared to that of the Outer Core Zone sites. Squaring each of these standard deviations produces variances that can be compared statistically. An F-test for equality of variances shows that the difference is significant (F = 8.78, p = .003). This analysis confirms the initial impression that the hemispherical hearths of the Outer Core Zone were much more variable in size than were their counterparts of the Inner Core. The simple hemispherical hearth is *the* basic intramural feature of Medio period architecture everywhere, but it appears to have been at its least variable and thus at its most standardized among the sites of the Inner Core Zone. Finally, it is clear that the basin hearths of Paquimé were much larger than those of the neighboring sites. Using figures provided for Paquimé (Di Peso et al. 1974:4:251–57), basin hearth volumes were calculated to average between 8 and 11 liters.

Platform hearths are the other major category of fire feature recognized by Di Peso and colleagues at Paquimé. Platform hearths, they wrote, "have been thought of as being typically Casas Grandean because of their unique association with the architecture of this archaeological zone" (Di Peso et al. 1974:4:255). The authors were aware that the term "unique" was not accurate, as they cite Henry Carey's early report (1931:252), which described three variants of platform hearths at a small Medio period pueblo located some 100 km south of Paquimé on the Babícora Plain. In the Casas Grandes area, however, platform hearths were known only from Paquimé. Subsequent excavations at Inner and Outer Core Zone sites revealed that platform hearths are an infrequent but consistent element of the architecture of neighboring communities.

Frequency data on the six types of platform hearths recognized at Paquimé are presented in table 4.7. Type 2A is a simple rectangular platform containing a fire pit and an ash box. Type 2B is a platform with only a fire pit and deep air vent. Type 2C is a platform with only an ash pit, the fire pit lying on the floor beside. Type 2D is a rectangular platform with two fire pits and an ash pit. Type 2E is a platform built into a room corner, with fire and ash pits. Type 2F is a circular platform with a central fire pit and no ash pit. Type 2G is a rectangular platform with a central fire pit, no ash pit, and a vent extending on both sides of the fire pit. These are illustrated in the Casas Grandes report (Di Peso et al. 1974:4:252, fig. 179-4).

It is evident from the table that the simple rectangular platform hearth with fire and ash pits in its surface is the most common kind in the region. Nearly 95 percent of the platform hearths recorded at Paquimé are of this type, and it is present at all neighboring sites where elevated fire features have been found. While it could be observed that Paquimé has the greatest variety of platform hearths, the preceding table shows that most of these different types are represented by a single example. The same is true at the investigated neighbors. The relative frequencies of platform hearths among the sites of the Core Zone can be expressed as a ratio of platform hearths to in-floor basin hearths (table 4.8).

These data show that platform hearths were much less common at all neighbors of Paquimé except for Site 242. This is an unusual case, however, as only four basin hearths were found there. This is very far below average for a Medio period pueblo, and it is part of our argument that Site 242 was occupied for a short time. Recall that Site 242 is a postulated control node established by Paquimé to manage agricultural production in its vicinity. Not only were platform hearths less common at neighbors than at Paquimé, but they were also simpler. Type 2A platforms were sometimes decorated with geometric designs molded into their upper surfaces (see Di Peso et al. 1974:4:255, fig. 181-4 for illustrations). Thirty Type 2A hearths and one Type 2G hearth were so treated, accounting for about 25 percent of all platform hearths at Paquimé. This elaboration was apparently unique to the central place, however, as no platform decoration has yet been found on any elevated fire feature among the investigated Inner and Outer Core Zone neighbors. Size is the last point of contrast between the platform hearths of Paquimé and those of its Core Zone neighbors. Descriptive statistics are presented in table 4.9, together with the same statistics from platform hearths among Core Zone neighbors.

TABLE 4.7 Platform hearth types and frequencies at Core Zone sites

		Inner Core			Outer Core	
Type	Paquimé	565	315	355	204	242
2A	114	1	2	1	3	2
2B	2	0	0	0	0	0
2C	1	0	0	0	0	1
2D	1	0	0	0	0	0
2E	1	1	0	0	0	0
2F	1	0	1	0	2	0
2G	1	0	0	0	0	1
?[a]	1	7	0	0	7	0
Total	121	9	3	1	7	4

[a] Hearths in this category were too badly damaged to classify.

TABLE 4.8 Ratios of platform to basin hearths at Core Zone sites

	Inner Core			Outer Core	
Paquimé	565	315	355	204	242
121/344	7/64	3/127	1/14	3/24	4/4
0.35	0.11	0.02	0.07	0.13	1.00

TABLE 4.9 Platform hearth descriptive statistics for Paquimé and its Core Zone neighbors

	n	Min. (cm)	Max. (cm)	Mean (cm)	Std. dev.
			Paquimé		
Platform length	60	42	94	76.9	11.1
Platform width	60	37	79	61.2	9.2
Platform height	60	2	8	5.7	1.5
Fire pit diam.	60	14	29	21.6	2.9
Fire pit depth	60	6	22	12.8	3.2
			Neighboring sites		
Platform length	8	30	92	68.0	17.2
Platform width	10	25	80	58.8	15.4
Platform height	9	5	12	8.1	2.7
Fire pit diam.	13	10	28	21.1	6.1
Fire pit depth	13	7	22	13.5	5.4

A related consideration is the size of the rooms in which platform hearths were found. In our sample of 60 platform hearths from Paquimé, mean room size with these facilities was found to be 26.6 m² (σ = 18.9; range 8–120 m²). The average-sized room at Paquimé was 25 m², with a standard deviation of 19.1 and a range of 1.4–120 m² (Whalen and Minnis 2009:74). Platform hearths at Paquimé thus occur across all room sizes without being confined to any single size category (e.g., the largest). The situation at the neighboring sites was found to be similar. There, the average platform-hearth-containing room area was 21.1 m² (σ = 11.4, range 8–56 m²). As at Paquimé, platform hearths at the neighboring sites occur across a broad range of small to large rooms.

Elsewhere (Whalen and Minnis 2001b, 2009) we have argued that platform hearths were part of an "architecture of power" displayed at Paquimé and at its administrative satellites, like the 242 community. Platform hearths were not found at small simple Sites 231 and 317, and they were rare at large Site 204. The recent Inner Core Zone excavations add a little to this picture. Platform hearths were present in small numbers at large Sites 565 and 315 and at small Site 355. The latter site also showed a mix of thick-walled and thin-walled architecture, and its few platform hearths were not consistently associated with either thick- or thin-walled rooms. As noted, the contrast between simple architecture and the architecture of power is not as pronounced in the Inner Core Zone as it was found to be in the Outer Core. It still seems, however, that platform hearths represent an especially elaborate type of intramural fire feature that may have had status implications.

Fire Feature Uses

The preceding discussion of intramural fire pit and hearth types leads to the question of their functions. First, we note that fire features, often in multiples, were present in nearly every Medio period room dug in Chihuahua. At Paquimé 484 fire features were found in 230 excavated rooms. Of the 259 rooms dug there, only 29 (11%) had no fire feature. At Outer Core Zone Site 204, only 3 of 31 excavated rooms (10%) had no intramural hearth or fire pit. All excavated rooms at Outer Core Sites 231 and 242 contained fire features, as did all but one of the rooms dug at Site 317. These figures allow us to estimate that 80–90 percent of Medio period rooms contained fire features. In the Inner Core large Site 565, medium Site 315, and small Site 355 continued this pattern, with 80 percent to 95 percent of all excavated rooms containing fire features. The only exception to this widespread pattern is small Inner Core Site 290. Twelve rooms were excavated there, of which six had fire features, and six did not. Moreover, some of the larger rooms at Site 290 lacked fire facilities. Some of the site's fire features were of the simplest sort: fires built directly on floor surfaces, without any pit. We assert earlier in this chapter that Site 290 was architecturally the simplest of those investigated here, and the paucity and ephemeral nature of its fire features reinforce this conclusion.

In general, fire pits and hearths were nearly ubiquitous in Medio period rooms because they served common essential domestic functions. Heating, illumination, and cooking were argued to be the roles played by the intramural fire features of Casas Grandes (Di Peso et al. 1974:4:251). Others (e.g., Lowell 1999; Reid and Whittlesey 1982) see a good deal of cooking being done inside pueblo rooms, while also acknowledging the multifunctional nature of the fire features. The in-floor fire pits just described for the primate center were large enough for all these tasks, and we agree with the implication that intramural fire pits were likely multifunctional. We suspect that the clay-lined fire pits composing most of the sample from nearly every site were so treated to increase their refractory properties, making them more efficient for heating and cooking. The rarer unlined fire pits may have been more casual constructions for illumination or for other short-term use. Lowell (1999) made a similar interpretation of the uses of lined and unlined basin fire pits in east-central Arizona at the Grasshopper and Chodistaas Pueblos.

The uses of platform hearths are less clear, and the facilities have no counterparts in existing fire feature studies (e.g., Lowell 1999; Riggs 2001; Shafer 2003; Sobolik et al. 1997). The fire basins of platform hearths were often heavily burned, but those at Casas Grandes were smaller and shallower than the in-floor basin fire pits. Fire pit volume for a sample of 60 platform hearths from Paquimé averages 0.4 liters, while the fire pit volumes of lined and unlined basin hearths were earlier shown to average 1.2 liters for the Inner Core sites and 1.7 liters for their Outer Core counterparts. This strongly suggests that platform hearths did not serve the full range of functions just ascribed to basin fire pits. In particular, the platform hearth fire basins seem too small for effective cooking, as the fire pit volumes of basin hearths all over the study area are three to four times the volumes of platform hearth fire pits.

The disparity noted earlier in this chapter in in-floor fire pit size between Casas Grandes and all its Core Zone neighbors is extreme, and it likely has behavioral implications. At this point, it is necessary to consider the factors that likely determined fire feature size at Casas Grandes or in any pueblo community. Several variables come immediately to mind, and these can be summarized under the headings of room size and cooking activities. There clearly is a general correlation between fire pit size (expressed here as pit area) and room floor area in the Medio communities discussed here. Casas Grandes has the region's largest rooms (mean area = 23.2 m^2), and these contain the region's largest fire pits (mean volume = 8–10 liters). The Inner and Outer Core Zone sites have much smaller rooms (mean area = 8.7 m^2), and they contain smaller fire pits (mean volume = 1.4 liters).

To test the validity of this apparent pattern, correlation coefficients were calculated between room floor area and fire pit areas. The resulting coefficients should have values near 1.0 if fire pits were built to fit room sizes. In fact, the correlation coefficients were less than 0.1 at all of the Inner and Outer Core Zone sites investigated here. This demonstrates that there is no relationship between fire pit areas and the floor areas of the rooms in which they were found. In other words, hearth size clearly does not depend on room size at any of the neighboring communities. We did not make similar calculations for Casas Grandes, although we suspect that the same result would be obtained.

Cooking activities have long been recognized as a strong influence on fire pit size (e.g., Ciolek-Torrello and Reid 1974). The relation is likely not a simple one, however, as noted in the study just cited. Variables influencing intramural fire pit size minimally include the number of people cooked for, the cooking technology used, and the presence of extramural cooking facilities like those documented in the Mimbres area (Shafer 2003; Sobolik et al. 1997). At present, we know too little about all these variables to be able to make convincing arguments. Outdoor cooking facilities, for instance, are known to exist on Medio period sites. Our regional surveys (Whalen and Minnis 2001a) noted the presence of extramural fire features around a number of pueblo room blocks. These ranged in size from small to very large, and there are some very large outdoor roasting pits at Paquimé itself. The cooking facilities of interest to the present discussion, however, are those likely to have served families or residential groups. Unfortunately, we still have almost no idea how this was done.

Room Function at Paquimé

An earlier study (Whalen and Minnis 2009:95–102) contains a discussion of the problems in assigning functions to pueblo rooms. The problem has been approached through architecture and through features and artifacts. Often-cited complicating factors, however, are the frequent remodeling of pueblo rooms in long occupation sequences and the uses of these rooms for more than one purpose during their histories. All excavated rooms at Paquimé were classed as either domestic, public, public-ceremonial, or ceremonial, but the published definitions of these room types (Di Peso et al. 1974:4:198) contain high levels of overlap and ambiguity. In addition, the classification does not mention storage rooms. The descriptions of a few Paquimé rooms contain the notation that they probably served for the storage of food or exotica. Nevertheless, storage rooms are not included in the summary tables showing the percentages of rooms across time that were devoted to the four functions just listed (Di Peso et al. 1974:4:198, 200).

The lack of defined storage rooms at Paquimé is inconsistent with other studies of pueblo communities. E. Charles Adams (1983:51) asserts that a traditional pueblo community should have two or three storage and granary rooms for each habitation room. A similar figure comes from the Turkey Creek Pueblo (Lowell 1991), where 132 storage rooms and 59 habitation rooms were identified. The storage-to-habitation room ratio here is 2.2. Other studies of pueblo room use show considerable variation in frequencies of storage rooms. At the NAN Ranch pueblo, 21 storage rooms were identified, versus 30 habitation rooms, for a ratio of 0.7 (Shafer 2003). The Broken K pueblo contained 17 rooms identified as storage spaces, while 42 others were classed as habitation rooms (J. Hill 1970). This storage-to-habitation room ratio is 0.4. At the Grasshopper Pueblo, Riggs (2001) also produces a storage-to-habitation room ratio of 0.4. Although they vary widely in the figures just given, all of these studies of historic and prehistoric southwestern pueblos recognize a substantial number of storage rooms. The classification used at Paquimé stands sharply apart from this pattern.

The four room classifications employed by Di Peso seem to have been based primarily on architectural characteristics and feature assemblages, although artifacts were also used to infer intramural activities. The following definitions were provided for the room types of Paquimé. Domestic rooms have fire hearths, bed platforms, and doors of all types but of the smaller sizes, and their floor levels contain food preparation tools. Public rooms have the characteristics of domestic rooms, plus entryways of larger size, stairways, colonnades, or large quantities of stored material such as shell. Public-ceremonial rooms have any of the characteristics of domestic and public rooms, plus subfloor corner caches and "other ceremonial materials." Ceremonial rooms have special associations with ball courts and other ceremonial features. In this classification, Di Peso and colleagues made no explicit use of room size, although this variable often plays a central part in studies of pueblo room function in the U.S. Southwest.

Accordingly, we used a multimodal histogram of room size as a starting point for a reconsideration of room function at Paquimé (Whalen and Minnis 2009:98–101). The following discussion is abstracted from the study just cited. Four room-size classes were defined from histogram modes. Class I rooms range from 1.4 to 34.9 m^2 of floor area, with a mean size of 17.6 m^2. Class II rooms are 35.0 to 63.9 m^2 in area, and their mean size is 47.1 m^2. Rooms of Class III measured 64.0 to 99.5 m^2, having an average size of 71.6 m^2. Last, Class IV rooms ranged from 99.6 to 120.0 m^2. An analysis of variance (see the study just cited for details) was used to compare the mean frequencies per room of element and feature values within size classes. The results of this analysis are summarized as follows. Rooms of Size Class I average 17.6 m^2 in floor area. They showed a number of statistically significant differences from the rest of the sample. They have fewer hearths, doors, and windows than do larger rooms. They also have the sample's lowest frequencies of platform hearths and "bed" platforms. Class I rooms never have subfloor caches, and nearly all are of simple shapes. Class I rooms, then, are the community's smallest, simplest, and least accessible spaces. We stress, however, that while Class I rooms are small by the standards of Paquimé, they include rooms up to nearly 35 m^2. These rooms are large in comparison to other southwestern pueblo rooms or to the rooms of Medio period sites of the Inner and Outer Core Zones.

Some of these Paquimé rooms could have been storage spaces. Of the 188 Class I rooms, 20 contain no hearths. These hearthless rooms range in floor area from 1.4 to 19.5 m^2, with a mean size of 9.6 m^2 ($\sigma = 4.7$). About 80 percent of the small hearthless rooms lack windows and wall niches, while about 70 percent have no bed platforms or subfloor burials. They are, in other words, the smallest and simplest rooms of Size Class I. These 20 rooms are not distributed evenly among the excavated parts of Casas Grandes. Instead, more than half of them occur in Units 6 and 12, while the rest are scattered thinly over all the other excavated room units. It is interesting to note that Units 6 and 12, respectively, contain low and medium frequencies of the bed platforms we earlier argued were intramural storage facilities. Even if all 20 of these rooms served for storage, however, they compose only 8.6 percent of the 231 excavated rooms in our sample. Other work in pueblos of the U.S. Southwest (e.g., Adams 1983) leads us to expect that more spaces should have been devoted to storage. This leads us to suspect that intramural food storage at Paquimé may not have been done in the manner characteristic of pueblos in the U.S. Southwest.

The largest rooms at Paquimé (Class IV) average more than 100 m² in floor area. There are only four of these rooms in the excavated sample, but they show several characteristics that set them apart. They have the sample's highest frequency of elaborate platform hearths, no subfloor caches were found in any of them, and this is the only category of room that contained no subfloor human burials. Very large rooms are commonly interpreted as communal or ceremonial facilities in studies of southwestern pueblo room function (e.g., Adams 1983; Cameron 1999; Shafer 2003). In fact, Di Peso characterized one of our Class IV rooms as a communal space of some sort (Di Peso et al. 1974:5:710). This is Room 45 of Unit 14, which had a floor area of 99.8 m². Inside the room were four adobe pillars of columns that may have supported a second-story balcony running around all four sides of the space. The other three rooms in Class IV did not contain such unusual features.

It seems likely that Class II and III rooms served a wide variety of purposes. The average floor areas of these two classes are, respectively, 47 m² and 72 m², so that they are large by Southwest pueblo standards. One of the Class III rooms is number 36 of Unit 14. It had 68 m² of floor area, and it was described by Di Peso et al. as "one of the most impressive rooms excavated in Unit 14" (1974:5:671). The room had a compound shape described by the excavators as a butterfly. Beneath its floor were eight caches of shell and stone jewelry. In fact, subfloor caches were most common in the rooms of Class III. Apart from a few rooms like the one just described, however, Class II and III rooms differed little from each other. Both contained a full range of architectural traits and features.

At the end of this analysis, however, we concluded that the Paquimé rooms do not sort into clear functional classes based on size and architecture, as there is a good deal of trait overlap among the size classes. There are several possible explanations for this situation. It may be that our classification system is inadequate or inappropriate, drawing as it does on the pueblos of the U.S. Southwest. This implies that we see Paquimé as the same kind of community as other southwestern pueblos, although it existed at a much larger scale. It could also be that the Casas Grandes rooms have been so extensively modified that their original functions are blurred. Unfortunately, questions of room function and storage remain imprecisely defined at the primate center.

Room Function at Neighboring Sites

The preceding discussion shows high levels of overlap and ambiguity in the original classification of Paquimé room functions. Compared to the central place, the neighboring settlements' rooms were always smaller; room shapes were usually simple quadrilaterals; alcoves were rare; floor features like platform hearths were present, but these platforms were almost invariably simple rectangles; and subfloor caches were almost nonexistent. Accordingly, the present study uses a simpler two-part classification for room function among the large and small neighboring settlements: general purpose versus special purpose rooms.

Almost all rooms at all sites fall into the general purpose category. This means that they served a range of functions associated with living, storage, heating, and other activities of daily life. They occur in a wide range of sizes, from a few square meters to 20 m², and they contain all sorts of fire features, wall niches, and doorways. A few rooms were classed as special purpose spaces. These are distinguished by characteristics that are especially elaborate or unusual in general purpose rooms. Subterranean floors, colonnades, pillars, and subfloor caches of unusual or exotic materials are examples. Rooms classed as special purpose were found in a wide range of sizes ranging up to 25 m², the largest of which is small compared to spaces at Paquimé. Special purpose rooms likely existed at many sites, as they likely served various public and ceremonial functions. Their low frequencies, however, make discovery a matter of chance in excavation. Even so, two of the three large Core Zone sites and one of the small ones contained such spaces. Each is described below.

Inner Core Zone Site 315, a close neighbor of Paquimé, had at least two special purpose rooms. Room 7 was a long, narrow space separated from the adjacent Room 8 by a row of three collared posts (figure 4.22). These posts averaged 22 cm in diameter, and together they spanned an opening of 10.5 m. The posts were placed about 2.2 m from the parallel adobe wall to the north. The east and west walls were of the same heavy adobe construction as the northern one. The covered space was about 23 m². There were many floor features, but they appear to belong to the later remodeling of the room, as we discuss later in this chapter. The colonnaded area of Room 7 opened from Room 8, which was also a long, narrow space, with an alcove at the east end. Its heavy adobe south wall stood 2.3 m from the colonnade row, as did the north wall of Room 7. The fact that there were no door openings in the Room 8 side of the unit suggests that it was the roofed interior space that opened via the three colonnades onto the possibly unroofed Room 7. There is no indication that the colonnade row supported a second story, as was often the case at nearby Paquimé.

Outer Core Zone large Site 204 provides an example of a similar special purpose space in the main room block. Room 21 is illustrated elsewhere (Whalen and Minis 2009:105,

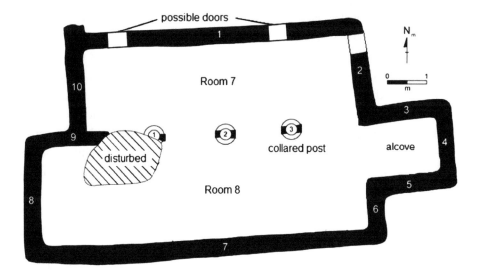

FIGURE 4.22 Special purpose Rooms 7/8 at Site 315.

fig. 3.17). The north side of Room 21 opened onto a plaza. At the room-to-plaza transition were two substantial adobe column bases. Each measured about 1.5 m long by 75 cm wide. The columns were hollow, formed by adobe cobs arranged in a rectangular shape around an empty center. Their original heights are unknown, but the surviving portions stood about 55 cm above the room floor. The columns' adobe footings extended about 15 cm beneath the room floor and into sterile soil. Similar columns at Paquimé were presumed to have extended up to the roof level, and the same may be true for the Room 21 columns. There was a north wall to the room, against which the columns abutted.

The floor area of Room 21 was nearly 24 m², placing it among the largest rooms dug at Site 204. Later, a small space was formed by a thin adobe wall that partially enclosed the northeast corner of Room 21. In this added space, at the base of the adobe column that formed part of its northwest wall, was a cache of manos in both used and blank (unused) forms. Also present in this small space was a second cache of two large bifaces and five Late Archaic projectile points. The points, at least, undoubtedly had been curated from the surrounding countryside, where they may still be found today. Both of these caches are illustrated in the 2009 volume (Whalen and Minnis 2009:105, figs. 3.15 and 3.16). The north wall of adjacent Rooms 19 and 22 was formed by the south wall of Room 21. Room 19 contained the largest cache of mano blanks thus far discovered outside Paquimé, while beneath the floor of Room 22 was the only macaw burial thus far found outside Paquimé. Room 21, then, not only has uncommon architectural features and caches, but is surrounded by unusual and exotic items.

Returning to Inner Core Site 315, a second special purpose space is Room 70 (figure 4.23). It lay about 30 m from the Room 7/8 colonnaded space, and it may be significant that both Rooms 7/8 and Room 70 lay in the part of the Site 315 room block that faced Paquimé, less than 1 km away on the other side of the Casas Grandes River. Room 70 was nearly square, measuring about 5 m on a side. Its floor area was about 25 m². In the center of this space were post collars. Three of them were preserved (Features 401, 407, and 409), but the fourth was destroyed by looting. Its position is estimated based on the other three. The four posts would have been arranged in a smaller square that was some 2.7 m on a side. Each posthole lay about 2.3 m from the corresponding room corner. Judging by the sizes of the three surviving adobe collars, the posts that they enclosed would have been about 22 cm in diameter. The postholes were about 30 cm deep. Each hole had a flat stone slab at its base. They were similar to the one illustrated earlier in this chapter (refer to figure 4.19b). These posts would have had a substantial support capacity, as would the room's 40 cm thick external adobe walls. There was, however, no indication of multistory construction.

Room 70 had a long and complex history of use. There were four floors, the lowest of which sat directly on sterile soil, some 25 cm below the ground level of its time. Three successive floors were laid over Floor 4, each separated by about 8 cm of fill. The roof-support posts originated from the lowest floor and extended through all subsequent surfaces. A total of 26 features lay on one or another of the floors, although none were recognizable on the poorly preserved surface of Floor 1. A few small simple fire pits were

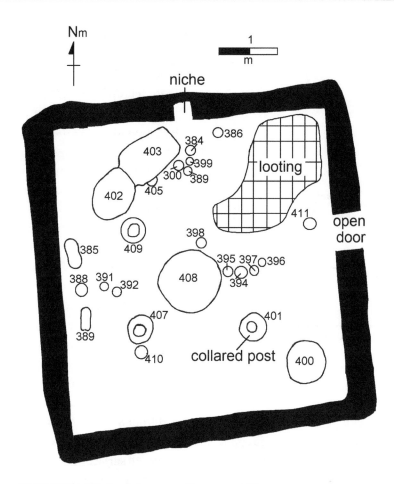

FIGURE 4.23 Special purpose Room 70 at Site 315.

scattered over Floor 2. Floors 3 and 4 contained the most interesting and diverse feature assemblage. Two burial pits originated from Floor 3. Feature 402 was a cylindrical pit about 75 cm in diameter by 110 cm deep. These dimensions are approximate, as part of the 402 pit was disturbed by the slightly later burial pit identified as Feature 403 (see figure 4.23). Feature 402 was sealed with a plug of adobe at the Floor 3 level. It contained the disturbed and almost completely disintegrated remains of a 20- to 30-year-old male. The body likely had been seated in a tightly flexed position, which is characteristic of Medio period interments. Several shell beads came from the grave fill, but these may have come from the intrusive feature 403 burial pit, where many such beads were found. There were no ceramic grave goods.

Feature 403 also originated from Floor 3. It was an irregularly shaped, elongated pit about 60 cm deep. It contained the incomplete and poorly preserved remains of two individuals. Sex could not be determined. All of the bones appeared to be those of adults, one of whom was around 22–45 years old. There were no ceramic grave goods, although about 130 small shell beads were scattered throughout the fill. Originating from the lowest floor, 4, was Feature 408, a circular burial pit that lay in the center of Room 70. The pit was about

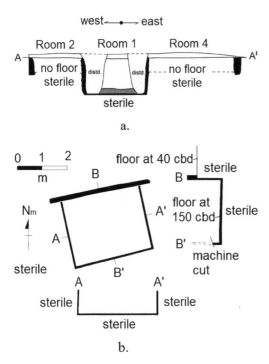

FIGURE 4.24 Subterranean Room 1 at Site 290.

1 m in diameter by 1.2 m deep. This burial pit contained a few craniofacial and long bone fragments, as well as several teeth. These represented three individuals, two adults of undetermined age and one child aged around 7–12 years. One of the adults was female, but the sex of the other could not be determined. Grave goods were two small polychrome vessels and one small Playas Red jar.

Finally, Inner Core small Site 290 contained a room to which we hesitatingly ascribe special function because of its unique construction. Subterranean Room 1 (figure 4.24) clearly was not a Viejo period pit structure. It was built against an existing east–west wall of the surface rooms. The room was excavated almost a meter into sterile soil on all four sides. The faces of the excavation were covered with a thin layer of adobe that ranged from 8 to 12 cm thick. There was no indication of an entryway into the room, although most of the south was lost to looting destruction. The floor of Room 1 was a single hard, smooth surface of grayish-white plaster that was 1.5 to 2 cm thick. This floor lay 150 cm below the site datum, while floors of all surface rooms ranged from 40 to 50 cm below the datum. Much of the floor was destroyed by looting, but one prepared feature survived. This was a well-made hemispherical fire pit with plastered interior surfaces. It contained a little ash, but its edges were not reddened. This lack of oxidation shows that the Room 1 fire pit was not used as heavily as many found in other locations. The abutment pattern of the north wall of Room 1 shows that it was built after the surface rooms, although the interval could have been brief. We suppose this because both Room 1 and the lowest floors of some of the surface rooms share the same CGAT building style.

We note that several subterranean rooms were excavated in Unit 9 at Paquimé. The floor of Room 2-9 lay about 100 cm below the existing ground surface. The room was quadrilateral, with 10 m² of floor area. The structure had thick stone and adobe walls on all four sides, and it was entered via a short stone-stepped ramp in the center of the east wall. The floor of quadrilateral Room 2-9 consisted of about 2 cm of adobe plaster laid down on sterile soil. There were no floor features, and there was little evidence of the function of this oddly constructed room (Di Peso et al. 1974:4:469–70). Paquimé Room 2-9, then, resembled Room 1 at Site 290 in depth, floor area, and floor construction. Its walls, however, were much more substantial than those of Room 290-1, nor did it have an entry ramp. Room 290-1 remains unique among the neighbors of Paquimé.

The End of the Casas Grandes Architectural Tradition

The CGAT characterized large and small sites in the eponymous area for as much as 250 years, although there was substantial variety in its execution. Paquimé was by far the most elaborate example of the tradition. By the end of the fourteenth century or early in the fifteenth, however, we see breakdown of the architectural tradition. Di Peso termed this time the Diablo phase at Paquimé, when, in his words:

> The colonnaded galleries, such as those in Units 14 and 16, and many of the large public thoroughfares that fingered through the city were taken over by the citizens, who put up crude adobe wall partitions to make living quarters of these once grand areas. The city water and reservoir system was no longer maintained but was left choked by debris and used as a burial area. More hopeless were the cistern drains, which emptied the enclosed plazas of rainwater. These, too, were permitted to go out of commission The great columned gallery (Room 44-14) that formed the south entrance filled with fallen wall debris, and the people built a crude series of steps on its surface in order to gain access to various upper floor rooms that were still habitable. (Di Peso 1974:2:666, notes 6–8)

These comments on the degenerate nature of Diablo building referred only to Paquimé, but our work among neighboring settlements shows that the disintegration of the CGAT was a widespread phenomenon. We found crude reconstructions or additions to CGAT buildings on many Inner Core Zone large and small settlements. It is interesting to note that this sort of construction does not appear to have been so common on the sites of the Outer Core Zone. As we discussed in chapter 3, small Outer Core Sites 231 and 317 might have been occupied for a few generations after the decline of large Site 204. The architecture of these small sites, however, does not appear to change from the CGAT style that characterized most of their occupation. Other Inner Core sites, in contrast, show several distinctive sorts of construction. One of these resembles Di Peso's Diablo phase building, representing the end of the CGAT. A second sort of building came sometime later and is a departure from the preceding style. We term this second building style the Post–Casas Grandes Architectural Tradition (PCGAT).

Site 315

The colonnaded Room 7/8 complex was described earlier in this chapter as a special purpose space. Three collared posts extended in a row across the longest dimension of the room. Toward the end of the room's use, a thin adobe wall with a door opening was built between the posts, dividing the space in two north and south halves. Di Peso described similar "Diablo phase" partitioning between colonnades at Paquimé, as just quoted. The height of the thin adobe wall is unknown, but its thickness suggests that it may have been low. Above it was likely a light jacal upper wall. There was one simple open door in the middle of the partition wall. The floor on both sides of the partition wall contained more

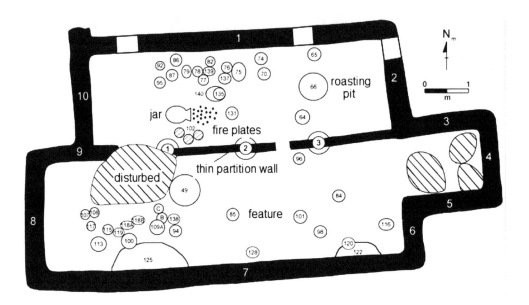

FIGURE 4.25 Small shallow hemispherical fire pits in Rooms 7 and 8.

than 30 features, most of which were small, shallow, lightly used fire pits (figure 4.25). Unfortunately, none of them gave dateable charcoal samples. Fire pits like these are usually found inside rooms, but their scattered distribution suggests that these small, casual fire pits were mostly built and used in the last stages of the rooms' occupation. They would then be contemporary with the thin wall joining the three collared posts.

One feature in Room 7 deserves special mention. Feature 66 was a small roasting pit filled with fire-cracked rock, and it was clearly dug through the floor of Room 7 (figure 4.26). Roasting pits are *never* found inside rooms, and the intramural presence of this one can be explained in two ways. First, Room 7 may have been unroofed, while the adjacent Room 8 was covered. An alternative is that Feature 66 was in use after the Room 7/8 complex was finally abandoned. Support for this hypothesis comes from the concentration of nearly all Room 7 intramural features in the western half of the space, far removed from Feature 66 on the room's east end. In short, we see Feature 66 as a PCGAT construction.

A comparable colonnaded space was described in Unit 6, Plaza 2, at Paquimé. There, seven posts were set in a row along the west side of Plaza 2-6, spanning an opening of 9.25 m. The postholes averaged 23 cm in diameter, and they were set at about 2.3 m from the parallel adobe wall to the west. This colonnaded space opened to the east onto Plaza 2-6, which is the location of the Viejo pit structures and early Medio surface structures discussed in preceding pages. Di Peso dated this colonnaded structure to the Early Medio period. Later, the spaces between the posts were filled by narrow adobe walls, converting the area into living rooms (Di Peso et al. 1974:4:317, fig. 226-4). The Site 315 Room 7/8 complex shows a similar sequence. There, a charcoal sample from one of the posts gives an age of 895 ±30 years BP, which is calibrated AD 1039–1215 (2σ). There were no Viejo period ceramics in this part of Site 315, indicating an early Medio age for the colonnade posts. The

FIGURE 4.26 Pit oven in Room 7 at Site 315.

rooms were in use through the Late Medio, and their modification began at the end of CGAT times (our Terminal CGAT), or what Di Peso termed the Diablo phase.

There is one more feature on the floor of Room 7, Site 315, that does not appear to have been simply utilitarian. Feature 102 (see figure 4.25) is a group of three bases of small ceramic jars found sitting on the floor of Room 7. They clearly belong to the last use of the room, and all three are likely contemporary. Each base forms a small shallow plate, all of which were heavily fire reddened. The extent of oxidation of each base suggests prolonged contact with hot coals, such as might be produced in incense burners. Simple space heating does not appear to have been their purpose, as we have never encountered similar features in other Medio rooms. To one side of the three fire dishes, and in likely association with them, a small Brownware jar lay on its side (see figures 4.25 and 4.27a). It once contained exotic and unusual items, including crystals, minerals, engraved stones, and stone pendants. These had been spread over the floor in front of it (figure 4.27b). This whole complex appears to date after the primary occupation of Room 7.

This find is almost identical to one from Paquimé, where a Brownware jar on a room floor contained a similar assortment of exotic and unusual items termed a "magician's kit" (Di Peso et al. 1974:7:292). A recent discussion sees such features as pieces of ritual technology, observing that "Southwest peoples attribute protection from witchcraft to the anima of ash, projectile points, minerals, ochre, and other artifacts.... [P]ast pueblo people deployed such technologies in rites of passage to close their pueblos and protect those who might come later from the potential dangers inherent in the materials left behind" (Walker and Berryman 2023:450). These authors contend that such manipulations of animate materials are common in abandonment situations worldwide, and it is a good explanation for

FIGURE 4.27 A ritual assemblage from the floor of Room 7, Site 315.

FIGURE 4.27 (*continued*)

the Room 7 discovery, accompanying the preceding discussion in this chapter of isolated human remains and their roles in closure rituals.

Further evidence of ritual closure or termination activity is extensive disturbance of human burials in several rooms at Site 315. Room 70 had a niche built into its north wall. In the niche were stacked a few splintered fragments of long bones. Their size shows them to belong to adults, and the bone thicknesses of several suggest leg parts. No articular surfaces were present. Another fragment was that of a distal humerus without visible epiphyseal fusion lines. Whether these remains came from one or several individuals could not be determined. There were no associated artifacts. The relation of the bones to the room's burial pits is unknown. Extensively fragmented human bone was scattered over the floor of Room 2, Site 315, although we found no burial pits close by, as we did in Room 70. This activity likely took place shortly after the rooms fell out of use, as floors and walls were still entirely exposed for bone scraps to be scattered over or arranged within a wall niche.

Site 355

This small room block mound is estimated to have contained 12 rooms, of which 6 were excavated (see chapter 3). The rooms were of typical CGAT construction, with walls ranging from 25 to 39 cm thick, collared posts, T-shaped doors, and numerous fire pits, including a platform hearth. Later, cruder construction is evident on the south side and around the southwest corner of the room block.

Room 1 was originally of typical CGAT construction, with well-finished walls and floors of a reddish brown adobe. Later, Room 1 and adjacent spaces were remodeled using adobe of a distinctive light gray color, as shown in figure 4.28a. New walls of this material were added, and existing walls were cut to a lower level and supplemented with the light gray adobe. Thick layers of this material were added to the floor and to the walls (figure 4.28b). This new adobe formed low, rough, irregular walls topped with large stones (figures 4.28c and d). The original CGAT walls appear to have been cut down to form level surfaces, after which light gray adobe and large stones were used to form new irregular walls. This construction is illustrated schematically in figure 4.28e. The later decomposition of these new walls is shown by the stone scatters in figures 4.28f and g. The white lines in these figures show the original reddish brown adobe walls of the CGAT construction. These were cut to level surfaces, and the PCGAT stones were added on top. More stones of 30 to 50 cm in maximum dimension were scattered about the south and west sides of the room block. Most lay fallen a little distance from the room block, but a few remained in their original positions atop the walls.

This kind of large stone construction was notably not part of other exterior or interior walls in this room block. It is apparent, therefore, that the gray adobe and large stones were not part of the original building. Instead, they represent a PCGAT style of building done later than the CGAT construction that underlay them. The distribution of large stones around the mound shows that this remodeling was limited to the southwest corner of the room block. Unfortunately, no dateable material was recovered from this remodeling, and

FIGURE 4.28 Remodeling at Inner Core small Site 355.

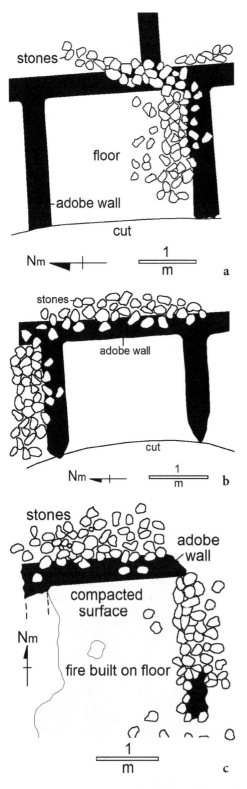

FIGURE 4.29 Original adobe walls and stones later piled atop them at Site 321.

there were no associated prehistoric ceramics or historic artifacts. It is apparent, however, that the remodeling occurred after the range of the room block's radiocarbon dates (see chapter 3), or sometime after the early 1400s.

Site 321

A second small site that shows a similar sort of piled-stone remodeling of a Late Medio CGAT occupation is Site 321, a small upland room block adjacent to the Ojo Vareleño drainage. Its room block mound measured about 24 m north–south by 22 m east–west. The mound's maximum height was about 35 cm. The center of the mound had been dug away by power machinery. This looting plus erosion exposed a number of adobe walls all over the mound. These were of typical small site Medio period construction. On the east side of the mound, this CGAT construction had been heavily remodeled by work similar to that of Site 355. That is, rooms were defined by CGAT adobe walls measuring 25–30 cm in thickness. These were later cut down to level surfaces about 25 cm high, onto which large field stones of about 10 to 30 cm in maximum dimension were piled to form room walls. These later collapsed, forming scatters similar to those just illustrated for Site 355. This situation is shown in figure 4.29. It is noteworthy that only a small portion of Site 321, about 20 percent of the whole, showed PCGAT construction. It clearly did not involve a remodeling of the entire room block but was confined to a few of the probably then-deserted rooms. The remodelers continued to use the original plastered floors of Site 321, but they built fires directly on these floor surfaces (figure 4.29c), without any of the fire features described earlier in this chapter for typical Medio period construction.

The chronology of the CGAT construction at Site 321 was discussed in chapter 3 of this volume. The four radiocarbon dates fell between the late 1200s and the early 1400s, or in the Late Medio period. The PCGAT construction presumably comes later, although probably soon after disuse of the rooms, as the original floors were still exposed. There were few ceramics from Site 321, and they are of little help in establishing chronology. More than 75 percent of them were Plain Brownwares, with small percentages of Textured (6%), Red-slipped (9%), Black and Black-on-red (0.3%), and Polychromes (8%). This is a typical Late Medio assemblage. It might have been associated with the CGAT construction of most of the mound, but the PCGAT occupants could have continued to use all or part of it, especially the Plain, Textured, and Red-slipped utility wares that make up 90 percent of the assemblage.

Site 290

Inner Core Site 290 is a small room block that was probably C-shaped. It had about 15 rooms in a low mound covering about 220 m² (see figure 3.7 for the site map). The site lies on a heavily eroded piedmont slope above the Casas Grandes River valley. The center of the room block, which we believe to have been a plaza, was destroyed by machine looting. A few adobe wall remnants were visible around the looted area. The sparse artifact assemblage included chipped and ground stone and ceramics. Most of the latter were Medio period utility wares, although a few sherds of Ramos Polychrome were present. The radiocarbon dates discussed in chapter 3 fall between AD 1300 and 1450 (cal., 2σ), which is consistent with the ceramics. The site was selected for investigation as a small simple residential site of Late Medio age.

Excavation revealed two distinctive types of architecture, the differences of which were visible in walls, floors, and floor features. The first type of construction was a simple version of CGAT, and we called it Type 1 architecture during excavation. The well-made walls were 25 to 35 cm thick (figure 4.30), and vestiges of adobe plaster survived in a few places. Floors were hard, smooth grayish-white plaster, and the few features they contained were simple hemispherical hearths of the familiar CGAT type (figure 4.31). This style of building closely resembles that found in the original construction of neighboring Inner Core small Sites 355 and 321. These two sites also showed partial reconstruction in the form of piled stones and refurbishment of some CGAT walls and floors with overlays of gray adobe, as discussed earlier in this chapter.

Site 290 shared some of these attributes, combined with a variant of PCGAT construction that we termed Type 2 building (figure 4.32). Here, adobe walls varied from 15 to 30 cm thick, but they were laid directly on the sterile ground. The unplastered surfaces of these Type 2 walls were irregular, and their adobe had a coarse, crumbly texture. The associated floors were thin and uneven, usually without the hard, smooth plastered surfaces of CGAT construction. Finally, these Type 2 floors contained almost no prepared intramural features. Instead, fires were built directly on floor surfaces (figure 4.33a), although a typical CGAT fire feature was found on a lower floor some 15 cm below the fire stain (figure 4.33b).

FIGURE 4.30 Walls and floors of CGAT Type 1 in Rooms 7 and 12 at Site 290.

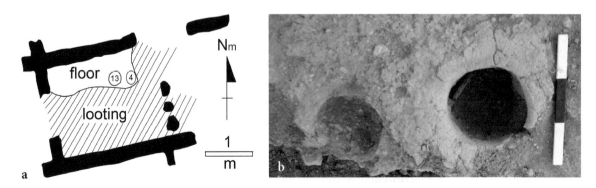

FIGURE 4.31 Hemispherical floor hearths of CGAT Type 1 in Room 10 at Site 290.

FIGURE 4.32 Thin, irregular walls of PCGAT Type 2 construction in Rooms 5 (a) and 8 (b) at Site 290. This adobe was coarse, with a good deal of small gravel in it. The thin walls were built directly on the ground surface, without footing trenches. It is distinctly different from CGAT construction.

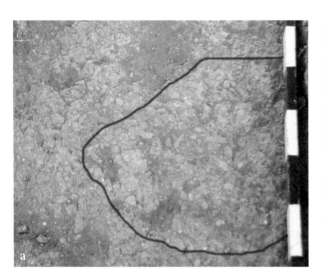 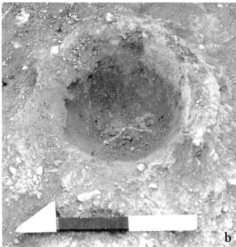

FIGURE 4.33 Fire feature succession in Room 7 at Site 290: (a) the stain of a fire kindled directly on the existing floor surface, without any hearth preparation, as sometimes seen in PCGAT construction; (b) a hemispherical hearth of the CGAT style that was built on a floor directly below the PCGAT feature.

This practice of building fires directly on floor surfaces was also seen at nearby Site 321. Overall, walls and floors of this Type 2 style were of noticeably different appearance than those found in CGAT building. There were, however, no large stones used to build up the original adobe walls at Site 290.

This contrasts with the refurbishment of neighboring small Sites 321 and 355. Despite their relatively coarse building style, a number of the Site 290 rooms showed a good deal of reconstruction and reuse. Some rooms, for example, had two or three closely spaced floors. The uppermost were of the Type 2 sort just described. Fires were built directly on these floor surfaces, without prepared fire pits. The lowest floor, in contrast, was harder and smoother, with CGAT-style hemispherical hearths. Rooms 6, 7, and 12 are good examples.

There also was some evident remodeling of original walls, as seen in Rooms 2 and 13. Here, layers of grayish adobe were applied over the reddish original walls. This technique also was seen in PCGAT construction at Inner Core small Site 355. Site 290 clearly had a complicated occupational history; the lowest floors of some rooms were fairly well made and contained CGAT-style hemispherical hearths, while floors closely overlying these were coarser and without prepared features.

Preceding pages describe construction in the Inner Core Zone that postdates the CGAT. PCGAT building, as thus far recognized, includes several types of remodeling of existing CGAT structures. Large colonnaded rooms at Site 315 were subdivided in thin adobe partitions built between the original columns, and a large roasting pit was dug into a portion of the floor of original Room 7. Likewise, many small fire pits were made and used in the floor of Room 7, making it likely that this was an unroofed exterior space adjacent to Room 8.

Also visible is rough overbuilding of CGAT walls and floors with layers of gray adobe. Sites 355 and 290 are examples. This material contrasts with the reddish brown adobe used in original CGAT construction. The consistent placement of the gray adobe over the reddish brown CGAT surfaces confirms its later date. It was found in only a few of the rooms of Sites 290 and 355, so it was not an overall refurbishment of the entire room block. In several cases, large stones were piled atop cut-to-level sections of existing CGAT walls, as at Sites 321 and 355.

It is noteworthy that this PCGAT construction was not conspicuous in the Outer Core Zone, although it was tentatively suggested (Whalen and Minnis 2009) that several of the small sites were occupied, without major architectural change, into the mid- to late fifteenth century.

Concluding Thoughts

This chapter considers the succession of architectural forms in the Core Zone, from pit houses through post-Paquimé remodeling of pueblo room blocks. Viejo pit structures have been found beneath all the large Medio sites excavated to date, including Paquimé, so there might be many more of them than have been detected on surface surveys. On these sites, there is a clear succession from pit structures to jacal surface rooms in the Late Viejo, but these light surface structures clearly continued to be used in later times, as several are accompanied by Medio period ceramics. Di Peso explained them as temporary housing for the Medio period builders of CGAT structures. We excavated a set of them on Inner Core Site 565, and associated ceramics and radiocarbon dates suggest that these surface structures had a long and complicated occupational sequence that extended from the Early Medio period into Late Medio times.

The CGAT did not originate with Paquimé, as Di Peso asserted. Rather, it extended from a simple form in the Early Medio through its Late Medio fluorescence at Paquimé and to its eventual decline. Late Medio Paquimé is its apogee and most elaborate form. Toward the end of the Medio period there are crude, simple additions to CGAT structures, although they were still made within the same architectural tradition and are accompanied by Late Medio period ceramics. Di Peso called this the Diablo phase at Paquimé, and we term it the Terminal CGAT (TCGAT) in the Casas Grandes area. Somewhat later, there was another episode of rough remodeling of edge portions of old pueblo room blocks, and this is not done within the CGAT. We refer to it as Post-CGAT, or PCGAT. At present, it is known only from the small settlements of the Inner Core. It is clear that the Casas Grandes area was not abandoned after the decline of Paquimé, and it is equally apparent that this was a complicated situation that we are just beginning to perceive. Succeeding chapters define material culture changes that accompanied these different architectural forms.

 *Chapter 5*

Medio Period Ceramics of the Core Zone

Di Peso and colleagues provided the first extensive description of the Medio period ceramic assemblage (Di Peso et al. 1974:6:77–316). They also introduced several ideas about its origin and distribution. The first of these is that the Medio period ceramic assemblage existed in its pure form only at Paquimé, while outlying sites had only simplified versions of it. Second is the notion that Paquimé and its Medio ceramic assemblage appeared and disappeared together. Work among the center's neighbors expands on and revises these ideas. This chapter shows that the distinctive Medio period ceramic assemblage is present all over the Core and Middle Zones, or up to 80 km north of Paquimé. Next, we consider Medio ceramics and chronology, noting progress to date and continuing concerns. One of these arguments is that the existence of the center and much of its ceramic assemblage may not have been as congruent as originally supposed. The last part of the chapter deals with a functional analysis of the Medio ceramics of the Core Zone.

The Distribution of Ceramic Wares in the Core Zone

At the broadest level, ceramics of the Medio period can be divided into four major ware groups based on surface color and treatment. These are Brown, Red, Black, and Polychrome. Black-on-red ceramics make up a fifth ware group that is extremely rare and will not be discussed here. The Brownware group has two major variants: Plain and Textured. The former subgroup consists of Brown vessels without surface decoration, forming one type. Textured Brownwares, the second subgroup, have the same paste as Plainware, but the necks and shoulders of textured vessels carry plastic decoration, including incising, scoring, punching, and several varieties of corrugations of narrow and broad coil widths. Below this decoration, body sherds are indistinguishable from Plain bodies. There are 11 named types of Textured Brownwares. Red-slipped (hereafter, Red) wares are identified by the red slip that covers them entirely or in part. There may be sparse plastic decoration in addition to the red slip. Lower areas of jars that are unslipped are indistinguishable from

Plain bodies. The Red ware group contains five named types. Black ware was fired in a reducing atmosphere, producing a dark surface that was often highly burnished, and surface decoration was rarely used. There is one type of Black ware. Polychrome wares carry a range of designs in black and red paints. There are nine named types of polychromes, excluding what Di Peso termed "Ramos variants" of several of the polychromes. We here exclude these variants because of their rarity. Plain, Textured, and Red utility wares make up the vast majority of every Medio period ceramic assemblage.

Now to be considered is the distribution and frequency of these ware groups and their constituent types in the Casas Grandes region. The first comparison is among sites of different sizes and locations in the inner or outer parts of the Core Zone (table 5.1). Although Paquimé is an Inner Core site, its ware frequencies are included as a separate line in the table with the caution that screening and collection practices were different from those used in our excavations.

Brownware sherds are overwhelmingly dominant all over the area, and this is evident from Paquimé to the smallest site. The Brownware total at Paquimé is a good deal smaller than those of the other excavated settlements. We hesitate to read much into this, however, as sherd collection strategies were not the same. At Paquimé, large-mesh screens of about 6 inches were used inconsistently. At the other sites shown in table 5.1, all of which we dug, we used mesh of 6 mm (1/4 inch) to screen all excavated deposits. The result was recovery of many more small sherds, the most numerous of which were Brownwares. All sherds greater than 2 cm in maximum dimension were identified at least to ware group.

A second factor is that large jars of Textured Brown and Red-slipped wares characteristically carried plastic decoration or red slip on their necks and shoulders. Lower parts of these vessels were undecorated and so were indistinguishable from the same parts of Plain Brown vessels, as all shared similar paste composition. Some of these brown body sherds surely were from Plain Brown vessels, but others equally certainly were from the lower parts of Red-slipped or Textured Brown vessels. As there was no way to make this distinction, all were tabulated as Brownwares. This doubtless increased the frequency of that class in our tabulations.

Earlier in this discussion, it was suggested that Brown and Red wares were the general purpose utilitarian vessels of the Medio ceramic assemblage. By the production step measure (Feinman et al. 1991), the costs of these common wares were relatively low. Predictably, these utilitarian general purpose wares were by far the most common on large and small

TABLE 5.1 Ceramic ware frequencies on large and small Core Zone sites

	Size class	Brown (%)	Red-slip (%)	Black (%)	Polychrome (%)	Total
Paquimé	Large	66.7	10.3	4.7	18.3	100.0
ICZ	Large	85.1	3.3	2.1	9.5	100.0
OCZ	Large	82.1	6.1	3.0	8.8	100.0
ICZ	Small	79.1	4.8	3.9	12.2	100.0
OCZ	Small	91.6	2.6	1.8	4.0	100.0

sites all over the Core Zone. In contrast, the rarer Black and Polychrome wares might be considered special purpose containers, with considerably more production steps and thus higher production costs. Data from table 5.1 shows that large sites of the Inner and Outer Core Zones had comparable polychrome frequencies. A surprise, however, is that polychrome ceramics were much more common on the small sites of the Inner Core than on their small Outer Core counterparts. In fact, the Inner Core polychrome frequency on the small sites is slightly larger than the large site figure anywhere in the Core Zone, excepting Paquimé.

It is predictable that large settlements should have more of the more expensive special purpose vessels, while small sites should have fewer of them. We are unsure how to explain the situation in the Inner Core, however. There was the suggestion in chapter 3 that the small sites of the Outer Core continued to be occupied into the sixteenth century, while the small sites of the Inner Core produced evidence of occupation beyond that of Paquimé, but not to the extent of the Outer Core small sites. These Outer Core settlements might have been occupied so much longer that the polychrome vessels' symbolic relevance and even their heirloom value were greatly diminished. Samples are small and data are sparse, however, and firmer conclusions must await more research.

Ceramic Type Distributions in the Core Zone

The four Medio ware groups contain 29 named types, descriptions of which are found in the Casas Grandes ceramic volume (Di Peso et al. 1974:6:108–316). One new polychrome type (White-Paste Babícora) was introduced by us (Whalen and Minnis 2009:121–22), for a total of 30 named ceramic types. We note that a few rare types (e.g., Casas Grandes Armadillo, Black-on-red, and Ramos-style variants of some polychromes) are not included in the present discussion.

The first diversity measure is a simple count of the number of types identified on each of the sites studied here (table 5.2). Predictably, all large sites of the Inner Core Zone (315 and 565) and of the Outer Core Zone (204) contained all 30 types. The same is true, of course, for the center of Paquimé. As a diversity index, we simply divide the number of types found on a site by 30. All the large Core Zone sites thus have the maximum type diversity score of 1.0 and so are not shown in the table. These data show that the small sites of the Outer Core (231, 242, and 317) all have the highest type diversity scores. In contrast, Inner Core small sites uniformly show the sample's lowest type diversity scores, averaging 0.75 (σ = .07). In contrast, those Inner Core small sites with PCGAT building (355, 290, and 321) show the lowest type diversity, averaging 0.47 (σ = 0.09). The highest type diversity score in the Inner Core (0.67 at Site 355) is less than the lowest type diversity score in the Outer Core (0.67 at Site 242).

The next question is whether all ceramic types are equally sparsely represented on PCGAT sites. The preceding table shows that they are not. Rather, the highest type diversity scores are found among the Brownware ceramics, with an average for CGAT small

TABLE 5.2 Small site ceramic type diversity scores

Site[a]	Arch. type[b]	All [30]	Brown [12]	Red [5]	Black [1]	Polychrome [9]
231 OCZ	CGAT	(23) 0.77[c]	(12) 1.00	(2) 0.4	(1) 1.0	(8) 0.89
		$n = 1{,}523$[d]	$n = 1{,}405$	$n = 28$	$n = 44$	$n = 46$
242 OCZ	CGAT	(19) 0.63	(9) 0.75	(2) 0.4	(1) 1.0	(7) 0.78
		$n = 4{,}733$	$n = 4{,}491$	$n = 75$	$n = 73$	$n = 84$
317 OCZ	CGAT	(22) 0.73	(12) 1.00	(3) 0.6	(1) 1.0	(6) 0.67
		$n = 3{,}715$	$n = 3{,}428$	$n = 168$	$n = 42$	$n = 77$
355 ICZ	PCGAT	(16) 0.53	(7) 0.58	(2) 0.4	(1) 1.0	(6) 0.67
		$n = 1{,}111$	$n = 1{,}004$	$n = 5$	$n = 54$	$n = 48$
290 ICZ	PCGAT	(13) 0.43	(8) 0.67	(1) 0.20	(0) 0	(4) 0.44
		$n = 642$	$n = 595$	$n = 28$	$n = 0$	$n = 19$
321 ICZ	PCGAT	(12) 0.40	(6) 0.50	(2) 0.40	(0) 0	(4) 0.44
		$n = 540$	$n = 6$	$n = 2$	$n = 0$	$n = 5$

[a] OCZ = Outer Core Zone; ICZ = Inner Core Zone.
[b] CGAT is Casas Grandes Architectural Tradition. PCGAT is Post-CGAT.
[c] (Number of types identified) / [number of types in that ware group] = type diversity score. Maximum value is 1.0.
[d] The sample size is n.

sites of 0.92 ($\sigma = 0.14$), while PCGAT small sites average only 0.58 ($\sigma = 0.09$). In addition, the preceding table shows that the six Red and Black types, while present on all CGAT small sites, are nearly absent on PCGAT sites. The average diversity score for these types on CGAT sites is 0.82 ($\sigma = 0.27$), while that of PCGAT sites is 0.33 ($\sigma = 0.41$). Last, the nine polychrome types are well represented on CGAT small sites, which have a diversity score of 0.78 ($\sigma = 0.11$). The PCGAT small sites, in contrast, contain only four to six of the nine polychrome types, for an average diversity score of 0.52 ($\sigma = 0.10$). Small PCGAT sites clearly have lower polychrome diversity in all their ceramic types than do their small CGAT counterparts.

But what about the frequencies of particular types within the broad ware groups? Our earlier analysis of deep midden deposits on Outer Core Zone large Site 204 showed useful change in type frequencies through time (Whalen and Minnis 2009:120, table 4.3). The lower levels of Site 204 test pits contained Plain, Textured, Red-slipped, and polished Black vessels, plus a few polychromes of the Babícora, White-Paste Babícora, Dublán, and Villa Ahumada types. All of these polychromes carried simple geometric designs painted in thick, imprecise lines of red and black paint. These designs occurred in continuous bands that encircled the vessel body. Mitch Hendrickson (2003:32) applies the term "Design Horizon A" to this style of painting. Others (e.g., Kelley and Larkin 2017:114) refer to it more simply as "Medio A," and we follow this usage here. Charcoal in these lower levels provided a date range of calibrated AD 1160–1280 (2σ). This ceramic assemblage time span was termed the Early Medio period.

The Late Medio period saw the addition of a new style of polychrome painting, although the Early Medio types continued in use. This new polychrome tradition is termed Design

FIGURE 5.1 Polychrome painting styles. The broad-lined, continuous style is termed Medio A, while the fine-lined, segmented style is Medio B. Reprinted by permission from Whalen and Minnis (2009:fig. 4.27).

Horizon B, or Medio B. Vessels painted in the Medio B tradition carry more motifs per vessel, and these were arranged into discrete segmented, or "paneled," areas around the vessel. Motifs are more complex, adding zoomorphic and anthropomorphic figures to the Medio A geometric designs. All this painting is done in a neat, precise, thin-lined style. Based on radiocarbon dates on either side of the appearance of Ramos Polychrome, we dated the beginning of the Late Medio period to roughly AD 1300. Vessels of the A and B styles are shown in figure 5.1.

The many types of Early Medio Plain, Textured, and Red utilitarian wares continued in use with little morphological change throughout the Late Medio period. Their persistence is likely due to their use in a wide range of domestic tasks, including cooking, serving, storage, and fermenting. Plain Brown, Scored, Incised, and Punched ceramics are ubiquitous in the 204 test pit levels, but there was a drop in frequency of corrugated vessels from 2.2 percent in early Medio levels to less than 1 percent in the uppermost Late Medio levels. This is consistent with others' arguments that corrugated ceramics decline in frequency throughout the Medio period (W. Hill 1992:98; Rakita and Raymond 2003:177). All CGAT sites, large and small, contain corrugated sherds, while none was found on the presumed PCGAT sites. This suggests a late chronological position for the PCGAT occupations.

Another rare ceramic type, Black-on-red, shows a similar pattern. We and others (Burd et al. 2004; Rakita and Raymond 2003) have argued that this type is diagnostic of the Late Medio period, although it so rare that it was not tabulated in the preceding tables. Most of the small sites studied here have one or two sherds of this type, while large sites have five to ten Black-on-reds in assemblages numbering thousands of sherds. Small PCGAT Sites 290 and 321, however, are the only ones in the present sample containing no Black-on-red pottery at all.

We next turn to polychrome type frequencies on the small sites. The polychrome types have the area's greatest potential as dating tools because of the complexity of their decoration and the associated opportunities for stylistic change. The midden data from Outer Core Site 204 showed several trends. First, Babícora Polychrome is present in all test pit levels, from earliest Medio through the end of the period, although it declines sharply in frequency. In Early Medio test pit levels, which we date from the late 1100s to the late 1200s or early 1300s, Babícora composes 70 to 100 percent of the polychrome total. Its near relative, White-Paste Babícora, together with Villa Ahumada and Dublán Polychromes, make up the rest of the assemblage in these early levels. This is the Outer Core Zone, and we now must ask to what extent is such a pattern recognizable elsewhere in the Inner Core?

New data from the Inner Core provides an answer. Ceramics and radiocarbon dates from large Site 315 formed a good stratigraphic progression from quite recognizable Early Medio assemblages through their equally clear Late Medio successors. The Early/Late Medio distinction holds, but with some difference. At Site 315, Babícora, White-Paste Babícora, and Villa Ahumada Polychromes were present in Early Medio levels, as expected, but Villa Ahumada Polychrome was the most common. It is worth emphasizing that Babícora, White-Paste Babícora, and Villa Ahumada Polychromes are all Medio A ceramics, characterized by banded broad-lined designs. Ramos Polychrome, of Medio B, behaved as predicted on Inner Core Site 315. As at Outer Core Site 204, it is entirely absent in levels belonging to the early part of the Medio period, after which it rises rapidly in frequency to about 60 percent of the polychromes by the mid-to-late fourteenth century. This observation leads us to the next area of inquiry.

Medio Period Ceramics and Chronology

Preceding pages defined Early and Late Medio period ceramic assemblages, but there was the possibility of additional chronological refinement (figure 5.2). Significant fluctuation in Ramos Polychrome frequencies was apparent throughout the Late Medio test pit levels at Site 204, offering the possibility to subdivide that period. Accordingly, we proposed a Late Medio I interval in which Ramos Polychrome made up 18 to 39 percent of all polychromes in a context, while Late Medio II levels contained 40 to 84 percent Ramos Polychrome. We calculated a ratio of Babícora to Ramos in hope of establishing another criteria for division of the Late Medio, since both polychrome types were present in quantity in test pit levels. For the Late Medio I test pit levels, the ratio had a mean of 1.8, while it was 0.6 for the Late Medio II levels (Whalen and Minnis 2009:127–28). This reflects the rising popularity of Ramos Polychrome and the declining frequency of Babícora.

We then compared the proposed Late Medio I and II midden ceramic frequencies to those of Paquimé (Whalen and Minis 2009:128, table 4.4). These deposits included material from contexts assigned by Di Peso to all three of his phases. We concluded that the Paquimé deposits, as a group, looked most like our Late Medio II time interval, which we tentatively dated from the late 1200s or early 1300s onward. We saw the apogee of the center

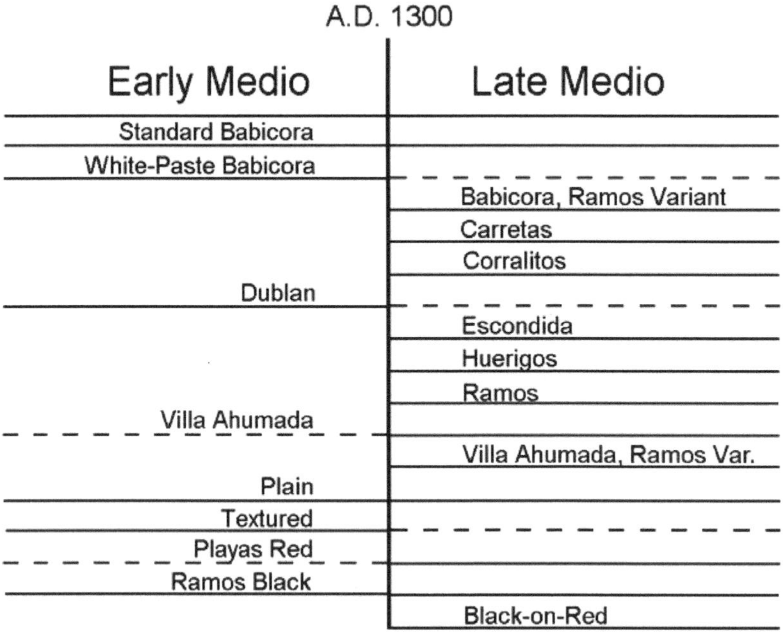

A.D. 1300

Early Medio	Late Medio
Standard Babicora	
White-Paste Babicora	
	Babicora, Ramos Variant
	Carretas
	Corralitos
Dublan	
	Escondida
	Huerigos
	Ramos
Villa Ahumada	
	Villa Ahumada, Ramos Var.
Plain	
Textured	
Playas Red	
Ramos Black	
	Black-on-Red

FIGURE 5.2 Early and Late Medio ceramic assemblages. The solid lines show strong presence of a type, while the dashed lines indicate reduced presence. (Reproduced from original figure: Whalen and Minnis 2009:149, fig. 4.9.)

in the 1300s, or about the Late Medio I/II juncture. Others similarly have concluded that most of Paquimé was a fourteenth-century phenomenon (e.g., Dean and Ravesloot 1993; Lekson 1984, 2000, 2008; Ravesloot et al. 1995; Schaafsma and Riley 1999). This is not to say that there were no deposits at Paquimé that fell into Early Medio or Late Medio I times. There may well have been, and we recognize that a large Late Medio II assemblage would mask all earlier components.

A more specific test of the proposed Late Medio I/II division was done at Site 204, using room fill, floor, and subfloor contexts for which radiocarbon date ranges were available. The following discussion is summarized from the original source (Whalen and Minnis 2009:129–34). A set of rooms from Area 1 in the center of the main room block mound (Whalen and Minnis 2009:15, fig. 1.5) had Early Medio (i.e., pre-1300) floor-contact date ranges. Lekson (2008:316, note 161) has requested clarification of the frequency of sherds of Gila Polychrome in the fill, floor, or subfloor levels of these purportedly Early Medio rooms. Gila Polychrome was imported from the southwestern United States, where it is well dated to AD 1300 and later. It would thus be a Late Medio II import in the Casas Grandes area, and there is a good deal of it at Paquimé. Reexamination of the ceramic data sheets for the Area A rooms, however, shows that no Gila Polychrome sherds came from any Area A context.

In agreement with the early floor-contact date ranges from the Area A rooms, deposits beneath these surfaces yielded ceramic assemblages that were readily classifiable as Early Medio. Room fill contained Late Medio assemblages in which the Ramos Polychrome frequency averaged 54 percent, a Late Medio II value. On the other hand, Babícora Polychrome frequencies were also high, averaging 39 percent of the polychrome assemblages, a value falling in between the proposed Early Medio and Late Medio I intervals. This discordance led us to envision Early Medio rooms filled with Late Medio trash. We could not confidently assign this trash to Late Medio I or II intervals, however.

A similar situation exists in the rooms of Area 4, Site 204. These Late Medio rooms on the east end of the main room block mound were less well built than those from other parts of the site. Walls were thinner and less regular, and wall footings were simply laid on the existing ground surface. Radiocarbon dates from three floor features were solidly Late Medio. There were no Medio subfloor features. In the room fill, we found a Late Medio II frequency of Ramos Polychrome (56%), several other polychrome types done in Design Style B that could occur in either the Late Medio I or II intervals, and a frequency of Babícora Polychrome (34%) that matched Early Medio and Late Medio I expectations. These results again cast doubt on the applicability of the proposed Late Medio I/II subdivision as a general regional pattern.

As the focus of this volume is on the large and small neighbors of Paquimé in the Inner Core Zone, we attempted to apply the proposed Early Medio/Late Medio and Late Medio I/II divisions to those ceramic collections. As noted earlier in this chapter, Inner Core Site 315 provides a large dated ceramic assemblage against which to test the ideas developed from the Site 204 midden seriation. The radiocarbon dates discussed in chapter 3 show that the occupation sequence of Site 315 extends from Viejo through the Early Medio and into Late Medio times. Of particular interest are Rooms 50 and 51 of Area B, an area lying on the southeast edge of the room block (refer to figure 3.1 of this volume). The Area B rooms were built in typical Medio period style. Walls were 30 to 40 cm thick; floors were hard, plastered surfaces containing lined hemispherical hearths; and other architectural elements included T-shaped doorways, wall niches, and adobe columns. Floor-feature and floor-contact dates from these rooms were, respectively, 640 + 30 and 595 + 50 years BP. The coeval test accepts the null hypothesis that both are dating the same event. Their average calendar date span is calibrated AD 1280–1410 (2σ), an interval falling into the Late Medio period.

Room 50 in Area B was built over a 30 cm thick layer of earlier trash fill, and several excavation units were extended through this trash layer. From the above-floor fill of Room 50 came nearly 4,000 analyzable sherds of many types. By analyzable, we mean pieces of at least 2 cm in minimum dimension. From the subfloor fill came a more limited assemblage of just over 1,100 sherds. Ceramics of the room fill levels were always dominated by Plain Brown and Textured types, making up 80 to 89 percent of each of the four levels' assemblage. Also present in some levels were Playas Red, Ramos Black, and Black-on-red, plus 281 Medio A and B Polychromes (table 5.3). All fill levels are combined, as there was no systematic fluctuation in types and frequencies among the four above-floor levels.

This Inner Core Zone assemblage certainly is Late Medio, which agrees with the radiocarbon date intervals just given. It does not, however, entirely match expectations from the Outer Core Zone Site 204 midden (Whalen and Minnis 2009:128, table 4.4). Ramos is a major polychrome type of the Medio B style, but it shares the top position with Villa

TABLE 5.3 Polychrome frequencies in intramural fill levels of Room 50, Site 315

Type	Count	%	Style
Ramos	107	38.1	B
Villa Ahumada	112	39.8	A and B
Babícora	37	13.2	A and B
White-Paste Babícora	13	4.6	A and B
Dublán	7	2.5	A and B
Babícora, Ramos style	2	0.6	B
Carretas	1	0.4	B
Corralitos	1	0.4	B
Escondida	1	0.4	B
Total	281	100.0	B

Ahumada, a Medio A Polychrome found in both the Early and Late Medio. At Site 204, in contrast, Ramos and Babícora Polychromes occurred at highest frequency, closely followed by White-Paste Babícora. The latter two are painted in Medio A style, and, like the Medio A Babícora Polychrome of the 204 test pits, they are found in both Early and Late Medio test pit levels. Ramos, of Medio B style, is always one of the most abundant polychromes in Late Medio times, but exactly which Medio A Polychrome is also in high frequency seems to be variable.

We also wish to know whether the new Inner Core Zone ceramics support the Late Medio I\II division that was postulated from the Outer Core Site 204 midden data. The frequency of Ramos Polychrome in the fill of Room 50 was 38.1 percent of the polychrome assemblage, falling about midway between the observed 29 percent Ramos of Late Medio I and the higher proportion of Ramos (61%) that characterized Late Medio II. The presence of the other polychromes shown in the preceding table is likewise ambiguous, as they occur in Late Medio I and II deposits at Site 204.

In the Site 315 assemblage from Room 50, Plain Brown and Textured dominate in every level. Also present were sherds of Playas Red, in both plain and textured varieties. It is interesting to note that Playas Red Textured types occur only in the above-floor levels. Below the floor, there is only plain, untextured Playas Red. Ramos Black makes up nearly 40 percent of the monochrome wares in the above-floor levels, declining steadily to about 9 percent by the floor level. Conversely, Corrugated Brown types steadily increase in frequency with increasing depth. In the surface level, corrugated sherds make up 26 percent of all Brown Textured types. By the floor level, this frequency increased to 39 percent, and it continued to increase to over 50 percent all through the subfloor levels. It has long been suggested that corrugated types became more common with movement further back in time. In contrast, Brown Scored and Incised types and their rubbed and patterned variants consistently make up 48 to 59 percent of Textured Brownwares, so that we see no correlation between Scored and Incised type frequencies and stratigraphic positions.

Sherds of imported ceramics were present in the above-floor levels, although there was no consistent pattern in their distribution. El Paso Polychrome, represented by 32 sherds, was the most common imported type. Almost all El Paso sherds were from vessel bodies. There was one rim sherd of the Late El Paso Polychrome variant, but we cannot be sure that all El Paso sherds came from late vessels. Also present were single sherds of Mimbres Classic Black-on- white, Chupadero Black-on-white, Gila Polychrome, and St. Johns Polychrome, all of which are well-dated imports from the adjacent U.S. Southwest. The Mimbres Classic Black-on-white sherd is the only one that does not belong to the Late Medio, but also present in these deposits are a few sherds of Viejo period Red-on-brown, which would be contemporary with the Mimbres fragment. We note that some of the Room 50 upper level deposits were mixed and churned from the extensive looting that took place all over the site.

Three subfloor levels in Room 50 and an adjacent area immediately to the south (i.e., toward the edge of the room block mound) produced a total of 1,103 sherds, and these were accompanied by a radiocarbon date of 760 ± 55 years BP. This corresponds to the interval of calibrated AD 1160–1300 (2σ), which falls almost entirely into the Early Medio period. As noted earlier, the subfloor ceramic collection came from a 30 cm thick layer of trash fill that formed the substrate on which the rooms were built. The subfloor ceramic collection was notably different from those of above-floor levels. Most sherds continued to be Brown Plain and Textured utilitarian types; corrugated sherds rose in frequency, while Ramos Black sherds declined to traces (i.e., to single sherds) in all subfloor levels. Playas Red Textured sherd types were entirely absent in these levels, which contained only the simple untextured type of that utilitarian ceramic.

The greatest difference between the above-floor levels and their subfloor predecessors, however, was in the polychrome assemblage. Broad-lined Medio A sherds composed nearly all of this group, including Babícora, Villa Ahumada, and White-Paste Babícora Polychromes. These Inner Core Zone data fit the Early Medio ceramic assemblage, as defined from midden test pits at Outer Core Site 204. The only exceptions in the Site 315 deposits were the presence of one sherd of Ramos Polychrome and three El Paso Polychrome body sherds, all in the uppermost subfloor level. We are inclined to attribute these to "leak-down" from the above-floor deposits, where 107 Ramos and 32 El Paso sherds were found. Subsequent subfloor levels contained no sherds of Ramos or El Paso Polychromes.

The above-floor deposits in Room 50 and vicinity, Site 315, are surely Late Medio, both by their date ranges and by their ceramic assemblage. In contrast, the subfloor fill deposits have an Early Medio date range, and they contain nearly all Medio A polychromes. Dublán Polychrome is the only one of this group to be unrepresented in the Room 50 sample, although it occurs in similar contexts elsewhere on the site. Untextured Playas Red, traces of Ramos Black, and increasing numbers of Brown Corrugated sherds make up the subfloor assemblage. This closely resembles the Early Medio assemblage that was defined from the Site 204 midden test pits.

Comparable deposits underlie other parts of Site 315. Subfloor excavations in Area D, on the northern edge of the room block mound, produced similar collections of Brown utility wares, untextured Playas Red, and a small number of the broad-lined polychromes of the Medio A style. To this Early Medio assemblage, in Late Medio times, is added everything else that Di Peso and colleagues described at Paquimé. This now appears to hold true in both the inner and outer parts of the Core Zone. The other result of the present inquiry is less promising. New Inner Core data support the Outer Core suspicion that the earlier proposed Late Medio I\II distinction may not be feasible. Relative frequencies of Ramos Polychrome might provide a measure of where an assemblage falls in the Late Medio, although this is so powerfully affected by assemblage size as to be of limited utility.

The Post-Paquimé Ceramic Assemblage

The last issue to be considered here is the ceramic signature of the end of the Late Medio period. As mentioned earlier in this volume, Ramos Polychrome and its Medio B variants appear to have carried a set of symbols relevant to a supernatural system that likely underlay Paquimé. Several sources (e.g., Whalen and Minnis 2009, 2012; Whalen and Pitezel 2015) assert that these images and the associated Medio B style of execution likely declined in relevance with the waning of Paquimé. In addition, Medio B vessels were distinguished by very fine painting, high polish, and high-temperature firing, all of which led Maria S. Sprehn (2003) to assert that many of them were produced by specialists. In a word, Medio B ceramics were high-cost wares with specific symbolic associations. They never constituted more than a small percentage of Medio period ceramics, so their removal due to high cost and decreasing relevance would leave intact the vast majority of the Medio ceramic assemblage, about 90 percent of which always consists of relatively inexpensive utilitarian wares that did not carry symbolism relevant to the supernatural system of Paquimé and thus need not be assumed to have fallen out of use with the decline of the center. The same point has been made from the perspective of southern Chihuahua (Kelley and Larkin 2017).

A post-Paquimé ceramic assemblage would also be undetectable in collections that included a Late Medio occupation component. Chapter 3 of this volume shows the presence of crude reconstruction of some rooms outside the Medio architectural tradition on all excavated small sites of the Inner Core Zone. A common pattern in the collapse of centralized, nucleated settlement systems is for the local population to disperse into small settlements. If this was so in the case of Paquimé, and if this dispersed population continued to use most of the Late Medio ceramic assemblage, then we would expect to see an archaeological record consisting of many small sites with Medio ceramics on their surfaces. This situation, together with the assumption that the entire Medio period ceramic assemblage was congruent with the existence of Paquimé, led to Di Peso's conclusion that the Casas Grandes region was empty after the collapse of the center. The scenario outlined in the preceding paragraph leads to a different conclusion. Moreover, we see no reason why what was surely one of the best and most productive areas in the entire region (Minnis and Whalen 2020) should have been left empty after the decline of Paquimé.

In conclusion, we make the following assertions. First, most of the Medio period ceramic assemblage existed before the rise of Paquimé in the late 1200s and early 1300s, or in Late Medio times. Second, in the Late Medio, a new and more complex set of elements and an associated painting style were added to the older Medio A painted ceramic assemblage. These new Medio B polychromes have been so extensively analyzed and discussed that they have come to represent Medio period ceramics. Yet, they make up no more than 10 percent of Late Medio assemblages. Most Medio period ceramic types appeared early in the period and continued in use for the next several centuries. Third, Medio B Polychromes, with their fine pastes and high standards of painting, were likely relatively expensive to produce. The waning of Paquimé and its associated belief system likely resulted in a decrease in production of these costly ceramics. Fourth, this situation likely had little effect on most of the Medio period ceramic assemblage. Assuming that people still needed utilitarian pottery vessels, what would be more logical than to continue to make them in their centuries-old traditions, most of which had nothing to do with Paquimé symbolism? Interestingly, there is some indication that manufacture of Medio-style Plain Brownwares and other aspects of life carried forward into early colonial times in the Casas Grandes River valley (Douglas and Brown 2023; Martínez Galicia 2016, 2024).

Analyzing Ceramic Vessels for Form and Function

Preceding pages considered the history and distribution of Medio period ceramics in the Core Zone of the Casas Grandes area. To be considered now are questions of the form and function of these vessels, which we approach through comparison and contrast of the large and small sites of the inner and outer parts of the Core. The Inner Core data are new in this volume, while those of the Outer Core were analyzed and discussed in a previous study (Whalen and Minnis 2009). Paquimé data are gleaned from the ceramics volume (Di Peso et al. 1974:5).

Ceramic vessel form and function analysis has been discussed at length (e.g., Hunt 2016; Rice 1987; Rye 1981; Sinopoli 1991; Skibo 1992). These and other studies identify three categories of relevant observations to be made on an archaeological assemblage. These are vessel form, vessel size, and use-wear. Each is categorized for the large and small sites of the Inner and Outer Core Zones. We expect to find indications of a wide range of domestic activities on large residential sites. Even so, there may be variability in their ceramic assemblages that can be related to organizational and integrative activities. These might include feasting, with its requisite large capacity for food preparation, serving, and storage, as well as special sorts of vessels that might have had ritual, ceremonial, or political significance. Some examples from Paquimé are effigy vessels, ceramic hand-drums, and imported vessels. In addition, we note in chapter 1 that we are concerned with estimating ranges of activities on the small residential sites that are the most numerous and least understood components of the Medio period settlement system. We turn now to Medio period vessel forms and their distributions across the Casas Grandes area.

Determination of Vessel Form from Sherds

Medio period ceramic assemblages everywhere in the region, including Paquimé, consisted almost entirely of globular or ellipsoidal vessels. We note that this is also the case in the Puebloan world of the adjacent U.S. Southwest. In fact, it has long been argued that the Medio period vessel shapes have much in common with the ceramics of the U.S. Southwest (e.g., Kidder 1916). This is not surprising from a utilitarian point of view, as simple rounded shapes without sharp corners are the easiest to build, dry, and successfully fire. They also transmit heat more uniformly and are less susceptible to cracking at angular corners (Rye 1981).

Vessels with flat bottoms, angular shoulders, sharp corners, carinated bodies, or effigy shapes are not common in any Medio assemblage. The few known examples come mostly from Paquimé, and their variety is illustrated in that site report (Rinaldo 1974a:3, fig. 1-6). These elaborate vessel shapes likely represented specific functions apart from the ordinary domestic tasks performed in every household. They never were major components of the assemblage, even at Paquimé, and they were still less common in the Core Zone neighbors. For example, of nearly 83,000 sherds recovered at large Outer Core Zone Site 204, only a handful were identifiable as coming from anything other than simple globular vessels. The same is true at Site 315 of the Inner Core Zone, where nearly 50,000 sherds were examined. We now turn to the utilitarian vessels that dominate all assemblages.

In any discussion of ceramic vessel function, it is desirable to identify sherds as coming from jars or bowls because each has distinctive uses. Jars and bowls are usually distinguished by (1) rim sherds, (2) the compound curves forming jar shoulders, and (3) the coarse and unevenly finished state in which jar interiors are often left. Jar and bowl rims are distinguishable, even in small sherds, and their relative frequencies in large ceramic samples can give a reasonable approximation of the proportions of these two major vessel forms. More common in any assemblage are body sherds from the middle and lower parts of their parent vessels. These do not contain the compound curves of shoulders, so interior surface finish can often be used to classify these sherds as coming from jars or bowls. Compared to bowls, jars frequently have coarse interior finish, often retaining smoothing or wiping marks. Quality of jar interior finish can be variable between assemblages, however, so it must be evaluated before using it as a criterion for dividing bowl and jar body sherds.

In John B. Rinaldo's (1974a:85) general discussion of the Medio period ceramics of Paquimé, he observes that the interior surfaces of jars "were frequently polished on surfaces near the rims and less well smoothed below." He also notes that Plainware (i.e., Plain Brown) jars showed the assemblage's highest frequency of poorly smoothed interior surfaces, and he notes that this also characterizes jars of other Brown Textured types, "which were less well smoothed to poorly smoothed except near the rim" (1974a:85). This seems to provide a convenient basis for jar/bowl distinction in Medio assemblages, as Plain and Textured Brown types always make up the vast majority of assemblages. In subsequent descriptions of Brown, Red, Black-on-red, and Black types, however, only about half of jar body sherds had coarsely finished interiors (Rinaldo 1974a:108–71). This suggests that interior finish is not reliable as a vessel form indicator. Coarsely finished body sherds likely come from jars, but the remaining 50 percent would be ambiguous as to vessel form.

Nevertheless, of the 581,866 sherds of these types at Paquimé, 100 percent were classified as jar or bowl pieces, without an ambiguous category. These figures are based on type-by-type tabulations made by Rinaldo (1974a:108–71). As just noted, rims and shoulders usually make up only about 25 percent of an assemblage, and such is assumed to have been the case at Paquimé as well. In addition to sherds, there were some whole vessels from the site, so it might be assumed that as much as 40 percent of the assemblage was classified on grounds other than interior finish. This leaves nearly 400,000 body sherds unambiguously classed as either jars or bowls. We could find no discussion of the classification rationale, but interior finish quality seems to be the only way this distinction could have been made across all types: smooth interiors denote bowls, while less-smooth interiors were jars.

We found this method of vessel form classification to be unacceptably ambiguous for the great majority of body sherds in our samples. As table 5.1 shows, Plain and Textured Brownwares constituted an average of 85 percent of assemblages all over the Core Zone, whether from large sites or small ones. Bowls of these wares have no interior decoration or slip, so we could only say that finely finished interiors likely came from bowls, while those with coarse interior surfaces likely represent jars. We were left, however, with a large number of simple body sherds of intermediate finish. These could have come from jars or bowls, and they typically made up about 65 percent of each ceramic assemblage. A large percentage of every site's sherd assemblage thus was ambiguous as to vessel form. It seems unlikely, therefore, that 100 percent of the vast assemblage from Paquimé could reliably be classed as jar or bowl sherds.

Accordingly, the most useful approach to vessel form classification in the present study's Medio period ceramic assemblage relies on rim sherd frequencies. Analyzed for this study were 9,502 rim sherds of all types from large and small Core Zone sites. All were readily classifiable as representing jars (8,973 sherds) or bowls (529 sherds). To these data, we add counts of bowl and jar rim sherds from Paquimé. These were presented for each ceramic type in tables of rim shape, but they are scattered throughout some 200 pages of the Paquimé ceramic volume. These tabulations for more than 47,000 sherds in the ware groups discussed earlier are assembled and presented in table 5.4. Plain Brown, Textured Brown, and Red-slipped vessels are the utilitarian pillars of the Medio ceramic assemblage, and they therefore make up most of the studied sherds. Black, Black-on-red, and Polychrome vessels are always rare. The Polychrome ware group discussed in this chapter consists only of the most common types (Babícora, Ramos, and Villa Ahumada), as these are the only ones found in any quantity on the sites studied in this volume. Included in table 5.4 are all the data relevant to several subsequent discussions. Some of the variables (e.g., volume, sooting) have not yet been introduced, so this table is referred to throughout the ensuing pages.

Jars and bowls are present in all ware groups, although their frequencies vary by group. The utilitarian Plain Brown, Textured Brown, and Red-slipped wares had between six

CHAPTER 5

TABLE 5.4 Jar and bowl rim sherd characteristics in the Core Zone, by ware group

Ware group[a]	# Rims	Form	J/B	B/J	Min., V[b]	Max., V[b]	Sooted	% Sooted
Plain Brown	16,164	Jar	6.3/1	—	0.3	46.0	8,719	54.1
	2,575	Bowl	—	0.2/1	0.2	10.0	1,375	53.4
Textured Brown	4,568	Jar	10.6/1	—	0.9	79.0	1,941	42.4
	431	Bowl	—	.01/1	4.3	6.0	249	57.7
Red-slip	9,094	Jar	8.4/1	—	0.4	30.0	3,257	35.8
	1,078	Bowl	—	0.1/1	0.3	28.0	194	18.0
Black[c]	1,056	Jar	0.4/1	—	0.4	3.9	—	—
	2,558	Bowl	—	2.4/1	0.1	5.3	—	—
Black-on-red	605	Jar	2.6/1	—	5.4	25.0	85	14.0
	234	Bowl	—	0.4/1	0.5	3.8	42	17.9
BRV[d] Polychromes	7,217	Jar	3.8/1	—	0.5	38.0	1,540	21.3
	1,883	Bowl	—	0.3/1	0.4	2.0	370	19.6
Total	47,463							

[a] Paquimé data assembled from Di Peso et al. (1974:6:108–216).
[b] Minimum and maximum vessel volumes in liters.
[c] There were no data on Black rim sooting.
[d] Babícora, Ramos, and Villa Ahumada.

and ten jar rim sherds for each bowl rim sherd, while the less common (and probably less strictly utilitarian) Black, Black-on-red, and Polychrome wares had fewer than one to almost four jar rim sherds for each bowl rim fragment. The high ratio of jars to bowls among the utilitarian wares is likely due to the wide variety of cooking and storage uses to which they were put. We emphasize that these counts of jar and bowl rim sherds represent pieces of vessels. Jars, especially those used for cooking, are expected to enter the refuse stream more often than bowls (e.g., Blinman 1989:116), so their sherds should outnumber bowl sherds by more than the actual ratio of whole jars to whole bowls present on a site at any specific time. With this caveat in mind, however, relative frequencies of jar and bowl sherds are still a useful measure of different sorts of activities in archaeological contexts (e.g., Blinman 1989; Blitz 1993; Mills 1999; Potter and Ortman 2004; Wills and Crown 2004).

The preceding figures apply to Medio ceramics all over the Core Zone. Next to be examined were rim sherd–based jar and bowl frequencies of utilitarian Plain Brown, Textured Brown, and Red-slipped wares, by Core Zone location and site size categories. Note that 75 to 80 percent of these totals are rim sherds from Plain Brown jars and bowls. All these data are shown in table 5.5.

In a series of X^2 tests using the data of table 5.5, the large sites of the Inner Core (315 and 565) were found to have significantly higher than expected frequencies of jars and lower than expected frequencies of bowls, while the large site of the Outer Core (204) reversed this situation ($X^2 = 5.6$, df = 1, $p = .018$). Among the small sites, those of the Inner Core (290, 321, and 355) showed a strong pattern of significantly lower than expected frequencies of jars, combined with higher than expected frequencies of bowls, while the small sites of the

Medio Period Ceramics of the Core Zone   141

TABLE 5.5 Frequencies of utilitarian jar and bowl rims by site size class and Core Zone position

Site	Size	Core Zone location	Jar sherd count	Bowl sherd count	Jar/bowl sherd ratio
Paquimé	Large	Inner Core	29,826	4,084	7.3/1
315	Large	Inner Core	1,223	230	5.3/1
565	Large	Inner Core	437	69	6.3/1
290	Small	Inner Core	23	10	2.3/1
321	Small	Inner Core	17	7	2.7/1
355	Small	Inner Core	32	16	2.0/1
204	Large	Outer Core	1,652	343	4.8/1
231[a]	Small	Outer Core	333	59	5.6/1
242[a,b]	Small	Outer Core	636	40	15.9/1
317[a]	Small	Outer Core	821	132	6.2/1

[a]Data from Jones (2002:75).
[b]Site 242 is seen as a Paquimé control node.

Outer Core (231, 317, and 242) reversed these frequencies with more jars and fewer bowls ($X^2 = 34.9$, df = 1, $p < .0001$).

Especially notable is small Outer Core Zone Site 242, which seems to have served as a control node, organizing upland agricultural production for Paquimé. This small site had an enormous I-shaped ball court, at the head of which lay the only platform mound known outside Paquimé. Site 242 also had an extraordinary ratio of about 16 jar sherds for every bowl sherd. The original study (Jones 2002) plausibly associated this pattern with storage and preparation of large quantities of food for public feasting in association with the ball court ritual. A similar disparity in the other direction is shown by the small settlements of the Inner Core, which have little more than two jar sherds for every bowl sherd. We note that all three small Inner Core sites show a good deal of PCGAT construction, as discussed in chapter 4 of this volume. We take this to be a post-Medio occupation of these sites, which does not appear to conform to the Medio period pattern just described.

The ratios just presented are comparable to those discussed elsewhere for several Pueblo II and III sites in the northern Southwest (Potter and Ortman 2004:177, table 10.1). Examined in that study are frequencies of Grayware jars used primarily for cooking, versus decorated Red and White ware bowls used for serving. From these data, we calculated jar-to-bowl sherd ratios of 4.5/1 for Pueblo Alto and 4.0/1 for Sand Canyon Pueblo. These values are comparable to, albeit somewhat lower than, those just reported for most of the large and small sites of the Paquimé Core Zone, which ranged from 4.8/1 to 6.2/1.

Vessel Volume Calculated from Rim Diameters

Vessel volume estimation in fragmentary ceramic assemblages is an often-discussed problem for which there is no entirely satisfactory solution. Several approaches rely on rim diameter measurement. The simplest of these reasonably assumes that larger orifices correlate with larger container volumes, allowing a general comparison of assemblages based on rim sherd diameter frequencies. A more specific approach is volume calculation using a regression formula developed from whole vessels of the same type and form. There are several limitations to this strategy, however. First, the vessels of a type or ware must be uniform enough that a constant relationship exists between orifice diameter and body volume. Some assemblages meet this expectation, while others do not. An earlier study (Whalen and Minnis 2009:163, table 5.2) developed regression-based formulas for calculation of whole jars and bowls of different ceramic ware groups from their orifice diameters. The predictive accuracy of the formulas is measured by R^2 values, with 1.0 as perfect predictability and 0 as no predictability whatsoever. For example, the value of R^2 for Plain Brown jars was .89, while that of Textured Brown jars was .83. Values of R^2 for jars and bowls of other ware groups were similarly high.

Even though such formulas exist, we are limited by the paucity of rim sherds large enough to yield reliable orifice diameter measurements. We found that sherds with at least 6 cm of rim circumference are required for reliable diameter estimates using circle gauges. The effect of this situation is that the totals of measured rims used in the present study are much smaller than the grand totals of all rim sherds just given in table 5.5. Unfortunately, the large assemblages of jar and bowl rims from Paquimé cannot be used in this study, as no orifice diameter measurements are included in the published data. Our only volume data, then, come from the whole vessels reported in the Paquimé ceramic study (Di Peso et al. 1974:6).

Brownware jars of Plain and Textured types are by far the most numerous components of Medio ceramic assemblages on all sites in all zones. From the large sites all over the Core Zone came 667 Brownware rims of appropriate size, while small sites yielded 275 specimens, for a total of 942. The volumes of Brownware utilitarian jars were calculated using the regression-based formula just discussed, and figures 5.3a and b show their size distributions on large and small Core Zone sites. Median jar volume (the heavy line in each box) is about the same on large and small sites. Likewise, the midspread, or middle 50 percent of values, as represented by the shaded boxes, is about 4 to 16 liters for large and small sites. The lower quartile (shown by the lines extending down from each box) is also about the same at a minimum size of about 1 liter. These figures likely approximate the range of jar sizes used in everyday household activities. The upper quartile of volume figures is shown by the lines extending up from each box. Large and small sites have some larger Brownware jars.

The situation is different for bowls (figure 5.3b). Median bowl size for large Core Zone sites of all sizes is around 2 liters. This set of bowl sizes seems to represent the ordinary household assemblage. Beyond this, only large sites contained large bowls with volumes of 5 to 6 liters. Assuming the use of bowls as mixing and serving vessels, the logical conclusion is that large settlements prepared and served food for larger groups than did small ones.

There is one interesting difference in jar volumes among the small sites of the Inner Core Zone. Figure 5.4 shows the spreads of Brown jar volumes from all small sites of the Inner Core, among which Site 290 stands out as having the smallest jars. All three of these small

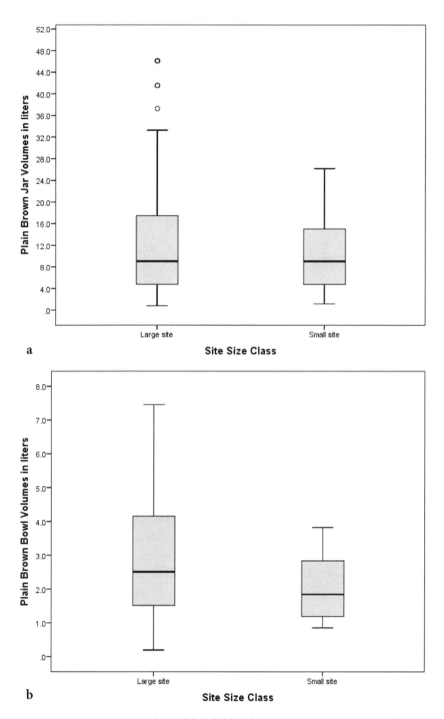

FIGURE 5.3 Brown jar (a) and bowl (b) volumes on Core Zone sites: All large Core Zone sites have a similar range of jar sizes. Three-quarters of the jars at large sites are less than 20 liters, which likely represents a common level of household usage. All large sites have jars as large as 60 liters, while the small sites of the Inner Core have about the same range. Plain Brown bowls are much larger on large Core sites than on small ones.

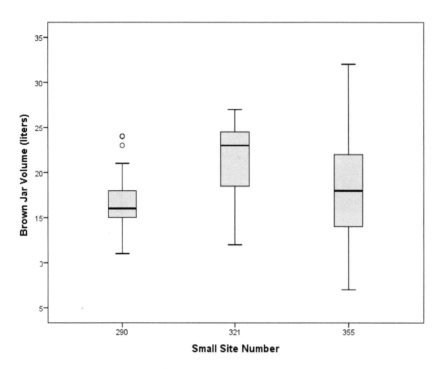

FIGURE 5.4 Brown jar volumes on small Inner Core sites. All show PCGAT construction. Site 355 has the widest range of volumes, but it also has the highest ratio of excavated CGAT to PCGAT deposits. Site 290 has the lowest ratio, as well as the smallest containers.

sites show evidence of PCGAT (Post–Casas Grandes Architectural Tradition) remodeling, but Site 290 is the most extreme example of this activity.

We do not have comparable data from the largest Inner Core settlement of all: Paquimé. There were over 16,000 Plain Brown jar rims in the studied sample (Rinaldo 1974a:111), but rim diameters were reported for no more than a few dozen whole vessels. Despite this paucity of data, the Plain Brown jars at Paquimé seem to show about the same range of sizes as those from neighboring large sites. Most Plain Brown jars were in the range of a few liters to nearly 50 L. Unlike the other Inner Core large sites, Paquimé had a few very large Plain Brown jars in the 50 to 70 L range. It thus appears that Paquimé shows the normal range of domestic jar sizes, plus some very large ones. From the published data, we unfortunately cannot say whether the proportion of large and very large jars at the center differed markedly from their frequencies at large neighboring sites of the Inner Core. There were more than 2,500 Plain Brown bowl rim sherds in the sample studied from Paquimé (Rinaldo 1974a:111), but only a few dozen rim sherd orifice diameters were reported. These data hint at a situation similar to that just described: many small bowls, plus some large ones in the 4 to 10 L range at Paquimé. The center thus seems to resemble its large Inner Core neighbors in Brownware bowl frequencies and size distributions.

Textured Brown jars were characterized by simple plastic decoration, including punched, scored, incised, and corrugated elements. It mostly occurs on necks and shoul-

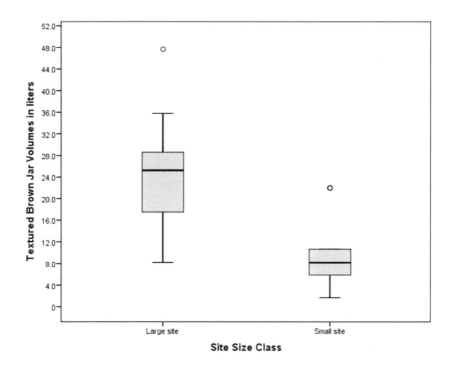

FIGURE 5.5 Textured jar volumes, by Inner Core site size class.

ders, but some vessels were corrugated over their entire surfaces. Undecorated body sherds of Textured types are identical to their Plain Brown counterparts. Textured sherds were rare in all the assemblages studied here, comprising about 9 percent of utilitarian jars on large and small sites all over the Core Zone. Distributions of Textured Brown jar volumes on large and small Inner Core sites are shown in figure 5.5. The pattern shown here is similar to that of Plain Brown jars in that the vessel size range is much greater on large sites. Moreover, the difference between Textured jar volumes on large and small sites is considerably more extreme than that of Plain Brown jars. This leads us to wonder whether Textured jars were more often used in commensal events than their Plain Brown counterparts. Textured bowl volumes could not be calculated in the original study (Whalen and Minnis 2009) as too few whole specimens were available for measurement and regression formula derivation. Unfortunately, therefore, we cannot compare Textured and Plain bowl sizes.

Red-slipped jars and bowls were found at large and small sites of the Inner Core Zone, although they made up only about 11 percent of these assemblages. The volume distributions of these jars by site size are shown in figure 5.6. As a group, they are smaller than the Plain and Textured jars that they accompany. Most Red-slipped jars were in the 10 to 25 L range. In a now-familiar pattern, median volumes and their midspreads are about the same on large and small settlements, although the largest vessels of 40 L and up occurred exclusively on large sites. Red-slipped bowls were rare, and they were present only on large sites, where their volumes ranged from about 2 L to a maximum volume approaching 20 L. Bowls with capacities of 20 L are very large ones, and their presence only at

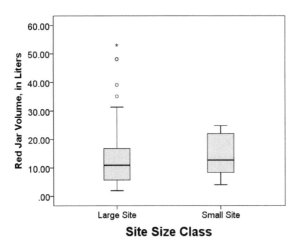

FIGURE 5.6 Red-slipped jar volumes, by Inner Core site size class. Large sites contained the widest range of volumes, plus all of the largest vessels.

large settlements follows the pattern of Plain Brown bowls. If the sample were sufficiently large, the same probably would be found true for Textured Brown bowls as well.

It is clear from the figures just presented that what we have termed utilitarian wares, that is, Plain Brown, Textured Brown, and Red-slipped wares, have similar distributions among the large and small sites of the Inner Core Zone. That is, the largest utilitarian jars and bowls are found only on large sites, while the assemblages of small settlements contain none of these very large containers. We presume that the small site utilitarian assemblages represent everyday domestic tasks, while the large sites show activity above the domestic level.

Polished black and polychrome vessels are described earlier in this chapter as nonutilitarian, with production costs considerably higher than those of Plain, Textured, and Red-slipped vessels. Both of these nonutilitarian wares are seen as associated with ritual practices in the Casas Grandes world (e.g., Rakita 2006; C. VanPool and VanPool 2007; Whalen and Minnis 2012). In the adjacent U.S. Southwest, it has been argued that elaborately painted vessels served symbolic roles in communal feasts among the Pueblo peoples (e.g., Mills 2004; Wills and Crown 2004). The Casas Grandes area counterparts of these southwestern painted vessels are polychrome bowls and jars. Succeeding discussion examines the sizes and distributions of these wares over the Core Zone.

All Black vessels recovered by the present study were jars containing from 2 to 15 L (figure 5.7). They were present but sparse on all large Inner and Outer Core sites, where there was a total of 48 rims of adequate size, but they were much rarer on all small sites. In the Outer Core, only 15 rims were found on sites 231, 317, and 242. In the Inner Core, Black sherds were entirely absent on small Sites 290 and 321, and they were represented only by one sherd at small Site 355. Again, we emphasize that these Inner Core small sites on which Black vessels were rare or absent all showed PCGAT modifications. Black vessel rims were present on small Sites 231 and 317 of the Outer Core Zone, both of which contained only CGAT construction. Previously, it was asserted that Black vessels were associated with ritual at Paquimé. If this is so, then we might conclude that little such activity took place at small Inner Core sites where there was evidence of the PCGAT modification.

Elaborately painted polychrome jars are present in small quantity on large and small Inner Core Zone sites, but like the polished black vessels just described, they do not follow the trend outlined for utilitarian vessels. Polychrome jar volumes for Inner Core sites, by size class, are shown in figure 5.8. There is clearly little difference. Most vessels on all sites

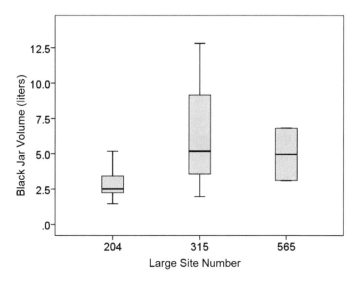

FIGURE 5.7 Black jar volumes on large Core Zone sites.

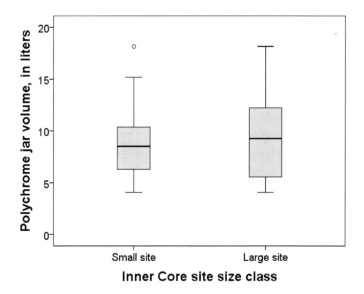

FIGURE 5.8 Polychrome jar volumes on Inner Core sites. The ranges of these volumes are similar for large and small sites. Most vessels were 7.5 L or less, but a few larger jars were found on sites of both size classes.

have volumes of 7.5 L or less, and a few larger jars are present on large and small settlements. We note that these so-called larger jars contained 10 to 12 L, so they are much smaller than the large jars of any utilitarian wares. Polychrome bowls are so rare in this sample that meaningful volume calculations cannot be made. Whatever their ritual associations may have been, the scarcity and small sizes of vessels with elaborately painted decorations do not appear to have played the public commensal roles that they did in the Southwest.

Vessel Diameters Estimated from Body Sherds

Another approach to vessel size estimation is based on body sherds, which are by far the most numerous in any assemblage. A common approach is to use trigonometric formulas to calculate the radius of a circle based on the height and chord of the arc formed by the curved body sherd. This radius can then be used to calculate the volume of the vessel using established formulas for the volumes of spherical, hemispherical, cylindrical, or ellipsoidal geometric solids (e.g., Rice 1987:221). A more rapid method is use of a set of templates of known diameters. These are fitted to the inner surface of the body sherd to estimate vessel diameter, and volume is calculated as just described. This method was introduced, tested, and applied in an earlier study (Whalen 1998), and the following summary is abstracted from that source.

Vessel diameter estimates from sherds would be quite accurate if the parent containers were perfect spheres or hemispheres. Unfortunately, hand-built globular or ellipsoidal vessels are rough spheres or ellipsoids, with flattened or bulging areas. Diameter estimates based on sherds from these irregular parts will naturally produce inaccurate results in both directions from the true value. Sherds from parts of vessels where shape changes—for example, shoulders of jars—will also yield inaccurate diameter estimates. While these irregularities or transitional areas are easy to see on whole vessels, they may be undetectable on sherds. There is no way to compensate for this limitation, especially when archaeological assemblages consist mostly of small sherds. To test the feasibility of translating dimensional estimates from pot sherds into individual vessel sizes, we used sherds from 15 jars with body diameters ranging from 13 to 43 cm. These were modern Mexican ceramics that were hand built to roughly spherical shapes. After true interior diameters were measured, each vessel was broken into large and small pieces, and a sample of sherds was randomly selected for diameter estimates. As accuracy of estimate diminishes with sherd size, it was necessary to set some lower limit on the pieces to be measured. By experimentation, 5 cm was selected as the minimum effective sherd size. An average of 23 sherds was measured for each vessel, for a total sample of 322.

These data are displayed in figure 5.9. Each figure represents the distribution of diameter estimates made on sherds from one vessel. The number within each box is the true interior diameter of each vessel. The heavy line inside each box is the median of the diameter estimates. The box itself encloses the midspread of the estimates. The lines extending from each box end mark the maximum dispersal of cases within one midspread's length of the upper and lower ends of the box. Extreme values are individually marked with dots.

The figure shows that measurements on sherds from the same vessels always yield a range of diameter estimates. The spread of these estimates also increases dramatically with vessel size, which is likely due to the difficulty of hand building large vessels to a high level of symmetry. In this test, the preceding figure shows that a sherd yielding an interior diameter estimate of 25 cm could have come from parent vessels of 18–26 cm in true interior diameter. Likewise, a sherd providing an interior diameter estimate of 35 cm could have come from any of the vessels with interior diameters between 30 and 43 cm.

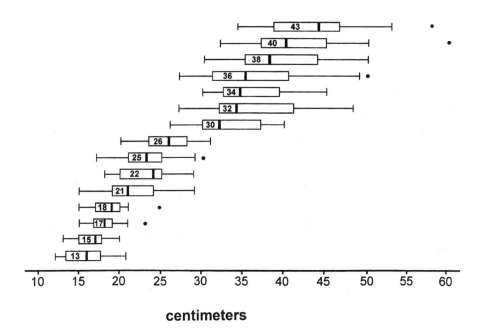

FIGURE 5.9 Diameter estimates from vessels of known sizes. Measurements on sherds from the same vessels always yield a range of diameter estimates. Each figure here represents the distribution of diameter estimates made on sherds from one vessel of known volume. The spread of these estimates also increases dramatically with vessel size. Originally published as figure 2, p. 222, in Michael E. Whalen, "Ceramic Vessel Size Estimation from Sherds: An Experiment and a Case Study," *Journal of Field Archaeology* 25:219–27. Reprinted by permission of Taylor and Francis Publishers.

It is clear that sherd-based diameter estimates cannot be used to recover the dimensions of individual parent vessels, unlike the rim sherd–based volume formulas introduced in preceding pages.

Despite this limitation, the preceding figure shows that diameter estimates permit comparative statements about ceramic assemblages. That is, although we cannot determine the volumes of individual containers, we should be able to reconstruct the composition of an assemblage in terms of broad vessel size categories. For example, we are unlikely to obtain diameter estimates of 40 cm from a set of vessels under 30 cm in true diameter. Likewise, we would expect to obtain some 50–60 cm diameter estimates from vessels of 36 cm and upward in true diameter. Compensating for this lack of precision is the ability to compare assemblages based on large numbers of body sherd measurements.

We now apply these concepts to Core Zone assemblages. Brownware and Red-slipped ware are considered to be utility vessels. They have to be combined for this measurement because it is not possible to say whether a brown body sherd came from a Plain vessel, or from the undecorated lower half of a Brown Textured or Red-slipped vessel. The paste is the same for all three, and all are counted as Plain Brown body sherds in the present analysis. The Outer Core data (Whalen and Minnis 2009) have been regrouped to conform to these categories.

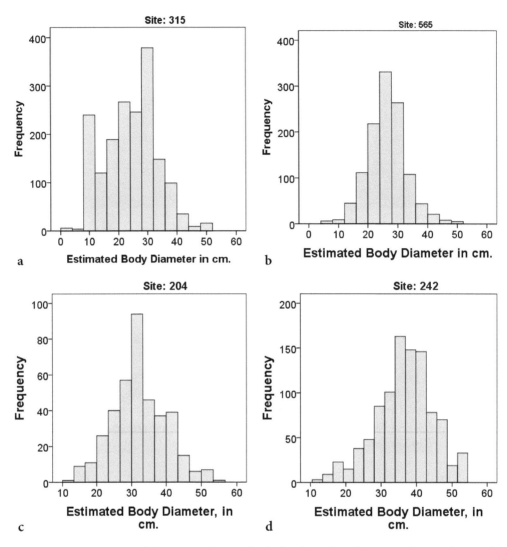

FIGURE 5.10 Estimated diameters of Brown body sherds on Core Zone sites, by size class. Both Inner and Outer Core distributions mostly contain vessels in the middle range of diameter groups, but Inner Core sites of all sizes gave diameter estimates that lean toward the smaller end of their range, while Outer Core distributions lean toward higher values.

Measurements of about 6,000 Brown body sherds have been grouped into five size classes, and frequencies are displayed for each class by position in the inner or outer parts of the Core Zone (figure 5.10). The Inner and Outer Core distributions are clearly not the same. Both contain mostly vessels in the middle range of diameter groups (i.e., 20 to 39 cm), but the centers of the two distributions are not congruent. Utilitarian body sherds from Inner Core sites of all sizes gave diameter estimates that lean toward the smaller end of their range. That is, they are skewed downward. The Outer Core large site's frequency distributions, in contrast, are skewed upward.

The significance of this imbalance was examined with a chi-squared test using the observed counts shown in table 5.6. For the table, $X^2 = 633.03$, df = 4, 2-tailed $p < .0001$.

TABLE 5.6 Frequencies of body sherd diameter groups on large sites, by Core Zone location

	Diameter group (cm)					
	10–19	20–29	30–39	40–49	50–60	Total
Inner Core observed count	499	1,971	1,305	157	18	3,950
Inner Core expected count	435	1,670	1,413	357	75	
Residual	5.4	16.2	–6.0	–18.5	–11.1	
Outer Core observed count	181	638	903	401	100	2,223
Outer Core expected count	245	939	795	201	43	
Residual	–5.4	–16.2	6.0	18.5	11.1	
Total	680	2,609	2,208	558	118	6,173

Residuals greater than 1.96 indicate that the difference in a cell is statistically significant. Here, all cells show significant differences between observed and expected counts. Positive residuals in a cell show that observed values were significantly greater than those expected under the null hypothesis of no significant difference. Negative residuals reflect observed values significantly smaller than those expected.

The large sites of the Inner Core Zone produced significantly more body sherd diameter estimates in the two smallest diameter categories, combined with fewer than expected counts in the three larger diameter categories. The large Outer Core site showed the opposite pattern: fewer of the smallest diameter categories and more of the largest ones. Vessels of all size classes are clearly present on all large sites, but the frequency difference is puzzling. Site 204 is a ball court community, but Inner Core sites 315 and 565 are not, relying instead on the courts of Paquimé for ceremonial functions. If data from Paquimé were included in the present analysis, the Inner Core sample frequency of larger diameter categories might be substantially increased, reversing the chi-squared test results. Unfortunately, none of the Paquimé sherds have been measured.

Vessel Function

After analyses of vessel forms and sizes, we now consider the uses to which they were put. Widely recognized indicators of use on ceramic vessels fall into two categories. The first is deposition of material on vessel surfaces. Extensive mineral layers might form on the interiors of water containers, for example. Certain types of cooking or heating activities could leave burned residues in portions of vessels' interior surfaces. Soot is deposited on the exterior surfaces of vessels heated over open fires. The second sort of use-wear is abrasion or erosion of vessel surfaces. This may be either mechanical or chemical. Abrasion is mechanical wear on parts of the interior surfaces of vessels. It may result from scraping or vigorous stirring of vessel contents. Chemical erosion, on the other hand, is deterioration of portions of vessels' interior surfaces. The softening of corn in alkaline water is one common source of interior surface erosion (M. Beck 2001; Di Peso et al. 1974:4). Another

152   CHAPTER 5

is fermentation, the acidic byproducts of which attack vessel walls (Arthur 2003). These use-wear traces are not visible all over the surfaces of ceramic vessels, and much depends on the particular characteristics of the local water supply, cooking activities, and storage practices. In the case of the Casas Grandes region's ceramics, we have found two indicators of vessel use to be widespread: soot on exterior surfaces and erosion of the interior surfaces. Each is considered below.

EXTERIOR SOOT

Carbonaceous deposits, or soot, on vessels' exterior surfaces shows that they were heated over wood fires, although it will not be deposited equally over vessel surfaces. David Hally (1983) defined the position over the fire of a ceramic cooking pot as the major determinant of the type and amount of soot accumulation on the exterior surface. James B. Skibo (1992:153–54) also considers different soot accumulation processes. These discussions refer to soot that is attached to vessel surfaces firmly enough that it cannot be rubbed off easily. Both authors agree that a dull black soot layer forms from the vessel's base upward on the lower exterior surface. The base of the vessel may show little or no soot if the deposited carbonaceous material is burned out in the high temperature to which the base is exposed. Base surfaces thus may be gray or only faintly black. Much depends on the distance of the vessel above the fire, on the intensity of heat, and on whether heat is produced by burning sticks or coals. Soot accumulates at its thickest on the midexterior surface of the vessel, where it is not burned away by close contact with the fire. It may have a thick, glossy appearance. Soot is more thinly deposited on upper exterior and shoulder surfaces. Long use produces thicker and more extensive soot deposits in the pattern just described.

The preceding discussion refers to whole vessels observed in ethnographic contexts. Archaeological sherd assemblages, however, are a more complicated problem. The uneven distribution of carbonaceous residue over cooking vessel surfaces means that body sherds of the same vessel will show different degrees of soot deposition. In assemblages characterized by globular or ellipsoidal vessel forms, it is often impossible to tell whether a sherd represents the lower, middle, or upper exterior surface of its parent vessel. The different soot zones just discussed thus cannot be identified with acceptable precision in sherd assemblages. Accordingly, this analysis coded sooting simply as present or absent.

A total of 14,695 body sherds were examined from Core Zone sites of all sizes. Of these, 9,850 body sherds had no observable soot on their exterior surfaces. A total of 4,845 body sherds showed some degree of soot accumulation. The great majority of these were Brownware fragments. Recall that these could have come from the lower portions of Plain Brown, Textured Brown, or Red-slipped vessels. A much smaller number of Black and polychrome jar sherds contributed to the examined total, a few of which were sooted. An earlier study (Whalen and Minnis 2009) analyzed frequencies of sooted body sherds on Outer Core Zone sites. The jar/bowl distinction used in that study is not continued here, as the great majority of body sherds either came from jars or were indeterminate, as discussed earlier in this chapter. The sooted sherd data presentation begun in the Outer Core Zone (Whalen and Minnis 2009:178–79, table 5.9) continues in table 5.7. Sooted body sherd frequencies

Medio Period Ceramics of the Core Zone

TABLE 5.7 Frequencies of exterior soot on Core Zone body sherds

Site	Core part	Size	Body sherds	Sooted sherds	Percentage sooted
Paquimé[a]	Inner Core	V. large	712,807	351,414	49.3
315	Inner Core	Large	5,095	2,018	39.6
565	Inner Core	Large	2,162	923	42.7
355	Inner Core	Small	1,108	345	31.2
321	Inner Core	Small	595	161	27.2
290	Inner Core	Small	281	41	14.7
204	Outer Core	Large	2,377	601	25.3
242[b]	Outer Core	Small	1,108	480	43.3
231	Outer Core	Small	736	111	15.1
317	Outer Core	Small	1,235	165	13.4

[a] Data from Di Peso et al. 1974:6:92–319.
[b] Site 242 is a ball court community and presumed Paquimé control node.

are tabulated for all Core Zone sites by size category and Core Zone location. Data from Paquimé are included.

The counts of sooted versus unsooted sherds from table 5.7 were used in a series of X^2 tests. Paquimé was found to have significantly more sooted sherds and fewer unsooted ones than its Inner Core large neighbors ($X^2 = 220.9$, df = 1, $p < .0001$). Large sites 315 and 565 of the Inner Core, in turn, had significantly more sooted sherds and fewer unsooted ones than did large Site 204 of the Outer Core ($X^2 = 178.28$, df = 1, $p < .0001$). Finally, the small sites of the Inner Core (290, 321, and 355) and Outer Core (231, 242, and 317) did not differ significantly in frequencies of sooted and unsooted sherds ($X^2 = 3.26$, df = 1, $p = 0.71$). It is not surprising that Paquimé had the highest frequency of sooted sherds, as that settlement also contained the area's largest complex of ritual architecture, as well as vast ovens for large-scale food preparation. All of this indicates an unmatched level of ritual and commensal activity. The relatively high levels of sooted sherds found at neighboring large Sites 315 and 565 might reflect their participation in food preparation for consumption during rituals at Paquimé. Neighboring Outer Core large Site 204 has a large I-shaped ball court, as does small Outer Core Site 242. A final X^2 test using the counts of table 5.7 shows that small Site 242 has significantly more sooted sherds and fewer without soot than does the much larger Site 204 ($X^2 = 114.7$, df = 1, $p < .0001$). In short, among the I-shaped Core Zone ball court sites considered here, Paquimé has the highest frequency of sooted sherds, followed by small Outer Core Site 242. Last in sooted sherd frequency is large Outer Core Site 204. All of these differences were shown to be statistically significant. Even though Site 204 is a sizable settlement with large ovens and an I-shaped ball court, it does not differ at a statistically significant level in frequency of sooted sherds from small Sites 231 and 317.

Earlier in this chapter, we suggest that these two small sites exemplify domestic activity at the household level, and it is surprising that large Site 204 is not much different from them in sooted vessel frequency. It is noteworthy, however, that Site 204 has a substantial

Early Medio occupation component, which we were not able to separate out for the previous analysis of sooted sherd frequency. Early Medio occupation is not in evidence at Paquimé, and it definitely does not exist at Site 242. If the ball game played in I-shaped courts was a phenomenon of the Late Medio period, then traces of the accompanying commensal activity should be much in evidence at Paquimé and at Site 242. Much of the occupation of Site 204, on the other hand, would have taken place before the popularity of the ball game and associated activities.

After consideration of frequencies of soot on sherds, we turn to the sizes of these sooted vessels. As only body sherds were used in this analysis, rim sherd–based regression formulas are not applicable. Instead, parent vessel diameters were estimated by fitting templates to body sherd interior surfaces. Unfortunately, Paquimé cannot be included in this part of the inquiry, as there are no diameter measurements on its sooted body sherds. The diameter estimates for body sherds with and without soot are shown in table 5.8. It is apparent from the table that sites all over the Core Zone have comparable ranges of sooted body sherd diameters only in the smallest vessels. These are 10–29 cm in estimated diameter. Reference to figure 5.9 shows that these are small to medium containers, and they probably represent household-level domestic use. It is in the larger vessel diameters that a difference is visible. The sites of the Inner Core have noticeably higher percentages of sooted vessels in the 30–60 cm ranges. These vessels are considerably larger than those with 10 to 29 cm diameters. Many households might have had a few pots of these sizes, but their disproportionate representation in the Inner Zone can be taken to reflect cooking activities at suprahousehold levels. The preceding discussion considered settlements of all sizes, and there remains the question of how sooted sherd diameter frequencies vary between large and small ones.

Figure 5.11 shows histograms of estimated body diameters for sooted sherds on each of the large sites of the Inner and Outer Core (315, 565, and 204), plus Outer Core small Site 242. Although it is not large, Site 242 has been interpreted as an Outer Core administrative node of Paquimé, where commensal activities likely took place. An analysis of variance compared the sooted sherd mean estimated diameters of these three large sites, showing that there is at least one significant difference ($F = 164.88$, $df = 2$, $p < .0001$). Tukey's post hoc test showed that each of the three sites differs significantly from the

TABLE 5.8 Distributions of diameter estimates for body sherds with and without soot

	Exterior soot?	10–19 cm (%)	20–29 cm (%)	30–39 cm (%)	40–49 cm (%)	50–60 cm (%)	Total
Inner Core	Soot	248 (49.9)	1,029 (49.8)	657 (64.9)	73 (48.7)	6 (46.2)	2,013
	No soot	249 (50.1)	1,037 (50.2)	355 (35.1)	77 (51.3)	7 (53.8)	1,725
	Total	497 (100)	2,066 (100)	1,012 (100)	150 (100)	13 (100)	3,738
Outer Core	Soot	207 (43.6)	926 (51.2)	903 (38.3)	257 (26.9)	44 (30.1)	2,337
	No soot	268 (56.4)	881 (48.8)	1,454 (61.7)	697 (73.1)	102 (69.9)	3,402
	Total	475 (100)	1,807 (100)	2,357 (100)	954 (100)	146 (100)	5,739

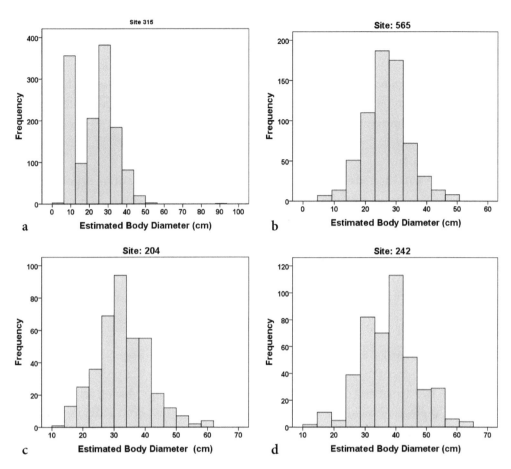

FIGURE 5.11 Estimated diameters of sooted vessels on Core Zone sites

other two ($p < .0001$ in every case), although all are arrayed around estimated diameters of about 30 cm.

An interesting pattern emerges with Site 315, as its estimated diameter histogram is multimodal (figure 5.11a). In addition to the peak around 30 cm, there is another one around 10 cm. In other words, hundreds of sherds from of small sooted jars at Site 315 stand out more distinctly than at either of the other large Core Zone sites. Reference to figure 5.10 shows that diameter estimates of about 10 cm likely come from the small hand-sized jars, which we estimate at up to 0.5 liters in volume. They are not large enough to store or prepare any appreciable quantity of food or drink, even at the household level, yet their sooted surfaces show that something was heated in them. Later in this chapter, we suggest a special use for these small sooted vessels. The situation at Paquimé is unknown, as this sort of analysis has never been done there.

In the Outer Core, 389 body sherds from large Site 204 (figure 5.11c) gave a sooted mean diameter estimate of 32.0 cm ($\sigma = 7.8$). Among the small Outer Core sites, 98 sherds from Site 231 give a mean diameter estimate of 29.8 ($\sigma = 8.8$). For Outer Core small Site 242, the corresponding figures are 419 sherds, and the mean diameter estimate is 38.0 cm ($\sigma = 8.7$);

and for Outer Core small Site 317, there are 138 sherds with a mean diameter estimate of 31.2 cm (σ = 8.0). The means just given were compared using analyses of variance, and a significant difference was detected (F = 4.597, p < .0001). Tukey's post hoc test shows that Site 242 differs significantly from the other three (p < .001 in every case). It had larger sooted vessels than the other three sites, which accords well with the postulated role of Site 242 as a Paquimé outpost in the Outer Core.

INTERIOR RESIDUES

Theobromine was detected in the interior walls of six out of ten sherds of small polychrome vessels from Site 315 (Crown and Hurst 2009; Crown et al. 2015). This residue could have come from several caffeine-containing plants that were used as ritual drinks by Indigenous people all over the Americas. Whatever the identity of the source plant (see chapter 8 of this volume for more discussion), consumption of an exotic drink may have been fairly common in at least one large community (Site 315) that was proximate to Paquimé. We do not have data on ritual drinks at any other Chihuahuan site, as only vessels from Site 315 have been tested.

INTERIOR SURFACE EROSION

Erosion of portions of the interior surfaces of Core Zone vessels was previously noted to result from two activities: (1) fermentation of cereals like corn, producing acidic byproducts; and (2) pregrind soaking of corn kernels in alkaline water. Both activities certainly could have taken place in the same communities. Corn was a major food source in NW/SW, so it would have been processed to a large extent. Fermented drinks like corn beer, however, were more common in public and ceremonial activities in northwestern Mexico than in the Southwest (e.g., Bruman 2000).

Ethnographic studies from South America (Parker and McCool 2015) to Africa (Arthur 2003) describe production of fermented drink in ceramic containers. All of these studies note that specialized vessels are used for fermentation. This is because the porous walls of the containers capture and hold yeasts that enhance fermentation of subsequent batches of beer (Parker and McCool 2015:375). With repeated use, the interior surfaces of these containers develop the erosion that Arthur (2003:524) characterizes as "a visible signature" of beer production. A similar observation was made using data from late prehistoric China (McGovern et al. 2005:256). Nevertheless, Parker and McCool (2015) show that interior surface attrition, while characteristic of fermentation, is not equally intense over the entire interior surface of the vessel. Photographs of African fermenting jars show the same situation: interior erosion affects discrete, dispersed areas of the vessels' interiors. Both studies raise an important point, however: some sherds from the same fermenting vessel might show significant surface erosion, while others would have none. It may be presumed that more intensive use of fermenting containers results in increasingly severe and widespread interior surface erosion. This, in turn, would increase the frequency of ceramic sherds showing substantial interior surface erosion.

Interior surface attrition of ceramic containers is found in the Casas Grandes area. The 2009 Outer Core study examined 2,652 body sherds from Late Medio levels of the midden test pits. This discussion is confined to the Late Medio, as that is the period of most of the Outer Core sample and all of that from the Inner Core. Most meaningful here is frequency of heavy interior pitting, as we have found this to be the most replicable observation and the most accurate reflection of vessel use. The 2009 Outer Core data is combined with new Inner Core counts of sherds with interior surface pitting in table 5.9. It is not surprising that Plain Brown, Textured Brown, and Red-slipped utilitarian vessels were heavily pitted at the highest frequencies. Much less common was heavy interior pitting on sherds from nonutilitarian Black (a little less than 1%) and polychrome vessels (a little more than 1%). The frequencies of vessels with heavy interior pitting are higher on average for almost all wares on Inner Core sites than on those of the Outer Core.

The preceding table does not consider differences in interior pitting among sites of different sizes and Core Zone locations. To obtain these data, we analyzed body sherds from all Inner and Outer Core sites studied in this volume, or 13,263 pieces. To this total were added 1,884 Plain, Textured, and Red-slipped body sherds from Paquimé. Jars and bowls are combined for this analysis (table 5.10).

These data lead to several observations about the activities that produced heavy interior surface pitting. If it were the product of everyday domestic activities, like the alkaline-water processing of corn, then we would expect to see heavily pitted sherds everywhere and in comparable frequencies. In fact, a different pattern is so clearly evident that it does not require statistical testing. First, large sites all over the Core Zone show considerably higher frequencies of heavily pitted body sherds than do their smaller neighbors. For large sites, this frequency is in the 6 to 8 percent range. For small sites, it is about 1 to 4.5 percent. The exception to this observation is Outer Core Site 242, a Paquimé control node, that has a heavily pitted body sherd frequency of 6.4 percent, matching those of large sites. It is interesting to note that the frequency of pitted sherds at Paquimé does not differ significantly from pitted sherd totals from near neighbors 315 and 565 . Finally, the small sites of the Inner Core have much higher frequencies of heavily pitted sherds, averaging 4.6 percent, while those of the Outer Core are almost absent at just over 1 percent. All of these are

TABLE 5.9 Interior surface pitting frequency in Medio ware groups

	Pitting	Plain (%)	Textured (%)	Red (%)	Black (%)	Poly (%)	Total
Inner	Little/none	2,625 (93.5)	873 (95.3)	186 (95.9)	93 (100.0)	600 (98.5)	4,047
Core	Heavy	183 (6.5)	43 (4.7)	8 (4.1)	—	9 (1.5)	243
Total		2,808	916	194	93	609	4,290
Outer	Little/none	1,796 (97.4)	274 (98.6)	100 (98.0)	337 (99.1)	86 (98.9)	2,593
Core[a]	Heavy	49 (2.7)	4 (1.4)	2 (2.0)	3 (0.9)	1 (1.1)	59
Total		1,845	278 (100.0)	102	340	87	2,652

[a] Outer Core data revised from Whalen and Minnis (2009:172, table 5.6.)

TABLE 5.10 Interior surface erosion by site size and location

Site	Core location	Site size	Sherds analyzed	Heavy pitting	Frequency (%)
Paquimé	Inner Core	Large	1,884	126	6.7
315	Inner Core	Large	3,737	243	6.5
565	Inner Core	Large	1,727	140	8.1
290	Inner Core	Small	642	24	3.7
321	Inner Core	Small	593	27	4.5
355	Inner Core	Small	1,108	52	4.7
204	Outer Core	Large	2,401	193	8.0
231	Outer Core	Small	733	8	1.1
242	Outer Core	Small	1,093	70	6.4
317	Outer Core	Small	1,229	16	1.3

relatively low percentages, but it has been observed that sherds with observable interior surface erosion are usually relatively rare, even where extensive production of fermented drink is known to take place (Parker and McCool 2015:376).

Data were cited earlier suggesting that more intensive use of fermenting containers produces increasingly severe and widespread interior surface attrition. This, in turn, would increase the frequency of ceramic sherds showing substantial interior surface erosion. The relatively high frequencies of body sherds with heavily eroded interior surfaces on all large sites of the Core Zone may thus be taken as frequent production of fermented drink. The same is true of small Outer Core Site 242, which has been characterized as a control node of Paquimé, using ritual and commensal activity to manage agricultural production in its portion of the uplands.

There are many studies of the uses of fermented drinks all over the world. Beer production and consumption is commonly important in the establishment and maintenance of social, economic, and political relations, especially in decentralized societies. Using data from Ethiopia, John W. Arthur (2003:519–21) shows that some beer consumption takes place in public festivities or ceremonies. He stresses, however, that beer production takes place at the household level, with wealthier and higher-status families doing most of the production and sponsoring most of the consumption. This is a logical observation, as staples like corn that are used for beer production must be obtained over and above ordinary domestic food requirements. The same is true of the facilities and labor needed to carry out frequent fermentation. Wealthier households are naturally best able to do this. It is the larger and more elaborate Late Medio period communities of the Core Zone that appear to excel in this activity.

Recently available is the first direct evidence of consumption of fermented drink at Paquimé. This is a study of microfossils recovered from the dental calculus of 110 human burials from Paquimé and other parts of the Casas Grandes area from Viejo through Late Medio times. Starch granules recovered from the dental calculus of several individuals showed damage from fermentation (King et al. 2017:368). The authors go on to argue that production and consumption of corn beer becomes visible in the archaeological record during the Late Medio period at Paquimé. This coincides with the rise of the center as a regional power, with all the social, economic, and political networking that building and maintaining such a position would entail. Our Core Zone ceramic data argue that large communities and control nodes were heavily involved in this process, while their small neighbors were less so.

Concluding Thoughts

We conclude this discussion with several observations. First, all 30 types comprising the Medio period ceramic assemblage occur at all investigated large sites, regardless of which part of the Core Zone they occupy. Second, the architecture-based division of small sites into CGAT and PCGAT categories in chapter 3 finds support in the ceramic distributions. Settlements dominated by CGAT architecture have higher ceramic type diversity all over the Core Zone. In contrast, all three small sites with a good deal of later, cruder PCGAT construction show substantially lower type diversity across all ware groups. Third, this diversity reduction does not equally affect all ware groups and types. PCGAT sites show their highest diversity of types in the utilitarian Brownware category. We note that these are the simplest of the Medio period ceramics in terms of the relatively small number of steps involved in their production. If any part of the Medio period ceramic assemblage survived the dissolution of Paquimé, these Brown types are the most likely candidates. Not only were they relatively easy to make, but their plastic decoration, when present, is simple, geometric, and nonrepresentational. They carry no images or symbols specific to Paquimé. They are what would remain, we argue, if the more complex element of Medio ceramics were reduced.

Next to be considered were questions of ceramics and chronology in the Core. Earlier work at Site 204 defined Early and Late Medio period ceramic assemblages and proposed that polychrome frequencies could divide the Late Medio period into subperiods, referred to as LM I and LM II. This scheme was applied to Outer Core Site 204, and Inner Core Site 315 provided an opportunity to test it at another large site. The floor and upper levels of Room 50 at Site 315 are Late Medio by their date ranges and by their Medio B ceramic assemblage. The subfloor fill deposits have an Early Medio date range, and they contain exclusively Medio A Polychromes. The rest of the subfloor ceramics closely resemble the Early Medio assemblage that was defined at Site 204. Likewise, the 315 Late Medio assemblage is the same as that described at Site 204 and at Paquimé. The Early/Late Medio division thus holds true in both the inner and outer parts of the Core Zone, but the proposed Late Medio I\II distinction, based on relative frequencies of Ramos Polychrome, is imprecise.

Also considered was the question of the persistence of the Medio ceramic assemblage after the decline of Paquimé. This chapter asserts that most of the ceramic types found at Paquimé appeared in Early Medio times and continued in use for the next several centuries. The types that likely disappeared with the collapse of the center were Medio B

Polychromes, which were both expensive to produce and the principal carriers of the symbolism of the belief system promoted by Paquimé. Their relevance would have decreased with the decline of the center. This situation probably had little effect on the majority of the Medio period ceramic assemblage, which carried no Paquimé symbolism. Since people still needed utilitarian pottery vessels, we propose that they continued to make them in their centuries-old tradition. In fact, it appears that manufacture of Medio-style Plain Brown wares carried forward into early colonial times in the Casas Grandes River valley.

The analysis of form and function in Medio vessels of the large and small sites of the inner and outer parts of the Core occupies the last part of the chapter. As much Paquimé data as possible was included. Medio period ceramic assemblages everywhere in the region, including Paquimé, consisted mostly of globular or ellipsoidal vessels, nearly all of which were jars or hemispherical bowls. In Medio assemblages, utilitarian Plain Brown, Textured Brown, and Red-slipped wares had six to ten jar rim sherds for each bowl rim sherd, while the less common Black, Black-on-red, and Polychrome wares had between one and four jar rim sherds for each bowl rim fragment. The small PCGAT settlements of the Inner Core had little more than two jar sherds for every bowl sherd.

Regression-based formulas were used to calculate vessel volumes from orifice diameters. Very large utilitarian Plain Brown, Textured Brown, and Red-slipped jars were found only on large sites, while the small settlements had no containers of this size. The small site utilitarian assemblages seem to represent everyday domestic tasks, while the large sites show activity above the domestic level. Black jars of small to medium sizes were present on CGAT sites, but sites with PCGAT construction had few or none of them. Small to medium polychrome jars were present on all sites, but polychrome bowls are so rare in this sample that meaningful volume calculations cannot be made. The scarcity and small sizes of vessels with elaborate painted decorations indicate that they did not have important display roles in public commensal events, as they did in the U.S. Southwest.

Indicators of use on ceramic vessels fall into two categories. The first is deposition of material on vessel surfaces. The second sort of use-wear is mechanical or chemical abrasion or erosion of vessel surfaces. Both are seen in Medio ceramics. Paquimé was found to have significantly more sooted sherds and fewer unsooted ones than its Inner Core large neighbors. Large sites 315 and 565 of the Inner Core, in turn, had significantly more sooted sherds and fewer unsooted ones than did large Site 204 of the Outer Core. Finally, the small sites of the Inner Core (290, 321, and 355) and Outer Core (231, 242, and 317) did not differ significantly in frequencies of sooted and unsooted sherds, although those sooted body sherds present at Site 242 had larger estimated body diameters than any of the other Outer Core sites.

Theobromine residue on the interior surfaces of a sample of polychrome jars from Site 315 likely came from caffeine-containing plants that are known to have been used as ritual drinks by Indigenous people. This is a largely unexplored area of inquiry, but it may be that consumption of ritual drink was fairly common in at least one large community, Site 315, that was proximate to Paquimé. We do not yet have data on ritual drinks at any other Chihuahuan site.

There is soot residue on vessel exterior surfaces at all sites studied here. Sooted vessels are mostly in the 20 to 30 cm estimated diameter range, which are medium to large vessels. These, we suspect, represent ordinary domestic food preparation. In addition to these ordinary containers, large sites all over the Core were found to have vessels of even greater volume. There was also a good deal of soot on these as well. Food preparation above the domestic level is indicated at all large sites of the Core, as well as at small Site 242, a postulated administrative outpost of Paquimé.

Erosion of portions of the interior surfaces of Core Zone vessels was taken to result from two activities: (1) fermentation of cereals like corn, producing acidic byproducts; and (2) pregrind soaking of corn kernels in alkaline water. Corn was a major food source that must have been processed on all large and small residential sites, but fermented drinks like corn beer were more likely to be used in public and ceremonial activities, seen at large sites all over the Core. Heavy interior pitting was taken to reflect repeated use of vessels in fermentation, a byproduct of which is acid. In Medio assemblages, Plain Brown, Textured Brown, and Red-slipped utilitarian vessels were heavily pitted in the highest frequencies. Much less common was heavy interior pitting on sherds from nonutilitarian black (a little less than 1%) and polychrome vessels (a little more than 1%). The frequencies of vessels with heavy interior pitting are higher on average for almost all wares on Inner Core sites than on those of the Outer Core.

The relatively high frequencies of body sherds with heavily eroded interior surfaces on all large sites of the Core Zone may thus be taken as evidence of frequent production of fermented drink. The same is true of small Outer Core Site 242, which has been characterized as a control node of Paquimé, using ritual and commensal activity to manage agricultural production in its portion of the uplands. We emphasize that all of these sites either had ball courts or were close to them. Commensal activity, including consumption of fermented drink, thus seems to have been associated with large communities and ball court ritual all over the Core Zone.

Small sites present a different picture. The architecture-based division of small sites into CGAT, TCGAT, and PCGAT categories is reflected in the ceramic type diversity data. Sites dominated by CGAT and TCGAT building everywhere have higher ceramic type diversity. In contrast, small Sites 290, 321, and 355 showed a good deal of the later, cruder construction that is termed PCGAT building. All three PCGAT sites are characterized by substantially lower type diversity scores. This diversity reduction, however, does not equally affect all ware groups and types. Sites of the PCGAT sort show their highest diversity of types in the utilitarian Brownware category, which are the simplest Medio period ceramics. Not only did they require relatively few production steps, but their plastic decoration, when present, is simple, geometric, and repetitive. They carry no images or symbols specific to Paquimé. If any part of the Medio period ceramic assemblage continued after the dissolution of Paquimé, we suggest these Brown types to be the most likely candidates.

 *Chapter 6*

Medio Period Lithics of the Core Zone

This chapter considers two broad categories of implements in the Core Zone, starting with the procurement of raw materials, production, and use of flaked stone implements, followed by examination of the same variables for their ground stone counterparts. Flaked stone assemblages were relatively simple, using minimally prepared cores for the expedient production of flakes. These flakes were extremely variable in size and shape, with little retouching, and few formal tools were seen. These characterizations also clearly apply to Paquimé as well as to the prehistoric Pueblo societies of the adjacent U.S. Southwest. Ground stone assemblages of the Core Zone are another matter. Some of these pieces are clearly utilitarian domestic implements (e.g., manos and metates), although they were produced in a range of levels of elaboration. Other pieces, like effigy stones and birdcage doors, apparently functioned in different spheres of life.

Raw Materials for Flaking and Grinding

The Sierra Madre Occidental is rich in volcanic rocks such as rhyolite, ignimbrite, andesite, and basalt. Siliceous sedimentary rocks form the subvolcanic structure over much of the region (Swanson et al. 2006:128). The Sierra Madre is estimated to consist of about 96 percent rhyolitic and andesitic volcanics, plus less than 0.2 percent sedimentary rocks (Hawley 1969:137, table 1). The mountain-to-basin transition zone, where Paquimé and its neighbors lie, is much like the mountain zone, with about 0.3 percent sedimentary rocks. The rocks of the basin zone include about 61 percent volcanics, 35 percent sedimentary stone, and about 3 percent basalt. Many deep drainages cut through the mountain zone's deposits, and these bring down a large variety of volcanic and siliceous stones. Basalt was a favored material for ground stone implements, and it has been characterized as one of the major suites of mid-Tertiary rocks in Northwest Mexico (Cameron et al. 1980:87). Other ground stone implements were made of locally available rhyolite, ignimbrite, andesite, felsite, and tuff. Populations of the Casas Grandes area clearly made use of a wide variety of lithic material that was available all over the eastern slope of the Sierra Madre, in its many deep-cut drainages, on its piedmont slope, and in the ranges of the basin zone. In fact, this pattern characterizes the entire region, extending at least from the southern Sierra Madre Occidental vicinity (MacWilliams 2001) to the Animas area in the north (Willhite 2016).

In addition to the materials just described, Medio populations made some flaked stone implements of obsidian, the sources of which are just beginning to be investigated. Rhyolite extrusions, when supercooled, produce volcanic glass. Millions of years of hydration of these glasses renders most of them unsuitable for flaking. Nevertheless, some usable obsidian survives as remnant nodules, seldom greater than 10 cm in diameter. Known as *marekanites*, or Apache Tears, these nodules erode out of mid- to late Tertiary rhyolite extrusions into Quaternary alluvium (Shackley 2005:14–15). Although never abundant, obsidian nodules are sufficiently widespread as to be described as "ubiquitous" in the northwestern Chihuahuan Basin and Range alluvia (Shackley 2005:81). Other sources of obsidian recently have been more intensively investigated. Source location, chemical characterization (Shackley 2005, 2021), and artifact analyses (Dolan et al. 2017) provide provenance information for the first time. Trace element characterization was determined by X-ray fluorescence on 116 obsidian artifacts from four Medio period sites of the Core Zone (Dolan et al. 2017), and these data were compared to known sources. The following discussion is abstracted from this source. Analyzed from Inner Core Zone large Site 315 were 65 pieces of obsidian. In the Outer Core Zone, 37 pieces came from large Site 204, 8 pieces from small Site 242, and 6 pieces from Site 317, another small occupation. Seven obsidian sources have been characterized in northeastern Sonora and northwestern Chihuahua, Mexico, while an eighth source is at Antelope Wells near the international border in southwestern New Mexico and extending into northwestern Chihuahua. The nearest six Chihuahuan sources lie 60–90 km from Paquimé. This places five of them in our Middle Zone. The sixth lies in the Sierra Madre, a little beyond the Middle Zone. The Antelope Wells source is about 130 km distant from Paquimé, in our Outer Zone. It is near the Joyce Well site, which lies on the northern edge of the Paquimé world (e.g., Skibo et al. 2002).

All six northwestern Mexican sources and the Antelope Wells source are represented in the analyzed sample of obsidian from Core Zone sites. Also present is obsidian from two unknown sources (Chihuahua A and B) and one from Sonora (Sonora A). The Chihuahuan A and B sources have elemental compositions similar to Antelope Wells, and they likely come from northwestern Chihuahua. Only one flake is assigned to the Sonora A source. It thus is clear that Core Zone Medio period obsidian has a wide range of elemental signatures that represent much of northwestern Chihuahua. This is a long-standing situation. Bradley Vierra (2020) sourced 80 obsidian artifacts from Cerro Juanaqueño, a Late Archaic hilltop site near Janos, in our Middle Zone. He found a similarly wide range of obsidian composition.

Also to be considered is how obsidian moved in northwestern Chihuahua. Researchers note several possibilities. One is direct procurement from the source; a second is collection of the obsidian nodules that weather out of the volcanic rock units all over the region. The third dispersal method is trade. Based on the small sizes of obsidian nodules all over the region, M. Steven Shackley (2005) asserts that the obsidian in artifacts of 5 cm or less cannot be assumed to have been procured directly from the primary source but are most likely to have been made on locally collected nodules. Local collection and direct procurement, however, are not mutually exclusive alternatives. In southcentral Chihuahua, on the southern edge of the Paquimé world, researchers estimate that 90 percent of their obsidian artifacts were collected as nodules within 1 km of where they were worked. They also note that a few pieces appear to have been brought into the area by trade (Fralick et al. 1998:1023). In the Core Zone sample, about one-quarter of the obsidian artifacts have the chemical signature of the Sierra Fresnal source, which lies about 60 km north of Paquimé and its neighbors. Sierra Fresnal obsidian nodules, however, are known to be distributed in alluvial and riverine gravels from the New Mexico border to Arroyo Seco, south of Paquimé (Dolan et al. 2017:560–61). The fact that all Core Zone obsidian artifacts are small argues strongly that obsidian was arriving there not in large pieces, but rather as small nodules. We note that all Core Zone large sites contained small whole nodules, partial nodules split by bipolar percussion, small debitage, and finished points. The same is true of Paquimé, where lists show the same array of nodules, cores, debris, and points. Clearly lacking in this discussion is trace element characterization of the obsidian from Paquimé. We predict that such work will show the same pattern as seen at nearby Site 315: pieces with a wide range of chemical signatures.

Previous Outer Core Chipped Stone Studies

An earlier volume (Whalen and Minnis 2009) examined nearly 27,000 pieces of chipped stone from Outer Core Zone Sites 204, 231, 242, and 317. Preliminary analyses were done on the entire dataset, which was sorted into flake, core, debris, and tool categories. Raw material was noted for each, as was whole or broken condition. The percentage of decortication served to sort flakes into primary (≥50% cortex), secondary (<50% cortex), and tertiary (no cortex visible) categories. Cores were defined as pieces bearing scars from removal of two or more flakes. Tools were pieces where use-wear or retouch was visible with little magnification. All other pieces were classed as debris. Detailed examinations were completed on about 38 percent of the total Outer Core Zone lithic dataset. Analyses began with notation of material type and measurement of flake, core, and tool dimensions. Other recorded flake characteristics are platform type, presence of platform lipping, dorsal surface flake scar direction(s), bulb prominence, and type of termination. Recorded for cores were direction(s) of flake removal, core shape, and evidence of utilization. Tools were classified into cutting, chopping, scraping, or perforating implements, projectile points, and preforms. Multifunction tools were recorded as such when recognized. All these data were used to monitor change in lithic assemblages from Early Medio to Late Medio, and to compare activities on large Outer Core Site 204 and its smaller neighbors 231, 242, and 317.

Early and Late Medio chipped stone data showed considerable similarity in technology, implement size, and raw materials throughout the period. Nearly 90 percent of all flakes were made from chert or fine-grained rhyolite, with much smaller percentages of basalt, chalcedony, and other materials. In Late Medio times, however, flakes were smaller, more of them were broken, and more striking platforms were shattered. More cores were broken, and more of them bore evidence of bipolar reduction. It was concluded that the Late Medio period at Site 204 showed more intensive reduction of lithic materials than was the case in the preceding Early Medio at that community.

A second level of analysis that is of more concern to the present study involved comparisons between Outer Core Zone large Site 204 and its small Outer Core neighbors 231, 242, and 317. All four sites showed many similarities in technique and raw material usage. Despite this homogeneity, however, significant differences were found between the chipped stone of Late Medio Site 242 and neighboring small Sites 231 and 317. Its size places Site 242 in the "small" category, but it was a ball court community and Paquimé administrative node. Found there was the smallest chipped stone assemblage of all the Outer Core sites. There were, however, higher frequencies of high-quality raw materials such as fine-grained chert and obsidian. Finally, Site 242 contained the Outer Core Zone's highest ratio of broken to whole flakes, plus fewer cores and less debris, than the other sites of its area. This suggests that at least some of the 242 lithics were made elsewhere and brought to the site. Outer Core sites 204, 231, and 317, in contrast, have the assemblages expected for on-site, expedient flake production. Similar conclusions have been reached in all extant studies of Medio period chipped stone assemblages (e.g., Gutzeit 2008; Mendez 2009; Peterson 2011; Rebnegger 2001; Rowles 2004; T. VanPool et al. 2000; Whalen and Minnis 2009; Willhite 2016).

New Inner Core Chipped Stone Studies

To these data and interpretations, we now add new lithic data from large and small Inner Core Zone sites. All of these occupations date to the Late Medio period. Paquimé is also a Late Medio site of the Inner Core, and enough of its chipped stone characteristics were published in the site report to show expedient core reduction like that just described in the Outer Core Zone. There are, however, no data comparable to the extensive analyses of other Inner and Outer Core Zone sites that make up the substance of this chapter. Although the Paquimé assemblage cannot be analyzed in the same detail as those of other Core Zone sites, comparisons and contrasts are made whenever possible.

Chipped Stone Frequencies

The first question is how chipped stone discard rates vary among the large and small sites of the Inner and Outer Core Zones. Lithic discard rates, or the frequencies of chipped stone of all sorts in contexts, are usually measured by dividing lithic counts by those of some other common artifact class, here ceramics, to produce a simple lithic frequency index that is comparable among sites. No interpretable differences were detected between Inner Core and Outer Core lithic assemblages of all sites combined.

When site size is the partitioning variable, however, a clear pattern emerges. Large Core Zone Sites 204, 565, and 315 have respective lithic discard or frequency indices of 0.9, 1.2, and 1.8. In contrast, small Core Zone sites 355, 317, 321, and 231 had lithic frequency indices of, respectively, 0.27, 0.33, 0.33, and 0.49. All four of these sites appear to be ordinary small residential localities. Small sites all over the Core Zone, then, show lithic discard rates that are barely half of those on large sites. A third group of lithic frequency index values are extremely low: Inner Core Site 290 scores less than 0.09, and Outer Core Site 242 has an index of 0.05. Neither appears to be a typical small residential locality. Site 290 has a high degree of PCGAT architectural modification (refer to chapter 4 for discussion). It also has low ceramic frequency and diversity, as discussed in chapter 5. Site 242, a small Outer Core residential locality, is a ball court community, and its rooms were built in clear imitation of the thick-walled architecture of Paquimé. It is seen as a ceremonial and administrative node that organized upland farming activity (Whalen and Minnis 2001b). Its ceramics were abundant, and they showed evidence of extensive preparation of fermented drink, which likely supplied public feasting (Jones 2002).

Raw Materials

Inner Core Zone sites, large and small, used the set of locally available raw materials described earlier in this chapter. Nowhere is there evidence of significant import of finer material, or of attempts to improve the workability of local stone by heat treating or other techniques like core platform grinding. In short, Medio populations took the abundant volcanic and sedimentary raw materials of their surroundings and used them as found. The three types of stone in highest frequency everywhere are chert, basalt, and rhyolite (table 6.1). Inner Core large and small sites show rhyolite/ignimbrite frequencies that are barely half of those from the Outer Core. This is likely because the Outer Core is closer to the mountain zone, with its vast supply of volcanic rocks. Outer Core sites also appear to have engaged in cultivation of agave or sotol on adjacent rocky slopes. This is attested to by the frequent presence of "agave knives" (S. K. Fish et al. 1992). These are heavy, medium to large tools usually made of medium-grained rhyolite and used in processing agavaceous plants. The Inner Core Zone sites studied here lie on the edge of the Casas Grandes River valley, where less land was suitable for agave production.

Assemblage Composition

Using the criterion applied earlier to the lithics of the Outer Core Zone, the new Inner Core lithic assemblage was divided into three broad categories: flakes and flake fragments, cores and their fragments, and angular debris. The counts and percentages of the full assemblage in each category by Core Zone location and site size class are shown in table 6.2. It is clear from the table that whole and broken flakes make up the vast majority of every assemblage. Cores and their fragments make up a small fraction of the totals. Debris is the most variable

Medio Period Lithics of the Core Zone

TABLE 6.1 Raw materials on large and small Core Zone sites

	Chert	Basalt	Rhyolite	Chalcedony	Ignimbrite	Obsidian	Total
Large ICZ	19,473	21,252	15,897	3,120	372	282	60,396
%	32.2	35.2	26.3	5.2	0.6	0.5	100
Small ICZ	676	530	463	137	226	32	2,064
%	32.8	25.7	22.4	6.6	10.9	1.6	100
Total ICZ	20,149	21,782	16,360	3,257	598	314	62,460
%	32.3	34.9	26.2	5.2	0.9	0.5	100
Large OCZ	11,049	1,527	8,874	881	87	63	22,454
%	49.2	6.8	39.4	3.9	0.4	0.3	100
Small OCZ	974	934	1,666	8	332	13	3,937
%	24.7	23.7	42.4	0.5	8.4	0.3	100
Total OCZ	30,522	22,779	24,771	4,001	459	345	82,877
%	36.8	27.5	29.9	4.8	0.6	0.4	100

TABLE 6.2 Composition of Core Zone lithic assemblages

Size	Location[a]	Flake[b]	Core[b]	Debris	Total
Large	ICZ	52,485	3,420	2,979	58,884
		89.2%	5.8%	5.0%	100.0%
Small	ICZ	1,649	123	480	2,252
		73.2%	5.5%	21.3%	100.0%
Large	OCZ	41,705	1,888	2,004	45,597
		91.4%	4.2%	4.4%	100.0%
Small	OCZ	3,488	382	597	4,467
		78.1%	8.5%	13.4%	100.0%

[a] ICZ = Inner Core Zone; OCZ = Outer Core Zone.
[b] Whole and fragmentary specimens.

assemblage component, ranging from a little over 4 percent to just over 21 percent of each assemblage total.

Predictably, large sites have the largest lithic assemblages, while small sites have the smallest. There is more variability, however, in the sizes of the small site lithic assemblages between the inner and outer parts of the Core Zone. One way to express this is to divide the larger assemblage total by the smaller. If the two were of equal size, the resulting size index would be 1.0. Lower index values indicate increasing difference in the assemblage sizes. For large sites all over the Core Zone, the size index value is 0.77, meaning that the smaller of the large site assemblages is 77 percent as large as the larger. In the Core Zone's small site case, the index is 0.50, showing that the smallest assemblage is only half as large as the largest. This small assemblage comes from Site 242, the Paquimé control node, but it should not be taken to show lower occupation intensity there than at neighboring small Sites 231 and 317. Instead, lithic density is better seen as gauging where an assemblage falls on the continuum from initial core reduction to the final stages of tool manufacture (e.g., Pecora 2001:177). By this logic, small sites of the Inner Core were not at exactly the same stage of core reduction as their Outer Core counterparts.

Cores

Core reduction and tool production represent two trajectories of stone knapping (e.g., Carr and Bradbury 2001:134; Hayden 2022:72; Hayden and Hutchings 1989:235; Johnson 1987:11; Kooyman 2000:57). The lithic debris of each trajectory has interpretable characteristics. Cores can be unprepared or prepared, the latter having flakes removed from a single surface or from two opposing surfaces. This directional, controlled process predetermines flake dimensions according to the prepared shape of the core. In contrast, flakes are removed opportunistically and in multiple directions from unprepared cores. These cores are typically irregular in size and shape, and they are reduced in a random fashion, using the best striking platform for the desired flake size and shape. Freehand hard hammer percussion is the rule in this expedient, uncontrolled process, which dominates the settlements of semisedentary or sedentary societies. This practice has been linked to plentiful local lithic resources and little need for specialized tools (e.g., Custer 1987:52–53). It is also argued to result from the stockpiling of partially reduced cores on residential sites. Flakes of many sizes and shapes can be removed, suiting the varied nature of on-site activities (Hayden 2022:71–72)

In the Medio period, cores and their fragments make up small fractions of their assemblages, never exceeding about 9 percent of the total count (refer to table 6.2). Chi-squared tests were done on frequencies of whole versus fragmentary cores on the large and small sites of the Inner and Outer Core Zones. The counts on which the tests are based are those of table 6.3.

The first chi-squared test compared core and core fragment frequencies on the large sites of the Inner and Outer Core Zones. The Outer Core Zone large site (204) contained significantly more whole cores and fewer fragments than expected under the null hypothesis of no significant difference. Large sites of the Inner Core Zone (315 and 565), on the other hand, had significantly fewer whole cores and more fragments than expected ($X^2 = 604.8$, df = 1, $p < .0001$). The second test compared frequencies of cores and core fragments on Inner and Outer Core Zone small sites, where assemblages were much smaller. Even so, the same pattern was observed. The small sites of the Inner Core Zone had significantly fewer whole cores and more fragments than expected, while the Outer Core Zone's small sites contained significantly more whole cores and fewer fragments than expected ($X^2 = 64.1$, df = 1, $p < .0001$). This is not a surprising result, as cores are usually discarded in processing areas rather than at residences (e.g., Custer 1987:52–53). The proximity of the large Outer Core site to the lithic-rich piedmont slope might explain its high number of whole cores. They were simply brought to the site. Inner Core Zone large sites, in contrast, lay farther out on the floodplain of the Casas Grandes River. They were farther from the lithic resources of the piedmont slope, and thus more intensive core reduction might be expected.

TABLE 6.3 Whole and fragmentary core frequencies on Core Zone sites

Site	Size	Location[a]	Whole cores	Core fragments
315	Large	ICZ	948	1,938
565	Large	ICZ	273	261
204	Large	OCZ	1,352	556
290	Small	ICZ	36	33
321	Small	ICZ	3	15
355	Small	ICZ	21	15
231	Small	OCZ	28	82
242	Small	OCZ	7	39
317	Small	OCZ	33	193

[a] ICZ = Inner Core Zone; OCZ = Outer Core Zone.

TABLE 6.4 Frequencies of core types, by site size and location

Size	Loc.[a]	Multidirec.	Bidirec.	Unidirec.	Rejuv. flake	Bipolar core	Total
Large	ICZ	59	10	26	9	27	131
		45.1%	7.6%	19.8%	6.9%	20.6%	100.0%
Large	OCZ	56	52	20	9	1	138
		40.6%	37.7%	14.5%	6.5%	0.7%	100.0%
Small	ICZ	17	7	11	1	10	46
		36.9%	15.2%	23.9%	2.2%	21.8%	100.0%
Small	OCZ	16	1	4	10	4	35
		45.7%	2.9%	11.4%	28.6%	11.4%	100.0%

[a] ICZ = Inner Core Zone; OCZ = Outer Core Zone.

Frequencies of cores of different types on the large and small sites of the Core Zone are shown in table 6.4. This core sample is much smaller than that of preceding analyses, as only a fraction of the entire assemblage received detailed examination. Even so, the largest single category of core type all over the study area and on sites of all sizes was clearly the multidirectional piece, on which at least three flakes were removed from different angles. Many of them (ca. 50%) were of irregular shapes, while others were roughly rounded (ca. 35%). Typically, they were large chunks of rhyolite, basalt, ignimbrite, or chert. Flakes were removed opportunistically without platform preparation, as is characteristic of expedient reduction.

Bifacial and unifacial cores were those with flakes removed from, respectively, two platforms at different angles or a single platform. Some of these were cores discarded early in the flake removal process, while others were tabular pieces. These cores range widely in frequency, from more than half of the assemblage at large Outer Core Zone Site 204 to 13 percent at small Outer Core sites. Inner Core large and small sites are more consistent at about 29 to 40 percent of the core assemblages. Many of these were sizable chunks of such common raw materials as rhyolite, basalt, and ignimbrite. In these cases, only a few flakes were removed before the core was discarded, either as unsatisfactory or because only a few flakes were needed, and raw material was plentiful. Tabular cores were most likely to be chert, which occurs in parent rock in thin veins. Chert that has eroded from its surroundings is found in small, thin, flat pieces. The flaking technique was adapted to the raw material shape.

The only attempt to increase the yield of cores was removal of large flakes to create new flat surfaces for further striking. These rejuvenation flakes usually had dorsal scars from previous flake removals. This was clearly not a common practice, however, as rejuvenation flakes amounted to only 4–5 percent of the core and core fragment assemblage all over the study area. Small Inner Core sites had even fewer rejuvenation flakes, at around 1.5 percent. The situation was dramatically different in the Outer Core Zone, where rejuvenation flakes found on small sites averaged over 20 percent of the core assemblage.

Bipolar core reduction appears to have been used to obtain flakes of very fine-grained material that was not abundant in the study area. Cores too small to hold and strike free-hand were rested on anvil stones and struck from above to split the piece into one or two usable flakes. Round or ellipsoidal nodules of obsidian, chalcedony, and chert were most often the objects of bipolar reduction in the study area. These pieces were typically less than 3 cm in maximum dimension, producing only one or two small flakes. The tiny projectile points of the Medio period, for example, were usually made of this fine stone. Bipolar reduction is found at all sites all over the Core Zone, but it was never a major strategy. Bipolar reduction was most consistently found in the Inner Core Zone, where it composed about 22 percent of the core assemblages on large and small sites (table 6.4). It has already been observed (see table 5.1) that Outer Core sites had higher frequencies of rhyolite and ignimbrite, which occur in large plentiful chunks all over the area. These are the stone types least likely to be reduced by the bipolar technique.

Flakes

Primary, secondary, and tertiary whole flakes were tabulated according to the percentage of cortex, as described earlier in this chapter. These data, plus the debris count, for large and small sites of the Inner and Outer Core Zones are shown in table 6.5.

The data just presented show similar sequences of core reduction at large sites all over the Core Zone. There were relatively few primary flakes and increasing numbers of secondary and tertiary pieces. A natural consequence of core reduction should be paucity of primary flakes, which in turn should be outnumbered by those of successive reduction stages. It might also suggest that material was already partly reduced when brought to these sites (e.g., Hayden 2022:72). Large Core Zone sites were also characterized by relatively high frequencies of broken flakes and by considerable amounts of debris. Both situations are explicable as natural consequences of core reduction. William Prentiss (2001:156) notes that many broken flakes are found when unprepared, amorphous, or expedient cores are reduced, and it has been shown that many Medio period cores were of this type.

TABLE 6.5 Flake and debris counts on Core Zone sites

Size	Loc.[a]	Primary	Secondary	Tertiary	Broken	Debris	Total
Large	ICZ	3,501	14,811	13,509	20,664	29,799	82,284
		4.3%	18.0%	16.4%	25.1%	36.2%	100.0%
Large	OCZ	3,095	7,078	11,364	19,898	20,004	61,439
		5.35%	11.5%	18.5%	32.3%	32.4%	100.0%
Small	ICZ	204	375	872	198	480	2,129
		9.6%	17.6%	41.0%	9.3%	22.5%	100.0%
Small	OCZ	375	570	2,450	93	597	4,085
		9.2%	14.0%	59.9%	2.3%	14.6%	100.0%

[a] ICZ = Inner Core Zone; OCZ = Outer Core Zone.

Interestingly, small sites all over the Core Zone have more primary flakes and many more tertiary flakes in contrast to large sites, but this pattern is accompanied by a large reduction in broken flakes. The proportion of debris is also lower on small sites than on large ones. This could be an artifact of less-intensive core reduction on small sites. Several have noted that relatively high proportions of shatter (or debris) are associated with core reduction, as opposed to tool preparation (e.g., Carr and Bradbury 2001:129; Hayden 2022:45; Pecora 2001:180; Prentiss 2001:163, 171). This accords well with the earlier finding that lithic discard rates were lower on small sites than on large ones all over the Core Zone.

RAW MATERIALS

Medio period chipped stone raw materials were tabulated and compared at the assemblage level in previous pages. In this section, however, we introduce a new comparative division of flake raw materials into three broad categories. Volcanic rocks of medium grain size are rhyolite, andesite, ignimbrite, and basalt, while siliceous materials like chert and chalcedony are fine grained and good for precise flaking. These two categories make up the vast majority of chipped stone materials used in Medio times. A third category is obsidian, a fine volcanic glass, small nodules of which are distributed widely but sparsely in the alluvia of northwestern Chihuahua. Counts and frequencies of the three raw material groups on the large and small sites of the Inner and Outer Core Zones are shown in table 6.6.

Chi-squared tests were conducted on some of the counts in table 6.6. The first comparison was of material frequencies on large and small sites. Large sites all over the Inner Core Zone were found to have significantly greater than expected frequencies of flakes of fine- grained siliceous stone, while frequencies of flakes made from medium-grained volcanic rocks are lower than expected under the null hypothesis of no significant difference in material frequencies. Large Site 204 of the Outer Core Zone is an exception. As table 6.6 shows, the two raw material classes are about equally represented in that site's flake assemblage. In contrast, small sites of the Inner and Outer Core Zones showed significantly greater than expected frequencies of flakes of volcanic stone together with lower than expected frequencies of siliceous stone flakes ($X^2 = 241.7$, df = 3, $p < .0001$).

TABLE 6.6 Flake raw materials on Core Zone sites, by size class

Site	Size	Core loc.[a]	Volcanic (%)	Siliceous (%)	Obsidian (%)
315	Large	ICZ	731 (61.2)	451 (38.4)	4 (0.4)
565	Large	ICZ	1,321 (53.4)	1,145 (46.2)	9 (0.4)
204	Large	OCZ	963 (49.7)	958 (49.4)	17 (0.9)
290	Small	ICZ	186 (80.2)	46 (19.4)	0 (0.0)
321	Small	ICZ	86 (92.5)	7 (7.5)	0 (0.0)
355	Small	ICZ	269 (70.2)	112 (29.2)	2 (0.5)
231	Small	OCZ	858 (79.8)	217 (20.2)	0 (0.0)
242	Small	OCZ	164 (52.1)	137 (43.5)	14 (4.4)
317	Small	OCZ	776 (60.9)	495 (38.8)	4 (0.3)

[a] ICZ = Inner Core Zone; OCZ = Outer Core Zone.

Siliceous raw material is widespread as small nodules and tabular pieces in the eroded Basin and Range alluvium, as noted earlier in this chapter. Presumably, therefore, this raw material was about equally available to large and small communities all over the Core Zone. Volcanic and siliceous stone were used differently in Medio period technology. Large coarse cutting and scraping implements were almost always made of medium-grained volcanic stone. Small sharp cutting, drilling, and scraping tools were invariably made of fine-grained siliceous stone or obsidian, the former being much more common than the latter. Both materials are present on large and small Core Zone sites, albeit at different frequencies. Both large Site 204 and all of the Core's small sites lie on or at the edge of piedmont slopes. This is prime agave-growing land, and it contains both features and artifacts relevant to this activity (e.g., Minnis and Whalen 2020:71; Whalen and Minnis 2009:194–95). Heavy tools of volcanic stones were especially useful here, but the presence of small sharp siliceous stone tools at all sites also emphasizes that a broad range of activities took place at large and small sites.

All large sites yielded obsidian flakes in trace quantities that did not differ significantly from expectation. Even so, it is notable that this rare material was better represented in the Outer Core Zone. Large Site 204 produced more obsidian flakes than both large Inner Core sites combined, except for Paquimé. Small administrative Site 242 also produced an unusually high frequency of obsidian flakes. Among the small sites of the Outer Core Zone, then, two of three had at least trace quantities of obsidian flakes. In the Inner Zone, in contrast, two of the three small sites had no obsidian at all. The paucity of obsidian among the nearest large and small neighbors of Paquimé, then, might have resulted from absorption by the primary center of much of what was available. The chipped stone assemblage from Paquimé is very small, numbering only around 3,700 pieces and attesting to the different collection strategy used there. Even so, there were more than 700 pieces of obsidian. This is a higher frequency than found at any other Inner Core Zone site. This, in turn, shows that many obsidian nodules were going into Paquimé, while few went out again. There is no indication, then, that Paquimé distributed obsidian to its neighbors. Indeed, given the ubiquity of the material, it is hard to imagine how the supply could have been controlled. Higher frequencies of obsidian at Outer Core Zone sites might be another part of the pattern recognized earlier in this volume: the Outer Core contains ball courts, large ovens, and birdcages (i.e., integrative features), which are absent in the Inner Core, save at Paquimé. No chemical characterization of Site 204 obsidian has yet been done to compare with recent work on Inner Core obsidian artifacts (Dolan et al. 2017). This may not be successful, however, given the ubiquity of obsidian nodules in Core Zone alluvia, all secondarily deposited from many primary sources.

FLAKE SIZES

The sizes of flakes are influenced by two factors. One of these is reduction intensity, as it is well known that flake size diminishes from the early to the late parts of the reduction continuum (e.g., Carr and Bradbury 2001:122, 134; Hayden 2022:45; Koldehoff 1987:169; Pecora 2001:180). A second significant determinant of flake size is the type of stone used. In the Casas Grandes area, for example, volcanic stones are present in pieces ranging from small to large. These flake sizes thus can vary widely. Siliceous stone is equally widespread, but it occurs in small to medium nodules or veins. These seldom exceed 15 cm in maximum dimension. The natural piece sizes of obsidian are smaller still. They occur sparsely but widely in nodules that are commonly 3 to 5 cm in maximum dimension. A few reach 10 cm, but these are rare. Piece sizes of siliceous stone and obsidian therefore preclude the existence of larger flakes.

Length, width, and thickness were recorded for complete flakes on large and small Core Zone sites. These data for each of the raw material groups, divided by Core Zone location and site size, are shown in table 6.7. Several observations may be made from these data. First, the means and standard deviations show that few flakes exceed 6 cm in maximum dimension. It was just remarked, however, that knappable volcanic stones occur all over the area in pieces much larger than this. The fact that most of the Core Zone flakes were 1 to 3 cm long suggests fairly small light tasks (e.g., Hayden 2022:124). A second observation is that flakes of volcanic stone are always longer, wider, and thicker than those of siliceous material or obsidian. This holds true across the entire Core Zone and among sites of all sizes, and it is a result of the raw material piece sizes just discussed. It is also likely influenced by reduction strategy, as volcanic stones of medium grain fineness were used for large, coarse, expedient implements, while siliceous stone and obsidian were used for smaller, sharper tools that were more often retouched. Large Outer Core Site 204 had flakes of volcanic stone that were longer and wider than those on Inner Core Zone large Sites 315 and 565. The pattern is almost the same among the small sites of the Inner and Outer Core. Flakes of the Outer Core small sites were, on average, longer and wider than those of the Inner Core. It has already been observed (see table 6.1) that Outer Core sites had higher frequencies of rhyolite and ignimbrite, which occur in large plentiful chunks, and which were the preferred material for large scraping and chopping tools. Large flakes have been noted to be characteristic of the early stages of core reduction (Kooyman 2000:52, fig. 3.1). Obsidian flake sizes were so sharply constrained by nodule size that their dimensions vary little everywhere.

TABLE 6.7 Flake dimensions on Core Zone sites, by raw material group

Site	Size	Core[a]	Volcanic stone				Siliceous stone				Obsidian			
			n	Length	Width	Thickness	*n*	Length	Width	Thickness	*n*	Length	Width	Thickness
315	Large	ICZ	712	26.3[b]	25.2	6.8	45	20.5	18.7	5.2	1	6.2	4.1	2.8
				10[c]	11.1	4.1	1	8.5	8.1	3.3		—	—	—
565	Large	ICZ	1,321	27.5	24.8	6.6	11	20.9	18.6	5.2	9	6.8	4.3	3.1
				11.4	11.9	4.0	45	7.5	7.0	2.9		1.7	0.7	0.8
204	Large	OCZ	1,176	32.9	28.9	7.2	10	19.0	17.0	5.1	9	5.6	4.0	2.4
				13.2	14.2	4.4	35	6.6	7.0	2.7		1.4	0.4	0.2
290	Small	ICZ	113	32.1	27.6	8.0	88	22.1	19.9	5.5	0	—	—	—
				12.7	12.2	4.0		8.9	7.2	2.8				
321	Small	ICZ	47	28.1	27.4	8.3	46	20.1	19.9	5.5	0	—	—	—
				13.1	12.4	4.5		8.8	7.7	3.0				
355	Small	ICZ	269	27.4	24.1	7.5	11	19.0	17.4	5.8	3	5.8	4.2	2.4
				10.7	10.9	3.7	1	6.2	6.2	2.7		2.0	1.3	1.3
231	Small	OCZ	100	35.1	28.6	6.1	22	26.1	27.7	5.5	0	—	—	—
				10.6	10.1	1.9		10.6	14.7	1.4				
242	Small	OCZ	42	42.2	34.3	6.3	23	31.5	26.9	6.1	14	5.1	3.9	1.3
				23.5	18.9	2.2		13.3	10.1	2.3		1.8	1.1	0.6
317	Small	OCZ	64	31.2	27.5	6.3	30	24.5	20.7	5.6	4	4.7	2.9	1.9
				12.8	11.5	1.9		10.1	10.6	1.8		1.2	0.7	0.8

[a] ICZ = Inner Core Zone; OCZ = Outer Core Zone.

[b] Mean, in millimeters.

[c] Standard deviation.

OTHER FLAKE ATTRIBUTES

Many have observed that flake characteristics provide important evidence of activities carried out on sites (e.g., Carr and Bradbury 2001:126–27). Some attributes of flakes shed light on the manner of working. Platform characteristics, dorsal scar patterns, and flake termination types might indicate hard hammer, freehand reduction of cores, as opposed to the more controlled flaking of biface production. Hayden and Hutchings (1989) provide criteria to distinguish between flakes produced by the two major trajectories of stone knapping, cited earlier in this chapter. Core reduction relies largely on hard hammer percussion, while soft hammer flaking is the norm in biface production. Observable features that distinguish between these two trajectories include characteristics of the striking platform as well as ventral surface lips and bulbs. Dorsal surface scar patterns and flake terminations may also be useful indicators (e.g., Odell 2004:53). Each is considered below for sites of the Inner Core Zone. Where possible, Outer Core Zone data are added for comparison. Some of these datasets were recorded decades ago, and not all of the same variables were used.

Striking Platform Condition

Preparation of the dorsal edge of the striking platform by abrasion or scrubbing is undertaken to strengthen the edges of cores, permitting removal of larger and better controlled flakes (Hayden 2022:43–44). Platform preparation of this sort is rare to absent all over the Core Zone, among sites of all sizes. This is in keeping with the amorphous core reduction strategy described earlier in this chapter. Beyond this, striking platforms will be either cortical, complex (also described as faceted) or smooth (Andrefsky 2005:94–95). As the term implies, cortical striking platforms retain at least some traces of the original stone cortex, and they likely represent the earlier stages of core reduction (Kooyman 2000:51–52). Faceted platforms bear multiple small scars from prior flake removals. Core reduction flakes show relatively few platform facets, while increasing numbers of them are seen in later, finer reduction. This is especially so in biface preparation trajectories (Carr and Bradbury 2001:133; Clarkson 2008:290; Odell 1989:172). Smooth platforms are often associated with unidirectional cores, where flakes are struck from one direction off single large flat surfaces (Andrefsky 2005:95).

Striking platform data for Inner Core Zone sites of all sizes, and for Outer Core Zone large Site 204, is tabulated in table 6.8. One condition is absent from the table, as we found no examples of platform preparation by abrasion. Small Outer Core Sites 231, 242, and 317 platform data were not tabulated in the same way as the other sites, so they are omitted from this table.

Chi-squared tests on cortical, faceted, and smooth striking platform counts of the Inner Core sites showed only that large settlements contained more platforms with cortex and fewer smooth platforms than expected under the null hypothesis of no significant difference, while small sites reversed this pattern but had more smooth platforms than expected ($X^2 = 70.17$, df = 2, $p < .0001$). It was argued in preceding pages that large sites likely contained stockpiles of roughly prepared amorphous cores for use as needed (Hayden 2022:72; Koldehoff 1987:169). It is thus not surprising to find flake striking platforms with at least

TABLE 6.8 Striking platform characteristics on Inner Core sites

Site	Size	Core[a]	Cortical	Smooth	Faceted	Shattered	Total
315	Large	ICZ	529	208	270	153	1,160
			45.9%	17.9%	23.3%	13.2%	100.0%
565	Large	ICZ	974	388	467	333	2,162
			45.0%	17.9%	21.6%	15.4%	100.0%
204	Large	OCZ	592	294	239	329	1,554
			44.5%	18.9%	15.4%	21.2%	100.0%
290	Small	ICZ	52	93	28	39	212
			24.5%	43.9%	13.2%	18.4%	100.0%
321	Small	ICZ	24	31	17	16	88
			23.7%	35.2%	19.3%	18.2%	100.0%
355	Small	ICZ	169	98	80	44	391
			43.2%	25.0%	20.5%	11.3%	100.0%

[a] ICZ = Inner Core Zone; OCZ = Outer Core Zone.

some cortex. The small site pattern is strongly influenced by Sites 290 and 321, which show low frequencies of cortical flake platforms together with high frequencies of smooth platforms. This could be a result of departure from the large site pattern of stockpiling cores in habitation areas. There is much less chipped stone in these sites, but their frequency of broken cores was shown earlier to be high. This seems like an indicator of heavy stone knapping on the small sites. Frequencies of shattered platforms were found not to differ significantly among the sites listed in table 6.8. This is predictable, as all over the region we see similar hard hammer, freehand reduction of amorphous cores of the same raw materials. Platform crushing or shattering is rare or absent in soft hammer flakes because of their diffuse area of impact (Hayden and Hutchings 1989:239).

Flake Surface Traits

Flake surface traits are divisible into ventral and dorsal surface aspects. Interior, or ventral, surface traits such as lips and bulbs are often cited as useful in identifying reduction trajectories (e.g., Odell 2004:53). The following paragraphs are abstracted from discussion by Brian Hayden and Karl Hutchings (1989:239–41). Hard hammer blows initiate compression cracking in the immediate vicinity of the point of impact, as large force is applied to a small area directly beneath the percussor. Soft hammer blows, in contrast, initiate bending cracks at a distance from the point of impact, as force is dissipated over larger area. Both of these flaking trajectories leave visible signs on flakes.

One of these is a lip, or a slight protrusion of the ventral edge of the striking platform. Lips are produced during the bending fractures associated with soft hammer knapping. The lower, or dorsal, surface of the flake is stretched by the impact, while the upper, or ventral, surface is compressed. The resulting fracture leaves a small lip or ridge on the compressed ventral surface, as has been illustrated elsewhere (Whittaker 1994:164, fig. 7.40). Bulbs are an associated feature of the ventral surfaces of hard hammer flakes. Lying just

TABLE 6.9 Lips and bulbs on Core Zone flakes

Site	Size	Core[a]	Lip		Bulb		
			Yes	No	Flat	Pronounced	Shattered
315	Large	ICZ	275 (23.6%)	889 (76.6%)	622 (53.3%)	512 (43.0%)	31 (2.7%)
565	Large	ICZ	831 (33.6%)	1,644 (66.4%)	1,147 (46.7%)	512 (43.9%)	40 (1.6%)
204	Large	OCZ	957 (42.1%)	1,315 (57.9%)	869 (38.2)	1,353 (59.5%)	52 (2.3%)
290	Small	ICZ	81 (35.1%)	150 (64.9%)	57 (24.7%)	147 (63.6%)	27 (11.7%)
321	Small	ICZ	33 (35.5%)	60 (64.5%)	22 (23.7%)	61 (65.6%)	10 (10.8%)
355	Small	ICZ	170 (39.9%)	256 (60.1%)	242 (52.6%)	191 (41.5%)	27 (5.9%)

[a] ICZ = Inner Core Zone; OCZ = Outer Core Zone.

below the lip, bulbs represent one side of the Hertzian, or conchoidal, fracture cone produced by concentrated force at the point of impact and crack initiation (Odell 2004:50). Pronounced bulbs do not characterize soft hammer flaking, again because of the diffuse area of impact force. All of these flake characteristics are visible on the Core Zone assemblages, as shown in table 6.9.

Chi-squared tests were conducted on the lip counts shown in table 6.9 for large Inner Core Zone sites (315 and 565) versus their small neighbors (290, 321, 355). Large sites were found to show significantly lower than expected frequencies of the lipping that is associated with soft hammer percussion, while small sites showed the opposite pattern of more than expected lipping ($X^2 = 15.71$, df = 2, $p < .0001$). The same result obtained when flakes were divided into volcanic versus siliceous stone. This is surprising, given that other indicators suggest more fine late-stage reduction on large sites than on small ones. There is opinion in the literature, however, that lipping is not as reliable an indicator of soft hammer percussion as is often asserted. Instead, lipping is seen as common with soft hammer percussion but not exclusive to it. For example, flakes with lips may be produced when very hard stone is struck (e.g., Andrefsky 2005:118; Kooyman 2000:79–80; Odell 2004:59).

Prominent bulbs are another indication of hard hammer percussion. They were common on the ventral surfaces of large and small sites of the Inner Core Zone, composing 40 to 60 percent of the sample. The situation appears to be similar for the small sites of the Outer Core Zone. There, Karen J. Rebnegger (2001:92) found prominent bulbs on nearly 80 percent of flakes from sites 231, 242, and 317. As these data were not tabulated by site, they do not appear in the preceding table. It has already been shown that the small sites of the Outer Core contained relatively high ratios of volcanic to siliceous stone. Volcanic stone was mostly used to make large coarse implements, while siliceous stone served for smaller, finer tools. It is therefore not surprising to find more evidence of hard hammer, early stage reduction on Outer Core small sites.

Chi-squared tests on the bulb condition frequencies of table 6.9 showed no significant difference in the frequencies of prominent bulbs among the large sites of the Inner and Outer Core Zones, or between the large and small sites of the same area. It is interesting to note, however, that the samples' lowest frequencies of flat bulbs come from small Sites 290 and 321. These have been shown to have substantial post-Medio architectural construction, and they appear to have less soft hammer reduction than other Inner Core sites. Another test, however, showed a significantly lower than expected frequency of shattered versus whole bulbs on large Inner Core Zone sites, while the small sites of the Inner Core had a greater than expected frequency of shattered bulbs (X^2 = 63.0, df = 2, p < .0001). This suggests somewhat more early stage hard hammer reduction on small sites than on large ones. Here, again, small Sites 290 and 321 stand out as having the sample's highest frequency of shattered bulbs.

Dorsal surface scars are produced by removal of previous flakes. All flake dorsal surfaces will show cortex, some pattern of scarring, or both (Andrefsky 2005:107). Pieces in the early stages of reduction are expected to have more cortex and relatively few flake removal scars. As reduction progresses, orientations of accumulating scars may be patterned (e.g., longitudinal, transverse, or medial) or irregular, as any suitable striking platform is used. Core rejuvenation by removal of a single large flake produces a new smooth but noncortical surface. Frequencies of dorsal surface characteristics for Inner Core Zone sites and for Outer Core large Site 204 are shown in table 6.10. We lack these site-by-site data for the small sites of the Outer Core Zone, so they are not included in the table.

Frequencies of the first three dorsal surface characteristics shown in the preceding table were compared for large and small sites of the Inner Core Zone. Large Inner Core sites were found to have significantly lower than expected frequencies of flakes with cortical dorsal surfaces, while frequencies of faceted and smooth dorsal surfaces were greater than expected. Small sites reverse this situation, with significantly greater than expected frequencies of cortical dorsal surfaces and lower than expected counts of faceted and smooth dorsal surfaces (X^2 = 667.3, df = 2, p < .0001). Brian P. Kooyman (2000:51) cites experiments demonstrating that the presence of dorsal cortex is indicative of early stage reduction, declining rapidly thereafter. All dorsal cortex in these experiments was gone midway through the reduction process. The chi-squared test just described thus hints at more early stage core reduction at small sites, combined with somewhat less of the finer flaking seen in late-stage reduction.

TABLE 6.10 Dorsal surface characteristics of the Core Zone

			Dorsal surface characteristics		
Site	Size	Core[a]	Cortical (%)	Faceted (%)	Smooth (%)
315	Large	ICZ	1,529 (45.6)	270 (23.3)	208 (17.9)
565	Large	ICZ	974 (45.0)	467 (21.6)	588 (27.2)
204	Large	OCZ	694 (44.7)	239 (15.4)	292 (18.8)
290	Small	ICZ	52 (24.5)	28 (13.2)	93 (43.9)
321	Small	ICZ	24 (27.3)	17 (19.3)	17 (19.3)
355	Small	ICZ	169 (43.2)	80 (20.5)	80 (20.5)

[a] ICZ = Inner Core Zone; OCZ = Outer Core Zone.

Flake Terminations

Flakes leave their cores in whole or broken conditions. Whole flake terminations (i.e., the shape of the distal end) can have either feather or hinge forms. Feather terminations represent the smooth termination of the fracture, and they are the desired outcome. Hinge fractures, on the other hand, occur when the detaching crack terminates by turning inward, leaving an irregular core surface that may be difficult to work with (e.g., Odell 2004:57). A step fracture results when the proximal part of a flake is detached from the core, while the distal part remains attached (Andrefsky 2005:20). This is also undesirable, as it leaves an irregular ridged core surface that may be difficult to work with (Odell 2004:57). Flake terminations thus tell something about both raw material quality and knapping success, which in turn reflects on the trajectory of reduction. Direct freehand hard hammer percussion on amorphous unprepared cores is widely known to increase the frequency of step fractures (e.g., Clarkson 2008:288; Goodale et al. 2008:318; Koldehoff 1987:166; Prentiss 2001:156).

Frequencies of flake terminations on Core Zone sites of all sizes are shown in table 6.11. On average, 49.9 percent of flakes had feather terminations (σ = 16.2). Hinge terminations averaged 28.8 percent of the sample (σ = 5.9), and an average of 13.5 percent showed step fractures (σ = 6.0). A Core Zone–wide chi-squared test on the termination counts of table 6.11 by site size showed that small sites had significantly greater than expected frequencies of step terminations, while large sites had fewer step fractures than expected under the null hypothesis of no significant difference (X^2 = 8.31, df = 1, p = .0039). Analyses of preceding pages showed that small sites evinced more early stage expedient reduction of amorphous cores, and their relatively high frequencies of step fractures is consistent with this situation. Last, the figures of table 6.11 show that Inner Core Zone small Sites 290 and 321 stand out for their high frequencies of step fractures and their relatively low counts of feather terminations. This has been a consistent pattern throughout this chapter: these small sites have a good deal of Post–Casas Grandes Architectural Tradition construction, and they differ from their neighbors in artifact assemblages as well.

TABLE 6.11 Flake terminations on Core Zone sites

Site	Size	Core[a]	Feather (%)	Hinge (%)	Step (%)	Total (%)
315	Large	ICZ	571 (49.3)	445 (38.4)	143 (12.3)	1,159 (100.0)
565	Large	ICZ	1,580 (64.6)	510 (20.9)	355 (14.5)	2,445 (100.0)
204	Large	OCZ	1,464 (72.0)	389 (19.0)	182 (9.0)	2,033 (100.0)
290	Small	ICZ	109 (47.8)	71 (31.1)	48 (21.1)	228 (100.0)
321	Small	ICZ	46 (49.4)	21 (22.6)	26 (28.0)	93 (100.0)
355	Small	ICZ	259 (57.8)	133 (29.7)	56 (12.5)	448 (100.0)
231	Small	OCZ	185 (60.4)	103 (33.7)	18 (5.9)	306 (100.0)
242	Small	OCZ	78 (57.1)	52 (34.4)	21 (13.9)	151 (100.0)
317	Small	OCZ	209 (61.3)	102 (29.9)	30 (8.8)	341 (100.0)

[a] ICZ = Inner Core Zone; OCZ = Outer Core Zone.

Chipped Stone Tool Analyses

All analyses of Medio period chipped stone assemblages point out the scarcity of recognizable tools on sites of this period. On Outer Core Zone large and small Sites 204, 231, 242, and 317, for example, macroscopic examination identified flakes that were used without retouching. Steep-edged pieces were used as scrapers, while fine-edged flakes served for cutting. These implements were made from locally available raw materials. This is entirely consistent with the expedient nature of Medio chipped stone technology.

To expand on these macroscopic characterizations, Keith Mendez (2009) carried out the Casas Grandes area's first microscopic analysis of a sample of 745 chert and rhyolite flakes from Outer Core Zone large Site 204. Mendez detailed sampling and analytical procedures, and the following discussion is abstracted from it. Low-power microscopic examination of flake edges revealed 150 utilized specimens, and these were compared to a collection of flakes known by experiment to have been used in specific tasks. Nearly all Site 204 specimens were single function pieces that were likely discarded after brief use. Multiple uses were identified on the same flake in only 10 cases. This pattern of brief use and rapid discard is consistent with the Medio period's expedient technology and with the area's abundant raw material.

The utilized pieces were classed as cutting, scraping, drilling, graving, and chopping tools. The majority of them (68%) were used for cutting various hard to soft materials. Most use-wear, however, was suggestive of the cutting of medium-hardness materials, including wood and fibrous plant matter. Much rarer was evidence of cutting soft material such as flesh and hides. This accords with what is known of Medio subsistence practices, in which vegetable foods such as corn, beans, squash, chile, and agave played major roles (Minnis and Whalen 2020:36). Meat has been argued to have played a much smaller role in the Medio period diet, and what there was of it came primarily from small to medium animals such as rabbits, antelope, and deer (Whalen and Minnis 2009:230). This processing is reflected in Mendez's (2009) lithic use-wear analysis. The results of this pioneering use-wear study, like other aspects of the chipped stone assemblages, will likely be found to characterize Medio communities throughout the area.

The use-wear study deliberately excluded two categories of tools that were also found on Core Zone sites: agave knives, also known as tabular knives, and projectile points. Studies of Outer Core Zone lithic assemblages (Rebnegger 2001; Rowles 2004; Whalen and Minnis 2009) showed that large and small sites had heavy hand-sized cutting and scraping tools made of locally abundant rhyolite. Similar tools were described as agave knives in the adjacent U.S. Southwest (S. K. Fish et al. 1992:83–84), and this study emphasized their roles in processing leaves and heads of agavaceous plants, which was a significant part of Medio period subsistence (Minnis and Whalen 2020:46). Tabular knives from the Outer Core Zone were especially abundant on the slopes above large Site 204, where agave cultivation likely took place in Medio times. The edges of these tools were roughly retouched to produce steep or fine scraping or cutting edges. They do not appear to have been used long, as scores of them littered the hill slope above Site 204.

FIGURE 6.1 Chert projectile points from Inner Core sites.

FIGURE 6.2 Obsidian projectile points from Inner Core sites.

A more finely retouched formal tool is the projectile point. These pieces were made of high-quality obsidian and chert. They are always small, measuring about 2 cm long by about 1 cm wide at the base. Their shapes are simple triangles. Basal notching or thinning was common but not ubiquitous, as was side notching. A sample of these points from Inner Core large Sites 315 and 565 is shown in figure 6.1. Others of the same sort from Outer Core large Site 204 are illustrated elsewhere (Whalen and Minnis 2009:197, figs. 6.2 and 6.3). This is also the common type of point at Paquimé, where points are classed in various types and subtypes (Rinaldo 1974b:391–97).

The point assemblage from Paquimé included 70 points and fragments that were of the small triangular sort. Twenty-five of these (36%) were made of obsidian, while the remaining 45 (64%) were of other fine siliceous materials such as chert, chalcedony, and jasper. This may not be a representative sample, however, due to the small size of the site's chipped stone assemblage. The entire three-year excavation at Paquimé produced a chipped stone collection of only 3,714 pieces. Of these 1,103 are classified as various sorts of tools, 122 as cores, and 2,611 as debitage (Rinaldo 1974b:341). We have suggested elsewhere that this collection strategy was biased toward retouched specimens (Whalen and Minnis 2009:184). In comparison, Sites 204, 231, 242, and 317 of the Outer Core Zone produced 26,694 pieces of chipped stone. A large difference in recovery strategies is clearly at issue.

The Paquimé data contrast with those of other Inner Core large Sites 315 and 565, where 56 small points were found (figure 6.2). Of this sample, 36 (64%) were obsidian, and 20 (36%) were fine-grained chert or other siliceous material. The sizes of obsidian points were doubtless limited by the dimensions of the available nodules. These were split by bipolar percussion, and points were carefully retouched from the resulting flakes. Fine-grained chert sometimes occurs as nodules reduced by bipolar flaking. These appear to be the only circumstances when bipolar reduction was used, as it is known to be a technique that gets the most from small or scarce raw material (e.g., Hayden 2022:76–78). Small triangular points, whether made of obsidian or chert, come almost exclusively from the large sites of the Core Zone, including Paquimé. A single small chert point was found on Outer Core small Site 317. The other small sites of the Outer Core, and all those of the Inner Core, yielded no points. It is also noteworthy that obsidian was more often used for point manufacture in the Inner Core Zone.

A second group of projectile points differs from the small triangular Medio period points just discussed. Most of the points and bifaces in this second group were made of chert and other familiar siliceous material, but they vary widely in size, shape, and style. Most are classifiable using typologies established in the U.S. Southwest. Some belong to the Late Archaic and early Ceramic times. In figure 6.3, points 1, 4, 8, 9, and 11 resemble the San Pedro style of the Late Archaic (see comparative examples presented by Hard and Roney 2020:96–102, figs. 6.6–6.8). Others are from early Ceramic times. Point 2 is of the Palmillas type, point 5 is the Figueroa type, 6 resembles Basketmaker II, and point 7 is likely Chiricahua style. These types are contemporary with the long-lived San Pedro style, and they represent a lengthy time span from the Late Archaic to the early Ceramic eras. Points 3, 10, 12, and 13 seem to belong, respectively, to the Harrell, Toyah, and Fresno types. These date between ca. 500 and 1200 BP, or during the Viejo period in the Casas Grandes area. Two points (1 and 2) were found in a subfloor cache at Site 315, and the rest were scattered through the deposits at Inner Core sites 315 and 565. At Outer Core large Site 204, six Late Archaic–type points and two bifaces were found cached together beneath the floor of a large colonnaded room (Whalen and Minnis 2009:104, fig. 3.16). In these cases, we see a widespread pattern of collecting earlier projectile points by later populations. If all people

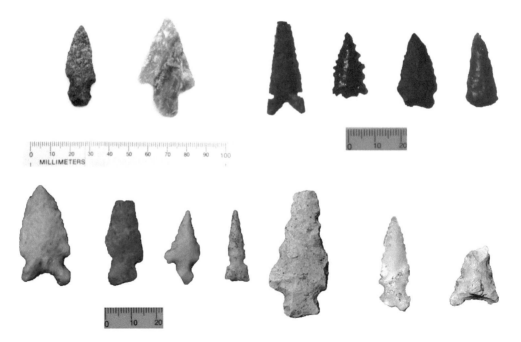

FIGURE 6.3 Curated early points found on Inner Core Sites 315 and 565.

Ground Stone Implements on Core Zone Sites

Implements of ground stone were clearly of great importance in the Medio period, as they were ubiquitous on sites of every size all over the Core Zone. The vast assemblage of over 7,000 pieces from Paquimé was the basis of an extensive typology and discussion (Rinaldo 1974b:38–335) that has guided all subsequent studies, including one comparing the ground stone collections from Paquimé and large Site 204 of the Outer Core Zone (McKay 2005). As the first step in this analysis, the 204 collection was sorted into the types established at Paquimé. This was readily accomplished, as nothing was found at Site 204 that did not have an already described counterpart at the principal center. The remainder of the study was a rank order comparison of the Paquimé and 204 assemblages. For each collection, ground stone implement categories were ranked in order of decreasing frequency, expressed as a percentage of the whole ground stone assemblage.

Because the Paquimé assemblage is many times larger than that of Site 204, it is not surprising to find that the larger sample shows much more variability than the smaller one (McKay 2005:45, table 6.2). Even so, the two assemblages were found to be alike in many ways. The difference between them, as Michael McKay's rank order table indicates, is produced mostly by the presence of several rare things that occur almost exclusively at Casas Grandes. These include cruciform objects, stone cylinders, effigies of several sorts, pipes, stools, rasps or ringing stones, altar stones, ceremonial axe and hammer heads, palettes, and decorated stone bowls, large stone disks, and slabs that were likely post bases, as well as birdcage doors and the stone plugs used to close them. We continue and expand on this inquiry by adding the three small sites of the Outer Core (231, 242, and 317) plus the four large and small Inner Core sites introduced in this volume (315, 565, 290, and 355). Note that Inner Core small Site 321 is omitted from this dataset, as almost no ground stone pieces were recovered there. Frequencies of ground stone implements on all these sites and at Paquimé are listed in table 6.12.

As the preceding table shows, manos and metates, which we term Group 1 implements, were by far the most common ground stone tools found on all sites. This is not surprising given their universal role as essential food preparation tools. Group 2 consists of small bowls and pestles, axes, mauls, polishing stones, and grooved shaft or bone awl smoothers. These represent other pieces of widespread technology. Ground stone Group 3 includes pieces with less obvious function, such as small pallets and disks, balls, effigies, pipes, stools rasps, altar stones, and decorated stone bowls. We consider these to be luxury or ceremonial items. Group 4 consists of architectural elements, prominently including birdcage doors and the stone stoppers used to close them. Heavy ground stone disks or slabs were used as post bases or caps in the Paquimé rooms. A fifth group consists of ground or

TABLE 6.12 Frequencies of ground stone implements on Core Zone sites

	Paquimé	315	565	204	290	355	231	317	242
Size, core location[a]	Very large, ICZ	Large, ICZ	Large, ICZ	Large, OCZ	Small, ICZ	Small, ICZ	Small, OCZ	Small, OCZ	Small, OCZ
Piece count	~6,000	255	238	562	9	10	18	20	32
Manos	26.3% (1,293)	50.2% (128)	50.5% (120)	53.9% (303)	44.5% (4)	20.0% (2)	53.5% (10)	60% (12)	62.5% (20)
Mano blanks	n.d. (100s)	0.8% (2)	—	3.9% (22)	—	—	—	—	—
Metates	6.6% (327)	13.8% (35)	21.0% (50)	13.9% (82)	33.3% (3)	30.0% (3)	27.8% (5)	20.0% (4)	3.1% (1)
Bowls/ mortars	4.4% (218)	10.2% (26)	5.0% (12)	4.4% (26)	—	30.0% (3)	—	5.0 % (1)	6.3% (2)
Pestles	4.0% (197)	3.1% (8)	5.9% (14)	2.5% (15)	—	10.0% (1)	5.5% (1)	5.0 % (1)	3.1% (1)
Axes	18.3% (904)	3.9% (10)	2.9% (7)	3.0% (18)	—	—	5.5% (1)	5.0% (1)	—
Mauls	3.3% (165)	5.1% (13)	6.3% (15)	1.9% (11)	—	—	—	—	—
Polishing stone	27.4% (1,352)	7.5% (19)	3.0% (7)	4.2% (25)	—	10.0% (1)	5.5% (1)	5.0% (1)	9.4% (3)
Grooved abrader	1.6% (84)	3.5% (9)	1.3% (3)	0.8% (5)	—	—	—	—	3.1% (1)
Balls	1.7% (75)	1.2% (3)	3.3% (8)	2.7% (16)	—	—	—	—	—
Effigies	1.7% (84)	0.4% (1)	—	0.5% (3)	—	—	—	—	3.1% (1)
(Many more)	n.d. (100s)	—	—	—	—	—	—	—	—
Birdcage doors	2.5% (125)	0.4% (1)	—	0.5% (3)	—	—	—	—	6.3% (2)
Cage door plugs	1.9% (95)	0.4% (1)	—	0.2% (1)	—	—	—	—	3.1% (1)

[a] ICZ = Inner Core Zone; OCZ = Outer Core Zone.

polished stone implements, containing beads, pendants, and other sorts of ornaments, but these are discussed in a later chapter.

Although ground stone implements were ubiquitous in the communities investigated here, they were not evenly distributed among the large and small sites of the Inner and Outer Core Zones. The Paquimé assemblage was by far the region's largest and most diverse, consisting of 36 major categories. Neighboring large sites showed markedly lower variety. Inner Core large Sites 315 and 565 contained, respectively, 19 and 14 of these categories, while Outer Core large Site 204 had 20. The number of artifact categories on small sites all over the Core Zone is only 4.3. As might be expected, the most common everywhere were Groups 1 and 2, with their obvious technological functions. Much less common were the luxury/ceremonial and architectural elements of Groups 3 and 4, and these were almost completely absent on small sites. The only exception to this is Outer Core small Site 242, on which we recorded 9 categories of ground stone implements, plus several of Groups 3 and 4. Site 242 is far from an ordinary small settlement, however. It has been characterized as a Paquimé control node with administrative and ritual functions.

As noted earlier in this discussion, the Paquimé data were collected differently from those of the other Core Zone sites shown in table 6.12. The Paquimé collection strategy was biased toward whole pieces, while all eight of the other Core Zone collections contain numerous fragmentary pieces, many of them identifiable to type. These were tabulated with the whole pieces, making those category percentages considerably greater than the whole piece–based Paquimé counts. Manos and their fragments, for example, make up 50 to 60 percent of assemblages. The Paquimé count is only about 25 percent, but it would be misleading to conclude that Paquimé had only half as many manos as its neighbors. Instead, the utility of the Paquimé column of table 6.12 is to emphasize the diversity of this large assemblage. As with other artifact categories, the intent of this discussion is to show how ground stone assemblages vary among sites of different sizes and in different parts of the Core Zone.

Group 1 food preparation tools (manos and metates) were almost always accompanied by small stone bowls and pestles, which were frequently found together. They probably played some small but important role in food preparation or in other technologies. Bowls and pestles were equally widespread at Paquimé, where they were found in every excavated room unit and all across the site's history (Rinaldo 1974b:39). Other utilitarian ground stone implements such as axes, mauls, polishing stones, and grooved shaft abraders were present on all large sites. They likely represent a range of common activities, such as chopping, pounding, and polishing of everything from pottery to bone awls. These implements were only sporadically present on small sites, however, none of which contained all of them. This implies a range of small site activities that was more limited than that of large sites. Small sites all over the Core Zone, then, do not appear to be simply miniature versions of large ones.

This is further evident in the distribution and frequencies of ground stone items of Groups 3 and 4, or those items that are not so clearly utilitarian. These were characterized in preceding pages as having luxury, symbolic, ceremonial, or architectural functions.

While they were always present on large sites, things of this sort were much rarer and of more limited variety than those from Paquimé. Effigies and birdcage door stones from Inner Core Zone sites are shown in figure 6.4. Note that the Paquimé column of table 6.12 shows only those Group 3 and 4 items that also occurred on at least some neighboring large sites. We emphasize that all of them were conspicuously absent on small sites all over the Core Zone, except for Site 242 and two birdcage doors and one stopper found on the surfaces of two small Outer Core Zone sites by the regional survey (Whalen and Minnis 2001a:130, fig. 4.12). Birdcage doors and stoppers, then, were more common on large and small sites of the Outer Core Zone than on their Inner Zone contemporaries, excepting Paquimé.

Raw Materials

Vesicular basalt was clearly the material of choice for ground stone implements at Paquimé. It was also widely used in the surrounding area, but not to the near-exclusive extent seen at the principal center. It has long been known that basalt is common in the Sierra Madre and in the adjacent Basin-and-Range Zone. There was likely quarrying of vesicular basalt, as some of the metates were made from pieces weighing 50 kg (T. VanPool and Leonard 2002:720). These are too large to have been collected from drainages. There was only this circumstantial evidence of vesicular basalt quarrying until recently, when a quarry with manufacturing debris and stone-reducing tools was found on the edge of the Casas Grandes River valley, some 6 km south of Paquimé (Searcy and Pitezel 2018). Michael Searcy and Todd Pitezel note the presence of other basaltic flows in exposed areas of the Cerro de Moctezuma, where the present quarry is located. Likewise, Todd VanPool and Robert D. Leonard (2002:720) noted other vesicular basalt sources in similar contexts in the area. Searcy and Pitezel began the work of chemical characterization of vesicular basalt from their quarry, but we still lack systematic reconnaissance of sources, combined with mineralogical and chemical characterization of the area's vesicular basalt flows.

The processes and priorities of vesicular basalt distribution remain unclear. VanPool and Leonard (2002) argued that manufacture and distribution of standardized vesicular basalt metates was a component of the Paquimé-focused economic system of Medio times. In reality, however, we have no indication that Paquimé controlled and distributed vesicular basalt tools. Our tabulations from the site report (Rinaldo 1974b:163–72) show that vesicular basalt was the material of nearly all metates recovered at Paquimé. A similar preponderance of this material is seen in the center's mano assemblage and in other ground stone implement categories. As with other categories of desirable commodities, the assumption has been that since Paquimé had more implements of vesicular basalt than any other community, it must have been the distribution center. Objections have been raised to this scenario with regard to marine shell and macaws (Whalen 2013, 2022), arguing that much went into Paquimé but little came out again. The center, in other words, absorbed rather than distributed certain classes of artifacts. It appears that carefully shaped grinding tools of vesicular basalt should be added to this list.

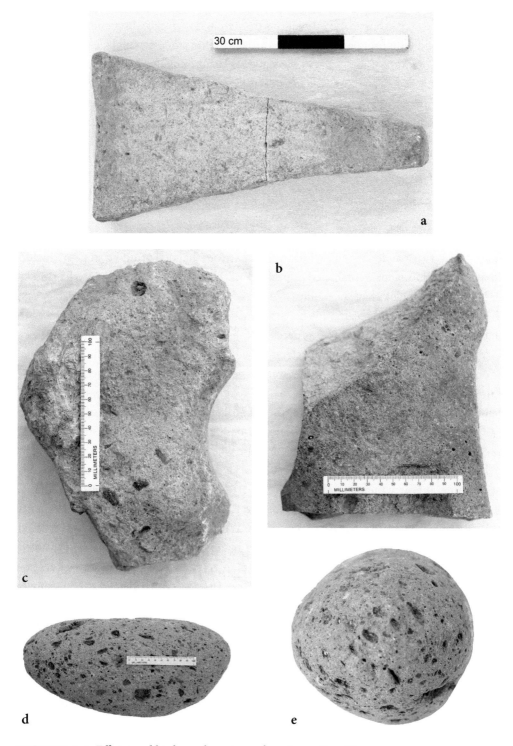

FIGURE 6.4 Effigies and birdcage door stones from Inner Core Site 315.

Specifically, some 98 percent of the manos and metates at Paquimé were of shaped vesicular basalt, according to our tabulations from Rinaldo's (1974b) discussion. That material represented no more than 49 percent of the grinding stone assemblage on large sites all over the Core Zone. Small sites in the same area had frequencies of these implements that did not exceed 14 percent. The only exception is Outer Core small Site 242, where 41 percent of the grinding stones were vesicular basalt. Site 242 was also the only small one with ground stone effigies and birdcage doors and stoppers, as Table 6.12 shows. This small administrative site, then, had a large site ground stone assemblage. We turn now to consideration of specific ground stone implements among Core Zone sites.

Manos

These ubiquitous tools are divisible into large and small categories. The former are often described as two-handed manos, while the latter are one-handed grinding stones (Rinaldo 1974b:172). Large manos were shaped by pecking and abrasion into blanks shaped like bricks or loaves. Mano blanks have been illustrated in several sources (e.g., Rinaldo 1974b:57–58; T. VanPool and Leonard 2002:711; Whalen and Minnis 2009:211) With use, the blocks wore into increasingly thin pieces. Some 85 percent of the manos at Paquimé were made of vesicular basalt, but this situation did not extend to neighboring communities, where an average of only 41 percent of the grinding stones were vesicular basalt. The highest frequency (54%) came from Outer Core Zone large Site 204, while on the large near neighbors of Paquimé, Sites 315 and 565, less than 45 percent of the mano sample was vesicular basalt.

Carefully shaped mano blanks of vesicular basalt showed a similar distribution. We presume that these blanks were given their shape where quarried, smoothed, and brought in bricklike form to Medio communities. It is not surprising that they were most numerous at Paquimé, although their exact number is uncertain. Rinaldo (1974b:172) observes that "a number" of mano blanks were found at the site. There were an additional 64 implements that he termed "block planes." An earlier study (Whalen and Minnis 2009:211–12) showed that these block planes closely resemble mano blanks. In fact, Rinaldo (1974b:57) noted that some of his block planes might be mano blanks. The second-largest known assemblage of mano blanks comes from Outer Core large Site 204, which yielded 23 blanks in its 592-piece assemblage. This is far fewer than Paquimé but far larger than the blank count at any other site. Large Inner Core Sites 315 and 565 together had a ground stone assemblage of 547 pieces. The assemblage varieties of all three sites were similar, as table 6.12 shows. Nevertheless, of the large Inner Core sites, 315 alone yielded just two vesicular basalt mano blanks, one of which is shown in figure 6.5. These numbers are again consistent with the idea of Paquimé as the principal consumer of vesicular basalt mano blanks, rather than the regional distributor.

The second category of mano is the small one-handed grinding stone found on Core Zone sites in numbers approximating those of their large counterparts. Compared to the large manos, the small ones were much more variable in size, shape, and raw material. This suggests that they were used in a wide range of activities ubiquitous in Medio period

FIGURE 6.5 A vesicular basalt mano blank from Inner Core Site 315.

FIGURE 6.6 Small manos from Inner Core Zone Sites 315 and 565.

communities. Some small manos were carefully shaped disks or ovals, while many others were simply minimally altered cobbles of convenient hand size. Most small manos were not made from vesicular basalt. Used instead was a wide range of fine-grained basalt, felsite, andesite, ignimbrite, and rhyolite, as shown in figure 6.6. Essentially, small manos were made of all local volcanic rocks that can be gathered in most drainages. Outer Core small Site 242 is again the only exception. There, about 30 percent (5/16) of the small manos were made of vesicular basalt.

Metates

The other ubiquitous category of ground stone tool is the metate, or grinding slab. Despite their central role in food preparation, metates were always much less common than manos for several reasons. First, they wear out more slowly than the smaller manos, requiring less frequent replacement and thus contributing less to the archaeological record. Second, metates or major parts of them were likely removed from their original sites from late prehistoric times to the present day. In the former case, they could be reused for grinding. Today, we have observed that whole or fragmentary prehistoric metates commonly adorn local gardens and courtyards.

The region's largest sample of metates comes from Paquimé, where a number of morphological types were defined (Rinaldo 1974b:162–69). To this we add a broader set of categories based on the extent of alteration of the original parent rock shapes. Shaped vesicular basalt metates, like the mano blanks just discussed, were hammered, pecked, and ground into blank shapes where they were quarried. Searcy and Pitezel (2018) detail the tools and shaping debris found on their newly discovered vesicular basalt quarry. This group includes variants of Rinaldo's Type I metates. VanPool and Leonard (2002) argued that shaped vesicular basalt metate blanks resulted from a standardized production process that was the work of specialized artisans. Unshaped metates make up Rinaldo's Type II and Type III categories. The first, basin metates, are thick chunks of rock with shallow oval central grinding basins. The second unshaped type contains thinner slabs of stone, again with oval central grinding basins. Both retain the original shapes of the parent rocks. Figure 6.7 illustrates these metate types.

Shaped metates make up nearly 98 percent of the reported total from Paquimé, and nearly all of them were vesicular basalt (Rinaldo 1974b:164–69). The situation is otherwise among neighboring communities. Shaped Type I metates and their fragments compose only 50 percent of the grinding stones collected on Inner Core large Sites 315 and 565. Of these, only 30 percent were made of vesicular basalt. The remaining 70 percent were made

FIGURE 6.7 Shaped and unshaped metates from Inner Core Site 315.

of other volcanic rocks, such as rhyolite, ignimbrite, andesite, and felsite. Outer Core large Site 204 presents a similar picture. Only 60 percent of its metates and fragments are of the shaped Type I sort, and only 50 percent of these were vesicular basalt, even at control center Site 242. The other 50 percent were made of the volcanic rocks just listed for the Inner Core Zone's large sites. Although Site 204 had many more vesicular basalt manos and mano blanks than both of the large Inner Core sites combined, this majority does not extend as far when considering shaped metates of that stone. All small sites of the Core Zone had even simpler assemblages. Among all five of them, there was one identifiable fragment from the side of a shaped Type IA metate. This is the type that was overwhelmingly dominant at Paquimé. The presence of a single Type IA fragment on small Inner Core Site 290 is difficult to interpret as it could have been picked up from other sites of the Inner Core. Recall from preceding chapters of this volume that Site 290 showed a great deal of PCGAT reconstruction, together with a restricted artifact assemblage. The other small sites of the Core Zone had few metate fragments, most of which were of the unshaped slab variety.

Other Ground Stone Implements

Beyond manos and metates, two fairly common categories of ground stone implements were found on all large sites and in smaller numbers on most of the small ones. These are polishing or abrading stones and stone bowls and their associated pestles. As Rinaldo (1974b:49) used the term, abrading stones were used in polishing everything from wood, bone, and stone to the surfaces of ceramic vessels. They were small implements that could be grasped by one hand, made from various raw materials, and their shapes were little altered from natural cobbles. They were common at Paquimé but less so at the other large Core Zone sites studied here (see table 6.12). Part of this imbalance is due to classificatory differences. There is sometimes an unclear division between abrading stones and one-handed manos. For example, McKay (2005:87) identified many abrading stones at Site 204, while we reassigned some of them to the one-handed mano category. Despite this classificatory difference, it is clear that polishing or abrading stones were important in Medio period technology. They were found on all large sites and on most of the smaller ones, and there is no significant difference in their frequencies between large sites of the Inner and Outer Core Zones.

The last common ground stone implement to be considered here is the stone bowl and pestle set. The small bowls were carefully pecked and ground to smooth symmetrical shapes. Many were circular, with diameters of 10 to 15 cm (figure 6.8). Others were square, measuring about 15 cm on a side. Both shapes had flat smooth bases. Their interior grinding basins are deep and finely finished, reflecting the square or circular shape of the piece. Wall and floor thicknesses were 2 to 3 cm. None of the bowls in this sample had any exterior decoration. These bowls are simpler counterparts of the assemblage found at Paquimé. There, most bowls were square or circular, but a few had oval, rectangular, and cruciform shapes. Other stone bowls at Paquimé showed finely finished exterior surfaces on which geometric designs had been cut and ground. Rinaldo (1974b:318) termed these "ceremonial bowls." None was found in our Core Zone sample. The same author observes, however, that there was sometimes little difference in finish between ceremonial bowls and those of the general category (Rinaldo 1974b:207). Ground stone bowls were often found in association with pestles (figure 6.8), indicating that they formed a functional complex. These pestles were as symmetrically shaped and finely finished as the vessels themselves. Pestles were either cylindrical or conical in outline. Of the latter group, the widest end formed the domed grinding surface. Pestles were sized in proportion to the bowls, measuring 10 to 12 cm long by 3 to 4 cm in diameter at the grinding end.

FIGURE 6.8 Stone bowls and pestles from Inner Core sites 315, 355, and 565.

The sizes of bowls and pestles suggest that they were used to grind small quantities of material. This sometimes involved heat, as Rinaldo (1974b:207) writes that "a considerable portion" of the stone bowls from Paquimé were sooted or burned. Other Paquimé bowls contained traces of the red, white, and yellow pigments that had been ground in them. Our smaller sample of bowls from neighboring sites did not include any that were burned or stained with pigments. The laborious shaping and fine finishing of these bowls and pestles would have consumed a good deal of labor, making them costly items that were likely employed for purposes beyond the purely utilitarian. We found no examples of crudely shaped or poorly finished bowls or pestles.

Stone Tool Use in Core Zone Settlements

Chipped stone cores, flakes, and debris were present on all Core sites, albeit at different frequencies. Predictably, large sites had the most chipped stone. Their discard rates, calculated as a ratio of chipped stone to ceramic pieces, were twice those of most small sites. We note that extremely low discard rates were found at Inner Core small Sites 290 and 321, which are occupations characterized by large amounts of PCGAT construction. Differences between these two small sites and their counterparts are outstanding throughout this discussion. Despite this variability, the same set of locally available raw materials were knapped at all Core sites. Medio people took the abundant volcanic and siliceous raw materials of their surroundings and used them as found. The three types of stone in highest frequency everywhere are chert, basalt, and rhyolite.

Core reduction and tool production represent two trajectories of stone knapping, and each produces interpretable characteristics in lithic debris. Most effort in all Medio period contexts was clearly on expedient flake production from amorphous cores. There was little biface production. The largest single category of core all over the study area and on sites of all sizes was multidirectional. Flakes were removed opportunistically by hard hammer percussion and without platform preparation. Fragmentary cores were common all over the Core, often outnumbering whole ones on large and small sites. Predictably, lithic discard rates were lower on small sites than on large ones all over the Core. Last, bipolar reduction is found at all sites all over the Core Zone, but it was never a major strategy. Although it is a simple, easy reduction technique, it was used only for chert, chalcedony, and obsidian. These are high-quality raw materials that occur in small nodules or veins. The bipolar technique was not used on large abundant pieces of volcanic stone.

Large sites all over the Core Zone showed similar sequences of core reduction. There were relatively few primary flakes and increasing numbers of secondary and tertiary pieces. Large Core Zone sites were characterized by relatively high frequencies of broken flakes and by considerable amounts of debris. In addition, we note that large sites all over the Inner Core Zone were found to have significantly higher frequencies of flakes of fine-grained siliceous stone, while frequencies of flakes made from medium-grained volcanic rocks are lower than expected.

Flake sizes are influenced by reduction trajectory and intensity and by the type of stone used. The expedient hard hammer core reduction just described for the entire Core Zone would produce flakes of various shapes and sizes, and intensive core reduction would produce increasingly small flakes and debris. The area's knappable stone also played a major role in limiting flake sizes. Volcanic stones like rhyolite, basalt, ignimbrite, and andesite are present all over the Core Zone in sizable pieces. Siliceous stone occurs in small to medium nodules or veins. The natural piece sizes of obsidian are smaller still. Not surprisingly, flakes of volcanic stone were always longer, wider, and thicker than those of siliceous material or obsidian. Most of the Core Zone flakes of all materials were 1 to 3 cm long, suggesting fairly small light tasks.

Large Core Zone sites contained a higher frequency of faceted platforms than did small ones. Extensive platform faceting is associated with soft hammer billet flaking. Large sites, therefore, might show evidence of more late-stage, finer scale knapping than would their small counterparts. One curious result of this chapter's statistical tests, however, is that large sites show lower frequencies of lipping, while small sites showed the opposite pattern of more lipping. This need not point unambiguously to more soft hammer percussion, as there is opinion in the literature that lipping is not exclusive to that technique. Hard hammer use on very hard stone, for instance, produces some lips. Prominent bulbs are another indication of hard hammer percussion, and they are common at large and small sites all over the Core Zone. Flat bulbs, and the implied billet flaking, were also found everywhere, although at lower frequencies. Again, small Inner Core Sites 290 and 321 showed the region's lowest frequencies of flat bulbs. These sites have substantial construction in the PCGAT style, and they appear to have even less soft hammer reduction than other Inner Core sites. Small sites 290 and 321 also stand out as having the sample's highest frequency of shattered bulbs, as well as high frequencies of step fractures and relatively low counts of feather terminations. In general, these two small sites seem to contain evidence of more expedient core reduction than do their neighbors.

A constant characteristic of Medio period lithic assemblages all over the Core Zone is scarcity of retouched tools. Instead, flakes were struck from amorphous cores and used, without retouching. This is borne out by microscopic use-wear analysis of a sample of chert and rhyolite flakes from Outer Core Zone large Site 204. Nearly all specimens were single function pieces that were likely discarded after brief use. Cutting, scraping, drilling, graving, and chopping actions were in evidence, although most use-wear was suggestive of the cutting of medium-hardness materials, including wood and fibrous plant matter. This accords well with what is known of Medio subsistence practices.

In addition to utilized flakes, another common type of tool was the agave knife, also known as a tabular knife. These are heavy hand-sized cutting and scraping tools made of locally abundant rhyolite. Their edges were coarsely retouched, but the surfaces of the stones were otherwise little altered. These tools were found on large and small sites all over the Core Zone. They were most common on Outer Core Zone sites, where agave is believed to have been grown.

The only finely retouched implement is the small triangular projectile point. These were made of high-quality obsidian and chert, and they come almost exclusively from the large sites of the Core Zone, including Paquimé. Found on large Core Zone sites is a second group of projectile points that are neither small nor triangular. Their styles place them in the Late Archaic and early Ceramic times. They demonstrate a long-lasting pattern of collection of earlier projectile points by later populations.

Inner Core Zone sites, even the large ones, yielded little obsidian compared to large Site 204 and small Site 242 of the Outer Core. More than 700 pieces of obsidian were recovered at Paquimé, vastly outnumbering the combined obsidian totals of the entire Core Zone. The abundance of obsidian at Paquimé, combined with its paucity among large near neighbors, shows that many obsidian nodules were going into Paquimé, while few went out again. There is no indication that Paquimé distributed obsidian to its neighbors. Indeed, given the ubiquity of the material, it is hard to imagine how the supply could have been controlled.

Like chipped stone, implements of ground stone were found on all Core Zone sites, although there were notable differences between the assemblages of large and small communities. Each size category is much alike. The Paquimé assemblage consists of 36 categories of ground stone implement. The number of artifact categories on large sites all over the Core Zone is 11.7, whereas the comparable figure for small sites is only 4.3. The only exception to this is Outer Core small Site 242, where 9 categories were found. It is clear that the range of small site activities involving ground stone tools was more limited than that of large sites.

Ground stone implements were divided into five groups, according to their frequencies on Core Zone sites. Group 1 contains manos and metates. These would have been basic to food preparation, and they are by far the most common ground stone tools found on all sites. Also fairly common are Group 2 implements, including small bowls and pestles, axes, mauls, polishing stones, and grooved shaft or bone awl smoothers. These represent additional pieces of everyday technology. Group 3 contains less obviously utilitarian pieces, such as small pallets and disks, balls, effigies, pipes, stools, rasps, altar stones, and decorated stone bowls. These were likely luxury or ceremonial items, and they occur on large sites. They are seldom found on small sites, except for administrative node 242 of the Outer Core Zone. Also limited to large sites and to administrative small Site 242 are Group 4 items. These are architectural elements: birdcage doors and the stone stoppers used to close them, plus disks or slabs that were used as post bases or caps in rooms. Group 5 contains ornaments such as beads and pendants. These are found only on large sites and on small Site 242, and they are discussed in chapter 7 of this volume.

The ground stone implements everywhere were made of basalt, both vesicular and fine grained, rhyolite, ignimbrite, andesite, felsite, and tuff. These materials are common in the Sierra Madre and in the adjacent Basin and Range Zone. In fact, basalts have been characterized as one of the major suites of mid-Tertiary rocks in Northwest Mexico. Medio populations thus made use of local stone that was widely available all over the eastern slope of the Sierra Madre. Vesicular basalt was clearly the material of choice for ground stone implements at Paquimé. It was also widely used in the surrounding area, but not to the near-exclusive extent seen at the principal center. For example, 98 percent of the manos and metates at Paquimé were of shaped vesicular basalt, while this material made up less than half of the grinding stone assemblage on large sites all over the Core Zone. Small sites in the same area had frequencies of these implements that did not exceed 14 percent. Small Outer Core Zone Site 242 is again an exception, as 41 percent of its grinding stones were vesicular basalt. An exceptionally close connection to the principal center has been suggested in this case. Still, Paquimé had most of the area's tools of vesicular basalt, and the scarcity of this material among its closest large neighbors argues against the idea that the center was a distributor. Previous discussion in this volume saw Paquimé as an absorber rather than a distributor of certain classes of artifacts. It is here argued that carefully shaped grinding tools of vesicular basalt should be added to this list.

This chapter and the preceding one discuss the most obviously utilitarian artifacts found on Core Zone sites: ceramics and lithics. The succeeding chapter considers exotic and sumptuary goods that likely functioned in other aspects of social life.

 *Chapter 7*

Exotic and Ritual Items and Facilities in the Core Zone

Paquimé has long been famous for its vast quantities of exotic and imported items, many of which appear to have been used in ritual and ceremonial activities. Such things are also found among the center's neighbors, and the question of this chapter is how exotic and ritual items were distributed among the large and small sites of the Core Zone, including Paquimé. The raw materials involved in the manufacture of some of these items include marine shell, copper, and minerals of various sorts, all of which were imported into the Casas Grandes area. Likewise, some of the macaws of Paquimé are not native to northwestern Chihuahua. Because Paquimé possessed all these things in such quantity and diversity, it has long been assumed to have accumulated and distributed them to neighboring communities. The argument of this chapter, however, is that although Paquimé consumed exotic materials and items on a vast scale, it distributed few or none to neighboring settlements. Even the largest of these neighbors possessed only bits of the finery of the principal center. Each category of exotica is considered below.

Shell

Frequencies of different sorts of shell items at Paquimé and among its large and small Core Zone neighbors are shown in table 7.1. Note that no shell was recovered from Inner Core Zone small Sites 290 and 321 or from Outer Core small Site 242, so these are excluded from the following table.

None of the neighbors had anything like the cache of millions of whole-shell beads found at Paquimé. Among them, the most common ornament type is the small shell bead, which occurs in several types. First among these is the flat disk bead. These were cut from pieces of shell, perforated in the center, and ground into circular outlines (figure 7.1a). Whole-shell beads are the next most common. Many of these are small univalve shells with the ends removed for stringing (figure 7.1b), while others, primarily small gastropods, were pierced through their sides (figure 7.1c). This latter type of whole-shell bead makes

TABLE 7.1 Shell items at Paquimé and its neighbors

	Inner Core Zone				Outer Core Zone		
Item	Paquimé[a]	315 (Large)	565 (Large)	355 (Small)	204 (Large)	231 (Small)	317 (Small)
Truncated shell bead	11,542 (14.3%)	4 (2.5%)	1 (6.7%)	—	6 (4.6%)	—	—
Whole-shell bead	3.7 million (—)[b]	4 (2.5%)	2 (13.3%)	—	17 (13.1%)	1 (5.9%)	—
Disk bead	41,994 (52.3%)	130 (86.9%)	—	1 (20.0%)	5 (3.8%)	—	—
Other type of bead	275 (0.3%)	—	—	—	1 (0.8%)	—	—
Tinkler	21,852 (27.3%)	5 (3.1%)	3 (20.0%)	3 (60.0%)	11 (8.5%)	—	—
Pendant	4,218 (5.2%)	5 (3.1%)	1 (6.6%)	—	17 (13.1%)	3 (17.6%)	1 (8.3%)
Bracelet	435 (0.5%)	2 (1.3%)	—	—	2 (1.5%)	—	—
Other worked pieces	183 (0.2%)	1 (0.6%)	4 (26.7%)	1 (20.0%)	23 (17.7%)	7 (41.2%)	5 (41.4%)
Unworked pieces	No data	—	—	—	48 (36.9%)	6 (35.3%)	6 (50.0%)

[a] Paquimé data compiled from Di Peso et al. 1974:6:401–526.
[b] Percentage not calculated for this table, as others would be reduced to near-zero.

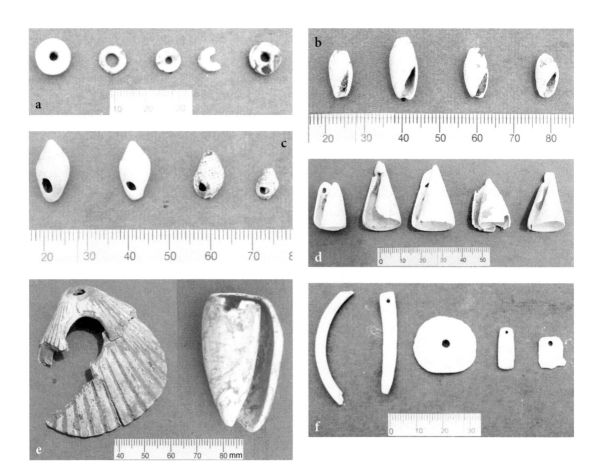

FIGURE 7.1 Shell ornaments from Inner Core Sites 315 and 565.

up the cache of millions at Paquimé. *Tinklers* are lower segments of univalve shells, cut so as to form a hollow cone (figure 7.1d). Pendants of various shapes were formed from cut-out pieces of shell (figure 7.1e), while bracelets are the outer rims of large bivalve shells (figure 7.1f). Other worked pieces assume various forms (figure 7.1f). Fragments of shell are shown in the table 7.1 as "unworked pieces."

These data show that large sites contain much greater quantity and diversity of shell ornaments than do their small neighbors. We note that shell ornament quantity and diversity at all large Core Zone sites was likely greater than that shown in table 7.1. All three of these sites were heavily looted over the past half century, and shell beads and bits were frequently found scattered over their surfaces. In particular, we were told by knowledgeable locals that large quantities of exotic materials were taken from Inner Core Site 315, which is the closest to Paquimé of any studied here.

The paucity of shell on small sites was most extreme in the Inner Core Zone. There, two of them (290 and 321) yielded no shell at all, while the third (355) had very little. Preceding chapters of this volume show that these three small sites were deficient in other artifact categories when compared to their counterparts of the Outer Core Zone (Sites 231 and 317). It was also demonstrated that all three small Inner Core sites showed a good deal of Post–Casas Grandes Architectural Tradition (PCGAT) construction, while there was none on the small Outer Core sites. It thus appears that some of the occupations of the small Inner Core sites postdated the time when shell was coming into the Casas Grandes area.

The shell found on Core Zone sites represents various genera, most of which are available in the Sea of Cortez, some 400 km (240 miles) from the Casas Grandes area. As usual, Paquimé far exceeds any of its neighbors in its diversity of shell. More than 50 genera were identified there, some of which are shown in table 7.2. Those selected for the table include all common genera, as well as all those identified on neighboring sites. A full account of the Paquimé shell is provided elsewhere (Di Peso et al. 1974:6:401–526). The first point of note in table 7.2 is that a few genera make up most of the shell at all sites, while other genera make up minute percentages of the entire assemblage. A second point is that among the Core Zone neighbors, large sites contained all common genera plus a few rarer ones. Small sites present a much simpler picture, containing only a few of the common genera. Especially noteworthy are the frequencies of freshwater shell on Core Zone sites. Many of these at Paquimé were *Rabdotis*, a terrestrial gastropod (Di Peso et al. 1974:6:405). Also present are pieces cut from the nacreous parts of freshwater mussel shells. These contribute only a small fraction of the center's shell assemblage, however.

The situation is otherwise at the center's neighbors. The total numbers of shell genera identified at Outer Core large Site 204 are shown in table 7.1. The inventory appears to be diverse, but the picture changes considerably when the recovered shell is divided into early and late contexts. Recall that the Early Medio period predates the ascendency of Paquimé, which dates to the Late Medio or after about AD 1300. The following discussion is abstracted from Whalen and Minnis (2009:241). Ten genera of marine shell were recovered from Site 204 deposits. Eight genera came from Early Medio midden levels or room deposits, whereas only two different genera were present in Late Medio contexts. By the

TABLE 7.2 Genera of shell found on Core Zone sites

		Inner Core Zone			Outer Core Zone		
Item	Paquimé[a]	315 (Large)	565 (Large)	355 (Small)	204 (Large)	231 (Small)	317 (Small)
Nassarius	3.7 mil (—)	2 (9.1%)	1 (5.9%)	—	1 (1.0%)	—	—
Conus	31,365 (62.6%)	6 (27.3%)	3 (17.6%)	3 (100%)	16 (16.5%)	1 (5.9%)	—
Olivella	11,856 (23.6%)	5 (22.8%)	1 (5.9%)	—	5 (5.2%)	1 (5.9%)	2 (15.4%)
Laevicardium	1,144 (2.2%)	—	—	—	1 (1.0%)	—	—
Glycymeris	590 (1.2%)	3 (13.6%)	1 (5.9%)	—	7 (7.2%)	—	—
Aquipectin	147 (0.3%)	2 (9.1%)	2 (11.7%)	—	—	—	—
Pyrene	(<0.1%)	1 (4.5%)	—	—	—	—	—
Trivia	(<0.1%)	—	1 (5.9%)	—	—	—	—
Argopectin	(<0.1%)	—	—	—	1 (1.0%)	—	—
Turritella	(<0.1%)	1 (4.5%)	—	—	1 (1.0%)	—	—
Cerithedia	(<0.1%)	—	—	—	1 (1.0%)	—	—
Petaloconchus	(<0.1%)	—	—	—	2 (2.1%)	—	—
Pinctada	(<0.1%)	—	—	—	4 (4.1%)	—	—
Freshwater	116 (0.2%)	2 (9.1%)	8 (47.1%)	—	58 (59.9%)	15 (88.2%)	11 (84.6%)

[a] Paquimé data compiled from Di Peso et al. 1974:6:401–526.

Late Medio period, then, Site 204 resembles small Sites 231 and 317 in its paucity of marine shell genera. At the same time, freshwater shell at Site 204 increased from 48 percent of the Early Medio to 78 percent by Late Medio times. This pattern shows wider access to marine shell in the Early Medio period. By the Late Medio, when Paquimé was ascendant, regional access to marine shell appears to have diminished sharply, and increasing use was made of freshwater shell.

Around half of the shell assemblage is freshwater at large Site 565 of the Inner Core (figure 7.2), most of which belongs to the Late Medio period. Small Outer Core Late Medio Sites 231 and 317 show an even heavier reliance on freshwater shell, which composes nearly all of both assemblages. The regional survey data support this conclusion as well, in that 75 percent of the identified shell on site surfaces was freshwater. Most of the ceramic assemblages of these sites contained Ramos Polychrome, demonstrating the presence of Late Medio occupation components. The only departure from this pattern is Inner Core large Site 315, where the frequency of freshwater shell is less than 10 percent. While this figure is much lower than that of any other Core Zone neighbor, it is still much larger than the Paquimé figure. It thus appears that, by Late Medio times, the center of Paquimé had come to dominate the shell trade in the Casas Grandes area, largely keeping the material for its own use.

We suspect that freshwater shell was not of equivalent symbolic value to marine shell for Late Medio people in the Casas Grandes area. Freshwater shell is available everywhere, but it was dramatically underused all over ancient Europe, Asia, and the Americas, even at sites located far inland (Classen 1998:235). This preference for marine shell over freshwater

FIGURE 7.2 Freshwater shell from Inner Core Site 565.

varieties probably has to do with the origin of marine shell in seemingly limitless bodies of water, a point that is supported by Cheryl Classen's (1998) survey of worldwide beliefs about shell and its efficacy. This leads us to wonder how shell was used as a resource in the political and prestige economies of the Casas Grandes area. The original supposition was that shell at Medio period Paquimé served primarily for trade rather than for local use, and this was seen as a major departure from the pattern of the preceding Viejo period (Di Peso et al. 1974:7:385). Ronna Bradley (1999) also developed an argument that saw Paquimé as an active shell trader rather than simply a passive recipient. Instead of interpreting shell as a purely commercial commodity, Paul Minnis (1988, 1989) asserted that the shell of Paquimé represented accumulation of elite wealth. Still others (e.g., P. R. Fish and Fish 1999; Whalen and Minnis 2001a) considered shell ornaments to be prestige goods, dispensed by Paquimé elites.

Most recently, the hoard of millions of perforated shells at Paquimé has been viewed in a different light (Whalen 2013). The following is abstracted from that discussion. The hoarded shells did not serve as displays of elite wealth, as they were kept in architectural contexts of limited accessibility and low visibility. The paucity of shell among the neighbors of Paquimé is not consistent with the idea that it was dispersed from the center through trade or prestige goods gifts. Rather, it was accumulated at Paquimé in a context that is explicable as the materialization of supernatural power. All over the prehistoric Americas, shell was seen as a powerful animate object that influences water and rain, blesses and revives, re-creates, and animates other objects and people. It also protects and sanctifies places, endowing them with power and creating sacred landscapes. There is the idea that the power of marine shell to do these things may be magnified by increasing its quantity. Last, low-quality shells may be as effective as fine specimens of rare species. Other researchers have characterized Paquimé as a ritually charged place of pilgrimage, and its vast shell deposits could have been accumulated over time through ritual deposition. In short, extant literature shows that accumulation of meaningful things is a common way to create, empower, and maintain scared places. Extant literature also shows that prehistoric sites of concentration of meaningful objects generally result from a number of iterations of ritual performances. The literature on sacred place creation stresses the common idea of intensification by repetition where ritual features and ritual deposits are concerned. The vast shell deposits at Paquimé are thus interpreted as objects deposited by repetitive ritual carried out over some portion of the life of the community.

In previous discussion of Outer Core Zone sites (Whalen and Minnis 2009:241–42), we considered the surprising absence of shell on Outer Core Site 242. The occupation is well dated to the Late Medio, and there is no indication of the PCGAT construction that was so prominent on small Inner Core sites. Nor does the absence of shell on Site 242 seem to be a function of small sample size, since as much earth was excavated there as at small Sites 231 and 317. Last, Site 242 was not heavily looted compared to its contemporaries. In all other aspects, Site 242 was an extremely elaborate community. It had thick-walled architecture, macaw cages, a ceramic assemblage indicative of feasting, and the largest ritual complex known outside Paquimé. The site was interpreted as an administrative satellite of Paquimé whose role was to organize agricultural productivity in its part of the uplands (Whalen and Minnis 2001b). If, as argued above, marine shell was an important component of the creation and maintenance of the scared-place status of Paquimé, rather than being a universal object of prestige and wealth, then its scarcity at neighboring communities is readily explicable. They were not the central sacred place.

Also relevant to this discussion are frequencies of shell genera identified at Paquimé and its neighbors. This postulated control of marine shell seems to have extended only to the neighbors of Paquimé in the Core and Middle Zones. Farther away, in the Outer Zone, the Joyce Well site contained more abundant marine shell of *Olivella*, *Glycymeris*, *Ostrea*, and *Nassarius* genera, while no freshwater shell was reported (Skibo et al. 2002:35). Accordingly, we conclude that Paquimé controlled the regional marine shell supply and made little of it available to neighboring communities. Beyond the limit of this control, in the Outer Zone, quantities of marine shell were somewhat larger.

Macaws

One of the most famous aspects of Paquimé is the many macaw bones found there. Ceramics of the time carry a good deal of macaw imagery, and the birds and their feathers were likely as significant in ritual at Paquimé as they were in the wider pueblo world. See, for example, the papers collected by Schwartz et al. (2022). Other aspects of macaw husbandry are less clear. Di Peso (1974:2:599) argued for macaw breeding on a vast scale at Paquimé, where he numbered more than 500 birds, most of which were assigned to the scarlet macaw species (*Ara macao*). If true, this would amount to the largest sustained feat of macaw breeding in the history of the world before modern times.

Many hundreds of macaw bones were recovered from Paquimé. Some were whole or nearly whole birds, although many more were scattered, fragmentary, and poorly preserved (McKusick 1974a:284). It is clear from the field notes and drawings that there were many commingled deposits. Nevertheless, about 80 percent of all remains—whole and fragmentary—were identified to the species level as either scarlet or military macaws. These identifications were based on a set of species-defining characteristics developed by Lyndon Hargrave, who used skeletal measurements to define nine species-distinguishing morphological traits in a control sample of seven birds. Later, Ellen Ruble (1996) tested this identification system on a new and much larger sample of 31 scarlet macaws and 18 birds of the military species. She made 33 of Hargrave's original skeletal measurements on the new sample. A series of t-tests of mean difference of these 33 measurements in the scarlet and military populations showed that only 12 (36%) showed statistically significant mean differences between scarlet and military macaw populations, while 21 (64%) did not. A cluster analysis on the 12 significantly differing characteristics shows that measurements do not fall into two groups, but rather fall into three, which might be termed large, medium, and small sets. In short, the analysis shows that macaws with largest wing and leg bones almost certainly are of the scarlet species, while about half to three-quarters of those with small measurements are likely military macaws, although this group probably includes a number of scarlet macaws. Finally, Rubel's data show a sizable central group of medium measurements that contains members of both species. Ruble rightly concluded that only the largest specimens can be confidently classified to the species level based on simple morphological measurements, while cases in the middle ground cannot. Scarlet macaws average somewhat larger than their military cousins, so that the two can be distinguished by statistical analysis of large datasets *containing specific bones*. The Paquimé macaw remains, however, were fragmentary, incomplete, and often commingled, so the same parts of the skeletons were not likely to have been available for the species classification of every one of the 80 percent of the remains identified to that level.

At Paquimé, Hargrave's criteria seem to have formed the basis of a dichotomous scarlet or military scheme. Ruble performed a discriminant analysis that was instructed to separate her large sample of modern macaw remains into *either* scarlet or military species based on skeletal measurements. *Given only two choices, the discriminant function assigned nearly all specimens to the scarlet species.* That is, the analysis was apparently lumping the large and medium bones into a "large" (or scarlet macaw) category, the remaining small bones being military macaws. We suspect that this is what happened in the visual sorting of macaw remains at Paquimé, producing the reported large majority of the scarlet species.

In sum, we believe that (1) both scarlet and military macaws were at Paquimé, as originally reported; but (2) species proportions remain uncertain. This is a significant issue, as one of the two species (military) came from a nearby area, while the other (scarlet) is native to a distant one. Unfortunately, it cannot be resolved with the extant data in hand, and DNA analysis is required.

Contrary to established interpretations, Paquimé does not appear to have been a significant distributor of macaws to surrounding populations (see arguments by Whalen 2022:230–32). Instead, the center was a consumer of the birds. Preceding pages of this volume make the same argument for finely finished vesicular basalt implements, obsidian, and marine shell. Extension of this conclusion to macaws is reinforced by the paucity of their remains or cage facilities among the neighboring communities of the Core Zone. To date, only one macaw burial has been found outside the principal center. This was at Outer Core Zone large Site 204, and it consisted of the complete remains of one juvenile macaw of undetermined species. It had been buried in a shallow simple pit beneath the floor of a small, otherwise unremarkable room. There were no offerings. This was the same sort of shallow simple pit grave that was used for the macaws of Paquimé. No other site of the Inner or Outer Core Zone has yielded any macaw remains.

Despite the absence of bird remains, cage door stones were somewhat more widespread in the Inner and Outer Core Zones without ever being common. The regional survey noted 15 mostly fragmentary specimens of cage door stones on site surfaces. These seem to have been unearthed by looters, so that more attractive examples may have been carried away. It is interesting to note that all 15 of these sites are in the Outer Core Zone. Most of their surfaces and outer edges were only partially smoothed, although Outer Core Site 242 produced the finely shaped example shown elsewhere (Whalen and Minnis 2001a:243, fig. 8.2a). Paquimé also has such finely worked cage door stones, and we originally suggested that the coarse ones were a "rural" variety. This no longer appears to be true, as fragments of the coarse variety were found on Inner Core Site 315 (figure 7.3), the nearest large contemporary neighbor of Paquimé.

In summary, macaw remains and cage features are abundant at Paquimé, rare at its nearest large neighbors of the Inner Core, and more abundant, though still sparse, on the large and small sites of the Outer Core Zone. This is the same pattern seen for ball courts, obsidian, vesicular basalt grinding tools, and marine shell. In all of our Core Zone excavations, however, we found no traces of the adobe-walled holding pens that were present in quantity at Paquimé. Again, the situation seems to be that many macaws went into the principal center, while few were present among its neighbors. The handful that were not absorbed by Paquimé seem best represented in the Outer Core Zone.

Copper

Paquimé produced what is by far the region's greatest quantity and variety of copper artifacts. Nearly 700 copper artifacts and scraps were found there, leading to Di Peso's original characterization of the community as a copper working center. Two techniques of copper working are in evidence in the New World in general and at Paquimé in particular. The first is cold hammer shaping of flat pieces from nuggets. Copper is soft and relatively pure, so nodules can be flattened, and impurities hammered off their edges. The resulting thin pieces can be cut and cold shaped into simple forms like strips, cones, pendants, and beads. The second technique is more involved. Lost-wax casting requires smelting, and the resulting material is poured into molds formed by wax pieces covered in fine clay. Di Peso envisioned both forms of copper work at Paquimé, but this claim has been convincingly disputed (Vargas 1995). The following discussion is abstracted from the source just cited.

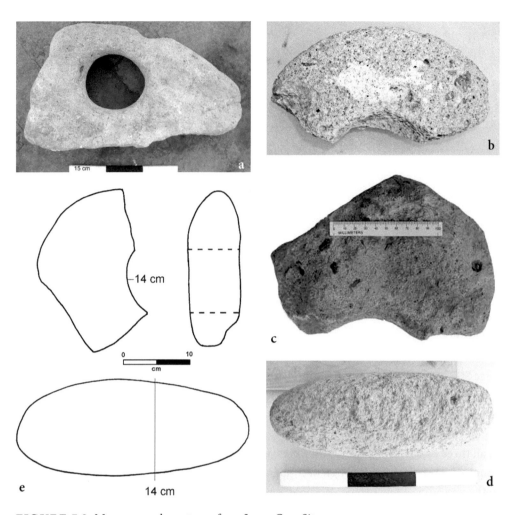

FIGURE 7.3 Macaw cage door stones from Inner Core Site 315.

Convincing evidence of copper smelting and casting is absent at Paquimé. Rather, the ornaments produced by this technique were imported already finished into the community, probably coming ultimately from western Mexico. Cold forming of simple shapes could have been done at Paquimé or elsewhere using imported copper sheets or even nuggets. Copper, then, appears to be an imported product rather than a local commodity, although source characterization work has yet to be conducted on northern Mexican copper deposits.

As at Paquimé, two kinds of copper ornaments were found among its Core Zone neighbors, although each was rare. Sometime before our excavations there, a cast copper bell was found on the surface of one of the small mounds (Mound B) of Outer Core Zone large Site 204. Edwin Sayles (1936a:59, plate XIX) illustrates three pendants, two bells, a wire ring, and a tinkler from the Ramos site. This is a community of four-room block mounds on the boundary between the Inner and Outer Core Zones. It has been heavily looted but never excavated by archaeologists. The site clearly had a rich and elaborate assemblage of exotica,

FIGURE 7.4 Copper pendant and ore fragments from Inner Core Site 315.

including finely ground bowls and pestles of vesicular basalt, a macaw cage door stone, shell, copper, turquoise, and various stone carvings. Were it not for Sayles's (1936a) report, however, we would have little idea of the variety of the site's exotica. It may well be that other sizable communities of the Core Zone (e.g., Sites 315 and 204) had similar assemblages before they were looted. At the time of our excavations at Sites 315 and 204, we were told that a great many elaborate things were taken by looters. The copper assemblage that we recovered from Site 315 is shown in figure 7.4. It consists of a simple pendant and four nuggets of raw copper. No copper came from site Inner Core Zone large Site 565, and only one cast copper bell is known from Outer Core Zone large Site 204. Copper from the Ramos site was described above.

Unfortunately, we cannot date most of the region's copper to Early Medio or Late Medio times. We are aware, however, that Sites 315, 204, and the Ramos site all have Early Medio occupation components, as demonstrated in the first two cases by radiocarbon dating and in all three cases by the ceramic assemblages. The Early Medio period predates the rise of Paquimé. There is also indication of copper in the Casas Grandes area before Medio times, in the preceding Viejo period. We note the presence of a bit of copper sheet plus a tinkler rolled from another piece of copper sheet at the Convento site (Di Peso et al. 1974:7:499). This is a Viejo period pit house and pit-house-to-pueblo transition village in the Casas Grandes River valley. The Convento site finds demonstrate that copper was coming into the area in the eleventh and twelfth centuries AD. This is long before the Medio period in the thirteenth century AD and even longer before the rise of Paquimé in the fourteenth century AD.

A scenario that is probable, although still unproved, is import of increasing amounts of copper from Viejo times onward. This is in line with the U.S. Southwest, where copper bells and other items were in circulation in the tenth, eleventh, and twelfth centuries AD. The Late Medio period of the fourteenth century AD clearly saw the apogee of this trade, and Paquimé may have achieved a near-monopoly on copper at the peak of its power, both as raw material and as finished ornaments. There might thus have been very little copper in circulation in the Casas Grandes area after the rise of the center. This remains unproved, although neighboring communities clearly had nothing like the abundance and variety of copper artifacts found at Paquimé. As with other exotica, the principal center seems more like a copper consumer than a distributor.

Turquoise, Crystal, and Other Minerals

Di Peso's original model of Paquimé as a major trade emporium connecting the U.S. Southwest and Mesoamerica envisioned a southward flow of turquoise in exchange for Mesoamerican commodities such as copper and scarlet macaws. A recent study (Thibodeau et al. 2018) casts doubt on this scenario. Lead/strontium ratios were used to characterize sources from a wide region, demonstrating that Aztec and Mixtec turquoise was not mined in the U.S. Southwest. It is more likely from Mesoamerican sources. Rather than being a trade item with societies to the south, turquoise appears to have been accumulated at Paquimé. It was worked into beads, pendants, and other tesserae, as well as blank pieces. In total, more than 4,000 pieces were found, making turquoise much more abundant than copper at Paquimé, while it was less common than marine shell. A few other minerals, such as quartz and calcite crystals, mica, hematite, petrified wood and fossil fragments, were found on the large Core sites. These data for Paquimé and its large Core neighbors are summarized in table 7.3. Turquoise is more plentiful in the Inner Core than in the outer part, and selenite is much more common in the Outer Core, although the numbers involved in this comparison are small. None came from the small sites of the Core, including small administrative Site 242 of the Outer Core Zone.

The massive imbalance of minerals between Paquimé and its Core Zone neighbors is clear from the table 7.3. Inner Core large Site 315 provided most of the Core Zone turquoise, of which there were 20 pendants and only 6 flat disk beads (figure 7.5a). A few turquoise pieces came from Site 355, the most elaborate of the Inner Core small sites. A number of large crystals of quartz were found at Site 315, the sizes of which suggest they were obtained from cave formations (figure 7.5b). A fragment of fossilized bone came from

TABLE 7.3 Minerals from large Core Zone sites

Mineral	Paquimé, ICZ[a]	351/565, ICZ	204[b], OCZ[c]
Specular hematite	14,192	1	4
Selenite	4,236	4	47
Turquoise	>4,000	20	13
Malachite	2,692	0	0
Quartz crystals	2,420	9	4
Fluorite	632	0	0
Serpentine	340	0	1
Calcite	274	7	4
Thenardite	272	0	0
Mica	57	8	14
Petrified wood, fossils	35	2	0

[a] Inner Core Zone.
[b] Data from Szarka (2006:tables 11 and 14).
[c] Outer Core Zone.

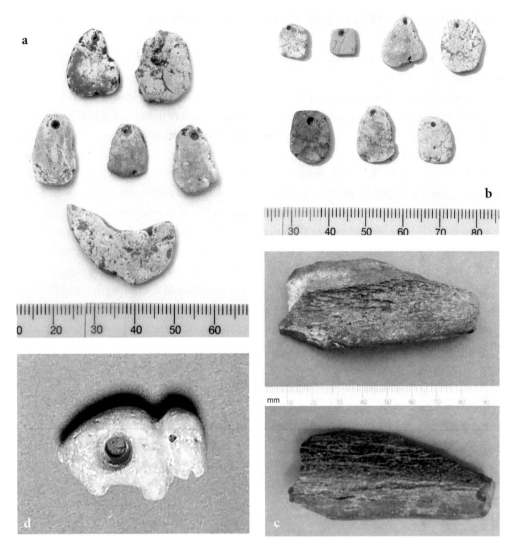

FIGURE 7.5 Minerals from Core Zone Sites 315 and 355.

Site 315 (figure 7.5c). Other minerals were worked into beads and pendants. Most of the latter were simple geometric forms, although a bison pendant came from Inner Core small Site 355 (figure 7.5d). Similar sorts of ornaments came from Outer Core Site 204, and they are illustrated elsewhere (Whalen and Minnis 2009:247, fig. 8.3; 25, fig. 8.4; and 253, fig. 8.7).

Concluding Thoughts

It is evident from the preceding discussion that Paquimé vastly exceeded its neighbors in quantity and variety of exotic and sumptuary goods and materials of all sorts. It is equally clear that nearly all sorts of exotica were present at much lower frequencies among the sites of the Core Zone. We do not see, however, a simple "gravity decline" in their frequencies with increasing distance from the principal center. This is what we would expect if Paquimé was a distributor of exotica and sumptuary items in a prestige goods situation. Rather, in every case we see (1) concentration at Paquimé; (2) absence or low frequencies of these things and facilities at Inner Core Zone neighbors; (3) a rise in the frequencies of all of them in the Outer Core Zone; and (4) return to zero or near-zero frequencies of exotica and sumptuary items in the Middle Zone. The sparse and sporadic distribution of exotica has been noted by others, who correctly observe: "Overall . . . the sumptuary goods present in the Casas Grandes region do not present distributions that conform to items either required by large segments of the population to mark widely observed rites of passage or utilized as regular payment for subsistence goods transported to the center as implied in a mercantile model" (Pailes and Searcy 2022:105).

The authors just cited are certainly correct in recognizing the sporadic distribution of exotica and sumptuary goods in the Casas Grandes area and beyond. Clearly, the great majority of people had little, even at Paquimé. We have noted elsewhere (Whalen and Minnis 2000:173) that most of the burials recovered at the center were not at all elaborate. The majority were interred in simple pit graves under room or plaza floors. Fewer than half of them (ca. 40%) had clearly associated mortuary offerings (Di Peso et al. 1974:8:363). About half of this group (ca. 20% of the burial sample) had only a ceramic vessel or two of common local types. A little jewelry of shell, copper, and other minerals was present in the remaining half of the furnished graves (ca. 20% of the total burial sample). There were few notable concentrations of sumptuary goods. Put another way, around 80 percent of the Paquimé burial sample had either one or two local ceramic vessels or no mortuary offerings at all. This is not an elaborately furnished group of burials. In fact, the most elaborate of known Paquimé interments contains nothing comparable to the wealth of some Mississippian burials, where a well-established system of hereditary ranking is presumed (e.g., Pauketat and Emerson 1997). If Paquimé had the sort of corporate communal leadership described for the Puebloan societies of the U.S. Southwest, then this sparse distribution of sumptuary goods is understandable. Status distinctions exist in such societies, but they are characteristically based on kinship and sodality structures, plus control of ritual knowledge and the associated paraphernalia. These roles are not strongly reflected in personal possessions, mortuary treatment, or elaboration of domestic structures, and such is observed to be the case at Paquimé. This argument is developed in more detail in the concluding chapter.

Chapter 8

Floral and Faunal Remains

Domestic and Community Food Economy and Ecology

This chapter examines two important issues in the history of the Casas Grandes culture as expressed in the Early and Late Medio periods, or from ca. AD 1175 through the early 1400s. The first is the production, distribution, and consumption of food in the region, and the second is anthropogenic ecology, or how the ancient people of the region affected their biotic environment In considering production and distribution in the region, we distinguish between two levels of activity. The first is the domestic economy that supported the vast majority of the population daily, and the second is the community economy that entailed the ritual and political use of food beyond individual household consumption. Its produce is often termed "staple finance" (D'Altroy et al. 1985:187–206). Plants and animals contributed to both economies. It has already been shown that the agricultural productivity and water availability, as well as the potential for irrigated agriculture, of the Casas Grandes River valley around Paquimé offered the potential of unusually bountiful yields for the domestic economy (Minnis and Whalen 2020). This, in turn, allowed aspiring leaders and social groups to fund status-building activities, such as hosting major ritual events through the use of surpluses, which is the community economy. In addition, the region is well suited for access to other resources in the extensive mountains of the Sierra Madre to the immediate west and on the vast desert plains and grasslands to the east.

The second topic we consider is anthropogenic ecology, or how the ancient people of the region affected their biotic environment. Given its reasonably dense human population, one would expect that the needs of the pre-Hispanic economy would significantly affect the local environment. Two instances for which we previously found data (Whalen and Minnis 2009:222–28) are deforestation due to heavy wood use and increase in weedy plants that thrive in the disturbed soils of cleared fields. These cumulative processes alter the quantity and variety of other resources. While the Casas Grandes region is bountiful, its resources were not equally distributed. Therefore, we focus on variation within and around the Core Zone, considering how settlements best suited for farming differed from those in less favorable locations. For example, some settlements with less access to high-quality land were able to use different plants and animals than those in favorable farming locations. This chapter first discusses plant remains, both propagules (seeds and fruits) and wood, after which faunal remains are considered. In each case, we first outline the critical issues that these data can address, then present the data, and finally compare them to research in other sites in the local region and beyond.

The collection strategy, laboratory methodology, data summaries, and analyses of the plant remains are presented in detail elsewhere (Minnis and Whalen 2020) and are abstracted and supplemented here. Propagule and wood counts for all the sites we excavated are presented in tables A.1–A.26 in the volume just cited. Because of the problems of differential preservation for organic remains in open sites, we discuss only charred plant propagules (seeds and fruits). This omits green and tuberous plants that were surely also in use, but which are not preserved for recovery in flotation samples. Quantities of remains are expressed by the ubiquity measure, which is the number of samples containing a specific taxon divided by the number of samples containing charred propagules. For example, a maize ubiquity score of 45 percent indicates that 45 percent of the charred propagule samples contained maize. Wood presents a different situation because the differences in preservation between types is much less than for propagules. For wood, we simply count the number of specimens of each type. We term this "abundance," so a score of 45 percent for pine would mean that 45 percent of the wood specimens identified are pine. The rationale for these analytic approaches is explained in more detail elsewhere (Minnis and Whalen 2020). Flotation samples were generally taken from specific contexts, such as hearths and other features. Because of the extensive looting of Medio period sites, our flotation sampling normally did not include room fill, most of which was disturbed and mixed by looting activity. Discussion of the faunal analysis methodology is available in other sources (e.g., Cannon and Etnier 1997; Loven 2016; Schmidt 2005; Whalen and Minnis 2009). Like plant remains, the types and quantities of animal remains are affected by the condition of the sites and the recovery techniques employed.

Plant Remains

Paquimé was uniquely well suited to produce surpluses because of its proximity to the most and best farmland along the Casas Grandes River floodplain. Inner Core Zone large Sites 315 and 565 occupy similarly excellent farming locations beside the same floodplain, while Outer Core Zone large Site 204 lies in an area of farmland that is limited in quantity and quality. There are interesting comparisons to be made in the ethnobotany of these differently situated settlements. We focus on the large settlements, as the quantity and variety of their organic remains far exceeds those of the neighboring small sites.

There is no doubt that floodplain farming would have been the area's most productive, although upland locations also have agricultural potential, as demonstrated by the region's many fields marked by rock retaining walls locally termed trincheras. Also present are fields dotted with rock piles that likely served as mulch, regulating the temperature and moisture of plants like agave and sotol (Minnis et al. 2006). These fields were not as productive as those along the watercourses, but they offered alternative farming localities for major crops, as well as other useful produce such as agave. In addition, upland settlements were closer to mountain resources.

Propagules for Food

Unfortunately, we cannot fully evaluate the macroplant remains from Paquimé, as the site was excavated before flotation became a standard part of archaeological work. Specimens from large beams at Paquimé were collected for dendrochronological dating, limited pollen analysis was undertaken, and some items of material culture (such as fibers) were found. Otherwise, few plant remains were recovered. This gives special importance to the assemblages from Sites 315 and 565 because they are the first flotation-based datasets from sites in the Casas Grandes River valley.

Although plant remains from Paquimé were rare, other archaeological data provide glimpses into its community economy. These are discussed in greater detail elsewhere (Minnis and Whalen 2020), but two examples demonstrate the importance of the community food economy. There are five exceptionally large underground ovens at Paquimé (Minnis and Whalen 2005). One is next to a ceremonial platform mound in Unit 9. These ovens were used to cook enormous amounts of agave or related plants. This scale of food preparation obviously transcends the needs and labor capacity of individual households, and it likely served for large commensal events.

Upland fields marked by linear stone walls are the second example. Based on our survey of such fields, we note that a small number are exceptionally large and are usually near ceremonial centers (Minnis et al. 2006). We interpret these as "chiefs' fields," or agricultural plots controlled by social leaders and worked communally. Their produce would have been used to fuel the staple economy, or the funds of power. Many flotation samples were collected from the excavations at Site 315, and data from them are shown in table 8.1. Flotation samples from the first years of excavation at Site 565 were also studied. No flotation samples from the second year of excavation from 565 have been analyzed.

Propagules from Site 315 represent 43.5 percent of those from all our excavations and 32.9 percent of the flotation samples studied. Those from 565 represent 17.0 percent of all propagules for all our excavations and 16.4 percent of the flotation samples analyzed. A complete inventory of all samples studied from all our excavations is presented in the original study (Minnis and Whalen 2020:116, table A.1). Carbonized material was very sparse at the small sites, and most of what there was served for radiocarbon dating. Inner Core large site data are presented in table 8.1.

Most of the remains shown in table 8.1 were of cultivated crops, including maize kernels and cob fragments, seeds of beans, squash, chile, cotton, and little barley, plus cotton fibers. Agave is included in this list as a possible cultigen. "Unknowns" are unidentifiable specimens. A similar list of cultigens for Outer Core Zone large and small sites was presented elsewhere (Whalen and Minnis 2009:220–21, table 8.1), and all Outer Core data used in the

TABLE 8.1 Summary of flotation samples from 315 and 565

Site	# Samples	# Propagules
315 Total	159	8,169
Area A	57	2,876
Area B	57	2,932
Area C	14	1,264
Area D	22	900
Area E	9	1,97
565 Total	82	3,217
Areas A/B	41	1,961
Area Z	41	1,256
Grand Total	**241**	**11,386**

following discussion come from that source. The gourd is the only cultivated plant from the region that was not found on Inner Core large sites, although it is reported from Paquimé (Cutler and Blake 1974:308). Gourd remains were also present at Outer Core large Site 204 and small Site 317. Chile seeds were found on Inner Core large Site 315, although none came from Outer Core settlements. In general, it is evident that populations all over the Core Zone used the same set of cultivated plants, including agave. The results shown in table 8.2 agree with the limited data from Paquimé. Di Peso characterized its people as "virtually vegetarian," basing their subsistence largely on corn, squash, gourds, and perhaps beans. Agave was also important food (Di Peso 1974:2:618). At Paquimé, other analysts observed, "corn specimens" were by far the most common type of plant remain, while squash, gourds, and cotton were also documented there (Cutler and Blake 1974:308). Noncultivated plants and animals supplemented the diet.

Maize remains are the most abundant all over the Core Zone and on sites of all sizes. The fact that maize kernels are so common in flotation samples is a clear indication of maize's role as the major dietary staple. Cupule fragments likely overstate the importance of maize in the diet because cobs were used as fuel and kindling, as shown in figure 8.1. On the other hand, the ubiquity of maize kernels most likely underrepresents the plant's dietary importance. In addition to its role as the basic food source of every household, maize likely played an important role in the community food economy or in a system of staple finance, and thus might be expected to be more common around Paquimé, where ritual and commensal activities were most evident.

Maize can be consumed as food or drink, and discussion in chapter 5 of this volume provides ceramic evidence for both. Interior surface pitting of large ceramic vessels is argued in chapter 5 to result from the acidic foam that is a byproduct of fermentation. The corn beer thus produced could have been consumed during commensal feasting at ritual events. Analysis of human dental calculus from Paquimé interments supports this picture: maize starch grains, some modified by fermentation (King et al. 2017). Apart from preparation of fermented drink, chapter 5 documents the presence of very large Brown and Red-slipped utilitarian jars on large Core Zone sites and on small Site 242, a presumed administrative

TABLE 8.2 Comparison of propagule ubiquity scores from Inner Core large Sites 315 and 565

Site 315 (*N* = 159)	Ubiquity	Site 565 (*N* = 83)	Ubiquity
Maize cupules	82.4	Maize cupules	84.3
Unknown	62.2	Maize kernels	30.1
Maize kernels	30.2	Unknown	24.1
Fabaceae (bean family)	29.9	Cheno-am	16.9
Gossypium hirsutum (cotton)	17.0	*Portulaca* (purslane)	13.3
Portulaca (purslane)	12.0	*Phaseolus* (bean)	10.8
Phaseolus cf. *vulgaris* (bean)	10.7	*Gossypium hirsutum* (cotton)	8.4
Shell	10.1	Shell	7.2
Poaceae (grass family)	8.8	*Chenopodium* (chenopod)	4.8
Opuntia (prickly pear)	6.3	*Atriplex* (saltbush)	2.4
Chenopodium (chenopod)	5.0	*Trianthema* (horse purslane)	2.4
Asteraceae (sunflower family)	4.4	*Cucurbita* rind (squash)	2.4
Gaura-type	3.8	Poaceae (grass family)	2.4
Capsicum annuum (chile)	3.2	Spine	2.4
Trianthema (horse purslane)	2.5	*Amaranthus* (amaranth)	2.4
Cucurbita rind (squash)	2.5	*Gaura*-type	2.4
Prosopis juliflora (mesquite)	2.5	Fabaceae (bean family)	2.4
Amaranthus (amaranth)	1.9	*Capsicum annuum* (chile)	1.2
Quercus (oak)	1.9	Euphorbia (spurge)	1.2
Hedioma-type	1.3	Geraniaceae (geranium family)	1.2
Helianthus (sunflower)	1.3	*Opuntia* (prickly pear)	1.2
Plantago (plantain)	1.3	*Agave* (agave)	1.2
Papaveraceae (poppy family)	1.3	*Echinocactus* (fishhook cactus)	1.2
Agave? (agave)	1.3	Asteraceae (sunflower family)	1.2
cf. *Cleome* (beeweed)	1.3		
Hordeum pusillum (little barley)	1.3		
Solanaceae (nightshade family)	1.3		
Brassicaceae (mustard family)	1.3		
Corispermum (bugseed)	1.3		

Source: Minnis and Whalen (2020:table 2.2).

node of Paquimé. The capacities of these vessels are far above that required for domestic cooking, so they likely served to prepare food for commensal events.

Agave is another plant that played a prominent role in the community food economy. It was cultivated in the Hohokam region of the U.S. Southwest, but we do not know whether such was the case in the Casas Grandes area. There, it could have simply been a frequently utilized wild plant. Although its remains are frequently found in our samples, agave was not nearly as common as maize. The ubiquity scores for agave remains are highest on Outer Core Zone sites, ranging from a low of 5.9 on small Site 242 to a high of 22.6 on small Site 231, while the score for Outer Core large Site 204 was 10.8. All these values are much higher than agave ubiquity scores shown in table 8.2 for Inner Core large Sites 315 and 565.

FIGURE 8.1 Burned maize cobs in a hearth on Site 315. The black bar is 10 cm.

The Outer Core Zone contains a good deal of the rocky upland terrain in which agave thrives. There are similar settings in the Inner Zone, although they are smaller.

Wherever agave was grown, substantial amounts were used by Medio populations. Agave, like maize, can be consumed as food or fermented drink, and large well-made pit ovens scattered over the Core Zone show that it was prepared at scales far beyond household requirements, most likely for the commensal events that accompanied ritual activities (Minnis and Whalen 2005, 2020). We have no direct evidence of what was cooked in these ovens, although agave baking is certainly the most likely explanation. There is a cluster of such facilities at Paquimé, among which the Unit 9 oven is the largest known in the NW/SW. It could have prepared enormous amounts of food, estimated at as much as 3,800 kg per cooking episode. There are several slightly smaller ovens at Paquimé as well, and their combined output of food would have been enormous. Apart from Paquimé, large ovens are rare in the rest of the Inner Core. Their frequency rises sharply again with movement to the Outer Core Zone, which contained most of the known examples of these facilities.

Cultivated produce was supplemented with wild plant foods, of which remains of more than 20 were recovered from Inner Core large sites. Especially common are weedy plants such as amaranth (*Amaranthus*), goosefoot (*Chenopodium*), and purslane (*Portulaca*), as well as less frequent ones such as sunflower (*Helianthus*), tansy mustard (*Descurainia*), and drop seed (*Sporobolus*). These weedy species are recognized as "disturbance taxa," and they are coproducts of agricultural intensification (Huckell and Toll 2004:61). Rises in frequencies of these weeds are taken to be "a predictable consequence of replacement of native vegetation by anthropogenic communities such as cultivated fields" (Huckell and Toll 2004:65). Potential foods also came from local plants, such as prickly pear (*Opuntia*), oak (*Quercus*), piñon (*Pinus cembroides*), mesquite (*Prosopis*), juniper (*Juniperus*), and hackberry (*Celtis*), all of which were also recovered from large Inner Core sites. Some of the same plant remains came from Outer Core Site 204, including mesquite, prickly pear, and piñon. In general, the large number of flotation samples from large sites produced long lists of taxa, whether located in the Inner or Outer Core Zone. Outer Core small Sites 231, 242, and 317 showed much lower diversity. All of the common cultivated food plants were present, although fewer wild plant taxa were identified. This is likely an artifact of sample size, as many fewer flotation samples were processed from small sites than from their large counterparts. Thus, we presume that Inner Core and Outer Core populations used the same range of cultivated food crops, plus various local wild plants.

Still, there were some differences. Little barley and the cultivated chile were recovered from Sites 315 and 565, although neither was found on any of the Outer Core's large or small settlements. The little barley is the first documented example of this poorly known cultigen in Mexico, and the chile is the first to be recovered from archaeological sites in the NW/SW. Also to be considered is cacao or yaupon holly, although their traces are found as residue on ceramic vessels. Each is discussed in greater detail below.

LITTLE BARLEY

Little Barley (*Hordeum pusillum*), a New World relative of cultivated barley, is a weedy annual with a wide distribution in North America, including the NW/SW, plus a limited distribution in Mexico (Lebgue and Valerio 1986). While we do not know if the modern distribution of little barley reflects its ancient distribution, it seems most likely that the Casas Grandes area was at or near the southern limit of the plant's natural range. Little barley matures in the late spring or early summer (K. R. Adams 2014; Bohrer 1991), and like most grasses, its seeds are primarily a source of starchy carbohydrates. There is evidence that it was cultivated by pre-Hispanic groups. Ancient naked grains of little barley, an indicator of domestication, have been found in eastern North America (Gremillion 2018), in the Hohokam region of southern Arizona (K. R. Adams 2014), and in southwestern Colorado (Graham et al. 2017), although it seems to have been a minor crop in all these areas. We recovered one naked little barley seed from Inner Core large Site 315. This is, to the best of our knowledge, the first evidence of that plant's cultivation in pre-Hispanic Mexico. It was recovered from a small oval hearth in Room 60. Also in the flotation sample were maize cupules and some unidentifiable seed fragments. There was nothing unusual about this feature or the room it was in. As we only have a single specimen from one provenance, little more can be deduced about little barley's use other than to note its presence and suggest that it was not a major crop. It needs to be noted that grass phytoliths recovered in dental calculus from Paquimé could have been from little barley or other grasses (King et al. 2017).

CHILE

The second plant of special interest is the cultivated chile (chili, *Capsicum annuum*). It has long been puzzling that chile was not found in the pre-Hispanic NW/SW. Most of the important Mesoamerican crops that could have been grown in the ancient NW/SW made their way there in pre-Hispanic times (Minnis 1985a, 1992), including plants such as corn, beans, squash, cotton, gourd, and perhaps amaranth. This points toward a free flow over millennia of crops between the NW/SW and groups farther south in Mexico, although chile was a puzzling exception. There is no obvious reason why the plant could not have been grown in the NW/SW. In Mesoamerica, pre-Hispanic chile remains are found as far north as La Quemada in Zacatecas (Paula Turkon, personal communication, 2016), and chile remains are common among some postcontact sites in the U.S. Southwest (Diehl et al. 2021; Minnis and Whalen 2010). This led to the conclusion that chile was not cultivated in the pre-contact NW/SW. It could have been transported easily over long distances. In fact, chile seeds would have been an ideal item for long-distance exchange. There are 120,000 seeds per kilogram, so that huge numbers of them could have been carried by a single individual. They also remain viable for long periods. In short, how cultivated chiles came into the NW/SW is still unknown.

Despite this limitation, we are beginning to develop a better idea of when chiles were in use thanks to their discovery at Inner Core Sites 315 and 565. We reported on the first chile seed recovered (Minnis and Whalen 2010), and subsequent analysis has identified more seeds on both large sites of the Inner Core Zone. The first specimen came from a subfloor deposit in a small room in Site 315. Analysis of flotation samples from a second excavation season at Site 315 and excavations at Site 565 yielded even more chile seeds. As many as 25 have been identified (table 8.3). All but one were recovered from five different domestic rooms at Site 315. One seed came from a domestic room at Site 565. In addition, a possible chile stem (peduncle) was noted in the flotation sample from Room 20 at Site 315.

The social context of chile use in the Casas Grandes area is not clear. Was it a normal part of domestic cuisine or was it a special item controlled by or restricted to certain segments of the population or certain types of events? Chile has been found on both large sites near Paquimé, although none has been reported from other sites in Chihuahua or Sonora. Likewise, the plant's remains are absent in the large number of flotation samples from sites in the U.S. Southwest. This might indicate that chile was an edible prestige good that was restricted to important settlements or people. On the other hand, its remains do not appear in what could be considered special or unique contexts at Inner Core Sites 315 and 565. There, they were found in small hearths and in subfloor trash deposits, or in ordinary contexts in and under typical domestic rooms. Data presented in table 8.3 show that a wide variety of other common plant remains accompanied the chile seeds.

It is noteworthy that the Room 50 chile seed was found in a subfloor trash deposit that both radiocarbon and ceramic types dated to the Early Medio, ca. AD 1150–1300. Other deposits with chiles had Late Medio dates, ceramics, or both. It thus appears that chiles were in use in the Casas Grandes area from Early Medio times onward, and they might have been a more common culinary ingredient than is suggested by the data just presented.

TABLE 8.3 Chile seeds from Sites 315 and 565

Site	Provenance	Context	Chile remains[a]	Other plant remains[b]
315	Rm. 20 Feat. 67	Circular hearth	1	Unknown specimen
315	Rm. 20 Feat. 331	Hemispherical hearth	3 (12)[c]	Maize cupules, purslane, grass family, vegetative shell
315	Rm. 24 Feat. 365	Hemispherical hearth	2 (8)	Chenopod, unknown specimen, cotton,
315	Rm. 50	Subfloor	1	Maize cupules and kernels, prickly pear, bean family, cotton, mesquite bean
315	Rm. 54	Subfloor	2	Bean family, maize cupules, maize kernels, grass family
565	Rm. 5 Feat. 47b	Hemispherical hearth	1	Maize cupules
Total			**10 (25)**	

Source: Minnis and Whalen (2020:table 2.3).

[a] The first number is the number of actual seeds recovered. Subsamples (25%) of two samples, from rooms 20 and 24, were sorted, so the number in parentheses is the estimated number of chile seeds present in the entire sample.

[b] Only charred propagules in the same flotation sample are listed here.

[c] One seed had attached tissue, and a likely chile peduncle was present in this sample.

This supposition is based on the fact that chile remains were present in both Inner Core sites where flotation samples were processed, while equally large samples of plant remains from Outer Core sites of all sizes yielded none at all. We are, therefore, led to suppose that chiles were reasonably common among the large Inner Core sites, while they were rare or absent in the Outer Core Zone. There is thus the possibility that chile cultivation was restricted to the Casas Grandes River valley, where it was a luxury food. It is unfortunate that we have no data on the presence of chiles at Paquimé, and resolution of the questions surrounding the use of that plant in the Casas Grandes area must await new findings.

CACAO OR YAUPON HOLLY

Research throughout the NW/SW (Crown and Hurst 2009; Crown et al. 2015) has documented what appears to be chemical residue of either cacao (*Theobroma cacao*), an important plant from Mesoamerica, or yaupon holly (*Ilex vomitoria*), a shrub used ritually by Indigenous communities in the U.S. Southeast. This holly is among the few plants native to North America that contain caffeine. Cassina, or black drink, a caffeinated beverage, was brewed from holly native to coastal areas from the Tidewater region of Virginia to the Gulf Coast of Texas. It was a valuable pre-Columbian commodity that was widely traded. Recent analyses recovered theobromine residue from shell cups indicating that it was being drunk at Cahokia, which is far outside the plant's native range (Hudson 2004).

Core Zone sites have provided no remains of either cacao or yaupon holly, but the presence of theobromine has recently been detected in the Inner Core. Only ten polychrome sherds from Site 315 were tested, but theobromine was detected on 40 percent of them (Crown et al. 2015). The sample of polychrome sherds used in this analysis was restricted to small polychrome jars, as these were thought most likely to have been special-use vessels. Despite the small, casual sample, its percentage of positive results is the highest of all tested sites in the NW/SW. This result hints at frequent use of some sort of caffeinated drink in the Inner Core Zone. In chapter 5 of this volume, we note that many polychrome jars on Inner Core sites were small, and some of them bore traces of exterior soot. Their small volumes make them unlikely to have been used for food preparation, but they might well have been used for heating small quantities of ritual consumables. Like the questions surrounding the use of chiles, those pertaining to cacao or yaupon holly drinks are fascinating, but they cannot be resolved without more data.

In summary, the food economy during the Medio period was heavily based on the cultivation of a wide range of crops. Maize was certainly the most important, but other important crops included beans, squash, gourd, cotton, and perhaps agave, plus minor crops such as little barley and chile. The seeds of weedy annuals such as goosefoot and pigweed are ubiquitous in the flotation samples. Many other wild plant foods were commonly eaten, including pine nuts, acorns, and the fruits of shrubby plants. These last wild plant foods may have had more dietary importance than is suggested by their limited presence in the archaeological record. The fact that several rara or previously unknown taxa have been detected on the Inner Core Zone's large sites suggests that plant use diversity was at its maximum in the Late Medio period among the nearest neighbors of Paquimé.

Differential Plant Use in the Core Zone

The preceding discussion suggests that similar food plants were in use all over the Core Zone, although their frequencies were not identical. To understand more about differences in plant uses in the Core, we contrast Inner Core large Site 315, a lowland site in the major river valley, with Outer Core large Site 204, an upland site located on the Arroyo la Tinaja. This is a secondary drainage, adjacent to which are extensive rocky piedmont slopes. Both sites have large flotation assemblages, which we compare using rank order analyses of ubiquity scores (table 8.4). The Spearman rank order score (r_s = .029) suggests that the assemblages are not statistically similar. If one does the same statistical test with only the taxa found in both samples, however, the results (r_s = 0.63) indicate a weakly significant similarity.

Much of the frequency difference in the preceding table is a product of the settlements' surroundings. At Site 204, there is less floodplain farming land but greater opportunity for growing and processing agave. The reverse is true at Site 315, where there is extensive opportunity for floodplain farming. This is reflected in agave ubiquity scores of 10.8 at upland Site 204 and 1.3 at lowland Site 315. The ubiquity scores for maize cupules (which are cob fragments), maize kernels, beans, and squash reverse this pattern. The respective scores of these plant remains on Site 315 are 82.4, 30.2, 10.7, and 2.5. On Outer Core large Site 204, the same scores, in the same order, are 70.7, 21.0, 1.9, and 1.3. Although cultivated cotton was not a food plant, it shows a similar disparity between the lowland and upland settings. Its ubiquity is 17.0 at lowland Site 315, but it is only 5.1 at upland Site 204. This may

TABLE 8.4 Comparison of propagule ubiquity scores from lowland (315) and upland (204) sites

315 (*N* = 159)	Ubiquity	204 (*N* = 155)	Ubiquity
Maize cupules	82.4	Maize cupules	61.6
Unknown	62.3	Unknowns	31.7
Maize kernels	30.2	Purslane	22.0
Bean family	30.0	Maize kernels	21.3
Bean	18.2	Cheno-am	17.1
Cheno-am	12.0	Chenopod	15.2
Purslane	12.0	Agave (?)	11.0
Shell	10.1	Amaranth	7.3
Grass family	8.8	Nightshade family	7.3
cf. *Gaura*-type	8.2	Cotton	4.9
Chenopod	6.3	Prickly pear	4.3
Prickly pear	6.3	Fabaceae	3.7
Chile	3.1	cf. Rattlebox	3.0
Mesquite	3.1	Shell	2.4
Horse purslane	2.5	Phaseolus	2.4
Squash rind	2.5	Gourd seeds	1.8
Sunflower family	2.5	Saltbush	1.2
Amaranth	1.9	Grass family	1.2
Oak	1.9	Poppy family	1.2
cf. *Hedioma*-type	1.3	Juniper	1.2
Sunflower	1.3	Mesquite	1.2
Plantain	1.3	Mexican piñon	1.2
Poppy family	1.3	Gourd rind	1.2
Agave (crop?)	1.3	Buckwheat	0.6
Saltbush	1.3	Dropseed	0.6
cf. Beeweed	1.3	Sunflower family	0.6
Little barley	1.3	Sumpweed	0.6
Nightshade family	0.6	Summer poppy	0.6
Mustard family	0.6	Grape	0.6
Stickleaf	0.6	Bugseed	0.6
Vervain	0.6		
Horse purslane	0.6		

Source: Minnis and Whalen (2020:table 2.3).

be explained by the relatively high water requirements of the cotton plant. While the same food crops were present, people clearly used them within the productive possibilities of their surroundings.

Wood

Wood is often ignored in ethnobotanical analyses, even though it is one of the most widely used resources for heat, cooking, and construction of structures and other items of material culture. For example, we have estimated that the inhabitants of Paquimé alone could

Floral and Faunal Remains

have required up to 800 million pounds of wood just for heating and cooking during the Medio period (Minnis and Whalen 2020). The amount of labor required to collect and transport this quantity of material is very substantial, particularly in a semiarid location with low woody biomass. Unfortunately, there are few extant data on this wood. Work at Paquimé took place before flotation was common, so the site's recovered wood was mostly from large architectural beams. Ninety-nine percent of these beams were large straight conifer trunks from the Sierra Madre west of Paquimé (Scott 1966). A very few other wood specimens were reported, including cottonwood (*Populus*), "cane" (probably *Phragmites*), "hardwood," juniper (*Juniperus*), and Douglas fir (*Pseudotsuga menziesii*).

We identified 2,044 individual pieces of wood from Inner Core large sites, as shown in table 8.5. They are from flotation and nonflotation contexts, and they account for 32.5 percent and 8.1 percent of the flotation wood identification from our project. The total wood counts for all sites we excavated are presented in another source (Minnis and Whalen 2020:130–42, tables A.27–A.52; table A.27 provides a complete summary of wood identifications).

Spearman's rank order correlation between sites 315 and 565 shows a strong similarity (r_s = .084). This is predictable, as both sites lie close together in the same river valley location. The wood inventory for each site is shown in table 8.6. There were 155 samples with wood from Site 315, while 37 came from Site 565. In general, the most abundant wood remains were pine (*Pinus*), cottonwood/willow (*Populus/Salix*), and oak (*Quercus*). Mesquite/acacia (*Prosopis/Acacia*) is one of the four wood types from two excavation areas (B and Z) at Site 565. Cottonwood and willow are found on waterways and floodplains, and the others are more common away from the river.

A Spearman rank order test comparing floodplain Site 315 and upland Site 204 show that the two have a weakly significant similarity (r_s = 0.57) (table 8.7). We interpret this to indicate that the woods used are generally similar between the two settings but with some minor differences attributable to variation in local flora. This is highlighted by the fact that

TABLE 8.5 Summary of wood identifications from 315 and 565

Area	# Identifications
Site 315	
A	860
B	620
C	145
D	293
E	126
Site total	**2,044**
Site 565	
A	176
B	141
Z	191
Site total	**508**

TABLE 8.6 Rank order comparison of wood remains in flotation samples from lowland Site 315 and upland Site 565

	Site 315		Site 565	
	Ubiquity	Abundance	Ubiquity	Abundance
Cottonwood/willow	1	2	1	1
Pine	2	1	2	2
Oak	3	3	3.5	4
Monocot	4	4	3.5	5
Diffuse porous	11	8	5.5	10
Mesquite/acacia	7	10	5.5	3
Unknown	8.5	12	7	6
Ring porous	6	6	8	9
Juniper	10	15.5	11	8
Dicot	5	5	11	13
Elm family/hackberry	—	—	11	12
Walnut	9	13.5	11	12
Semi-ring porous	8.5	7	11	7
Saltbush	17	17	15.5	15.5
Common reed	16	15.5	15.5	12
Piñon	13.5	13	15.5	15.5
Sycamore	13.5	11	15.5	14.5
Gymnosperm	13.5	14	15.5	14.5

TABLE 8.7 Rank order comparison of wood remains in flotation samples from lowland Site 315 and upland Site 204

Taxon	Site 315	Site 204
Pine (*Pinus*)	2	2
Oak (*Quercus*)	3	1
Cottonwood/willow (*Populus/Salix*)	1	5
Piñon (*P. cembroides*)	9.5	4
Monocot	4	12
Dicot	5	4
Agave (*Agave*)	12	10.5
Walnut (*Juglans*)	9.5	8.5
Juniper (*Juniperus*)	7	8.51
Sycamore (*Platanus*)	9.5	7
Gymnosperm	9.5	6
Mesquite/acacia (*Prosopis/Acacia*)	6	10.5

Outer Core small Sites 231 and 317 had only one specimen of cottonwood/willow out of the 711 wood specimens identified from flotation. Both sites, we note, lay far from floodplains.

The most interesting pattern from the wood data is the large percentage of pines. In this figure, we do not include piñon pine, which grows at lower elevations, closer to our study areas. Rather, these are pines from the Sierra Madre, some of the most distant wood resources from our sites. That pines were used for roof construction is not surprising, as no local trees could produce the necessary strong straight timbers, although the wood served for more than construction. Earlier work (Whalen and Minnis 2009) showed that a large amount of pine was burned in intramural hearths in Late Medio times. Burning of debris from preparing roof beams is unlikely, as the pine pieces in our flotation samples were small to medium branches. Moreover, it would have been most efficient to transport completely trimmed beams from the Sierra Madre. Instead, we think that the dense population in the Paquimé region over several centuries denuded most of the local woody plants useful for fuel. This would cause people to acquire firewood from more distant sources. Mountain pine in the form of charcoal would weigh little and could have been transported relatively easily and in quantity to the lowlands. Charcoal is ideal for intramural heating and cooking, as it produces little smoke.

Some support for this idea comes from Outer Core large Site 204. The following discussion is abstracted from the original source (Whalen and Minnis 2009:228). The community today lies in an open setting surrounded by grass and shrubs, although this does not seem to have been the original environment of the area. Instead, we envision that the surrounding hillslopes had heavier coverings of oak, piñon, and juniper than is presently the case. These are the woods that were most commonly found in Early Medio contexts at Site 204. The abundance of all these woods declines in the Late Medio, likely representing decreasing native tree cover in the site's environs. The Late Medio decline in use of oak, piñon, and juniper was compensated for by an increase in pine, mesquite, and cottonwood/willow. Mesquite, cottonwood, and willow still grow today in and around the bottom of the adjacent arroyo. The pine comes from higher elevations, as just discussed. The Arroyo la Tinaja, on which Site 204 lies, is one of the major corridors from the lowlands up into the Sierra Madre, so it appears that the Late Medio inhabitants of Site 204 were using some lower quality local woods from shrubby plants, while obtaining high-quality pine from farther away. As just noted, a feasible strategy for importing large quantities of pine to the lowlands involves reducing it to charcoal in the mountains prior to its transportation to the lowlands. We do not have comparable Early and Late Medio data from the sites of the Inner Core Zone. Even so, we suggest similar processes were at work, as reflected in the high frequency of pine in the sites' mostly Late Medio deposits.

Anthropogenic Ecology of Plant Populations

This is a complex topic, as environmental effects due to human activity can have intentional or unintentional consequences. There are examples of both from the southwestern United States (e.g., K. R. Adams 2017), and from northwestern Chihuahua (Minnis and Whalen

2020; Whalen and Minnis 2009). Significant ecological consequences are predictable based on the large number of settlements in the semiarid Casas Grandes region by the Late Medio period, or after about AD 1300. We have documented anthropogenic ecological changes in the Outer Core Zone through diachronic changes in plant and wood use from Early Medio to Late Medio times. Preceding discussion in this chapter cites the increasing Late Medio presence at Outer Core Site 204 of the weedy annuals known as "disturbance taxa," including amaranth, chenopods, and purslane. Our 2009 study of Outer Core Zone large Site 204 showed that the ubiquity of these disturbance taxa remains was about 24 percent in the Early Medio period, rising to 38 percent in the Late Medio (Whalen and Minnis 2009:223). This points to increasing soil-disturbing activities around the 204 settlement, probably reflecting increased field clearing. The ubiquity score sum of Inner Core disturbance taxa is 18.9 at Site 315 and a comparable 20.5 at Site 565. Neither of these scores is as high as that of Outer Core Site 204 in the Late Medio period. We do not know whether similar processes of field expansion took place in the Inner Core by the Late Medio. It might not have been as necessary, in the Inner Core, as there is considerably more high-quality floodplain land available there than around Outer Core Site 204.

A second indicator of anthropogenic change comes from wood taxa frequencies. In preceding pages, we argue that the most likely explanation for the large amounts of mountain pine being used as fuel in Late Medio times was a result of overharvesting locally available fuel sources, such as oak, piñon, and juniper, by a dense population. Wood remains also point to increasing impoverishment of the wet areas along the Outer Core Zone's Arroyo la Tinaja. The stratified midden deposit at Site 204 showed that only one taxon of floodplain plant, cottonwood/willow, was found in the Late Medio upper test pit layers. In contrast, three taxa, cottonwood/willow, elm, and sycamore, were recovered from the Early Medio lower test pit levels.

Stresses on native flora could have been exacerbated by the use of large quantities of resources for the increasingly large community economy. Two specific stressors may be envisioned. These are the large quantities of agave baked in the large ovens for commensal events, and the preparation of extensive "chiefs' fields," or communally worked plots, which would have removed native vegetation and increased weedy annuals. Both of these are phenomena of the Late Medio period, when we expect environmental stress to have been most pronounced in the Casas Grandes area. In conclusion, evidence for anthropogenic change is substantial for the Outer Core Zone. Unfortunately, the situation is less clear for the Inner Core, where we do not have as robust an Early Medio sample with which to compare the Late Medio. The late period, however, was the time of maximum population, so that human-induced environmental deterioration should be most evident then.

A REGIONAL COMPARISON

It is interesting to compare data from the Casas Grandes area with those from southern Chihuahua. The common Casas Grandes–area terms Viejo and Medio are used to classify these southern manifestations, although they differ considerably from their northern counterparts. In comparative discussions, therefore, we refer to the two archaeological records as Northern Viejo and Northern Medio for the Casas Grandes area and Southern Viejo and Southern Medio for southern Chihuahua. The Southern Viejo pit structures are larger and more elaborate than those known from the Northern Viejo in the Casas Grandes area. Other discussion highlights differences in the Medio, or pueblo, remains from the south, contrasting these with those from the north (Kelley and Phillips 2017).

Archaeobotanical data offer additional support for the northern/southern distinction. The following information is summarized from the original analysis of southern Chihuahua plant remains (K. R. Adams 2017). Those populations were using maize, supplemented by wild plant foods. At their highest values in the Southern Viejo and Southern Medio periods, maize ubiquity scores are in the 50 to 60 percent range, with somewhat higher scores in the Southern Viejo period than in succeeding times. We have no Northern Viejo maize ubiquity scores, but those from the Northern Medio period are about 70 to 85 percent. The same food crops were in use, but the preceding observation suggests a substantially higher dependence on maize in the northern area than in the southern one. Southern wood remains tell a story of overexploitation of the local woods and great reliance on the more distant pines, as in the northern area. The ubiquity of pine in Southern Viejo deposits is 41.5 percent, rising to 66.5 percent by Southern Medio times. The Casas Grandes area and southern Chihuahua thus have both similarities and differences in their archaeological records, suggesting different developmental trajectories that have yet to be fully explored.

Faunal Remains

The first extensive faunal dataset in the region came from Paquimé. While many different animals were identified, sporadic and limited recovery techniques make it difficult to compare those data with faunal assemblages from recently excavated sites. In modern excavations, remains are routinely retrieved by screens with fine mesh, usually one-quarter inch. Many deposits excavated at Paquimé were unscreened, so that small bones and bone fragments would not have been recovered. In fact, we do not know whether animal bone was collected routinely or sporadically. We suspect the latter, as the reported sample from the entire excavation is only 2,689 animal bones (McKusick 1974b:245, fig. 299-8). The large percentage of bone identified to at least the genus level (McKusick 1974b) is likely an indication of the completeness of the bones. This, in turn, suggests a collecting strategy biased toward larger and better-preserved specimens. The recently excavated faunal assemblages from the neighboring sites come from completely screened deposits; they recovered many more small bone fragments, and they therefore have a much higher percentage of unidentifiable bones.

Animals in the Domestic and Community Food Economies

The sporadic recovery pattern just described for Paquimé likely increased recovery of bones from large animals such as bison, elk, and deer. As a result, the faunal remains were originally taken to indicate a focus on procurement of large game, especially bison (e.g., McKusick 1974b:245). Di Peso and colleagues' (1974:8:243) assertion that bison were the primary source of meat protein through much of the life of Paquimé is frequently repeated in today's literature.

This is unlikely to have been the case, however, as argued in a previous study (Whalen and Minnis 2009:229–30), the ideas of which are summarized here. There were 152 bison bone fragments recovered at Paquimé. This is about 6 percent of the site's total bone sample of 2,689. These 152 bones were combined into a "minimum faunal count" (MFC) of 29 bison and 19 unspecific bovids, for a total of 48 animals (Di Peso et al. 1974:8:242). MFC is equivalent to the modern MNI, or minimum number of individuals represented in a context. Given that there were 152 bone fragments, each of the 48 individuals produced by MNI was represented by an average of 3.2 bones, which were described as only cranial and postcranial fragments. Nevertheless, these were assumed to be 48 complete bison, each of which yielded about 645 pounds of meat. The total is about 31,000 pounds of bison meat available for consumption at Paquimé. Total estimated weight of Medio period meat is given as 59,699 pounds, of which 52 percent is estimated to have come from bison (McKusick 1974b:244, figs. 297–98). From these figures came the idea that bison were a major source of meat in the settlement.

There are two significant problems here. The first is estimation of 48 whole animals at Paquimé based on the MNI counts from a number of contexts around the site. The error comes from summing MNI estimations from multiple contexts. It is illustrated as follows: fragments of one bison are scattered among four different features on a site. Based on these, an MNI number estimate of one bison is correctly derived for each feature. These MNI values of one bison represented in each of the four features are then *inappropriately* summed to produce a total MNI estimate of four bison on the site. There is wide agreement in the zooarchaeological literature that MNI estimates are not additive, as they are based on portions of individuals, not on whole specimens.

Nevertheless, the summing of many MNI values is clearly what was done for bison at Paquimé, almost certainly producing a substantial overestimate of their abundance. Based on extant data, we cannot say how many bison were represented at Late Medio Paquimé, but we can be confident that the number was fewer than 48. The second unacceptable assumption is that the entire meat weight of the estimated number of bison was present at Paquimé. This obviously was assumed in the site report, where an MNI of one (represented on average by 3.2 bone fragments) is interpreted as one whole bison, which equals 645 pounds of meat available for consumption at Paquimé, times 48. Such an assertion is insupportable, and it must be concluded that the role of bison meat as a protein source was greatly overestimated at Paquimé.

If people did not depend heavily on bison, then what meats did they consume? The most common types by percentage of MFC were antelope (32.1%), deer (16.6%), jackrabbits (13.8%), dogs (6.9%), rats (5.3%), and cottontails (4.9%). Bison and possible bison bones were present in small quantities (3.4%–5.6%). These data demonstrate a focus on small and medium-sized animals, which is a common pattern all over the adjacent U.S. Southwest (e.g., Driver 2002; Spielmann and Angstadt-Leto 1996). Antelope and deer were by far the most common game animals at Paquimé, together accounting for nearly half of the faunal remains. The addition of rabbits raises this proportion to about two-thirds of the faunal assemblage. If such also was the case at Paquimé, which had the most and best of so many things in the Casas Grandes area, what was the situation at other settlements of the Inner and Outer Core Zone?

Our excavations at four Outer Core Zone sites yielded 773 elements from large Site 204, and 391, 81, and 327 elements, respectively, from small Sites 231, 242, and 317. These represent 32 taxa of animals that were not equally distributed among the four settlements. A total of 20 faunal taxa came from large Site 204, compared with 12, 6, and 15, respectively, from small Sites 231, 242, and 317 (Whalen and Minnis 2009:231, table 7.9). The comparatively small number of taxa from Site 204, despite extensive excavations, may indicate that there was simply not as wide a variety of fauna available in the Outer Core's upland setting. We cannot say whether this limitation was ecological or social. The Outer Core sites, for instance, have no antelope remains and very few of deer, although those desirable game animals are found at Paquimé. Instead, Site 204 and its small neighbors, sites 231 and 317, have more rabbits, rats, squirrels, other rodents, and unidentified small mammals. The people of the Outer Core Zone, then, do not seem to have had as rich an assemblage of animal protein as those of the Inner Core Zone.

There is one exception. Small Outer Core Site 242 had more large mammal bones that are possibly bison (38%), and medium to large bones that most likely come from deer (18.5%) compared with small Sites 317 (1.5% and 0.0%) and 231 (1.0% and 0.0%), also of the Outer Core. Elsewhere (Whalen and Minnis 2001a, b) we describe 242 as a site with a unique combination of features: a large I-shaped ball court with the only platform mound outside Paquimé, an adobe room block built in a thick-walled style we have called an "architecture of power," large rooms, many platform hearths, and at least one macaw cage door stone. Although only a few dozen people could have lived there, Site 242 lay beside an exceptionally large system of agricultural terraces. The productivity of this system would have greatly exceeded the needs of the small 242 community, as well as requiring much more labor than so few people could have provided. The occupation of Site 242 was closely coincident with that of Paquimé, and we see this site as a node or agent of Paquimé, one of its roles being the organization of upland agricultural production. In chapter 5 of this volume, we note that Site 242 had a ceramic assemblage indicative of commensal activity. The large percentage of large and medium to large animal remains and the lack of diversity of faunal taxa recovered is best interpreted as the selective consumption of the most preferred meats. This pattern also suggests that the large number of large animal and large-medium remains from Paquimé may not be due to solely differential recovery, but rather reflects access to better meats that may have been in use during feasting events.

Faunal remains from Inner Core Zone large Site 315 and small Site 355 have been analyzed (Loven 2016). A total of 867 bones were identifiable, which is about half the total number recovered (table 8.8). These represent 37 animal taxa, of which 26 are identified at least to the genus level. The data are compiled from Loven (2016:37, 51, tables 1 and 2). The measure of abundance is the number of identified specimens (NISP). This is an

TABLE 8.8 Faunal remains from Inner Core Sites 315 and 355

Taxon	Common name	Site 315		Site 355	
		NISP	% NISP	NISP	% NISP
Lepus sp.	Jackrabbit	200	23.07	8	1.64
Sylvilagus sp.	Cottontail	98	11.30	15	3.08
Antilocapra americana	Pronghorn antelope	1	0.12	—	—
Odocoileus sp.	Deer	1	0.12	—	—
Ursus sp.	Bear	1	0.12	—	—
Procyon lotor	Raccoon	1	0.12	—	—
Mephitis sp.	Skunk	1	0.12	—	—
Thomomys sp.	Pocket gopher	1	0.12	—	—
Neotoma sp.	Woodrat	1	0.12	—	—
Cynomys sp.	Prairie dog	1	0.12	—	—
Artiodactyla indet.	Artiodactyl	35	4.04	42	8.62
Canis sp.	Dogs and coyotes	2	0.23	3	0.62
Canis familiaris	Dog	—	—	1	0.21
Peromyscus sp.	Mice	2	0.23	2	0.41
Ondatra zibethicus	Muskrat	—	—	1	0.21
Geomys sp.	Pocket gopher	2	0.23	1	0.21
Vulpes sp.	Fox	—	—	1	0.21
Salientia indet.	Frogs and toads	31	3.58	2	0.41
Meleagris gallopavo	Turkey	7	0.81	—	—
Falco sp.	Falcon/kestrel	1	0.12	—	—
Corvus sp.	Raven/crow	1	0.12	—	—
Anas sp.	Duck	1	0.12	—	—
Buteo sp.	Hawk	1	0.12	—	—
Cathartes aura	Turkey vulture	1	0.12	—	—
Athene cunicularia	Burrowing owl	1	0.12	—	—
Hesperiphona vespertina	Evening grosbeak	1	0.12	—	—
Icterus galbula bullockii	Bullock's oriole	2	0.23	—	—
Testudinata indet.	Turtle	5	0.58	—	—
Serpentes indet.	Snakes	1	0.12	—	—
Crotalus sp.	Rattlesnake	1	0.12	—	—
Very small mammal	Mouse to rat size	24	2.77	—	—
Small mammal	Prairie dog to cottontail size	37	4.27	11	2.26
Small-medium mammal	Jackrabbit to raccoon size	51	5.88	27	5.54
Medium mammal	Bobcat to fox size	54	6.23	19	3.90
Medium-large mammal	Dog to deer size	167	19.26	237	48.70
Large mammal	Deer to bear size	106	12.23	108	22.2
Small bird	Finch to quail size	4	0.46	6	1.23
Medium bird	Crow to hawk size	15	1.61	—	—
Large bird	Vulture to turkey size	4	0.46	2	0.41
Fishes	Fish	2	0.23	1	0.21
NISP Total		**867**	**100.00**	**487**	**100.00**

observational unit for the entire site. The minimum number of individuals (MNI) is an interpretive unit that should be based on the NISP (Klein and Cruz-Uribe 1984:28; Lyman 1994:99). The NISP percentage provides a good comparative measure of taxon abundance for the entire site.

These Inner Core large site and small site assemblages are noticeably different. Large Site 315 shows a wide range of taxa, including many birds and creatures of the nearby river and its banks, such as ducks, fish, and turtles. Even so, rabbits and small to medium animals made up nearly half of the bone assemblage at Site 315, which resembles Outer Core Site 204's assemblage in its high frequency of rabbits and other small to medium animals. Rabbits were clearly important resources at Inner and Outer Core sites and beyond. For instance, rabbits made up by far the largest proportion of the faunal remains at the Villa Ahumada site in the desert lowlands east of Paquimé (Cruz Antillón et al. 2004). A large difference between Inner Core Site 315 and Outer Core Site 204 is the frequency of medium to large animal remains. At upland Site 204, they are less than 5 percent of the assemblage, while the same figure at Inner Core Site 315 exceeds 25 percent of its assemblage. This is also the case at Outer Core Paquimé-agent Site 242 and at Paquimé itself. Larger animals thus seem most common on those settlements with the closest ties to Paquimé.

Inner Core small Site 355 is close to Paquimé as well, but its faunal assemblage is different in two ways. The most common categories of bones in descending order are medium or large mammal, large mammal, indeterminate artiodactyls that likely were deer and antelope, cottontails, and then jackrabbits. Both the dominance of larger animals and the large proportion of cottontails compared to jackrabbits are atypical. We suggest that these differences were produced by the occupational history of Site 355. This small site was built in the Late Medio, but it has a strong component of remodeling done in the Post–Casas Grandes Architectural Tradition (see chapter 3). Some of its faunal assemblage, then, may have been accumulated by the later inhabitants of the site. The ecology of the Casas Grandes River valley might have been somewhat different after the depopulation of Paquimé, as native vegetation returned to the formerly cleared fields. Such a situation is indicated by the presence at 355 of more cottontails than jack rabbits, the former preferring areas with heavier brush cover, while the latter thrive in open spaces. This small community's higher frequencies of medium to large animals might also reflect the decline of Paquimé, with the exceptional quantities of larger game consumed by that community. Remains of several bird taxa are represented in the Inner Core faunal assemblage. Most are minor components of the whole, although two taxa stand out. These are macaws and turkeys, which were important during the Late Medio period at Paquimé. Macaws are considered in chapter 7 of this volume, and we turn now to the other most numerous bird taxon in Casas Grandes area assemblages: turkeys.

Turkeys

Turkeys were commonly kept in Puebloan societies of the adjacent U.S. Southwest, and remains interpreted as 323 turkeys come from Paquimé (Di Peso et al. 1974:8:288–289, figs. 322–28; McKusick 1974a:274–75, figs. 310–18), This apparently substantial number led to the idea of large-scale turkey breeding there (Di Peso 1974:2:602). The same idea was echoed by McKusick (1974a:273–74), who termed the community's turkey breeding "a major industry." More recently, turkey breeding was characterized as being at "an industrial scale" by Lekson (2008:211). In reality, however, we do not know how many turkeys there were in that community. Their numbers almost certainly have been significantly overestimated in the same way as macaws (chapter 7) and bison: that is, by the erroneous practice of summing MFC (or MNI) estimates for all the site's provenances. Di Peso and colleagues' bird burial figure (1974:8:288–89, figs. 322–28) shows this clearly. In each of the burial categories, MCF (MNI) estimates are transposed into equivalent numbers of birds. Fragments thus become whole turkeys. A single example is the "miscellaneous remains" category, the bones of which are described as "sparse and fragmentary" (Di Peso et al. 1974:8:305). There is an MFC (MNI) estimate of 37 turkey entries in this sparse and fragmentary category, which is transposed to 37 whole birds to make up the reported total of 323. Many other remains come from "mixed carcass" contexts, in which it is not clear which bones were present and how many of the reported number of birds were reasonably complete. In short, we cannot estimate the actual number of turkeys in the community without reanalysis and consideration of the NISP. These data are not provided in the Casas Grandes report, however, and we can now be confident only that 323 is an overestimate.

But even if the unacceptable total of 323 birds is used, the turkey population at Paquimé would have been equaled or surpassed at other late prehistoric communities in the region. The reported total from the Arroyo Hondo Pueblo, New Mexico, is 384 individuals, while that of the nearby Pueblo Encierro is 342 (Lang and Harris 1984). The remains of about 900 turkeys were found at the Gran Quivira pueblo (McKusick 1980), and early Historic Spanish accounts report flocks of hundreds of birds in the Piro pueblos (Schroeder 1968). The turkey population of Paquimé, even by the original overestimation, is not outstandingly large. In fact, it might be rather small compared to contemporary communities in the U.S. Southwest.

TURKEY BREEDING AND TRADING AT PAQUIMÉ

Turkeys are native to wide areas of the highland NW/SW and Mesoamerica (Schorger 1966:43 and 49), including the mountains immediately west of Paquimé. At least some turkeys are considered to have been domesticated in the NW/SW (Speller et al. 2010), although the distinction between their domestic and wild forms has recently been termed "an oversimplification" based on genetic data (Lipe et al. 2016:97). In any case, large-scale turkey breeding was and still is envisioned at Paquimé. Evidence used to support this claim includes (a) the large numbers of turkeys of all ages found in the community; (b) the presence of turkey eggshells; and (c) facilities taken to be breeding or roosting bins (Di Peso 1974:2:734, note 21).

Data from the site report (McKusick 1974a:274–75, figs. 310–18) show that about 88 percent of turkey remains at Paquimé were classed as adults, while the remaining 12 percent were juveniles or immature birds. How many of the juvenile remains were those of turkey chicks is unknown. A study of wild turkeys shows that two clutches of eggs per year is common for laying hens, while domestic turkey hens may lay eggs all year (Schorger 1966:263). Data cited by Windes (1987:680) show that a brood of turkeys usually contains one hen and four to eight chicks. This suggests that a breeding population of turkeys, especially one managed by humans, should contain a larger number of young birds than is reflected in the data from Paquimé.

It is notable, however, that the mostly adult set of turkey remains at Paquimé is matched elsewhere in the region. At Big Juniper House, Mesa Verde, Colorado, turkeys make up 97 percent of identified avian bones, and adult birds comprise about 87 percent of identifiable bones and about 71 percent of the MNI (Swannack 1969:160, table 11). Adult turkeys are also the most common at the Grasshopper Pueblo of east-central Arizona (Olsen 1990:47). Data on late prehistoric turkey populations from all over the NW/SW thus show a similar pattern of mostly adult turkeys. This might reflect differential preservation of the remains of chicks, or it could be attributed to trade in subadult birds as opposed to a significant amount of local breeding.

Since wild turkeys are found in much of the highland NW/SW, there exists the distinct possibility that birds were captured from the wild and kept in Pueblo communities as a supplement to the pueblo-dwelling turkeys that also existed in the region (Lipe et al. 2016; Speller et al. 2010). The Tarahumara Indians of the mountain zone adjacent to Paquimé demonstrate the feasibility of wild turkey capture. This account is cited by the avian faunal analyst who made the original study of the turkeys of Paquimé (McKusick 1974a:274). "The turkey (*siwi*) in a domesticated state is not often seen among the Tarahumaras. However, plenty of turkeys are found wild in the sierra and brought home by the Indians. They are fed and carefully raised until they become quite tame and do not try to run away. It is not even necessary to clip their wings" (Bennett and Zingg 1935:23).

But what of other cited evidences for extensive breeding of birds in the community? The presence of turkey eggshells was taken in the Paquimé report as proof of on-site breeding (Di Peso 1974:2:734, note 21; McKusick 1974a:274), but there are several problems with this proposition. First, eggshells alone provide no direct evidence of bird breeding, as argued specifically for turkeys (Beacham and Durand 2007:1611). This study used electron microscopy to examine structural features of samples of modern and prehistoric turkey eggshells, documenting features of the shells that indicate the degree of development of the embryo. The authors convincingly maintain that the only definitive evidence of turkey breeding is shell determined to be from hatched eggs (Beacham and Durand 2007:1620). Unfortunately, the study was confined to a small sample of prehistoric turkey eggshells from the Salmon Ruin of northwest New Mexico. The study determined that some shell was from hatched eggs while other fragments were not. Certainly, this is a promising technique for future applications.

The second point relevant to turkey husbandry at Paquimé is the sheer quantity of shell recovered in site excavations. Many eggshell fragments have been recovered at sites in the northern U.S. Southwest, including Chaco Canyon, Mesa Verde, and Sand Canyon. For example, the Sand Canyon excavations have yielded more than 2,500 eggshell fragments (Munro 1994:94–95), while turkey eggshell fragments from the Pueblo Alto site, Chaco

Canyon, numbered 1,942 (Windes 1987:681). We do not know how many eggshells were involved in the Paquimé study. The analytical report refers to nine shell samples of unspecified size that appear to be from turkey eggs. The identifications, however, are phrased in terms of individually provenanced specimens, of which nine are from Medio period contexts at Paquimé (McKusick 1974a:281–82). Whether nine pieces of shell or nine batches of shell were identified, it does not appear that Paquimé yielded eggshell fragments in the thousands, as did other just-cited pueblos. It could be that most of the eggshell fragments from Paquimé were not collected due to the lack of fine screening throughout the site's excavation. Alternatively, the gathering of wild turkey eggs could easily account for a small total from Paquimé, and this practice is documented for the nearby Tarahumara (Bennett and Zingg 1935:23). In any case, the extant eggshell from Paquimé should not be taken as evidence of significant turkey production, as it traditionally has been.

A piece of evidence of intensive turkey husbandry that is missing from Paquimé is dung. No accumulations of turkey dung are reported from the site, in marked contrast to other areas farther north. At the Long House ruin at Mesa Verde, Colorado, there was an area about 40 m long and 13 m wide where deposits of turkey dung ranged from 0.6 to 1 m in depth (Munro 1994:99). Assuming an average depth of 0.75 m, this is nearly 400 m³ of turkey dung. Other turkey enclosures at Mug House, Mesa Verde, covered about 10 square meters, the floors of which "consisted largely of consolidated turkey droppings" (Rohn 1971:44). Thick layers of turkey dung and feathers are also reported from Big Juniper House and Mesa Verde, as well as from Johnson Canyon Pueblo III contexts to the south of Mesa Verde (Munro 1994:99). Cyler Conrad (2021:646) identifies the localized accumulation of dung as one of the best indicators of turkey penning, regardless of the type of space or associated materials.

Also present at sites in the northern part of the U.S. Southwest are gastroliths, or gizzard stones, which are small rocks swallowed by many birds (including turkeys) to assist the gizzard in reducing such tough foods as seeds. The stones are retained in the gizzard until they are ground away or until the bird dies and decomposition releases the stones into the archaeological record. Gizzard stones are frequently reported from sites of the Pueblo II and III periods in the northern part of the U.S. Southwest (Munro 1994:97, 44), although they are unreported in the southern Southwest and in Northwest Mexico, including Paquimé. Whether the birds are kept in confinement or in some type of free-range setting might explain the observed situation. This is suggested because of the correlation between the presence of gizzard stones and of large quantities of turkey dung. The Long House ruin at Mesa Verde, Colorado, produced both gizzard stones and the remarkable quantity of dung described in a preceding paragraph.

The about 1 m² features classified by Di Peso as turkey roosting pens at Paquimé are much smaller than other such facilities in the U.S. Southwest. This does not disqualify them as pens or nesting boxes, but they are also entirely dung-free. The Paquimé pens open onto a large plaza, but no dung deposits were reported there, either. This situation is similar to other pueblos in the Mogollon area. Grasshopper of east-central Arizona has many turkey bones but no identified pens or dung deposits. The same is true of the Classic

Mimbres pueblos of southwestern New Mexico. It was opined decades ago that the absence of recognizable turkey confinement areas from central Arizona through the Mimbres area shows a different pattern of turkey husbandry than is reflected in the dung-filled pens of the PIII northern pueblos (Reed 1951:201). The northern Pueblo III situation resulted from confinement of many turkeys for long periods. A similar interpretation of intensive turkey production in the late Pueblo world is found in recent literature (Driver 2002:151–60). In contrast, the southern pattern of substantial numbers of turkey bones but few or no dung deposits and gizzard stones suggests some less-intensive, shorter-duration, or lower-confinement approach to turkey husbandry. It has been observed that turkeys need not be kept caged, as they can be tethered (Conrad 2021:640) or allowed to roam and forage for themselves (Munro 1994:58). This option, however, may be limited by factors like numbers of turkeys or ownership patterns of the birds. By all indicators discussed here—eggshells, gizzard stones, and dung deposits—Paquimé more closely fits the southern pattern of turkey management. Moreover, data presented earlier in this chapter show that Paquimé did not have more turkeys than many other contemporary pueblos in the U.S. Southwest. The present study, then, does not see good evidence for either large-scale breeding or trading of turkeys at or from Paquimé.

Turkey remains are sparsely represented among the neighbors of Paquimé. Jeremy Loven (2016) identified seven bones as turkey and four "large bird" remains from Site 355 that could be turkeys or some other large bird. None of the Outer Core sites have such remains. In southern Chihuahua, the Babícora Basin's El Zurdo site yielded a faunal assemblage with many turkey bones. This is due mostly to the recovery of five intact turkey burials. Removing those, turkey remains account for 6.8 percent of the El Zurdo bones. After turkey remains, the next most common taxa were jackrabbits, cottontails, and medium-sized artiodactyls, likely antelope and deer (Hodgetts 1996). The El Zurdo site deposits cover the Southern Viejo and Southern Medio periods.

USES OF TURKEYS IN THE CASAS GRANDES AREA

Turkeys played multifaceted roles in the Puebloan societies of the U.S. Southwest, as sacrifices, sources of feathers, and food resources. These roles are not mutually exclusive, although Di Peso et al. (1974:8:269–71) and McKusick (1974b:273, 2001:43) saw the turkeys of Paquimé as sacrificial animals and providers of feathers but not as food sources. This distinction of use exists in the U.S. Southwest as well, where there are few indications that turkeys were eaten prior to about AD 900. After that date, consumption was added to the birds' other uses (Badenhorst and Driver 2009; Hargrave 1965). Shortages of wild game, especially artiodactyls, it is argued, were offset by intensification of turkey consumption by Puebloan peoples (e.g., Driver 2002:158; Grimstead et al. 2016:129; Spielmann and Angstadt-Leto 1996:92). Turkey consumption increased in later prehistory at Chaco Canyon's Pueblo Alto, Arroyo Hondo, Homol'ovi, Mesa Verde, and the pueblos of the Rio Grande Valley, to name a few examples. Rabbits and similar small game were used as protein supplements as well, but turkeys provide much more meat per animal, while still supplying the settlements' need for feathers.

But how can turkey consumption be detected in the archaeological record? Louise Senior and Linda Pierce (1989:251) provided a useful list of observations that point to use of turkeys as food, as well as others indicating nonfood use of the birds. All are summarized in the following discussion. Butchering marks or burning on turkey bones are obvious signs that turkeys were eaten, but they may not always be present on the bones of consumed birds. Some parts of the skeleton require more dismemberment by cutting than do others, so it is essential to specify which bones were examined to support arguments for or against butchering. More subtle is the crushing of cancellous ends of long bones, a practice designed to release high fat concentrations when the bones are boiled. "Such smashed bones would be evidence of 'butchering' of turkeys even though cut marks would not be present on the bones" (Senior and Pierce 1989:251). Extensive disarticulation of remains suggests that turkeys were eaten. Missing tibiotarsal ossified tendons, or splints, indicate consumption, as these skeletal elements are removed with the meat in which they are embedded. Hargrave (1965:162) discusses this at length. Turkey consumption should result in few fully mature or aged birds in the population. Females are less likely to be eaten because of their smaller size, lower fat content, and breeding potential. There are also observations pointing toward nonfood use of turkeys (Senior and Pierce 1989:251). These include articulated skeletons, differential treatment of turkey remains, and ossified tendons (or splints) still attached to the tibiotarsal remains. The turkey population should include mature and aged birds, and the sex ratio might be more balanced than in situations of consumption.

The Paquimé dataset meets some of the expectations, both for and against turkey consumption. Others cannot be examined with the MFC (MNI) dataset, which is the only one presently in hand. These include crushing of cancellous ends of long bones, tibiotarsal splint frequencies, and the birds' ages at death. No specific data are provided for the many hundreds of turkey bones from the site, for which there is simply the statement that "there is no evidence of food use" (McKusick 1974a:275). Paquimé is reported to contain the burials of many articulated whole turkey skeletons, but unfortunately there are no published photographs or drawings of these turkey burials. By examination of those made for macaws in the original field notebooks (Whalen 2022:234–35), it was determined that many of the birds included in the analytical categories of "relatively complete" and "articulated" were, in fact, only fragments of skeletons. Is the situation similar for turkeys? If so, then the number of articulated whole turkey burials would be significantly smaller than the reported figure, and there would be substantially more scattered disarticulated turkey bones in the site. The turkey bones from Paquimé are in urgent need of further study to support or correct extant interpretations.

Anthropogenic Ecology of Animal Populations

Large numbers of humans in the Casas Grandes region by the Late Medio period, or after ca. AD 1300, likely had a considerable effect on the abundance and distribution of animal populations. The high frequency of rabbits versus large game could be indicators of overhunting the immediate region. The greater number of jackrabbits versus cottontails could be evidence of the removal of ground cover, which cottontails prefer. Turkeys become more common in the Late Medio, and some of them might have been used for food, as they were in other overhunted parts of the pre-Hispanic U.S. Southwest. Loven (2016) has suggested that the increase in medium to large mammal remains at Site 355, a Late Medio site that appears to have been occupied after the depopulation of Paquimé, could reflect a rebound from intense hunting pressure if the human population was smaller than it was during the florescence of the principal center.

Concluding Thoughts

Our analyses are somewhat limited by the incompatible recovery methods used at Paquimé, the most important site in the region. Nonetheless, we can draw some conclusions about the domestic and community food economies. The people of the study area used a wide range of plants and animals for food, fuel, rituals, and material culture. Farming was certainly the economic mainstay of settlements all over the Core Zone. Similar crops were grown, albeit under different environmental conditions, including major river floodplain, small tributaries, and upland settings dependent on rainfall alone. Maize was undoubtedly the most important crop, used as a daily staple and probably also for production of corn beer for use in commensal events. Other cultivated plants that have been found in the Casas Grandes area include squash, gourd, cotton, beans, and perhaps agave. Cultivated little barley and chile remains are present as well, but we do not know whether these two plants were cultivated as ordinary food sources or whether they played some more special ceremonial roles in the community economy.

Cultivated foods were supplemented by collection of wild plant foods. The edible seeds of weedy plants such as amaranth and portulaca are common in flotation samples. Although they are useful food plants, this weedy vegetation is termed *disturbance taxa*, as they thrive when there is substantial soil disturbance. By the Late Medio period, we envision large dense populations and consequent efforts to intensify agricultural production. This would naturally involve increased field clearance, in turn promoting the spread of weedy disturbance taxa. We also emphasize that green and tuberous foods were probably consumed, although their remains are unlikely to be recovered by flotation. Another supplement to subsistence in the Casas Grandes area was hunting, increasingly directed toward small mammals such as rabbits and other rodents. This is a common pattern seen all over the U.S. Southwest. Turkey production was a commonly used subsistence supplement in the U.S. Southwest, and we see no reason that it should not have been so in the Casas Grandes area. There, current opinion is that these birds were used primarily for feather production and ritual sacrifice, not as a food source, although further research is needed to verify or correct this idea. In any case, we suspect that animal foods were not a major component of the diet. Instead, high-quality meats of antelope, deer, bison, and perhaps turkey may have been restricted to certain social groups or to special occasions.

Settlements farther from Paquimé in the Outer Core Zone seem to have had a more impoverished faunal assemblage than did their contemporaries of the Inner Core, including Paquimé. Turkeys also seem to have been restricted to the Inner Core Zone. They were kept at Paquimé, and they were also present at neighboring Site 315.

Abundant wood charcoal remains from our sites offer insights into the use of plants for fuel, a major need not often recognized by archaeologists. Nearly a billion pounds of wood might have been required for fuel by the inhabitants of Late Medio Paquimé, and this figure does not include wood used for other purposes or wood required by the numerous communities in the surrounding region. Local woods were heavily used, including those found along the floodplain, mostly cottonwood/willow but also sycamore and elm. Away from the floodplains, utilized woods included juniper, oak, mesquite/acacia, and piñon pine.

The most interesting wood pattern is the wide use of pine, a wood found in the Sierra Madre to the west. Pine was used for roof beams, as it provided the long straight timbers needed for the often large spans of rooms at Paquimé. It is less obvious why pine was so frequently used as fuel. A likely explanation is that high Late Medio usage lead to deforestation of the areas closest to the sites, requiring wood to be obtained farther afield. Some pine could have been carried down to the lowlands by seasonal flooding in watercourses descending from the Sierra Madre. Mountain pine could also have been supplied as charcoal, which would be much easier to transport to the lowlands. This would require at least some economic ties between mountain populations and those of the Casas Grandes area.

Plant and animal remains are not the only way to study pre-Hispanic diet. Isotopic analyses of dental enamel and bone collagen from human remains at Casas Grandes sites have been analyzed to investigate dietary variation among Late Medio period people and between the Viejo and Late Medio periods (McConnan Borstad 2021). Courtney McConnan Borstad's research concludes that there was a similar diet among different groups and across time. It was based on maize, with animals and wild plants important dietary components. In general, this isotopic analysis is consistent with conclusions based on carbonized plant remains and animal bones.

We found clear evidence of environmental changes due to human activity. The increase in weedy plants, the surprisingly large use of pine wood for fuel, and the shift in importance of cottontails to jackrabbits are all reflective of human environmental modification. These processes should have reached their maximum in the Late Medio period, or after ca. AD 1300. Yet, we see only the maximum-effect end product of anthropogenic ecological change that started sometime earlier. More research is clearly needed (Minnis and Whalen 2015).

Finally, we return to the nature of the social, ritual, and power structures in the Casas Grandes tradition. While the study of plant and animal remains is most valuable for other questions about ecology and subsistence in the Casas Grandes area, these datasets also provide some insights into broader topics. For instance, plants and animals were not only food or utilitarian commodities. In addition, they played roles in the formation and maintenance of social relationships. For example, there is the argument that Paquimé, well situated in a very productive part of the Casas Grandes River valley, had an ecological advantage that enabled production of the surplus used to fund the aspirations of competing groups or individuals in this middle range society. Some plants and animals, from chile to bison and other medium to large game animals, may have been more common at Paquimé and its nearest neighbors. These special foods likely both reflected and reinforced the prominence of their consumers. Although cacao would fit nicely among the other high-quality foods used in the Inner Core, we cannot yet suggest such a pattern, as only Inner Core sites have been tested for its presence. Beyond these, a general increase in agricultural productivity would have been essential to provide the staple finance supporting the commensal events associated with ritual and the maintenance of the social order in Late Medio times.

# Chapter 9

Paquimé and Its Neighbors

Community Formation and Fragmentation

Chapter 1 of this volume reiterates what has been a principal research question since the beginning of our work in the Casas Grandes area in 1989: How and to what extent did Paquimé affect its near and distant neighbors? This is certainly a large and multifaceted problem, the solution of which is a task beyond the scope of any single project or set of projects. It is best tackled through investigation of many smaller questions that build toward a larger solution. The present volume's focus is on three questions. First, what were the occupational histories of the nearest large and small neighbors of Paquimé, and how do these compare with that of the principal center itself? Second, what levels of complexity and functional diversity did these neighbors maintain, especially the large ones near Paquimé? Third, how did Paquimé relate to its nearest neighbors?

There are several possibilities for the occupational histories of these nearest neighbors. Do they represent a pre-Paquimé population that was drawn into the rising center, resulting in the abandonment of many sites by the fourteenth century? Were they active components of a settlement system that was contemporary with the florescence of Paquimé? Or do they represent settlements that grew up after the demise of the center? Clearly, there are variants of each of these questions where large and small settlements are concerned. The nearest neighbors of Paquimé were recorded during the intensive survey (Whalen and Minnis 2001a), but their surface ceramics identify them only as Medio period. More detailed investigation of their occupational histories could not be done without excavation and chronometric dating. Even with such studies, we remain at a disadvantage, as radiocarbon dating is the only effective and large-scale chronometric technique at our disposal. We have nothing approaching the precision and variety of dating techniques in the adjacent U.S. Southwest.

In addition, it is essential to learn more about what these large and small neighbors were like in terms of their complexity, or the types and varieties of functions that they discharged in their settlement systems. All of the sites studied here lie in the Core Zone, which the settlement pattern study (Whalen and Minnis 2001a) argued to have been the most effectively integrated part of the Paquimé regional system, but were all of them fairly alike within the hierarchical size categories established by the settlement pattern survey? Here it is essential to distinguish between several different types of hierarchies, or ranked structures: "Global-regional-local climate is an example of a scalar hierarchy: any level can affect any other. The American court system is an example of a control hierarchy: decisions at higher levels affect the operations of lower levels" (Crumley 1995:2).

There is a clear scalar hierarchy among the neighbors of Paquimé. It is a size-ranked structure, ranging from very large to very small settlements, but how can this be interpreted? Crumley observes, "Scalar hierarchies are routinely mistaken for control hierarchies" (1995:2). That is, the simple position of an element in a structure is given meaning without considering the number and kind of functions that it might have discharged. Consequently, the pattern of settlements of different sizes in the Casas Grandes area should not simply be assumed to represent a control hierarchy without seeking further indicators of activities that should be associated with management. Finally, to what extent did Paquimé exert centralized control of its neighbors, and how far did such centralization extend? The intent of this concluding chapter is to consider the implications of these questions for the large and small sites of the Inner and Outer Core Zones.

Site Occupational Histories

Our dataset consists of 238 radiocarbon dates secured from our work at large and small Core Zone sites over the past several decades. An earlier study (Whalen and Minnis 2009:45–67) considered the occupational histories of Outer Core Zone large Site 204 and its small Outer Core neighboring sites 231, 242, and 317. That study used what has come to be called the "Dates as Data" approach introduced by Rick (1987) and widely applied thereafter. Here, date frequency histograms are used to monitor the occupational histories of areas or sites. The assumption of this approach is that the number of dates produced by a context is broadly reflective of the magnitude of its occupation. Date ranges (i.e., the mean age with standard deviations on either side) are plotted as horizontal lines. Vertical lines are drawn across the horizontal ones at regular intervals, here, 25 years. Histogram bars are then formed from the number of horizontal lines intersected by each vertical one. This approach has been criticized (e.g., as summarized by Crema 2022:1388– 89) when date frequencies were taken as proxy measures of population size, and we acknowledge the validity of that discussion. Assuming, however, that the date sets in hand are reasonable samples of their contexts, the frequency histograms are useful ways to compare occupational histories of different sites or areas. The 2009 study presented a calibrated date frequency distribution for Outer Core large Site 204, which is reproduced here as part of figure 9.1.

Figure 9.1, top, suggests an initial occupation of Outer Core Site 204 in the Viejo period (ca. AD 1000 to the late 1100s), after which date frequencies rise rapidly through the Early Medio (ca. late 1100s to AD 1300). After a peak around 1300, the 204 date frequencies decline through the Late Medio, or after ca. AD 1300. None of the date ranges extend further than the early 1400s at this site. From these data, we argue that a substantial part of the

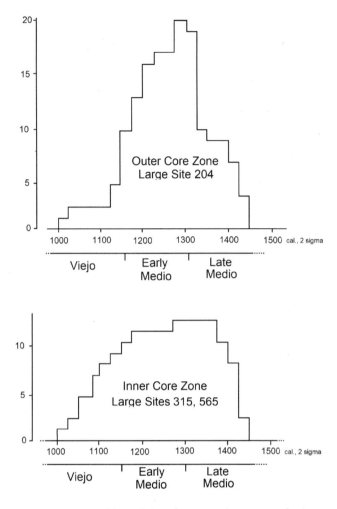

FIGURE 9.1 Calibrated date frequency histograms for large Core Zone sites.

occupation of Site 204 took place in Early Medio times. There was Late Medio occupation as well, of the main room block mound and of the two smaller room blocks that lay at either end of the oblong main mound. The 2009 study suggested that at least some of the population from Site 204 might have been drawn into the rising Late Medio center of Paquimé.

A date frequency histogram for large Inner Core Zone sites 315 and 565 is shown in the lower part of figure 9.1. They are combined here to increase the number of dates. The pattern is notably different from that of Outer Core Site 204. The Inner Zone has a substantial number of Viejo period dates, and date frequencies rise rapidly through that period to the mid- to late 1100s or 1200, which is the opening of the Early Medio period. Date frequencies continue to increase through the 1200s, peaking around 1300, or the opening of the Late Medio period. This peak holds through the 1300s, declining rapidly after AD 1400 and reaching zero by the mid-1400s. The interesting point of difference between the large Outer Core Site 204 and large Inner Core sites 315 and 565 is the prevalence of Late Medio dates. These decline at Site 204, while they remain at high levels at both Inner Core large Sites 315 and 565. The significance of this pattern for the present study is that the nearest large neighbors of Paquimé do not decline in size as the principal center rises. This answers a question posed at the end of an earlier volume (Whalen and Minnis 2009:277). The Outer Core situation, in contrast, suggests the opposite pattern. It might be argued that the populations closest to Paquimé are those most likely to be absorbed by its growth. In fact, this does not appear to be the case. We do not see a situation in which the principal center absorbs most of the surrounding population, emptying its immediate surroundings.

Absence of large near neighbors is often seen in settlement systems that are strongly dominated by a powerful center. For example, the Mississippian center of Moundville was a primate center at its peak (ca. AD 1300–1450). Survey shows that there were no other large neighbors in the Black Warrior River valley then, when only small hamlets and farmsteads existed (Welch 1998:138). The same is true on a more dramatic scale at the Mesoamerican center of Teotihuacán in the Early Classic period (Sanders et al. 1979). The primate centers in both of these cases showed high levels of centralization and powerful, comprehensive integration of surrounding populations. The Moundville case has been termed an "apical" hierarchy (R. A. Beck 2003), where substantial power is directed outward from the head settlement, strongly affecting regional demography and settlement characteristics. It has long been assumed that Paquimé had apical characteristics (e.g., Di Peso 1974:2:314–15). A corollary assumption was that the hierarchy of size among Medio communities represented a control hierarchy in a strongly integrated system, but we now doubt this interpretation. Some time ago, we observed that site size and complexity are not strongly correlated in the Casas Grandes Core Zone (Whalen and Minnis 2009:150–51), so that the Core Zone neighbors of Paquimé seem better described as components of a scalar hierarchy.

We turn next to the occupational histories of the small sites, both the Inner Core examples studied in this volume and those of the Outer Core that were reported on in the 2009 study. Do these Inner and Outer Core settlements show growth and occupation patterns similar to those of their large neighbors? Figure 9.2 suggests that they do not. All over the Core Zone, small sites had no Viejo period dates, and few of their date ranges extended back to the Early Medio. Occupations at all investigated small sites, then, were phenomena of the Late Medio period, or of times after ca. AD 1300. How long these occupations lasted is now the question, and the histograms of figure 9.2, when compared to those of the large sites (figure 9.1), hint at somewhat longer occupations of the small sites, relative to their larger counterparts.

Continued occupation of these sites would not be in accord with the established view (Di Peso 1974:2), in which the abandonments of Paquimé and the Casas Grandes region were simultaneous. That model rests on the assumption that the life of Paquimé was congruent with that of its ceramic assemblage across the area. The one was the other, so that both grew, flourished, declined, and finally ceased together. The fact that only Medio period ceramics are found in the Casas Grandes area, then, was taken to signify regional abandonment after the fall of the principal center. In contesting this interpretation, we

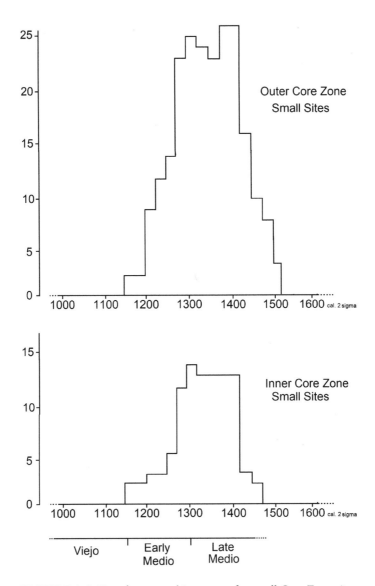

FIGURE 9.2 Date frequency histograms for small Core Zone sites.

argue in this volume that much of the ceramic tradition did not fall out of use with the decline of Paquimé. Rather, we see continued use of utilitarian ceramics that always make up most of the Late Medio assemblage.

This was accompanied by a cruder version of the Casas Grandes Architectural Tradition. Preceding discussion in this volume asserted that Paquimé was largely a phenomenon of the 1300s and that it had declined significantly by the early 1400s (e.g., Phillips and Gamboa 2015:163–64; Schaafsma and Riley 1999:244). Di Peso's Diablo phase remodeling of the Medio Architectural Tradition at the principal center thus likely dates to the early 1400s, and perhaps even to the last years of the 1300s. This Late Medio remodeling was not confined to Paquimé. Large neighbor 315 had similar construction, all of which was done within the Casas Grandes Architectural Tradition (CGAT), as shown in chapter 4.

There was evidently a second round of remodeling, which we have termed the Post–Casas Grandes Architectural Tradition (PCGAT).

All three of the small sites of the Inner Core Zone showed crude PCGAT remodeling of their original CGAT building style. There is a hint that this PCGAT building took place sometime after the Diablo phase work at the larger sites. This activity was mostly undated, but one radiocarbon sample secured from part of the rebuilding on small Site 355 gave a date of 570 + 30 radiocarbon years BP, or calibrated AD 1306–1424 (2σ). The radiocarbon date intersects a "wiggle" in the calibration curve at two points, defining two date ranges. The first is 1306–1364, with an associated probability of 57.7 percent, and the second is 1385–1424, with a still-strong probability of 37.7 percent. In keeping with strategy described in chapter 3, we took the earliest and latest dates to produce a range of 1306–1424, but there is a good probability that the true date extends into the first quarter of the fifteenth century. In addition, in chapter 8, we cite opinion that the increase in large animal remains at Inner Core small Site 355 might represent a "rebound" of the valley's ecology after the abandonment of the large settlements. The PCGAT building was done while the CGAT walls and floors were not yet covered by heavy infill, as noted in chapter 3. Both of these observations hint at a time interval on the order of decades between the Diablo phase end of the CGAT and the PCGAT building.

Unfortunately, given the limits of our present chronological control, we can only say that by the early 1400s, all investigated small sites of the Inner Core Zone showed crude PCGAT architecture, attenuated assemblages of Late Medio period pottery, and chipped and ground stone assemblages that were relatively sparse and simple. We therefore reject the original model in which the Medio period, as defined by its distinctive ceramics, ends when the CGAT falls out of use. There is Medio period pottery with the PCGAT building. We presently cannot say how long these occupations continued, but they appear to have been occupied longer than the large sites of the Inner Core. The situation is more confusing among the small sites of the Outer Core Zone. There are 27 radiocarbon date ranges from these sites, 16 of which have 2σ upper limits extending at least to 1425. Eleven of these reach 1450, and some extend into the 1500s and 1600s. Typical Late Medio ceramics were found on all of them. All these dates were presented and discussed in an earlier study (Whalen and Minnis 2009:60–67). At that time, we noted that five of the dates had standard deviations of more than ±100 years, and these are the ones that extend into the 1500s and 1600s. All of these large-sigma dates were processed decades ago by the same laboratory. Dates on the same sites were recently processed by two other laboratories, producing deviations of ±40 to 60 years. The late ends of these new date ranges, then, do not extend so far toward Historic times. It is certainly possible that Medio period ceramics continued to be made for generations after the demise of the center, but the five dates in question are too shaky a basis for such a proposition. Accordingly, we omit them here. We emphasize, however, that doing so does not move the upper limits of occupation back into the early 1400s. As figure 9.2 shows, there still remains the possibility of small site occupation in the mid-1400s and into the 1500s. Such remnant occupations have long been suggested for the Casas Grandes area by other researchers (e.g., P. Fish et al. 1994:163; Wilcox 1999:121).

This discussion of the occupational histories of the large and small neighbors of Paquimé reaches the following conclusions. First, there were large Late Medio settlements lying within a few kilometers of Paquimé and contemporary with it. At its fourteenth-century peak, Paquimé *did not* absorb the immediately surrounding population. Second, occupations of the Inner and Outer Core large sites do not appear to extend much beyond the early 1400s. Others have argued that substantial occupation of Paquimé itself did not extend much beyond the early 1400s (e.g., Phillips and Gamboa 2015; Schaafsma and Riley 1999). The large Inner and Outer Core settlements, including the principal center, thus seem to have had similar histories of decline. In contrast, there is an apparent difference in the earlier histories of these settlements. Large Site 204 of the Outer Core Zone seems to reach its occupational peak by ca. AD 1300, which is the end of the Early Medio or the beginning of the Late Medio. Occupation continues thereafter, although it appears to decline through Late Medio times, reaching its end by the early 1400s. Large Inner Core sites 315 and 565 do not follow this pattern. Their peaks come in the Late Medio, but they are sustained through the period, declining only in the late 1300s or early 1400s. This is the same pattern seen at Paquimé.

Our third point is that the investigated small settlements of the Core Zone do not exactly follow either of these growth and decline patterns. Their occupations are entirely Late Medio, and both Inner Core and Outer Core small sites have date ranges whose extreme ranges extend, respectively, to AD 1450 and 1500. We stress that all these sites contain Late Medio ceramic assemblages. They have few of the Ramos Polychrome ceramics that we argue carry symbolic messages relevant to Paquimé and its ritual system. After the decline of the principal center, these esoteric design elements might have lost relevance to remaining populations. Some vessels bearing the symbols might have been retained as heirlooms, but it is likely that they were not produced after the decline of Paquimé. Most of the Medio period ceramic tradition is utilitarian, however, and it may have been used in the Casas Grandes area for generations after the demise of Paquimé by small populations in scattered hamlet or rancheria settlements.

Di Peso argued for persistence of an attenuated form of the Late Medio ceramic assemblage among a dispersed "refugia" population outside the abandoned Casas Grandes area during what he termed the Robles phase (Di Peso 1974:2:758). This concept has been criticized (e.g., Phillips 1990; Phillips and Carpenter 1999), with scholars asserting that the phase has no adequate chronological or artifactual definition, and that the post-Paquimé deposits classed as Robles by Di Peso are actually Late Medio. The idea that scattered populations continued to use Late Medio ceramics long after the decline of Paquimé is thus not a new one, but we add another aspect to it, arguing that post-Paquimé occupations are to be found in the Casas Grandes River valley, as well as in more distant locations. In fact, there is good indication that ceramics indistinguishable from Casas Grandes Plain Brown were in use at early colonial period Indigenous sites associated with the Mission of San Antonio de Padua in the Casas Grandes River valley (Martínez Galicia 2016, 2024).

The Organization of the Core Zone

Based on findings of the regional survey project (Whalen and Minnis 2001a), we defined an Inner Zone that lay within about 30 km of Paquimé. Found here were the most Paquimé-like of the Medio period settlements, exhibiting common architecture, material culture, site size hierarchies, and facilities for commensal and ritual activities. These things were poorly represented or entirely absent in the more distant Middle Zone, and such observations led to perception of the Inner Zone as the most integrated part of the Paquimé interaction sphere. Even so, there did not seem to have been a uniform hegemony over all of that area. For example, although there were large Medio period settlements within about 15 km of Paquimé, only that central community had ritual and commensal facilities. This contrasts with the wide distribution of such facilities between about 15 and 30 km from Paquimé. These observations argued against a uniform control over the entire Inner Zone. Apparently, there were differences in organization and integration within that area, but the 2001 survey volume did not pursue the idea beyond suggesting that the more distant part of the Inner Zone had a different and looser organization than the part within about 15 km of Paquimé. Note that Wilcox (1999) termed this distance the "limit of daily interaction," as it is about as far as a person on foot can travel and return in a single day. Subsequently, the Inner Zone designation was renamed the Core Zone. The area within the 15 km limit of daily interaction around Paquimé was the Inner Core Zone, while the Outer Core lay between 15 and 30 km from the central community.

Later, excavations at one large settlement and several small ones in the Outer Core Zone led to more specific conclusions about its organization (Whalen and Minnis 2009:274–78). This examination of economic indicators, ritual facilities, demographic data, and site size hierarchies led us to suggest that the entire Core Zone was tightly tied to Paquimé by different control strategies, including (1) monopoly of ritual and commensal activities in the Inner Core Zone; (2) absorption of once-autonomous Outer Core communities like Site 204, with their own ritual and commensal facilities, into the Paquimé-focused social-religious-economic system; and (3) establishment of new special purpose settlements that served the needs of Paquimé. Site 242 is such an example. Even with these ideas, much remained unknown about the Inner Core settlements that were the nearest neighbors of Paquimé.

The present volume's analyses began with the sites of the Inner Core Zone. At every point in the analysis, data from Paquimé and its large and small neighbors were compared to information from sites previously studied in the Outer Core. This volume's analyses added some new ideas, while revising or discarding old notions. These are summarized here under four headings: (1) Community richness in the Core Zone, (2) reconsideration of the Medio period and the Paquimé community, (3) relations between Paquimé and more distant areas, and (4) the end of Paquimé and Medio period culture. Each is elaborated on below.

The Relative Richness of Core Zone Settlements

Chapter 1 of this volume outlines a strategy for evaluating settlement richness, providing a number of variables relevant to settlements' ranges of function and thus to their relative levels of complexity. The assumption is that more complex settlements discharged more functions than simpler ones. Organizational and integrative activities, whether political, economic or ceremonial, are chief among these. Preceding chapters analyze several different kinds of data from the large and small Core Zone neighbors of Paquimé, and the present discussion applies these data to the list of indicators of community richness and variety of function. Our comparisons begin with Paquimé and extend outward to progressively more distant Core Zone neighbors.

The first characteristic is presence of an "architecture of power," expressed at Paquimé as multistoried room blocks with extremely thick walls that enclosed large rooms, some of which were of intricate shapes. The walls of Paquimé averaged 64 cm for one-story constructions and 85 cm for multistory buildings. This is certainly more than was required by wall stability concerns. To demonstrate this, we cite the marked reduction in wall thickness all over the site during Di Peso's final Diablo phase, as the architecture of power was no longer the dominant building style. At its apogee, however, the thick walls of Paquimé were not matched at any Core Zone settlement. In chapter 4 we show that large Core Zone sites were characterized by walls between 25 cm and 35 cm thick. We note that some walls at Inner Core large Site 315 reached thicknesses of 40 cm, while most others were in the usual 25 to 35 cm range. Even at their thinnest, these walls were solid, substantial constructions. They would have been stout enough to support the domestic activities that were likely carried out on rooftops (Whalen et al. 2010:536). The nearest contender for Paquimé-like wall thicknesses is Outer Core Zone small Site 242, where average wall thickness was 52 cm throughout the room block. We emphasize that all walls of neighboring settlements appear to have been built with the same techniques as those of Paquimé.

About 24 percent of the rooms excavated at Paquimé were of elaborate shapes, a few having as many as 14 walls in butterfly configurations. Some rooms were also unusually large at more than 100 m² of floor space. Despite this elaboration, most of the Paquimé rooms (ca. 76%) were of simple quadrilateral or L shapes, with average floor areas of less than 30 m². Although they were not dominant, very large rooms and those of elaborate shapes occurred often enough to be conspicuous components of the architecture of power at Paquimé. Like extreme wall thickness, large and intricately shaped rooms were uncommon among the center's Core Zone neighbors. As at Paquimé, most rooms everywhere were of simple quadrilateral or L shapes. Outer Core small Site 242 stands out with a single room of elaborate configuration. All the rooms at Site 242 were larger than usual among Core Zone communities, although they did not come close to the largest spaces at Paquimé. Most rooms, then, were built by the same technique and were of the same range of shapes everywhere in the Core Zone. Paquimé stands out as having very thick walls, a few very large rooms, and a few rooms of intricate shapes. There were three stories of rooms in several parts of the settlement.

Ritual architecture is another outstanding feature of Paquimé. The community is famous for its large I-shaped ball court, platform mounds, water shrine, and large reservoirs. Other researchers see additional ball courts and a serpent effigy mound in the community. No Inner Core settlement has any of these features, although some of them reappear in the Outer Core Zone. There, large Site 204 and small Site 242 both have I-shaped ball courts. In addition, small Site 242 has a small platform mound at one end of the ball court. This is the only such ball court–mound combination known in the region, apart from at Paquimé. In room size, room shape, wall thickness, and ritual architecture, Outer Core small Site 242 is a miniature version of its contemporary, Paquimé. This is a very different situation than seen at Outer Core ball court Site 204.

In addition to ritual architecture, which presumably functioned at the public level, there are many small pieces of ritual paraphernalia at Paquimé. These range from ceramic and stone human, bird, and animal effigy figures to pipes, phalli, and intricately shaped stone slabs that have been termed altar pieces. These are sparsely represented on Inner Core large sites, where only Site 315 had an altar stone. None was found on large Inner Core Site 565, or on any Inner Core small site. Concentration of these items at Paquimé and their near absence at all Inner Core neighbors is the situation. The case is different in the Outer Core. At large Site 204 were found pipes, altar stones, and a stone effigy head in roughly human form. Outer Core small Site 242 produced a finely made stone phallus. No ritual paraphernalia came from Outer Core small Sites 231 and 317.

The public ritual centered on ball courts likely involved preparation of food and drink for commensal events. Present at Paquimé are very large ovens that likely served for agave baking on a vast scale. This activity is illustrated and discussed elsewhere (Minnis and Whalen 2020:46–57). Only one other facility of this size and type is known from the Inner Core Zone. The Site 299A oven lies in a prime agave-growing area on the upper piedmont slope above the Casas Grandes River valley. The nearby spring (the Ojo Vareleño) carried water via canal to the large reservoirs of Paquimé, so we may assume a close link between the center and the Ojo Vareleño area. Similar ovens are much more common in the Outer Core Zone, where two lie close to the I-shaped ball court of large Site 204. The very elaborate small Site 242, however, does not have a large oven. Instead of agave baking, its copious evidence of large-scale fermented drink preparation (Jones 2002) might reflect a focus on corn beer in commensal contexts. Already prepared agave might have been brought to Site 242 as necessary, as examples of large ovens are scattered over the Outer Core Zone's piedmont slopes. Some occur alone while others are associated with Medio period settlements like Site 317 (for a complete list, see Minnis and Whalen 2020:128–29). Large-scale agave baking thus appears to have been more widespread in the Outer Core Zone than in the Inner Core. This is partially because the Outer Core includes more of the rocky piedmont slopes that were favorable to the activity. Even so, what large-scale agave baking there was in the Inner Core was concentrated at Paquimé.

The funds of power are maintained everywhere by large storage facilities, whether built into a settlement's architecture or in large ceramic vessels. Attached to the rooms at Paquimé were many alcoves with enclosing tops and fronts. These were referred to by Di Peso as "bed platforms," but they have been reinterpreted as storage facilities. Each enclosed several cubic meters, and their combined volume is considerable. A few alcoves were present on all the large sites of the Inner and Outer Core Zone, as well as on Outer Core small Site 242. All lack enclosing front walls, and whether they had upper coverings is questionable. Even if all of them were classified as storage areas, their combined volumes would have been insignificant. Small rooms of a few square meters in floor area were used as food storage spaces in the pueblos of the U.S. Southwest. Such rooms are present on Core Zone sites of all sizes, although they lack evidence of use for storage. Large ceramic vessels have been used for storage, and these could have been placed anywhere in the inhabited spaces. Very large jars are found only on large sites in the Core Zone, although they seem too few to have contained enough resources to fuel the activities of power. The preceding discussion does not argue that no large-scale storage took place on major Core Zone sites. Except for Paquimé, however, we have no indication of large-scale storage capacity in any of these settlements.

Most of the Inner and Outer Core Zone sites studied here also lack evidence of preparation of food at a scale above the household. None, for example, had extraordinary numbers of grinding implements. Even so, one notable difference among Core Zone sites described in chapter 5 is elevated frequencies of exterior soot and interior vessel wall erosion (or pitting) on utilitarian Brownware jars at Paquimé and at Outer Core Zone ball court sites 204 and 242. Presence of more sooted vessels implies more than the ordinary level of cooking, and higher than usual levels of interior surface erosion are linked to increased production of fermented drink. Food and drink are important components of commensal gatherings in many contexts worldwide. It is significant that indications of food and drink production at larger than usual levels are found in association with ball courts all over the Core Zone. Large Inner Core neighbors of Paquimé that do not have ball courts likewise lack high frequencies of sooted and pitted jars.

Imported luxury items and exotica, such as nonlocal ceramics, marine shell, copper, turquoise, and macaws, are abundant at Paquimé, as are the stone cage door plugs that are indicative of macaw husbandry. These items were present at Inner Core large Site 315, although they were less common at Inner Core large Site 565 and entirely absent at small Sites 290, 321, and 355 (see chapter 7). No Inner Core large settlement contained anything like the quantity and variety of exotica found at Paquimé. There is a similar scarcity of exotic and sumptuary items in Outer Core Zone settlements. There, large Site 204 contained turquoise, copper, marine shell, and macaw cage door stones, but always in small quantity. Also found in a 204 room was the only macaw burial yet discovered outside Paquimé. Outer Core small Site 242 has been cited in preceding discussion as the near equal of large Site 204 in indicators of richness and functional variety. Interestingly, however, it yielded few imported and exotic items. There was a macaw cage door stone, but turquoise, copper, marine shell, and imported ceramics all were absent. Outer Core small Sites 231 and 317 contained small quantities of shell, but no other luxury or exotic items were present.

Another category of luxury item includes desirable material of local origin but of limited distribution. Both obsidian for fine chipped stone implements and vesicular basalt for various grinding tools are available in the Casas Grandes region. We would expect all sites to possess these desirable materials if access were free and universal, but this is far from the case. Paquimé yielded large quantities of both materials, and preceding discussion in this volume cites models in which Paquimé controlled the regional supply, redistributing some of it to neighboring communities. The small quantities of both materials at large Inner Core sites 315 and 565, the center's nearest neighbors, are inconsistent with such a scenario. Rather, we argue that Paquimé consumed these materials in quantity while it redistributed little among its nearest neighbors. Both obsidian and vesicular basalt implements increase slightly in frequency on Outer Core Zone large Site 204 and small Site 242. At the same time, they are rare or absent on Outer Core small Sites 231 and 317.

It has been suggested that the frequency of Ramos Polychrome pottery, with its highly symbolic zoomorphic and anthropomorphic designs, is a useful measure of participation in a ritual-based system of community organization focused on Paquimé. As a percentage of all polychromes, Ramos is abundant at Paquimé, amounting to about 68 percent of all polychromes. Its frequency falls sharply at the two Inner Core large neighbors, sites 315 and 565, where Ramos averages only about 38 percent of polychromes (see chapter 5). In the Outer Core, the frequency of Ramos Polychrome is slightly more common at large Site 204, where it makes up 43 percent of polychromes, but the comparable figure is only 29 percent at small Site 242. All other small Inner Core and Outer Core sites showed low frequencies of Ramos.

Finally, our systematic collections from the surfaces of surveyed sites showed that Ramos Polychrome was well represented in the Middle Zone, at 51 percent of all polychromes. It is evident, therefore, that there is not a simple decline in Ramos Polychrome frequency as we proceed outward from Paquimé. The Outer Core and the Middle Zones have, on average, more of what has been termed "the signature ware" of Paquimé, while less is present at the settlements closest to Paquimé in the Inner Core, or at those which show direct association with it, as at Site 242 in the Outer Core. It has been argued that the highly symbolic designs of Ramos Polychrome formed a "visual language" used by elites to communicate the precepts of a unifying ritual system (Townsend 2005:17). If this is so, then it is curious that the nearest large neighbors of Paquimé had less of it than more distant ones. It could be that those settlements proximate to Paquimé were already firmly enmeshed in the center's organization. If ideology is to be used to finance an organization, emphasizes Brian Billman (2001:182), dissemination of ideological messages must be extended to the widest possible audience. Shared symbols, Billman continues, are an effective means of ideological dissemination.

To summarize and visually present the preceding discussion of indicators of community richness, we have expanded on the simple ranking system used to compare settlements in an earlier study (Whalen and Minnis 2001a:150–51). Paquimé, of course, will rank highest, serving as the standard of comparison for all other communities. We assign an arbitrary value of 5, meaning "plentiful," to each of the variables in table 9.1. Other sites received

TABLE 9.1 Richness scores for Core Zone sites

Variables	Paq.	315	565	204	231	242	317	290	321	355
Thick walls	5	1	1	1	0	3	0	0	0	0
Large rooms	5	1	1	1	0	3	0	0	0	0
Elaborate room shapes	5	2	2	1	0	2	0	0	0	0
Ritual architecture	5	0	0	3	0	4	0	0	0	0
Ritual paraphernalia	5	1	0	3	0	2	0	0	0	0
Large ovens	5	0	0	4	0	0	1	0	0	0
Large storage areas	5	1	1	1	0	1	0	0	0	0
Very large jars	5	1	1	1	0	1	0	0	0	0
High jar/bowl ratio	5	2	2	2	2	4	2	1	1	1
Sooted/pitted jars	5	1	1	2	1	4	1	1	1	1
IA metates	5	1	1	1	0	0	0	0	0	0
Mano blanks	5	1	0	2	0	0	0	0	0	0
Turquoise	5	2	1	2	0	0	0	0	0	0
Marine shell	5	2	1	1	1	0	1	1	0	0
Copper	5	1	0	1	0	0	0	0	0	0
Macaws	5	1	1	3	0	1	0	0	0	1
Obsidian	5	1	1	2	1	2	2	0	0	0
Vesicular basalt tools	5	1	1	2	1	3	0	0	0	0
High Ramos Poly. freq.	5	1	2	2	2	2	1	1	1	1
Imported ceramics	5	2	2	2	0	0	0	0	0	1
Total	**100**	**23**	**19**	**37**	**8**	**32**	**8**	**4**	**3**	**5**

lower variable scores, as appropriate, with 0 indicating "none found." The resulting total scores are displayed as a bar chart (figure 9.3). It is obvious from the figure that no large site has anything like the richness of Paquimé. Even so, large sites are generally richer than small ones, which is an entirely predictable result.

Figure 9.3 demonstrates considerable difference between the inner and outer parts of the Core Zone. Large sites of the Inner Core show much lower richness than Outer Core large Site 204, presumably due to absorption of many organizational and integrative functions by Paquimé. This conclusion also implies substantial dependence by the large Inner Core neighbors on the principal center. There likely was a different situation in the Outer Core Zone, where large Site 204 maintained its own ritual architecture, ritual paraphernalia, and large-scale food preparation facilities. More of what we consider to be organizational and integrative functions were discharged by Outer Core Site 204 than by its Inner Core counterparts.

Small Core Zone sites are still more variable. One of them, Outer Core small Site 242, has a complexity score that rivals that of large Site 204 and surpasses those of Inner Core large Sites 315 and 565. We have always seen the 242 settlement as an agent of Paquimé, serving to organize terrace-based agriculture in its part of the uplands. Thus, it is by no means a typical small settlement. Small Outer Core sites 231 and 317 are more likely typical minor settlements. In the Inner Core, small Site 355 and the unexcavated parts of Site 321 likely represent typical small settlements, with later, cruder remodeling of its CGAT

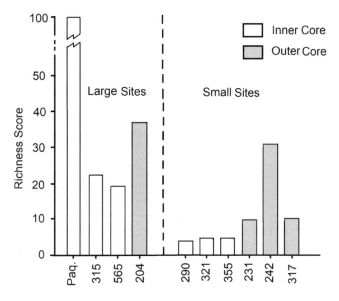

FIGURE 9.3 Bar chart of Core Zone richness scores.

construction. Inner Core small Site 290, on the other hand, seems to present a simpler situation. Most of its architecture is cruder than what we recognize as CGAT-style building, and in preceding pages, we term it the Post–Casas Grandes Architectural Tradition (PCGAT) style. Its artifact assemblages, too, are small and simple. Substantial PCGAT construction is visible on all three of the Inner Core Zone small sites studied here: 290, 321, and 355. Interestingly, we do not see this extent of PCGAT remodeling on the small sites of the Outer Core Zone. It may be that there was greater continuity in the Outer Core Zone, while the Inner Core showed brief abandonment and recolonization, using what we term PCGAT building. This is a complex issue for future research.

The Medio Period, Reconsidered

In Di Peso's (1974:2) original and highly influential interpretation, the Medio period material culture was defined as that of Paquimé. It appeared in purest form in that community, spreading outward in simplified form. This is consistent with the original interpretation of the center as owing many of its characteristics to external stimuli from Mesoamerica. We now see a different picture, as we are able to divide the original period into two time intervals, termed the Early Medio and the Late Medio. Note that these do not correspond with the three phases into which Di Peso originally divided his Medio period at Paquimé, all of which would fall into our Late Medio interval. In the new division, the Early Medio extends from the late 1100s to the middle or late 1200s. It is pre-Paquimé. The Late Medio dates from the mid- to late 1200s, and it contains the florescence of Paquimé together with the associated architectural and material culture traits described there. We see substantial Early Medio antecedents for much of what was found at Late Medio Paquimé.

The Early Medio is best represented at Outer Core Zone large Site 204, and this settlement is used to exemplify the period. We stress, however, that the Early Medio is a regional phenomenon. In chapter 4 of this volume, we show that there is substantial Early Medio occupation at not only Outer Core Zone large Site 204 but also at Inner Core Zone large Sites 315 and 565 and probably at Paquimé as well. The Early Medio situation discussed here thus is presumed to have been an early pueblo phenomenon of the Casas Grandes area. It develops out of the preceding Viejo period's pit houses and pit-house-to-pueblo transitional culture. The significance of the Early Medio period is that, while it predates the florescence of Paquimé, it contains a good deal of what Di Peso considered the unique culture of that center.

Discussion in chapter 4 of this volume shows that Early Medio adobe architecture was very similar to that of the Late Medio. Early Medio walls were built with the same English cobb technique found all over the region and at Paquimé itself. Early Medio rooms had T-shaped doorways and a few architectural embellishments, like adobe stairs. Late Medio constructions all over the Casas Grandes area carried on this building style, while adding some more elaborate features, such as alcove storage, platform hearths, wall niches, collared posts, and colonnaded areas. The architecture of Paquimé, we contend, is an extreme amplification and elaboration of this preexisting architectural tradition. This position is in contrast to Di Peso's, who saw it as a new building style imported from Mesoamerica. This is an understandable conclusion, as he had only the simple Viejo style of thin walls and jacal superstructures as predecessor to the massive adobe walls of Paquimé. The picture is different when the transitional Early Medio building style is added.

Architectural elaboration is not the only Paquimé trait presaged in the Early Medio period. The same is true of most of the ceramic assemblage described at Paquimé and since found to occur at Early and Late Medio settlements in the Casas Grandes area. Almost all of the ceramic assemblage described at Paquimé has Early Medio antecedents, as shown in chapter 5. The ceramics found at Early Medio sites 204 and 315 include all of the utility wares and some of the polychromes attributed to Paquimé. Utility wares always compose about 90 percent of any ceramic assemblage, whether Early Medio or Late Medio, and there are few differences in early or late examples of these wares, including those from Paquimé. Polychromes such as Babícora, White-Paste Babícora, and Dublán exist from the Early Medio onward. Not present in Early Medio assemblages, however, are polychromes bearing the elaborate anthropomorphic and zoomorphic imagery that was presumably linked to Mesoamerica. Ramos Polychrome and its variants were new symbol-carrying types added to the preexisting Early Medio assemblage and seldom making up more than 10 percent of an entire Late Medio ceramic collection. Some 90 percent of the assemblage described at Paquimé, in other words, existed in similar form in the preceding Early Medio period.

Other aspects of material culture show similar continuity from Early Medio times through the existence of Paquimé. In Early Medio deposits at Outer Core Zone Site 204, for instance, marine shell imported from the shores of the Sea of Cortez is present in moderate quantity. It was presumably obtained by local communities, such as 204. By the

Late Medio, however, the frequency of marine shell in that settlement drops nearly to zero, while freshwater shell increases in frequency. We and others (e.g., Classen 1998:235) see freshwater shell as a second-class substitute for shell of marine varieties. We do not know if this change took place in other Late Medio settlements in the area. It was surely not so at Paquimé, however, which seems to have absorbed most of the area's Late Medio supply of marine shell. That settlement likely dominated shell trade for its own use, leaving little scope for the local community shell procurement of the Early Medio period. Significantly, however, the same material (marine shell) from the same place (the Sea of Cortez) was in use as a sumptuary commodity in the Early Medio, some time before its massive accumulation at Paquimé.

Additional objects described at Paquimé as "ritual paraphernalia" were much less common in Early Medio deposits than in their Late Medio successors at Site 204. This hints at a lower or less visible level of ritual activity in Early Medio contexts, followed by an increase in such activity in the Late Medio. Even so, the quantity or quality of ritual paraphernalia at any of the Late Medio neighbors never rivaled that of Paquimé. The same could be said of another category of nonlocal exotica: macaws. These birds, or the distinctive remains of their cages, are reported on in chapter 7. There, we note that they have to date been found only in Late Medio contexts. A single macaw bone has been reported from Viejo deposits at the Inner Core Zone Convento site, showing that the birds were at least known then. Some might have been present in Early Medio times. No settlement, however, rivals the many macaw remains at Late Medio Paquimé.

Two other materials, obsidian and vesicular basalt, suggest a more controlled or centralized pattern of procurement in the Late Medio. Obsidian, a high-quality tool-making material, is available as small nodules all over the Casas Grandes area. The diminutive size of obsidian projectile points, debitage, and core-bearing fragments show that they were fashioned from these nodules. The Early Medio levels of the deep midden deposits at Site 204 contained about 90 percent of the small number of recovered obsidian pieces, while Late Medio levels had very little (Whalen and Minnis 2009:214). Late Medio Paquimé contained the lion's share of obsidian points, tools, and debitage, again suggesting domination of the acquisition of this popular material. The reverse is true of vesicular basalt, used at Site 204 for a few Early Medio grinding tools but for more implements in the succeeding Late Medio. It is significant that there were no neatly finished mano blanks in Early Medio deposits at 204 or in contemporary deposits at Site 315. Grinding stones were present in these contexts, but they were invariably made of rhyolite, andesite, or other common local materials. Finely shaped grinding implements, plus mano and metate blanks, all of vesicular basalt, were concentrated at Paquimé. Searcy and Pitezel (2018) have outlined a model in which Paquimé controlled the production of these implements and consumed most of them.

We do not know whether the ball game was played in the Early Medio, although it certainly was by Late Medio times. There are several kinds of ball courts in the NW/SW. The open court consists simply of two parallel rows of stones, without end features. At the other extreme is the classic I-shaped court, formed by earth and stone embankments. Earlier discussion (Whalen and Minnis 2009) cited Mesoamerican data showing that simple open courts are the older form that was later supplemented—but not replaced—by more elaborate I-shaped playing fields. In the NW/SW, the I-shaped court is associated with Paquimé, where at least one massive example was built. Ball courts have not been directly dated, although Harmon (2005, 2006) uses a morphological analysis to argue that simple open courts were the precedent form in the NW/SW, later supplemented by courts of T and I shapes. This line of thought makes conceivable the idea that simple open ball courts were in use in Early Medio times. The presence of Mesoamerican notions in the Early Medio is a topic yet to be adequately explored.

A final feature of public activity is the large oven. These ovens are interpreted as vast facilities producing food and the substance for fermented drink for commensal events. Nearly every known example was radiocarbon dated to the Late Medio, and all of these burned pine fuel. In chapter 4 of this volume, however, we present a very large oven, newly dug in the Inner Core Zone. This facility dated to the Early Medio, and it was fueled by mesquite. If the extant sample is any indication, these large ovens were rare in the Early Medio, while they were much more common in Late Medio times. This situation hints at a lower level of public ritual in the Early Medio as opposed to the Late Medio. We note that Late Medio Paquimé has a group of these huge facilities, the capacities of which far exceed those of any other settlement. Once again, Late Medio use of large ovens is presaged in the Early Medio period. We follow these observations with models of Early and Late Medio development in the Casas Grandes area.

An Early Medio Developmental Scenario

The preceding Viejo period population was increasingly agricultural, their settlements focusing on the region's watercourses. This pattern was to characterize all subsequent occupations, from prehistoric times to the present day. On this base, the Early Medio population built a larger and more intensively agricultural adaptation. We envision a relatively small Early Medio population in a productive environment. This sets the stage for what Robin A. Beck Jr. (2003:651) has termed "persuasive aggregation" by leaders of larger local communities, like sites 204, 315, 565, and Paquimé. Persuasive aggregation occurs in settings of relatively open residential mobility. Leaders or faction heads in different settlements compete to attract and hold followers and supporters through combinations of gifts, bribes, and promises. They engage in corporate, cooperative, group-oriented, group-building activities. Their economic base is staple finance built through production of agricultural surpluses to use in public contexts such as ritual and feasting. In addition, assistance might be provided to followers in hard times. The political environment is fluid, competitive, unstable, and characterized by shifting alliances in an uncentralized region. We postulate that all of this was taking place across the Casas Grandes area in the late 1100s to the late 1200s and among people sharing the Early Medio culture pattern. Other opinion is beginning to see the Late Medio as an outgrowth of Early Medio times as well:

"Hence, rather than Paquimé fluorescing and producing a wider Medio period hinterland, it appears that Medio period culture was in place as a regional entity by around AD 1200, and it is out of this shared 'social field' . . . that Paquimé's complexity develops in the Late Medio period" (Cunningham 2017:182).

A Late Medio Developmental Scenario

By the late 1200s, population had increased substantially, producing the scalar hierarchy of settlements observable all over the Core and Middle Zones. This is the time and context of the ascendancy of Paquimé. At this point, it is appropriate to ask why this settlement should have emerged from the preceding Early Medio competition as the central place. It has often been noted that Paquimé lies in a very good position for agriculture. It is located where the Casas Grandes River valley first widens into a substantial floodplain. Nearly all of the Inner Core Zone's prime farming land thus lies downstream from Paquimé. In an earlier scenario (Whalen and Minnis 2001a), Paquimé enjoyed a productive advantage over its peers. We now suggest that the settlement reached a sort of "first among equals" status in Early Medio times.

Late Medio Paquimé appears to have grown quickly, undoubtedly through population aggregation. Many have noted that there was a good deal of population migration, movement, and redistribution in the late prehistoric and protohistoric U.S. Southwest (e.g., E. C. Adams and Duff 2004; Lyons 2003; Spielmann 1998), and there is no reason to suppose that Northwest Mexico was markedly different. The extent to which the people who formed Paquimé were local or from more distant areas is still being debated (e.g., Kemp 2010; Lekson 2000, 2015; Offenbecker 2018; Snow et al. 2011; Waller et al. 2018). Whatever their origins, many people would have been needed to build the center and to fuel its funds of power through their work. In addition to attracting new people, Paquimé would have also needed to enlarge existing productive facilities. This was evidently done by several means. Canal irrigation of the Casas Grandes floodplain expanded in Late Medio times (Doolittle 1993:143; Minnis and Whalen 2022:64).

Another sort of productive intensification is in evidence in the Late Medio, one example of which are chiefs' fields around Paquimé in the Inner Core Zone, as discussed in chapter 8. Another example is Outer Core Zone small Site 242's vast system of agricultural terraces. This settlement likely served to organize farming in a sparsely populated part of the uplands. We have already seen that Site 242 was a Paquimé lookalike, although it was inhabited by no more than a few dozen people; it had an enormous I-shaped ball court, a platform mound, and copious evidence of preparation of large quantities of food. The settlement pattern survey recorded no large field systems in the adjacent Middle Zone. The absence in the Middle Zone of ball courts and, presumably, the associated ritual and commensal activities might explain the observed situation. That is, economic intensification among the Puebloan societies of the southwestern United States frequently occurred in support of ceremonial activities, in what has been termed a "ritual mode of production"

(Cunningham 2017:198; Spielmann 2002:196). By this logic, the absence of ball courts should reduce the frequency of productive intensification facilities.

Paquimé became a particularly elaborate built environment. A number of its characteristics, from general architectural style and ceramic assemblage to ritual and feasting facilities, had origins in the preceding Early Medio regional culture. Even so, we emphasize that Paquimé expanded and amplified these traits to create a unique setting. Present there was very elaborate and overbuilt architecture, although it was constructed largely within the CGAT style. Room count was much higher than any contemporary settlement, and many of the rooms were larger than the regional norm, some of intricate shapes. There were vast ceremonial and feasting facilities, including ball courts, platform mounds, and large ovens. Exotic, imported, and sumptuary goods were accumulated at Paquimé. An old idea that we should discard was that this material was used as prestige goods distributed among neighboring communities. It is now clear that most of what went into Paquimé stayed there, making the settlement a consumer rather than a distributor of exotic and desirable things. Others (e.g., Cunningham 2017:193; Pailes and Searcy 2022:107) make the same point. Such also seems to have been the case at other NW/SW centers, like Chaco (e.g., Plog et al. 2017:298).

Associated with the rise of Paquimé was a new ideology, the symbolism for which was displayed on vessels of Ramos Polychrome and its variants. This new set of symbols certainly had Mesoamerican antecedents, and ball courts of the classic I shape also seem to have been part of this package. Di Peso saw this as evidence of introduction of complete Mesoamerican ritual complexes in the Casas Grandes area, and others since have echoed and expanded on this idea (e.g., Mathiowetz 2018). In contrast, we argue that local people perceived Mesoamerican symbols as powerful talismans, used them to serve local ends, and were unconcerned with the substantial belief systems surrounding these symbols in their home contexts. Whatever the case, a new and potent package of ritual and ceremonialism appears to have developed around Late Medio Paquimé. It was likely a central component of influence on neighboring settlements, serving both to emphasize and legitimize social power differentials (e.g., Lipe 2002:203; Skibo et al. 2002:174).

All the while, however, Inner Core Zone large neighbors of Paquimé continued to exist only a few kilometers away in the Casas Grandes River valley. Moreover, these neighbors do not decline in size as the central community grows. They were nowhere near as large or elaborate as Paquimé, although there were luxury goods in them. We were told that a large quantity of ceramics, minerals, shell, and other valuables had been looted from Site 315 in the recent past, and our excavations there recovered more exotica than was found at, for example, Outer Core Zone Site 204. Even so, it is clear that neither Site 315 nor any of the other Inner Core Zone neighbors had ceremonial or feasting facilities. All of these, on a large scale, were concentrated at Paquimé. The problem before us is to reconcile the rise of the vast and elaborate built environment of the central place with the continued occupations of its large near neighbors.

The Paquimé Community

The solution, we suggest, is a revision of the concept of what constituted Paquimé. For Di Peso and subsequent researchers, the site of Paquimé was the unit of analysis and interpretation, although recent work on communities and their recognition in the archaeological record provides new ideas. A community has long been seen as a location in which there is regular face-to-face social interaction (Murdock 1949). There is consensus that a community is not necessarily a single settlement or place (Pauketat 2000:19; Rautman 2014:140). In the archaeological record, Mark Varien and James Potter (2008:2) note, "settlement clustering has been a primary criterion for the analytical definition of ancient communities since the concept was first applied." This spatial proximity of settlements allows the daily face-to-face interaction among community members. In short, then, community members are individuals dispersed among different settlements who interact regularly with each other in patterns of obligation and reciprocity (Adler 2002:38; Ortman 2008:125; Wills and Leonard 1994:xv). In the Paquimé case, this concept fits well with our Inner Core Zone's definition as the 15 km limit of daily interaction. A community thus is a social entity, not simply a spatial cluster of material remains (Yaeger and Canuto 2000:9). It is part of an identity-forming process (Pauketat 2000:35) that exists in the minds of its members (Ortman 2008:126; Preucel 2000:61), hence, the definition of a community as "a conjunction of people, place, and premise" (Yaeger and Canuto 2000:15).

There is not necessarily harmony in communities. In addition to being identity builders and maintainers, communities have also been described as "wracked with tensions and inequalities," and as "crucibles" containing the interaction of multiple and potentially incompatible identities, such as factions, kinship, village ties, and personal interests (Pauketat 2008:241; Yaeger and Canuto 2000:17). Communities are volatile places, where social relations are continually contested as individual members "pursue goals that are contingent, sometimes contradictory, and constantly changing" (Isbell 2000:245). Communities, therefore, are unstable and fluid, since they emerge as outcomes of conflicts of component group and societal interests (Preucel 2000:61).

In creating and maintaining communities in the face of these tensions, Scott Preucel (2000:73) stresses the importance of public symbolic acts. There are many such symbols, but chief among them is the built environment. Architecture is a potent statement in the social negotiation of community (Pauketat 2000:33), as it is a tangible expression of the prevailing social order (Mehrer 2000:45–46; Ryan 2008:70). The main pueblo at the Grasshopper ruin, for example, has three distinct room blocks, each containing about 100 rooms and an associated plaza. These are interpreted as the coming together of three social units (Fish et al. 1994:160) to form the larger community. The built environment thus both symbolizes and reinforces the prevailing social structure. Similar architectural symbolism may characterize Paquimé. It has long been known that there are three peaks in that community's main room block mound, one each in Units 8, 16, and 14. These are surrounded and connected by lower building remains. The pattern is clear at the site today, as it was to earlier visitors. An observer noting the three peaks of Paquimé in the 1850s commented, "At first, I believed that there were separate buildings . . . as there were three large heaps, apparently unconnected, each having portions of erect walls. But on closer examination, I found that they had been connected by a low range of buildings, which may merely have been courts, as they were of but one story" (Bartlett 1854:353). As suggested at Grasshopper Pueblo, the three peaks at Paquimé may represent social units that were founders and principal components of that community.

In addition to the built environment's symbolic character, Rautman (2014:4) observes that it facilitates ceremonial events, expresses ritual concepts, and helps to create and reinforce a shared public or official culture. Common beliefs in the sacred constitute a powerful unifying force (e.g., Rappaport 1971, 1999), and these beliefs are often expressed as shared symbols. These symbols may be anything from monumental architecture to elements of ceramic decoration. Frequently, vessels with symbolic iconography show and emphasize collective beliefs, as they are relatively cheap to produce and can be widely disseminated. In short, the built environment and its symbol systems are potent expressors of connection among different groups of people. Some communities have central settlements or places. In fact, Ortman (2008:126) asserts that "ancient pueblo communities were strongly associated with places." This is where the built environment and its associated symbolism are permanently on display to all community members. Our suggestion is that Paquimé and its near neighbors of the Inner Core Zone formed such a community.

Inner Core Zone settlements were dependent on Paquimé for ritual and public functions, as only that central place had ritual architecture, very large-scale food preparation facilities, and a great deal of hoarded exotica and sumptuary goods. Paquimé, in turn, likely depended on the labor and production of community members to supplement that of its own population. We still envision a political economy based on staple finance, involving a great deal of public ritual and commensal activities. Paquimé clearly monopolized exotic and imported goods, sharing very little with other community members. This is understandable if, as suggested by Pailes and Searcy (2022:146–49), these goods functioned primarily as status markers in ritual and ceremonial contexts. A recent study of Puebloan social organization asserted that there are two broad categories of Pueblo people: the ceremonially rich and the ceremonially poor, and that these categories have deep historical roots (Ware 2014:44–46). We may be seeing this distinction between the people of Paquimé, with their concentrations of exotic and sumptuary goods, and the population of the wider community. But was the Paquimé community limited to the Inner Core Zone? How should we determine the boundaries of a community? How was community related to political centralization?

Relations Between Paquimé and Its Neighbors

In the literature on communities, it is noted that the spatial scale of societies is frequently larger than the network of places where people interact on a daily face-to-face basis. Ortman (2008:153–54) emphasized this reality by distinguishing "place" from "space." The former exists at a community scale of direct frequent contact, while the latter is a supra-community scale of interaction among people of more diverse individual and group interests and priorities. Similar distinctions have been made by others, who see a community as characterized by "first-order" interactions, or those among local residential groups that regularly interact. In contrast to these first-order interactions is the more inclusive "larger community of interests," or the "larger social sphere" (Lipe 1999:33; Varien 1999:19–23). The people in these larger units share a common cultural tradition that is significant because it is "part of the historically constituted structure that shapes the actions of individuals and their interactions with others" (Varien and Potter 2008:16).

In the Paquimé case, the Outer Core Zone and the adjacent Middle Zone would fall in the "larger community of interests," beyond first-order, or daily, interactions. In chapters 4 and 5 of this volume, we show that the same architectural and ceramic tradition is found consistently all over the Inner and Outer Core and Middle Zones, or up to about 100 km from Paquimé. The same is true at the Galeana site and surrounding settlements in the Middle Santa Maria drainage southeast of Paquimé, as well as at the Río Gavilán Camposanto site on the eastern slope of the Sierra Madre Occidental. In both of these areas are settlements with the architectural tradition and ceramic assemblage seen in the Core and Middle Zones around Paquimé. In addition, the Río Gavilán Camposanto site has an I-shaped ball court. No courts were found at Galeana, although a few are known from other nearby parts of the Santa Maria drainage (Cruz Antillón and Maxwell 2017:182). These, we suggest, were the fringes of the "larger community of interests," or the social sphere surrounding Paquimé. Apparently lacking, however, is the uniformity and intensity of interaction found in the Paquimé community of the Inner Core Zone. Beyond the Inner Core, we see a fragmented social landscape, in which there was considerable variability in the extent to which communities shared interests with Paquimé. Neither can we say with certainty that these settlements in outer areas were related to Paquimé in the same way.

There seem to be few such sites in the low desert to the east, and our brief reconnaissance in the Outer Zone, near the U.S./Mexico border, found settlements with both similarities and differences in architecture and ceramic styles (Whalen and Minnis 2001a:78–80). The adjacent Animas area of southwestern New Mexico also contains similarities to and differences from the Casas Grandes tradition. For instance, a table of Joyce Well ceramic type identifications (McCluney 2002:36) shows that 30 percent of that site's ceramic assemblage was not classifiable in the typological system that comprehends everything in areas nearer Paquimé. To balance this, Joyce Well shows similarities to the CGAT, and there are several simple open ball courts on this and other Animas sites. The Animas area, then, seems to represent a northern periphery of the Paquimé interaction sphere, in which the Casas Grandes culture was expressed in a simpler form as compared to areas closer to the Core Zone. We consider the Animas area, plus Villa Ahumada to the east and Babícora to the south, to have been distantly linked to Paquimé but beyond the reach of any organization emanating from that central place.

The most clearly seen part of the Late Medio larger community of interests is the Outer Core Zone, lying some 15–30 km from the Paquimé community. We envision no frequent face-to-face interaction with the Paquimé community or domination by it. Instead of Di Peso's model of a uniform hegemony emanating from Paquimé, we now see a more fluid, fragmented situation. This is based on the reappearance of ball courts and large feasting ovens in the Outer Core Zone after their absence at Inner Core Zone sites except Paquimé. As we have noted in previous studies (Whalen and Minnis 2001a, 2009), most of the ball courts and large ovens known in the Core Zone come from its outer part. They are not as elaborate as the facilities of the Paquimé community, but they are far more numerous. In a relevant Mesoamerican study (Santley et al. 1991), Late Postclassic ball courts were found to have been most common in areas that lacked strong centralized control and that were fragmented into competing units. The effect of increased political centralization was suppression of factional competition, with a consequent reduction in ball court numbers.

The absence of ball courts among the Inner Core Zone settlements and their concentration at Paquimé may be taken as a sign of that area's centralization around the principal center. The Outer Core Zone, where many ball courts reappear, was likely more fragmented into competing local units and less integrated into a polity focused on Paquimé. We acknowledge this departure from our original notion of closer integration of the Outer Core Zone into a Paquimé-focused regional system (Whalen and Minnis 2001a, 2009). In contrast to this position, Marcel J. Harmon (2005) takes the many courts of the Outer Core as a sign of increasing connection with Paquimé. He interpreted the area's simple open courts as an early variant of the ball game, while those of T and I shapes were associated with a new version of the contest that was prompted by Paquimé. In Mesoamerica, simple open courts are also earlier than those of I shapes, but the latter courts do not replace their simpler predecessors. Instead, I-shaped courts are added to the existing set of facilities. The ball courts of the Animas area's Joyce Well site, for example, are certainly associated with a Late Medio occupation. Within the Casas Grandes area, then, presence of ball courts of T and I shapes *might* be taken as one measure of association with Paquimé. Beyond this, however, the situation is even less clear. An I-shaped ball court has recently been reported from a site in the Santa Clara area, some 130 km from Paquimé, and the researcher who recorded it argues that "The existence of an 'architecture of power' well outside the core area around Paquimé identified by Whalen and Minnis suggests that emergence of new systems of authority in the late Medio period may have been a regional phenomenon" (Cunningham 2017:183).

We have taken the same position, positing that Paquimé arose out of a regional Early Medio cultural tradition that contained many of the characteristics originally attributed to outside influences. The scale of analysis, in other words, is gradually shifting from the "unique" place of Paquimé and its extensive impact on its hinterland to a regional perspective that views the center as one of a number of prominent communities in Northwest Mexico, none of which achieved the sort of panregional hegemony that for so long has been attributed to Paquimé. Pailes and Searcy (2022) take a similar position .

It is evident that the Outer Core Zone settlements maintained relations with the Paquimé community of the Inner Core Zone, as we have seen that they shared a common cultural tradition from Early Medio times onward. Even so, regular frequent first-order contacts with the Paquimé community seem unlikely due to the distance separating the inner and outer parts of the Core Zone, as also suggested by the fact that Outer Core Zone settlements maintained their own ritual and public facilities. In the absence of first- order contacts, we suggest that there were different kinds of relations between the Paquimé community and its Outer Core Zone neighbors. One type of interaction is relations between the central place and prominent Outer Core Zone neighbors like Site 204. Analyses in this volume and elsewhere (Whalen and Minnis 2009) showed that large Site 204 was one of the most elaborate settlements in the Outer Core Zone. In fact, it might well have been the center of a community of its own, as a number of small Medio settlements exist in its vicinity. The 204 settlement has an underlying Viejo period occupation, a substantial Early Medio occupation, and a Late Medio presence that was reduced but still significant. The large I-shaped ball court likely belongs to the Late Medio occupation of the settlement, and a large oven near the court gave Late Medio radiocarbon dates (Whalen and Minnis 2009:59, table 2.10). The Late Medio occupants of Site 204 had macaws, vesicular basalt grinding stone blanks, and a modest quantity of exotic and sumptuary goods, although some of these, like marine shell, apparently became less common as Paquimé reached its apogee. Also present in the 204 settlement was Ramos Polychrome pottery, with its elaborate symbol system. It is evident, then, that people of the Outer Core Zone 204 community participated in the ritual system that might have been promoted by Paquimé. It was equally clearly not part of the closely integrated Inner Core community that depended on Paquimé for public and ritual activities.

Another large, still-unexcavated settlement in the Outer Core Zone might have been the central place of yet another community. This is the Alamito site, or Site 178, located some 18 km from Site 204 and about the same distance from Paquimé. The Alamito site lies on the broad piedmont slope above the Palanganas River, which is a major tributary of the Casas Grandes River. The site consists of several large and small room block mounds, plus a sizable ball court of the simple open style. Near the court is a large oven. A number of smaller settlements lie in its immediate vicinity. The Alamito site has been described and illustrated elsewhere (Whalen and Minnis 2001a:156, fig. 5.7). Both Site 204 and the Alamito site were classed as heads of local Outer Core Zone settlement clusters in the 2001 study, reflecting the fragmented nature of the lands beyond the immediate sphere of influence of Paquimé.

A second and more direct type of relationship between Paquimé and its Outer Core Zone neighbors is reflected at small Site 242, a small settlement of 10–15 rooms. It could not have housed more than a few dozen people, yet it was built in a style imitative of Paquimé. Its walls were quite thick, enclosing large rooms. At least one of the rooms was of an elaborate shape. Architectural features included alcoves, T- shaped doorways, and well-made platform hearths. The diminutive 242 settlement was almost as well provided with exotic and sumptuary goods as was the much larger 204 settlement. Also present at Site 242 was a very large I-shaped ball court, at one end of which lay the only platform mound yet recorded outside Paquimé. The 242 settlement lies on a broad piedmont slope above the Palanganas River. There are only a few small Medio sites in the vicinity, but a vast system of agricultural terraces was constructed there. These productive facilities were far larger than necessary for a single small settlement like 242. The terraces themselves are undated, but they are presumed to be Late Medio age (Minnis et al. 2006). Radiocarbon dates from Site 242 show that the site was not occupied before the florescence of Paquimé or long after its decline. The settlement is too far from the Inner Core Zone (ca. 22 km) for first-level interaction with the Paquimé community. Nevertheless, architecture, ritual facilities, ceramics, exotica, and symbolism at Site 242 are all of the shared style. We note that 242 contains the only ritual architecture for some distance around, although it does not have a large oven. In chapter 2, we review the interpretation of this settlement as an agent of Paquimé, reaching into a sparsely populated part of the Outer Core uplands to organize agricultural productivity. We see it as part of the Late Medio productive intensification required by the growing center of Paquimé. The site is the only known example of its kind, however, and it does not demonstrate extensive Paquimé control of the Outer Core Zone. We see incursion rather than extensive domination, in other words. Doubtless there were still other sorts of interactions and relationships between Paquimé and other Outer Core settlements. The presence of scattered ball courts and large ovens all point to a fragmented political landscape in which we see no indication of centralized control.

The End of Paquimé and the Medio Period

There is growing opinion that Paquimé had declined considerably by the early 1400s, probably retaining no more than a remnant population (e.g., Phillips and Gamboa 2015; Schaafsma and Riley 1999). The authority of the center, then, lasted some 100–150 years. New osteological work (Casserino 2009) argues conclusively against the Paquimé massacre and subsequent regional abandonment hypothesis originally proposed by Di Peso, so we must seek other explanations. One promising direction of inquiry is the nature of the authority of Paquimé and its implication for the center's demise. Billman (2001:185) plausibly maintains that ideology, particularly in the form of control over systems of belief, is at the beginning of all political organization, regardless of the power bases ultimately controlled by emerging leaders. These power bases, with their sociopolitical hierarchies and linearization of control, do not appear to characterize the aggregated Puebloan societies of the U.S. Southwest. Rather, authority was based on pervasive kinship systems, comprehensive sodality structures, and ideology, including management of ritual and control of ritual knowledge (e.g., Adams and Duff 2004:13; P. Fish et al. 1994; Spielmann 2002; see also the papers collected by C. VanPool et al. 2006). Application of such ideas to Paquimé moves us away from the original elite-dominated, wealth-financed control hierarchy model based on Late Postclassic Mesoamerican societies.

Instead of elite-driven systems of wealth finance at Paquimé, a kin-oriented (or household-level) mode of production based on staple finance is appearing more likely. A longer discussion of this concept is provided by Cunningham (2017). As emphasized in the study just cited and by Pailes and Searcy (2022:105), the concentration of exotic and sumptuary goods at Paquimé, together with their paucity in the hinterlands, argues against the wealth finance and prestige goods distribution models that have long dominated the literature. In lieu of dependence on powerful wealthy elites in network authority models, researchers are turning to what Gary Feinman (2001:156) describes as an alternative pathway to power: inclusive, group-building strategies and cooperative labor organization, in what has been termed a corporate mode of organization. Finance is of the staple variety that supports public ceremonialism and the associated feasting that Stanish (2009:109) describes as one of the most common features of collective human behavior, providing important material and social benefits to people in cooperative groups. Facilities for large-scale food preparation are in evidence in the vast ovens at Paquimé and in the extensive storage capacity we argue to have existed there.

There are managers and some status differentiation in corporate systems of organization, although their authority is not comprehensive and is based largely on the kinship and ideological control just mentioned. Characteristically, such inequality is not strongly displayed in house construction, personal possessions, or mortuary practices. This is the situation seen at Paquimé, where there is not much evidence for elite people in the architecture, artifact distributions, or mortuary practices in the center (e.g., Pailes and Searcy 2022; Whalen and Minnis 2000). This has led to confusion and contention about the nature and extent of "eliteness" at Paquimé, since leadership, power, and prestige in societies of this sort are highly variable and likely to produce an ambiguous archaeological record (Graves and Spielmann 2000:47). Instead of among the people of Paquimé, such status distinctions as existed perhaps were to be found between the Paquimeans, the founders of the great city and the owners of its rituals, and the rest of the Inner Core population.

For ideology to be effective as an organizing principle, it must be materialized, or its concepts transformed to physical form (DeMarrais et al. 2004). This is done through ceremonial events, using exotic and sumptuary goods and symbols, and through some aspects of architecture. In the Casas Grandes area, these include marine shell, macaws, copper, turquoise, and other minerals, plus Mesoamerican-derived symbols, practices such as the ball game, and architectural elements such as platform mounds. Contrary to earlier thinking, exotica represents not elite wealth or prestige goods, but rather sacred, animate objects that served to sanctify and empower the central place in which they were concentrated. This argument is elaborated at Paquimé for marine shell (Whalen 2013) and for architecture (e.g., C. VanPool and Newsome 2012; T. Van Pool and C. Van Pool 2016). A model for movement of exotic goods without elite control among the centers of Northwest Mexico has recently been provided (Pailes and Searcy 2022:127–28).

But why should such ritual leadership emerge and flourish? This question is explored elsewhere (Stanish 2009), and the following discussion is abstracted from that source. Emergent leadership in midlevel societies cannot plausibly be viewed as a one-sided exploitative affair to gratify the ambitions of elite managers, as means of coercion are frequently not evident. Instead, both leaders and followers benefit from cooperative structures. Leaders gain prestige, which is imbued with authority. Authority, in turn, can be used to control at least some aspects of peoples' behavior. Followers reap benefits as well, since cooperative, coordinated labor increases productivity, making more staple finance available for public works and ceremonies and the associated feasting. Participants thus receive material, ritual, and social benefits, fostering a sense of community.

When successful, this strategy allows the cooperating group to expand at the expense of other, less organized people, absorbing them into the corporate structure and forcing changes in the cultural landscape. Participants must cede a little autonomy to the central authority, but they are usually willing to do so for the received benefits. In R. A. Beck's (2003) consensual model, the ceded authority is mostly ritual. Such structures, however, are tenuous and often short-lived. Stanish (2009:117) observes that the ethnographic record is replete with instances of people leaving cooperative labor organizations and rejecting the control of managerial elites. The trick is to balance the demands of cooperative effort with the interests of component groups. Such systems may, in fact, have built-in failure points, as the requirements of managerial elites exceed the perceived benefits of participation. We suggest that these ethnographic cases provide a model for the disintegration and abandonment of Paquimé.

This suggestion differs considerably from the long-standing model of massacre of the Paquimé population and subsequent abandonment of the Casas Grandes region (Di Peso 1974:2:320–25). Di Peso's view was clearly of abandonment in its classic, traditional sense, of failure and retreat, as an event brought about by unmanageable catastrophe. In lieu of a massacre, scholars have sought another explanation for the center's demise: environmental degradation coupled with increasing social pressures (e.g., Whalen and Minnis 2001a:196–204). In chapter 8 we review some examples of anthropogenic environmental change, without detecting anything of major proportion. More recent perspectives on abandonment are quite different. For example, Margaret Nelson and Gregson Schachner (2000:178) cite opinions characterizing abandonment as a strategic process of population redistribution in response to social or natural environmental pressures. All long-term adaptive cycles require reorganization, of which abandonment may be seen as an example (Nelson et al. 2006:403). The abandonment of sites and regions is well known in world prehistory, and it has been especially common in the U.S. Southwest. There, many large aggregated farming communities, including Paquimé, were abandoned in late prehistoric times (e.g., P. Fish et al. 1994; Hegmon et al. 1998; Lipe 2002; Nelson et al. 2006; Nelson and Schachner 2000; Varien 1999).

Aggregated, communally focused groups have competitive advantages, although they are also wracked with tensions as the demands of cooperative effort confront the interests of component groups. In the absence of effective control hierarchies, southwestern aggregated communities relied on pervasive kinship systems (both real and fictive), on comprehensive sodality organizations, and on ritual control as their sources of managerial authority (Adams and Duff 2004:13; Cameron 2010:361; P. Fish et al. 1994:138), but these control mechanisms are of limited capacity. Should they weaken, a common result of unmanageable social tensions is community fission and relocation of its members (Inomata and Webb 2003:4; Nelson and Schachner 2000:179). This process may be a protracted one, in which social and environmental pressures felt over years produce gradual community disintegration.

From this recognition comes the current perception of abandonment as an adaptive process rather than as a sudden response to overwhelming catastrophe. The latter can certainly occur, as in the case of Pompeii, but gradual abandonment is much more common, as Cameron and Tomka (1993:4) argued. It is interesting to note that gradual abandonments produce archaeological signatures that differ from those of sudden events. Gradual abandonment may be reflected in substantial accumulations of uncleared domestic trash on the floors of empty rooms, while sudden abandonments do not allow removal of valuable or useful objects, or the accumulation of much floor debris (Cameron and Tomka 1993; Nelson and Schachner 2000; Schiffer 2003). In short, the present consensus seems to be that abandonments are commonly demographic reorganizations that occurred as results of cumulative human decisions made under changing social and natural circumstances. They can involve long-distance migration of large population segments to other regions, or short-distance movements within the same region. In both cases, especially in short-distance moves, abandonment of settlements does not necessarily involve the disappearance of a people, relinquishment of place ownership, or the extinction of their cultural tradition, according to opinions summarized by Nelson and Schachner (2000:169). An excellent and relevant example of this comes from the Mimbres area of the U.S. Southwest. The following discussion is abstracted from the original source (Hegmon et al. 1998). The mid-1100s AD saw the abandonment of all large aggregated villages of the Classic Mimbres culture. The traditional view was that this abandonment also marked the end of the Mimbres culture, especially reflected in its Black-on-white ceramic tradition. Recent research in the eastern Mimbres area, however, shows the relocation of residents of aggregated Classic Mimbres villages into many small dispersed hamlets. People in these small settlements continued to use Mimbres-style architectural elements and ceramics after AD 1150. This situation is discussed in resilience theory terms elsewhere (Redman 2005; Nelson et al. 2006:404–5), emphasizing the assertion that processes of abandonment are general rather than specific to particular cultures or regions (Tomka and Stevenson 1993:191).

There is good indication that this pattern of dispersal of large aggregated populations into smaller scattered units was not unique to the Mimbres area. In fact, major abandonments in many parts of the Southwest were succeeded by ephemeral, low-visibility remains of continued occupation. Specifically, the fifteenth century saw abandonment of several areas of formerly dense populations, although remnant occupations extended up to the sixteenth century (P. Fish et al. 1994:163). We emphasize that the discussion just cited specifically included the Casas Grandes area.

Current literature also shows that apparently "abandoned" areas and settlements often continued in use and significance. Curation, or artifact scavenging, collecting, and recycling are significant factors in formation of the archaeological record subsequent to settlement abandonment, especially where short-distance moves took place (Tomka and Stevenson 1993:193). Not only artifacts continued to be significant to relocated populations.

Settlements are recognized as highly symbolic, leading to many revisitations after abandonment. Modern Hopi and Zuni people, for example, revisit villages where they once resided to collect resources and perform rituals. In these cases, the villages are perceived as still inhabited by deceased ancestors (Nelson and Schachner 2000:182). Even groups that are not direct descendants of the original residents may attach high symbolic value to abandoned settlements (Inomata and Webb 2003:7; Schiffer 2003:xii). Earlier in this volume, we suggest that the post-abandonment activities documented at Inner Core Site 315 represented symbolic actions in still-significant contexts.

In fact, it is our contention that much of the preceding discussion is applicable to Paquimé and the Casas Grandes area. In the Late Medio, Paquimé was a large aggregated community that must have been formed by assembly of people from the Core Zone and, likely, outsiders. The site of Paquimé offered a very elaborate built environment containing large quantities of sumptuary goods, local and foreign symbolism, and large ritual and commensal facilities. There is a clear tripartite division of the main room block mound, possibly reflecting the union of social groups to form the nucleus of the community. These things would be *pull* factors drawing people into the community and creating a social and environmental situation very different from the Early Medio situation. A lesson here is that our explanations need not always rely on *push* factors forcing people into aggregated situations and holding them there.

Nonetheless, preceding discussion (e.g., Whalen and Minnis 2000; Pailes and Searcy 2022) argued that no extreme level of social differentiation is evident in the housing, possessions, or mortuary treatment of the people of Paquimé. The situation, we contend, more closely resembles differentiation in the Pueblo societies of the Southwest than the original analog, which was the strongly hierarchical societies of Late Postclassic Mesoamerica. Paquimé thus would have been ripe for the sorts of social tensions common to aggregated populations that lack strong, comprehensive control hierarchies. In making this argument, however, we do not deemphasize environmental degradation and stress. The Outer Core Zone study (Whalen and Minnis 2009:218–36) noted that efforts at subsistence intensification are evident in the Core Zone during Late Medio times. This was presumably in response to the escalating cost of maintaining Paquimé and its social, economic, and ritual systems. Environmental degradation and subsistence stress were factors in better-studied abandonments in the U.S. Southwest, for instance, in the Grasshopper region of east-central Arizona and in the Mimbres area of southwestern New Mexico (P. Fish et al. 1994:162; Minnis 1985b), and the same was likely true for the Casas Grandes area. Economic stress also exacerbates social tensions.

Perceiving the disintegration of Paquimé as a redistribution of population rather than as a catastrophic collapse and flight helps to resolve a long-standing puzzle. Di Peso's model saw abandonment of the entire Casas Grandes area as coincident with the sack of Paquimé and the massacre of a portion of its population. Osteological work renders the massacre model invalid (Casserino 2009), but there remains the question of abandonment of what surely was an area of exceptional agricultural potential, as described elsewhere (Minnis and Whalen 2020).

We do not have the extensive environmental monitoring of the adjacent U.S. Southwest, but there is little indication of general environmental collapse and devastating crop failures in the Casas Grandes area. Recent thinking, however, argues that such would not have been necessary to produce substantial population movements. William Lipe (2002:232) models a situation in which leadership in kin groups or religious sodalities depended at least in part on the ability to store and redistribute surplus food production. In such a case, even moderate declines in productivity would create conflicts between crop-producing households and individuals or groups using this productivity to support their social power. Both the social and economic orders thus are weakened, a result of which is that households begin to pull away from the central place in the gradual abandonment process described in preceding pages.

We cannot say with certainty that all former Paquimé population remained in the area, but it is likely that a significant part did so. Earlier in this volume, we note the presence all over the Casas Grandes area of small residential sites with Medio period ceramics on their surfaces. Using the regression formula discussed in chapter 2, we estimated that the small sites of the area contained as many as 3,000 rooms. This is many more than we estimate for Paquimé (Whalen et al. 2010). All of the six Core Zone small sites studied in this volume dated to the Late Medio period, and we argue that most of them were occupied longer into the fifteenth century than Paquimé and the other large settlements. We cannot, of course, say that all of the Casas Grandes area's small sites are Late Medio, or that 100 percent of their rooms were occupied through the fifteenth century. Even so, we assert that there were many small sites of Late Medio times all over the Casas Grandes area, with many habitation rooms among them. Thus, there were places for many people to disperse into. In the Mimbres case discussed earlier, small residential sites were formed though remodeling of field houses and seasonal sites (Hegmon et al. 1998; Nelson 1999). Small site rooms in the Casas Grandes area were smaller than those of Paquimé, but so were the vast majority of the habitation rooms at large sites all over the Core Zone.

Along with this redistribution of population, we see continued use of the Late Medio ceramic tradition, 90 percent of which consisted of utilitarian wares. Possibly reduced in frequency were the polychrome vessels that carried the elaborate symbolism associated with Paquimé, although remnant populations commonly curate things from abandoned settlements. We note that Di Peso was constrained to postulate abandonment of the Casas Grandes area upon the disintegration of Paquimé. He viewed Paquimé and its material culture as coincident. The one was the other, and both were heavily shaped by outside influences. It should also be noted that Di Peso's models were constrained by lack of fine chronometric data. Accordingly, the fact that only Late Medio period ceramics are visible on site surfaces all over the area was taken as proof of regional abandonment.

An alternative view, presented in this volume and elsewhere (Cunningham 2017), sees Paquimé as an especially elaborate Late Medio outgrowth of a preexisting Early Medio regional culture. In this case, there is no necessity to assume that the culture pattern vanished entirely when its most prominent center declined. The Medio period cultural tradition might have been carried on in attenuated form by a dispersed remnant population in the many small room blocks of the Core and Middle Zones. In addition, the present study of Inner Core Zone small sites describes crude remodeling in a Post-Medio Architectural Tradition. People clearly reoccupied some of the rooms, constructing sloppy additions of masonry and an adobe that differed markedly in color from that of the Casas Grandes Architectural Tradition. There may have been even greater continuity in some of the ceramics. There is evidence that Brownware pottery found on several small sites of the Spanish colonial period was very much like that found at Paquimé and its neighbors. Di Peso termed this colonial Brownware "San Antonio Plain," but statistical comparison of ceramic pastes shows that it does not differ significantly from the Plain Brown pottery of the Late Medio period (Martínez Galicia 2016, 2024). All these observations lead to the idea of a people continuing to inhabit the Casas Grandes area after the demise of Paquimé, especially in its resource-rich Inner Core Zone. In addition, early Spanish colonial–era documents contain numerous petitions for land title by Indigenous groups citing their ancestral occupation of the Casas Grandes area (Martínez Galicia 2024).

Concluding Thoughts

There has been a welcome resurgence of work in the Casas Grandes area by a number of researchers over the past several decades. These efforts have modified many long-standing ideas about Paquimé and the regional organization around it. There has been an explanatory shift from hegemonic models of an extensive, comprehensive dominance by Paquimé to simpler, more limited authority strategies that more resemble the Puebloan societies of the U.S. Southwest than the Late Postclassic polities of Mesoamerica. No one denies that there were Mesoamerican-inspired things and ideas in the NW/SW. Rather, the continuing debate is about how and to what extent they shaped local cultures, and positions have been taken on all sides of the issue. However this debate is ultimately resolved, models of the Puebloan sort offer refreshing alternatives to the traditional notions of coercive power directed downward by wealthy elites in an apical hierarchy. In fact, it is likely that much of the trouble that we have had in understanding Paquimé and its regional impact comes from attempts to fit an increasing body of knowledge into the traditional model of an elite-managed, wealth-financed network strategy in which Paquimé was at the top of a strong regional control hierarchy. In this volume, we contend that models of corporate organization show alternate pathways to power that better fit the Paquimé archaeological data. We find ourselves in agreement with Feinman (2001:173), who writes, "Corporate formations have tended to create interpretive enigmas for scholars reliant for explanation on the axis of complexity alone." We believe that many of the original ideas about Paquimé are more appropriate for Mesoamerican settlements than for the present case. In short, we conceive Paquimé as a mostly Puebloan phenomenon, although one with a heavier-than-usual overlay of Mesoamerican concepts and symbolism. In leaning toward the Puebloan form of organization, we do not deny that Paquimé was able to accomplish feats of organization of very impressive magnitude, but strong corporate, cooperative organizations are capable of large works, if only for a brief time. The Chaco Canyon Great Towns are such examples. Other researchers certainly will disagree, and the issue is far from resolved. As for the regional status of Paquimé, some of our colleagues have noted "there is a fairly clear break between those researchers who see Paquimé's exceptionalness as self-evident and thus meriting unique explanation, and those who see it only as the grandest example of a regionally common pattern" (Pailes and Searcy 2022:106). We clearly fall into the latter camp, but the controversy continues, and the last words on these issues have certainly not yet been written. In fact, we think it appropriate to end the present volume with the still-applicable words we used a quarter-century ago to conclude the survey volume: "It is sobering to reflect that the Chaco Canyon phenomenon [of the U.S. Southwest] is certainly one of the best studied and most precisely dated in the entire world, yet there is still considerable debate among Chacoan scholars about the exact nature of the regional polity that formed there. The [Paquimé] polity, in contrast, stands generations of work behind its Chacoan counterpart" (Whalen and Minnis 2001a:207).

References Cited

Adams, E. Charles. 1983. The Architectural Analog to Hopi Social Organization and Room Use, and Implications for Prehistoric Northern Southwestern Culture. *American Antiquity* 48:44–61.

Adams, E. Charles, and Andrew Duff. 2004. Settlement Clusters and the Pueblo IV Period. In *The Protohistoric Pueblo World, A.D. 1275–1600*, edited by E. Charles Adams and Andrew Duff, pp. 3–16. University of Arizona Press, Tucson.

Adams, Karen R. 2014. Little Barley (*Hordeum pusillum* Nutt.): A Pre-Hispanic New World Domesticate Lost to History. In *New Lives for Ancient and Extinct Crop*, edited by Paul Minnis, pp. 179–91. University of Arizona Press, Tucson.

Adams, Karen R. 2017. Ancient Plant Use in West-Central Chihuahua. In *Not So Far from Paquimé: Essays on the Archaeology of Chihuahua, Mexico*, edited by Jane Holden Kelley and David A. Phillips Jr., pp. 81–98. University of Utah Press, Salt Lake City.

Adler, Michael. 2002. The Ancestral Pueblo Community as Structure and Strategy. In *Seeking the Center Place: Archaeology and Ancient Communities in the Mesa Verde Region*, edited by M. Varien and R. Wilshusen, pp. 24–39. University of Utah Press, Salt Lake City.

Adler, Michael. 2012. Negotiating the Village: Community Landscapes in the Late Prehistoric American Southwest. In *Inscribed Landscapes: Marking and Making Place*, edited by B. David and M. Wilson, pp. 200–16. University of Hawai'i Press, Honolulu.

Aitken, M. J. 1990. *Science-Based Dating in Archaeology*. Longman, London.

Andrefsky, William, Jr. 2005. *Lithics: Macroscopic Approaches to Analysis*. 2nd ed. Cambridge University Press, Cambridge.

Arthur, John W. 2003. Brewing Beer: Status, Wealth, and Ceramic Use Alteration Among the Gamo of Southwest Ethiopia. *World Archaeology* 34:516–28.

Badenhorst, Shaw, and Jonathan C. Driver. 2009. Faunal Changes in Farming Communities from Basketmaker II to Pueblo III (A.D. 1–1300) in the San Juan Basin of the American Southwest. *Journal of Archaeological Science* 36:1832–41.

Bartlett, John. 1854. *Personal Narrative of Explorations and Incidents in Texas, New Mexico, California, Sonora, and Chihuahua*. D. Appleton, New York.

Beacham, Bradley, and Stephen R. Durand. 2007. Eggshell and the Archaeological Record: New Insights into Turkey Husbandry in the American Southwest. *Journal of Archaeological Science* 34:1610–21.

Beck, Margaret. 2001. "Archaeological Signatures of Corn Preparation in the U.S. Southwest." *Kiva* 67:187–218.

Beck, Robin A., Jr. 2003. Consolidation and Hierarchy: Chiefdom Variability in the Mississippian Southeast. *American Antiquity* 68:641–61.

Benfer, Robert A. 1968. An Analysis of a Prehistoric Skeletal Population, Casas Grandes, Chihuahua, Mexico. Ph.D. dissertation, Department of Anthropology, University of Texas–Austin.

Bennett, Wendell, and Robert Zingg. 1935. *The Tarahumara: An Indian Tribe of Northern Mexico*. Publications in Anthropology, Ethnological Series. University of Chicago.

Billman, Brian. 2001. Understanding the Timing and Tempo of the Evolution of Political Centralization on the Central Andean Coastline and Beyond. In *From Leaders to Rulers*, edited by Jonathan Haas, pp. 177–204. Plenum, New York.

Blitz, John. 1993. Big Pots for Big Shots: Feasting and Storage in a Mississippian Community. *American Antiquity* 58:80–96.

Blinman, Eric. 1989. Potluck in the Protokiva: Ceramics and Ceremonialism in Pueblo I Villages. In *The Architecture of Social Integration in Prehistoric Pueblos*, Occasional Paper No. 1, edited by W. Lipe and M. Hegmon, pp. 113–24. Crow Canyon Archaeological Center, Cortez, Colorado.

Bohrer, Vorsila L. 1991. Recently Recognized Cultivated and Encouraged Plants Among the Hohokam. *Kiva* 56:227–35.

Bradley, Ronna. 1999. Shell Exchange Within the Southwest: The Casas Grandes Interaction Sphere. In *The Casas Grandes World*, edited by C. Schaafsma and C. Riley, pp. 213–28. University of Utah Press, Salt Lake City.

Brand, Donald D. 1933. The Historical Geography of Northwestern Chihuahua. Ph.D. dissertation, Department of Geography, University of California, Berkeley.

Bronk Ramsey, Christopher. 2021. OxCal v4.4.4. Research Lab for Archaeology, University of Oxford.

Bruman, Henry J. 2000. *Alcohol in Ancient Mexico*. University of Utah Press, Salt Lake City.

Burd, Karen, Jane Kelley, and Mitch Hendrickson. 2004. Ceramics as Temporal and Spatial Indicators in Chihuahua Cultures. In *Surveying the Archaeology of Northwest Mexico*, edited by G. Newell and E. Gallaga, pp. 177–204. University of Utah Press, Salt Lake City.

Butler, Barbara. 1971. The People of Casas Grandes: Cranial and Dental Morphology through Time. Ph.D. dissertation, Department of Anthropology, Southern Methodist University, Dallas.

Cameron, Catherine M. 1999. Room Size, Organization of Construction, and Archaeological Interpretation in the Puebloan Southwest. *Journal of Anthropological Archaeology* 18(2):201–39.

Cameron, Catherine M. 2010. Advances in Understanding the Thirteenth-Century Depopulation of the Northern Southwest. In *Leaving Mesa Verde: Peril and Change in the Thirteenth Century Southwest*, edited by T. Kohler, M. Varien, and A. Wright, pp. 346–64. University of Arizona Press, Tucson.

Cameron, Catherine M., and Steve Tomka (editors). 1993. *Abandonment of Settlements and Regions: Ethnoarchaeological and Archaeological Approaches*. Cambridge University Press, Cambridge.

Cameron, Kenneth, Maryellen Cameron, William C. Bagby, Elizabeth J. Moll, and Robert E. Drake. 1980. Petrologic Characteristics of Mid-Tertiary Volcanic Suites, Chihuahua, Mexico. *Geology* 8:87–91.

Cannon, Michael D., and Michael A. Etnier. 1997. Report on the Analysis of Faunal Materials. In *Reconocimiento Regional Paquimé, 1996*, edited by M. Whalen and P. Minnis. Manuscript on file at the Department of Anthropology, University of Tulsa, Oklahoma.

Carey, Henry A. 1931. An Analysis of the Northwestern Chihuahua Culture. *American Anthropologist* 33:325–74.

Carr, Philip, and Andrew Bradbury. 2001. Flake Debris Analysis, Levels of Production, and the Organization of Technology. In *Lithic Debitage: Context, Form, and Meaning*, edited by William Andrefsky, pp. 126–46. University of Utah Press, Salt Lake City.

Casserino, Christopher. 2009. Bioarchaeology of Violence and Site Abandonment at Casas Grandes, Chihuahua, Mexico. Ph.D. dissertation, Department of Anthropology, University of Oregon, Eugene.

Casserino, Christopher, and Elizabeth Mills. 2009. "Site 315: Human Skeletal Remains." Report on file in the Department of Anthropology, University of Tulsa.

Ciolek-Torrello, Richard, and J. Jefferson Reid. 1974. Change in Household Size at Grasshopper. *Kiva* 40:39–48.

Clarkson, Chris. 2008. Changing Reduction Intensity, Settlement, and Subsistence in Wardman County, Northern Australia. In *Lithic Technology: Measures of Production, Use, and Curation*, edited by W. Andrefsky, pp. 286–316. Cambridge University Press, New York.

Classen, Cheryl. 1998. *Shells*. Cambridge University Press, Cambridge.

Conrad, Cyler. 2021. Contextualizing Ancestral Pueblo Turkey Management. *Journal of Archaeological Method and Theory* 29:624–65.

Contreras Sánchez, Eduardo. 1986. *Paquimé: Zona Arqueológica de Casas Grandes*. Gobierno del Estado de Chihuahua, Chihuahua City, Mexico.

Corruccini, Robert. 1983. Pathologies Related to Subsistence and Settlement at Casas Grandes. *American Antiquity* 48:609–10.

Crema, E. R. 2022. Statistical Inference of Prehistoric Demography from Frequency Distributions of Radiocarbon Dates: A Review and a Guide for the Perplexed. *Journal of Archaeological Method and Theory* 29:1387–1418.

Crown, Patricia L., Jiyan Gu, W. Jeffrey Hurst, Timothy J. Ward, Ardith D. Bavenec, Syed Ali, Laura Kebert, Marlaina Berch, Erin Redman, Patrick D. Lyons, Jamie Mereweather, David A. Phillips, Lori S. Reed, and Kyle Woodson. 2015. Ritual Drinks in the pre-Hispanic US Southwest and Mexican Northwest. *Proceedings of the National Academy of Sciences* 112(37):11426–42.

Crown, Patricia, and Jeffrey Hurst. 2009. Evidence of Cacao Use in the Prehispanic American Southwest. *Proceedings of the National Academy of Sciences* 106:2110–13.

Crumley, Carole. 1995. Heterarchy and the Analysis of Complex Societies. In *Heterarchy and the Analysis of Complex Societies*, edited by R. Ehrenreich, C. Crumley, and J. Levy, pp. 1–5. Archaeological Papers No. 6. American Anthropological Association, Washington, D.C.

Cruz Antillón, Rafael, Robert D. Leonard, Timothy D. Maxwell, Todd L. VanPool, Marcel J. Harmon, Christine S. VanPool, David A. Hyndman, and Sidney S. Brandwein. 2004. Galeana, Villa Ahumada, and Casa Chica: Diverse Sites in the Casas Grandes Region. In *Surveying the Archaeology of Northwest Mexico*, edited by G. E. Newell and E. Gallaga, pp. 149–75. University of Utah Press, Salt Lake City.

Cruz Antillón, Rafael, and Timothy Maxwell. 2017. La Provincia Oriental de Casas Grandes. In *La Cultura Casas Grandes*, edited by R. Cruz Antillión and T. Maxwell, pp. 177–90. INAH Chihuahua, Secretaría de Cultura de Chihuahua, Gobierno del Estado de Chihuahua, Chihuahua City.

Cunningham, Jerimy J. 2017. The Ritual Mode of Production in the Casas Grandes Social Field. In *Modes of Production and Archaeology*, edited by Robert Rosenswig and Jerimy J. Cunningham, pp. 174–206. University Press of Florida, Tallahassee.

Custer, Jay. 1987. Core Technology at the Hawthorne Site, New Castle County, Delaware: A Late Archaic Camp. In *The Organization of Core Technology*, edited by J. Johnson and C. Morrow, pp. 45–62. Westview, Boulder, Colorado.

Cutler, Hugh, and L. Blake. 1974. Corn from Casas Grandes. In *Casas Grandes: A Fallen Trading Center of the Gran Chichimeca*, vol. 8, edited by C. Di Peso, J. Rinaldo, and G. Fenner, pp. 308–15. The Amerind Foundation and Northland Press, Dragoon and Flagstaff.

D'Altroy, Terrance, Timothy K. Earle, David L. Browman, Darrell La Lone, Michael E. Moseley, John V. Murra, Thomas P. Myers, Frank Salomon, Katharina J. Schreiber, and John R. Topic. 1985. Staple Finance, Wealth Finance, and Storage in the Inka Political Economy. *Current Anthropology* 26:187–206.

Dean, Jeffrey S., and John C. Ravesloot. 1993. The Chronology of Cultural Interaction in the Gran Chichimeca. In *Culture and Contact: Charles C. Di Peso's Gran Chichimeca*, edited by A. I. Woosley and J. C. Ravesloot, pp. 83–104. The Amerind Foundation and University of New Mexico Press, Dragoon and Albuquerque.

DeMarrais, Elizabeth, Chris Gosden, and Colin Renfrew. 2004. *Rethinking Materiality: The Engagement of the Mind With the Material World*. McDonald Institute for Archaeological Research, Cambridge University, Cambridge.

Diehl, Michael, Deil Lundin, Robert B. Ciaccio, and J. Homer Thiel. 2021. The Native American Adoption of Chilies During the 18th Century in Arizona. *Kiva* 87:168–89.

Di Peso, Charles C. 1974. *Casas Grandes: A Fallen Trading Center of the Gran Chichimeca*. Vols. 1–3. The Amerind Foundation and Northland Press, Dragoon and Flagstaff.

Di Peso, Charles C., John B. Rinaldo, and Gloria J. Fenner. 1974. *Casas Grandes: A Fallen Trading Center of the Gran Chichimeca*. Vols. 4–8. The Amerind Foundation and Northland Press, Dragoon and Flagstaff.

Dolan, Sean, Michael Whalen, Paul Minnis, and Steven Shackley. 2017. Obsidian in the Casas Grandes World: Procurement, Exchange, and Interaction in Chihuahua, Mexico, CE 1200–1450. *Journal of Archaeological Science Reports* 11:555–67.

Doolittle, William. 1993. Canal Irrigation at Casas Grandes: A Technological and Developmental Assessment of its Origin. In *Culture and Contact: Charles C. Di Peso's Gran Chichimeca*, edited by A. I. Woosley and J. C. Ravesloot, pp. 133–52. The Amerind Foundation and University of New Mexico Press, Dragoon and Albuquerque.

Douglas, John. 2000. Exchanges, Assumptions, and Mortuary Goods in Pe-Paquimé Chihuahua, Mexico. In *The Archaeology of Regional Interaction*, edited by M. Hegmon, pp. 198–208. University Press of Colorado, Boulder.

Douglas, John, and Linda Brown. 2023. Reevaluating the Suma Occupation in the Casas Grandes Valley, Chihuahua, Mexico. *American Antiquity* 88:125–43.

Drennan, Robert, Adam Berry, and Christian Peterson. 2015. *Regional Settlement Demography in Archaeology*. Eliot Werner, Clinton Corners, N.Y.

Driver, Jonathan. 2002. Faunal Analyses. In *Seeking the Center Place: Archaeology and Ancient Communities in the Mesa Verde Region*, edited by Mark D. Varien and Richard H. Wilshusen, pp. 143–62. University of Utah Press, Salt Lake City.

Feinman, Gary. 2001. Mesoamerican Political Complexity: The Corporate-Network Dimension. In *From Leaders to Rulers*, edited by J. Haas, pp. 151–74. Plenum, New York.

Feinman, Gary, Steadman Upham, and Kent Lightfoot. 1991. The Production Step Measure: An Ordinal Index of Labor Input in Ceramic Manufacture. *American Antiquity* 46:871–84.

Fish, Paul R., and Suzanne K. Fish. 1999. Reflections on the Casas Grandes Regional System from the Northwestern Periphery. In *The Casas Grandes World*, edited by C. Schaafsma and C. Riley, pp. 27–42. Salt Lake City: University of Utah Press.

Fish, Paul, Suzanne K. Fish, George Gumerman, and J. Jefferson Reid. 1994. Toward an Explanation for Southwestern "Abandonments." In *Themes in Southwest Prehistory*, edited by G. Gumerman, pp. 135–64. Advanced Seminar Series, School of American Research, Santa Fe, New Mexico.

Fish, Suzanne K., Paul R. Fish, and John Madsen. 1992. *The Marana Community in the Hohokam World*. Anthropological Papers of the University of Arizona 56. University of Arizona Press, Tucson.

Fralick, Phillip, Joe Stewart, and Arthur MacWilliams. 1998. Geochemistry of West-Central Chihuahua Obsidian Nodules and Implications for the Derivation of Obsidian Artifacts. *Journal of Archaeological Science* 25:1023–38.

Frost, Dawn A. 2000. Architecture as Chronological Marker: Testing Di Peso's Assumptions at Paquimé, Chihuahua, Mexico. Master's thesis, Department of Anthropology, University of Tulsa.

Goodale, Nathan, Ian Kuijt, Shane MacFarlan, Curtis Osterhoudt, and Bill Finlayson. 2008. Lithic Core Reduction Techniques: Modeling Expected Diversity. In *Lithic Technology: Measures of Production, Use, and Curation*, edited by W. Andrefsky, pp. 317–38. Cambridge University Press, New York.

Graham, Anna F., Karen R. Adams, Susan J. Smith, and Terrence M. Murphy. 2017. A New Record of Domesticated Little Barley (*Hordeum pusillum* Nutt.) in Colorado: Travel, Trade or Independent Domestication. *Kiva* 83:414–42.

Graves, William, and Katherine Spielmann. 2000. Leadership, Long-Distance Exchange, and Feasting in the Protohistoric Rio Grande. In *Alternative Leadership Strategies in the Prehispanic Southwest*, edited by B. Mills, pp. 45–59. University of Arizona Press, Tucson.

Gremillion, Kristen J. 2018. *Food Production in Native North America*. Society for American Archaeology Press, Washington, D.C.

Grimstead, Deanna N., Amanda C. Reynolds, Adam M. Hudson, Nancy J. Akins, and Julio L. Betancourt. 2016. Reduced Population Variance in Strontium Isotope Ratios Informs Domesticated Turkey Use at Chaco Canyon, New Mexico, USA. *Journal of Archaeological Method and Theory* 23:127–49.

Guevara Sánchez, Arturo. 1991. *Gia Oficial: Paquimé y Cuarenta Casas*. INAH_SALVAT, Mexico City.

Gutzeit, Jennifer. 2008. The Chipped Stone Assemblage from Cerro de Moctezuma: Implications for Lithic Assemblage Variability in the Casas Grandes Region, Chihuahua, Mexico. Master's thesis, Department of Anthropology, University of Tulsa, Oklahoma.

Hally, David. 1983. Use Alteration of Pottery Vessel Surfaces: An Important Source of Evidence for the Identification of Vessel Function. *North American Archaeologist* 4:3–26.

Hard, Robert, and John Roney. 2020. *Early Farming and Warfare in Northwest Mexico*. University of Utah Press, Salt Lake City.

Hargrave, Lyndon. 1965. Turkey Bones from Wetherill Mesa. In *Memoirs No. 19*, pp. 161–66. Society for American Archaeology, Washington, D.C.

Harmon, Marcel J. 2005. Centralization, Cultural Transmission, and "the Game of Life and Death" in Northern Mexico. Ph.D. dissertation, Department of Anthropology, University of New Mexico, Albuquerque.

Harmon, Marcel J. 2006. Religion and the Mesoamerican Ball Game in the Casas Grandes Region of Northern Mexico. In *Religion in the Prehispanic Southwest*, edited by T. L. VanPool, C. S. VanPool, and D. A. Phillips, pp. 185–218. Altamira, Walnut Creek, California.

Hawley, John. 1969. Notes on the Geomorphology and Late Cenozoic Geology of Northwestern Chihuahua. In *The Border Region, Chihuahua and the United States: Twentieth Annual Fall Field Conference Guidebook*, edited by D. Cordoba, S. Wengerd, and J. Shomaker, pp. 131–42. New Mexico Geological Society, Albuquerque.

Hayden, Brian. 2022. *Understanding Chipped Stone Tools*. Eliot Werner, Clinton Corners, New York.

Hayden, Brian, and Karl Hutchings. 1989. Whither the Billet Flake. In *Experiments in Lithic Technology*, edited by D. Amick and R. Mauldin, pp. 235–57. BAR Series No. 528. British Archaeological Reports, Oxford.

Hegmon, Michelle, Margaret Nelson, and Susan Ruth. 1998. Abandonment and Reorganization in the Mimbres Region of the American Southwest. *American Anthropologist* 100:148–62.

Hendrickson, Mitch J. 2003. *Design Analysis of Chihuahuan Polychrome Jars from North American Museum Collections*. BAR International Series 1125. Archaeopress, Oxford.

Hill, James. 1970. *Broken K Pueblo: Prehistoric Social Organization in the American Southwest*. Anthropological Papers No. 18. University of Arizona Press, Tucson.

Hill, Warren. 1992. Chronology of the El Zurdo Site, Chihuahua, Mexico. Master's thesis, Department Archaeology, University of Calgary.

Hodgetts, Lisa M. 1996. Faunal Evidence from El Zurdo. *Kiva* 62:149–70.

Huckell, Lisa, and M. Toll. 2004. Wild Plant Use in the North American Southwest. In *People and Plants in Ancient Western North America*, edited by P. Minnis, pp. 37–114. University of Arizona Press, Tucson.

Hudson, Charles M. 2004. *Black Drink: A Native American Tea*. University of Georgia Press, Athens.

Hunt, Alice. 2016. *The Oxford Handbook of Archaeological Ceramic Analysis*. Oxford University Press.

Inomata, Takeshi, and Ronald Webb. 2003. Archaeological Studies of Abandonment in Middle America. In *The Archaeology of Settlement Abandonment in Middle America*, edited by Takahashi Inomata and Ronald Webb, pp. 1–12. University of Utah Press, Salt Lake City.

Isbell, William. 2000. What We Should Be Studying: The 'Imagined Community' and The 'Natural Community.' In *The Archaeology of Communities: A New World Perspective*, edited by M. Canuto and J. Yaeger, pp. 243–66. Routledge, New York.

Johnson, Jay. 1987. Introduction. In *The Organization of Core Technology*, edited by J. Johnson and C. Morrow, pp. 1–12. Westview, Boulder, Colorado.

Jones, Jenna F. 2002. "Ceramics and Feasting in the Casas Grandes Area, Chihuahua, Mexico." Master's thesis, Department of Anthropology, University of Tulsa, Oklahoma.

Kelley, Jane. 2017. The Viejo Period. In *Not So Far From Paquimé: Essays on the Archaeology of Chihuahua, Mexico*, edited by J. Kelley and D. Phillips Jr., pp. 29–53. University of Utah Press, Salt Lake City.

Kelley, Jane, and Karen Burd Larkin. 2017. Pottery Studies. In *Not So Far From Paquimé: Essays on the Archaeology of Chihuahua, Mexico*, edited by J. Kelley and D. Phillips Jr., pp. 99–119. University of Utah Press, Salt Lake City.

Kelley, Jane, and David Phillips Jr. 2017. Medio Period Sites in the Southern Zone. In *Not So Far from Paquimé: Essays on the Archaeology of Chihuahua, Mexico*, edited by J. Kelley and D. Phillips Jr., pp. 54–80. University of Utah Press, Salt Lake City.

Kemp, Brian. 2010. Evaluating the Farming/Language Dispersal Hypothesis with Genetic Variation Exhibited by Populations in the Southwest and Mesoamerica. *Proceedings of the National Academy of Science* 107:6759–64.

Kidder, Alfred V. 1916. The Pottery of the Casas Grandes District, Chihuahua. In *The Holmes Anniversary Volume: Anthropological Essays*, pp. 253–68. Private printing, Washington, D.C.

King, Daniel, Michael Searcy, Chad Yost, and Kyle Walker. 2017. Corn, Beer, and Marine Resources at Casas Grandes, Mexico: An Analysis of Prehistoric Diets Using Microfossils Recovered from Dental Calculus. *Journal of Archaeological Science Reports* 16:365–79.

Kintigh, Keith W. 2002. *Tools for Quantitative Archaeology: Programs for Quantitative Analysis in Archaeology*. Published by K. W. Kintigh, Tempe, Arizona.

Klein, Richard, and Kathryn Cruz-Uribe. 1984. *The Analysis of Animal Bones from Archaeological Sites*. University of Chicago Press, Chicago.

Koldehoff, Brad. 1987. The Cahokia Flake Tool Industry: Socioeconomic Implications for Late Prehistory in the Central Mississippi Valley. In *The Organization of Core Technology*, edited by J. Johnson and C. Morrow, pp. 151–86. Westview, Boulder, Colorado.

Kooyman, Brian P. 2000. *Understanding Stone Tools and Archaeological Sites*. University of Calgary, Alberta.

Kunsel, Christopher, and Alan Outram. 2004. Fragmentation: The Zonation Method Applied to Fragmented Human Remains from Archaeological and Forensic Contexts. *Environmental Archaeology* 9:85–97.

Lang, Richard, and Arthur H. Harris. 1984. *The Faunal Remains from Arroyo Hondo Pueblo, New Mexico: A Study in Short-Term Subsistence Change*. Arroyo Hondo Archaeological Series, vol. 5. School of American Research, Santa Fe, New Mexico.

Lebgue, Toutcha, and Alfonso Valerio. 1986. *Manual para Identificar las Gramineas del Chihuahua*. Gobierno del Estado, Chihuahua City.

Lekson, Stephen. 1984. Dating Casas Grandes. *Kiva* 50:55–60.

Lekson, Stephen. 1986. *Great Pueblo Architecture of Chaco Canyon, New Mexico*. University of New Mexico Press, Albuquerque.

Lekson, Stephen. 1999. *The Chaco Meridian: Centers of Political Power in the Ancient Southwest*. AltaMira, Walnut Creek, California.

Lekson, Stephen. 2000. Salado in Chihuahua. In *Salado*, edited by J. S. Dean, pp. 275–94. The Amerind Foundation and University of New Mexico Press, Dragoon and Albuquerque.

Lekson, Stephen. 2008. *A History of the Ancient Southwest*. School for Advanced Research Press, Santa Fe, New Mexico.

Lekson, Stephen. 2015. *The Chaco Meridian: One Thousand Years of Political and Religious Power in the Ancient Southwest. Second Edition*. Rowman and Littlefield, Lanham, Md.

Lekson, Stephen, Michael Bletzer, and A. C. MacWilliams. 2004. Pueblo IV in the Chihuahuan Desert. In *The Protohistoric Pueblo World, A.D. 1275–1600*, edited by E. Adams and A. Duff, pp. 53–61. University of Arizona Press, Tucson.

Lipe, William. 1999. Introduction to *The Sand Canyon Archaeological Project: A Progress Report*, edited by W. Lipe, pp. 23–35. Occasional Paper No. 2. Crow Canyon Archaeological Center, Cortez, Colorado.

Lipe, William. 2002. Social Power in the Central Mesa Verde Region, A.D. 1150–1290. In *Seeking the Center Place: Archaeology and Ancient Communities in the Mesa Verde Region*, edited by M. Varien and R. Wilshusen, pp. 203–32. University of Utah Press, Salt Lake City.

Lipe, William D., R. Kyle Bocinsky, Brian S. Chisolm, Robin Lyle, David M. Dove, R. G. Matson, Elizabeth Farmer Jarvis, Kathleen Judd, and Brian M. Kemp. 2016. Cultural and Genetic Contexts for Early Turkey Domestication in the Northern Southwest. *American Antiquity* 81:97–113

Long, Austin, and Bruce Rippeteau. 1974. Testing Contemporaneity and Averaging Radiocarbon Dates. *American Antiquity* 39:205–15.

Loven, Jeremy. 2016. Utilization of Faunal Resources at Site 315 and Site 355: Casas Grandes, Chihuahua, Mexico. Master's thesis, Graduate Faculty in Anthropology, Eastern New Mexico University, Portales.

Lowell, Julia C. 1991. *Prehistoric Households at Turkey Creek Pueblo, Arizona*. Anthropological Papers of the University of Arizona No. 54. University of Arizona Press, Tucson.

Lowell, Julia C. 1999. The Fires of Grasshopper: Enlightening Transformations in Subsistence Practices Through Fire-Feature Analysis. *Journal of Anthropological Archaeology* 18:441–70.

Lyman, R. Lee. 1994. *Vertebrate Taphonomy*. Cambridge University Press, New York.

Lyons, Patrick. 2003. *Ancestral Hopi Migrations*. University of Arizona Press, Tucson.

MacWilliams, Arthur. 2001. Beyond the Reach of Casas Grandes: Archaeology in Central Chihuahua. In *From Paquimé to Mata Ortiz: The Legacy of Ancient Casas Grandes*, edited by G. Johnson, pp. 55–64. Museum of Man, San Diego.

Margolis, Michael. 2007. The Isolated Human Bone from Grasshopper Pueblo. Master's thesis, Department of Anthropology, University of Arizona, Tucson.

Martínez Galicia, Marco Antonio. 2016. Plainware Textural Analysis and Cultural Continuity of the Casas Grandes Tradition after the Collapse of Paquimé, Chihuahua, Mexico. Master's thesis, Department of Anthropology, University of Tulsa, Oklahoma.

Martínez Galicia, Marco Antonio. 2024. "After Paquimé: Indigenous Life During the Early Spanish Colonization of Casas Grandes, Northern New Spain, in the XV Century." Ph.D. dissertation, Department of Anthropology, University of Tulsa, Oklahoma.

Mathiowetz, Michael. 2018. The Sun Youth of the Casas Grandes Culture, Chihuahua, Mexico (AD 1200–1450). *Kiva* 84:367–90.

McCluney, Eugene. 2002. The 1963 Excavation. In *The Joyce Well Site on the Frontier of the Casas Grandes World*, edited by James Skibo, Eugene McCluney, and William Walker, pp. 11–98. University of Utah Press, Salt Lake City.

McConnan Borstad, Courtney. 2021. Diet and Dietary Variation at Prehistoric Casas Grandes, Mexico. Ph.D. dissertation, Department of Archaeology, University of Calgary.

McGovern, Patrick, Anne Underhill, Hui Fang, Fengshi Luan, Gretchen Hall, Yu Haiguang, Chen-Shan Wang, Cai Fengshu, Zhijun Zhao, and Gary Feinman. 2005. Chemical Identification and Cultural Implications of a Mixed Fermented Beverage from Late Prehistoric China. *Asian Perspectives* 44:249–75.

McKay, Michael W. 2005. Observing Social Complexity within the Paquimé Polity: A Comparison of Ground Stone Implements from the La Tinaja Site and the Site of Casas Grandes, Chihuahua, Mexico. Master's thesis, Department of Anthropology, University of Oklahoma, Norman.

McKusick, Charmion. 1974a. The Casas Grandes Avian Report. In *Casas Grandes: A Fallen Trading Center of the Gran Chichimeca*, vol. 8, edited by Charles C. Di Peso, John B. Rinaldo, and Gloria J. Fenner, pp. 273–84. The Amerind Foundation and Northland Press, Dragoon and Flagstaff.

McKusick, Charmion. 1974b. The Mammalian Remains from Casas Grandes. In *Casas Grandes: A Fallen Trading Center of the Gran Chichimeca*, vol. 8, edited by Charles C. Di Peso, John B. Rinaldo, and Gloria J. Fenner, pp. 243–46. The Amerind Foundation and Northland Press, Dragoon and Flagstaff.

McKusick, Charmion. 1980. Three Groups of Turkeys from Southwestern Archaeological Sites. In *Contributions in Science of the Natural History Museum of Los Angeles County*, vol. 330, pp. 225–35. Natural History Museum, Los Angeles.

McKusick, Charmion. 2001. *Southwest Birds of Sacrifice*. Arizona Archaeologist No. 31. Arizona Archaeological Society, Globe.

Mehrer, Mark. 2000. Heterarchy and Hierarchy: The Community Plan as Institution in Cahokia's Polity. In *The Archaeology of Communities: A New World Perspective*, edited by M. Canuto and J. Yaeger, pp. 44–57. Routledge, New York.

Mendez, Keith. 2009. Stone Tool Use in the Casas Grandes Region: Use-Wear Analysis of a Medio Period Chipped Stone Assemblage from Site 204, Chihuahua, Mexico. Master's thesis, Department of Anthropology, University of Tulsa, Oklahoma.

Mills, Barbara. 1999. Ceramics and the Social Context of Food Consumption in the Northern Southwest. In *Pottery and People: Dynamic Interactions*, edited by J. Skibo and G. Feinman, pp. 99–114. University of Utah Press, Salt Lake City.

Mills, Barbara. 2004. Identity, Feasting, and the Archaeology of the Greater Southwest. In *Identity, Feasting, and the Archaeology of the Greater Southwest*, edited by B. Mills, pp. 1–26. University Press of Colorado, Boulder.

Mindeleff, Victor. 1891. "A Study of Pueblo Architecture: Tusayan and Cibola." *Annual Report of the Bureau of American Ethnology* 8:3–288.

Minnis, Paul E. 1985a. Domesticating Plants and People in the Greater Southwest. In *Prehistoric Food Production in North America*, edited by R. Ford, pp. 309–39. Anthropological Papers 75. University of Michigan, Museum of Anthropology, Ann Arbor.

Minnis, Paul E. 1985b. *Social Adaptations to Food Stress: A Prehistoric Southwestern Example*. University of Chicago Press, Chicago.

Minnis, Paul E. 1988. Four Examples of Specialized Production at Casas Grandes, Northwestern Chihuahua. *Kiva* 53:181–93.

Minnis, Paul E. 1989. The Casas Grandes Polity in the International Four Corners. In *The Sociopolitical Structure of Prehistoric Southwestern Societies*, edited by S. Upham, K. Lightfoot, and R. Jewett, pp. 269–305. Westview, Boulder, Colorado.

Minnis, Paul E. 1992. Earliest Plant Cultivation in Desert North America. In *Origins of Agriculture: An International Perspective*, edited by W. Cowan and P. Watson, pp. 121–41. Smithsonian Institution Press, Washington, D.C.

Minnis, Paul E., and Michael E. Whalen. 2005. At the Other End of the Puebloan World: Feasting at Casas Grandes, Chihuahua, Mexico. In *Engaged Anthropology: Research Essays on North American Archaeology, Ethnobotany, and Museology*, edited by M. Hegmon and B. Eiselt, pp. 114–28. Anthropological Papers No. 94. University of Michigan Museum of Anthropology, Ann Arbor.

Minnis, Paul E., and Michael E. Whalen. 2010. The First Prehispanic Chile (*Capsicum annum*) from the U.S. Southwest/Northwest Mexico and Its Changing Use. *American Antiquity* 75:245–57.

Minnis, Paul E., and Michale E. Whalen. 2015. *Ancient Paquimé and the Casas Grandes World*. University of Arizona Press, Tucson.

Minnis, Paul E., and Michael E. Whalen. 2020. *The Prehispanic Ethnobotany of Paquimé and Its Neighbors*. University of Arizona Press, Tucson.

Minnis, Paul E., Michael E. Whalen, and R. Emerson Howell. 2006. Fields of Power: Upland Farming in the Prehispanic Casas Grandes Polity, Chihuahua, Mexico. *American Antiquity* 71:707–22.

Munro, Natalie D. 1994. An Investigation of Anasazi Turkey Production in Southwestern Colorado. Master's thesis, Department of Archaeology, Simon Fraser University, Vancouver, B.C.

Munro, Natalie. 2007. Domestication of the Turkey in the American Southwest. In *The Subsistence Economies of Indigenous North American Societies: A Handbook*, edited by B. Smith, pp. 543–55. Smithsonian Institution, Washington, D.C.

Murdock, George. 1949. *Social Structure*. Macmillan, New York.

Nelson, Margaret. 1999. *Mimbres During the Twelfth Century: Abandonment, Continuity, and Reorganization*. University of Arizona Press, Tucson.

Nelson, Margaret, Michelle Hegmon, Stephanie Kulow, and Karen Schollmeyer. 2006. Archaeological and Ecological Perspectives on Reorganization: A Case Study from the Mimbres Region of the U.S. Southwest. *American Antiquity* 71:403–32.

Nelson, Margaret, and Gregson Schachner. 2000. Understanding Abandonments in the North American Southwest. *Journal of Archaeological Research* 10:167–206.

Newell, Gillian, and Emiliano Gallaga (editors). 2004. *Surveying the Archaeology of Northwest Mexico*. University of Utah Press, Salt Lake City.

Nilsson Stutz, Liv, and Lars Larsson. 2016. Disturbing the Dead: Archaeothanatological Analysis of the Stone Age Burials at Zveijnieki, Latvia. *Journal of Archaeological Science Reports* 10:715–24.

Noguera, Eduardo. 1930. *Ruinas arqueológicas del Norte de México; Casas Grandes, (Chihuahua), La Quemada, Chalchihuites (Zacatecas)*. Publicaciones de la Secretaría de Educación Pública, Mexico City.

Odell, George. 1989. Experiments in Lithic Reduction. In *Experiments in Lithic Technology*, edited by D. Amick and R. Mauldin, pp. 163–98. BAR Series No. 528. British Archaeological Reports, Oxford.

Odell, George. 2004. *Lithic Analysis*. Kluwer Academic/Plenum, New York.

Offenbecker, Adrienne. 2018. Geographic Origin, Status, and Identity at Paquimé, Northwest Chihuahua, Mexico. Ph.D. dissertation, Department of Archaeology, University of Calgary.

Olsen, John. 1990. *Vertebrate Faunal Remains from Grasshopper Pueblo, Arizona*. Anthropological Papers No. 83. University of Michigan Museum of Anthropology, Ann Arbor.

Ortman, Scott. 2008. Action, Space, and Place in the Castle Rock Community. In *The Social Construction of Communities: Agency, Structure, and Identity in the Prehispanic Southwest*, edited by M. Varien and J. Potter, pp. 125–54. Altamira, New York.

Ottaway, B. S. 1987. Radiocarbon: Where We Are and Where We Need to Be. *Antiquity* 61:136–38.

Pailes, Matthew. 2017. Northwest Mexico: The Prehistory of Sonora, Chihuahua, and Neighboring Areas. *Journal of Archaeological Research* 25:373–420.

Pailes, Matthew, and Michael Searcy. 2022. *Hinterlands to Cities: The Archaeology of Northwest Mexico and Its Vecinos*. Society for American Archaeology Press, Washington, D.C.

Parker, Bradley, and Weston McCool. 2015. Indices of Household Maize Beer Production in the Andes: An Ethnoarchaeological Investigation. *Journal of Anthropological Research* 71:359–400.

Pauketat, Timothy. 2000. Politicization and Community in the Pre-Columbian Mississippi Valley. In *The Archaeology of Communities: A New World Perspective*, edited by M. Canuto and J. Yaeger, pp, 16–43. Routledge, New York.

Pauketat, Timothy. 2003. Resettled Farmers and the Making of a Mississippian Polity. *American Antiquity* 68:39–66.

Pauketat, Timothy. 2008. The Grounds for Agency in Southwest Archaeology. In *The Social Construction of Communities: Agency, Structure, and Identity in the Prehispanic Southwest*, edited by M. Varien and J. Potter, pp. 233–50. Altamira, New York.

Pauketat, Timothy, and Thomas Emerson. 1997. *Cahokia: Domination and Ideology in the Mississippian World*. University of Nebraska Press, Lincoln.

Pecora, Albert M. 2001. Chipped Stone Tool Production Strategies and Lithic Debris Patterns. In *Lithic Debitage: Context, Form, and Meaning*, edited by William Andrefsky, pp. 173–91. University of Utah Press, Salt Lake City.

Peterson, Elizabeth. 2011. Chipped Stone Assemblage from Site 315: Variability Within Lithic Collections in the Casas Grandes Region, Chihuahua, Mexico. Master's thesis, Department of Anthropology, University of Tulsa, Oklahoma.

Phillips, David, Jr. 1990. A Reevaluation of the Robles Phase of the Casas Grandes Culture, Northwest Chihuahua. Paper presented at the 55th Annual Meeting of the Society for American Archaeology, Las Vegas, Nevada.

Phillips, David, Jr., and John Carpenter. 1999. The Robles Phase of the Casas Grandes Culture. In the *Casas Grandes World*, edited by C. Schaafsma and C. Riley, pp. 78–83. University of Utah Press, Salt Lake City.

Phillips, David, Jr., and Eduardo Gamboa. 2015. The End of Paquimé and the Casas Grandes Culture. In *Ancient Paquimé and the Casas Grandes World*, edited by P. Minnis and M. Whalen, pp. 148–71. Amerind Studies in Anthropology. University of Arizona Press, Tucson.

Plog, Stephen, Carrie Heitman, and Adam Watson. 2017. Key Dimensions of the Cultural Trajectories of Chaco Canyon. In *The Oxford Handbook of Southwest Archaeology*, edited by B. Mills and S. Fowles, pp. 285–305. Oxford University Press, New York.

Potter, James, and Scott Ortman. 2004. Community and Cuisine in the Prehispanic American Southwest. In *Identity, Feasting, and the Archaeology of the Greater Southwest*, edited by B. Mills, pp. 173–91. University Press of Colorado, Boulder.

Prentiss, William. 2001. Reliability and Validity of a "Distinctive Assemblage" Typology: Integrating Flake Size and Completeness. In *Lithic Debitage: Context, Form, and Meaning*, edited by William Andrefsky, pp. 147–72. University of Utah Press, Salt Lake City.

Preucel, Scott. 2000. Making Pueblo Communities: Architectural Discourse at Kotyiti, New Mexico. In *The Archaeology of Communities: A New World Perspective*, edited by M. Canuto and J. Yaeger, pp. 58–77. Routledge, New York.

Rakita, Gordon. 2006. Ancestors and Elites: Emergent Complexity, Ritual Practices and Mortuary Behavior at Paquimé, Chihuahua, Mexico. In *Religion in the Prehispanic Southwest*, edited by C. Van Pool, T. Van Pool, and D. Phillips Jr., pp. 219–34. Altamira, New York.

Rakita, Gordon, and Gerry R. Raymond. 2003. The Temporal Sensitivity of Casas Grandes Polychrome Ceramics. *Kiva* 68(3):153–84.

Rappaport, Roy. 1971. Ritual, Sanctity, and Cybernetics. *American Anthropologist* 73:59–76.

Rappaport, Roy. 1999. *Ritual and Religion in the Making of Humanity*. Cambridge University Press, Cambridge.

Rautman, Alison. 2014. *Constructing Community: The Archaeology of Early Villages in Central New Mexico*. University of Arizona Press, Tucson.

Ravesloot, John C. 1988. *Mortuary Practices and Social Differentiation at Casas Grandes, Chihuahua, Mexico*. Anthropological Papers of the University of Arizona No. 49. University of Arizona Press, Tucson.

Ravesloot, John C., Jeffrey S. Dean, and Michael S. Foster. 1995. A New Perspective on the Casas Grandes Tree-Ring Dates. In *The Gran Chichimeca: Essays on the Archaeology and Ethnohistory of Northern Mesoamerica*, edited by J. Reyman, pp. 240–51. Ashgate, Aldershot, UK.

Rebnegger, Karen J. 2001. Lithic Technology, Craft Production, and Site Variation in the Casas Grandes Region. Master's thesis, Department of Anthropology, University of Oklahoma, Norman.

Redman, Charles. 2005. Resilience Theory in Archaeology. *American Anthropologist* 107:70–77.

Reed, Erik K. 1951. Turkeys in Southwestern Archaeology. *El Palacio* 58(7):195–205.

Reid, J. Jefferson, and Stephanie M. Whittlesey. 1982. Households at Grasshopper Pueblo. *American Behavioral Scientist* 25:687–703.

Reimer, Paula J., William E. N. Austin, Edouard Bard, Alex Bayliss, Paul G. Blackwell, Christopher Bronk Ramsey, Martin Butzin, et al. 2020. The IntCal20 Northern Hemisphere Radiocarbon Age Calibration Curve (0–55 cal kBP). *Radiocarbon* 62:725–57.

Rice, Prudence. 1987. *Pottery Analysis: A Sourcebook*. University of Chicago Press.

Rick, John. 1987. Dates as Data: An Examination of the Peruvian Radiocarbon Record. *American Antiquity* 52:55–73.

Riggs, Charles R. 2001. *The Architecture of Grasshopper Pueblo*. University of Utah Press, Salt Lake City.

Riley, Carroll L. 2005. *Becoming Aztlan: Mesoamerican Influence in the Greater Southwest, A.D. 1220–1500*. University of Utah Press, Salt Lake City.

Rinaldo, John B. 1974a. Medio Period Ceramics. In *Casas Grandes: A Fallen Trading Center of the Gran Chichimeca*, vol. 6, edited by Charles C. Di Peso, John B. Rinaldo, and Gloria J. Fenner, pp. 77–316. The Amerind Foundation and Northland Press, Dragoon and Flagstaff.

Rinaldo, John B. 1974b. Medio Period Stone Artifacts. In *Casas Grandes: A Fallen Trading Center of the Gran Chichimeca*, vol. 7, edited by Charles C. Di Peso, John B. Rinaldo, and Gloria J. Fenner, pp. 38–481. The Amerind Foundation and Northland Press, Dragoon and Flagstaff.

Rodrigues, Teresa, and Hoski Schaafsma. 2008. Isolated Human Remains and the Archaeological Visibility of Prehistoric Ritual Practices in the American Southwest. In *Reanalysis and Reinterpretation in Southwestern Bioarchaeology, School of Human Evolution Research Papers No. 59*, edited by Ann Stodder, pp. 27–44. Arizona State University, Tempe.

Rohn, Arthur. 1971. *Mug House, Mesa Verde National Park, Colorado. Archaeological Series 7D*. National Park Service, Washington, D.C.

Rowles, Ryan A. 2004. Stone Tool Manufacture, Craft Specialization, and Intrasite Variation at the Arroyo La Tinaja Site (204) in the Casas Grandes Region, Chihuahua, Mexico. Master's thesis, Department of Anthropology, University of Oklahoma, Norman.

Ruble, Ellen. 1996. Macaws in the Prehistoric Southwest. Master's thesis, Department of Anthropology, Northern Arizona University, Flagstaff.

Ryan, Susan C. 2008. Constructing Community and Transforming Identity at Albert Potter Pueblo. In *The Social Construction of Communities: Agency, Structure, and Identity in the Prehispanic Southwest*, edited by M. Varien and J. Potter, pp. 69-88. Altamira, New York.

Rye, Owen. 1981. *Pottery Technology: Principles and Reconstruction*. Manuals on Archaeology 4. Taraxacum, Washington, D.C.

Sanders, William, Jeffrey R. Parsons, and Robert S. Santley. 1979. *The Basin of Mexico: Ecological Processes in the Evolution of a Civilization*. Academic Press, New York.

Santley, Robert S., Michael J. Berman, and Rani T. Alexander. 1991. The Politicization of the Mesoamerican Ballgame and Its Implications for the Interpretation of the Distribution of Ball Courts in Central Mexico. In *The Mesoamerican Ballgame*, edited by V. Scarbrough and D. Wilcox, pp. 3–24. University of Arizona Press, Tucson.

Sayles, Edwin B. 1936a. *An Archaeological Survey of Chihuahua, Mexico*. Medallion Papers No. 22. Gila Pueblo, Globe, Arizona.

Sayles, Edwin B. 1936b. *Some Southwestern Pottery Types*. Series 5. Medallion Papers No. 21. Gila Pueblo, Globe, Arizona.

Schaafsma, Curtis F., and Carroll L. Riley. 1999. Analysis and Conclusion. In *The Casas Grandes World*, edited by C. F. Schaafsma and C. L. Riley, pp. 237–49. University of Utah Press, Salt Lake City.

Schiffer, Michael. 2003. Foreword to *The Archaeology of Settlement Abandonment in Middle America*, edited by Takeshi Inomata and Ronald Webb, pp. xi–xviii. University of Utah Press, Salt Lake City.

Schmidt, Kari. 2005. Faunal Remains for Site 204 and 242, Chihuahua, Mexico. Manuscript on file with the Department of Anthropology, University of Tulsa, Oklahoma.

Schorger, Arlie. 1966. *The Wild Turkey: Its History and Domestication*. University of Oklahoma Press, Norman.

Schott, Michael. 1986. Radiocarbon Dating as a Probabilistic Technique. *American Antiquity* 57:202–30.

Schroeder, Albert. 1968. Birds and Feathers in Documents Relating to Indians of the Southwest. In *Collected Papers in Honor of Lyndon Lane Hargrave*, edited by Albert H. Schroeder, pp. 95–114. Papers of the Archaeological Society of New Mexico 1. Museum of New Mexico Press, Santa Fe.

Schwartz, Christopher, Stephen Plog, and Patricia Gilman (editors). 2022. *Birds of the Sun: Macaws and People in the U.S. Southwest and Mexican Northwest*. Amerind Studies in Anthropology. University of Arizona Press, Tucson.

Scott, Stuart D. 1966. *Dendrochronology in Mexico*. University of Arizona Press, Tucson.

Searcy, Michael, and Todd Pitezel. 2017. Explorations in Viejo Period Archaeology at the Vista del Valle Site in Chihuahua, Mexico. In *Shallow Pasts, Endless Horizons: Sustainability and Archaeology*, edited by J. Favreau and R. Patalano, pp. 138–43. Proceedings of the 48th Annual Chacmool Conference. The Chacmool Archaeological Association of the University of Calgary.

Searcy, Michael, and Todd Pitezel. 2018. An Ethnoarchaeological Perspective on Ground Stone Production at the Santiago Quarry in the Casas Grandes Region, Chihuahua, Mexico. *Latin American Antiquity* 29:169–84.

Senior, Louise, and Linda Pierce. 1989. Turkeys and Domestication in the Southwest: Implications from Homol'ovi III. *Kiva* 54(3):245–59.

Shackley, M. Steven. 2005. *Obsidian: Geology and Archaeology in the North American Southwest*. University of Arizona Press, Tucson.

Shackley, M. Steven. 2021. Distribution and Sources of Secondary Deposit Archaeological Obsidian in Rio Grande Alluvium, New Mexico, USA. *Geoarchaeology* 36:808–25.

Shafer, Harry. 2003. *Mimbres Archaeology at the NAN Ranch Ruin*. University of New Mexico Press, Albuquerque.

Sinopoli, Carla. 1991. *Approaches to Archaeological Ceramics*. Plenum, New York.

Skibo, James B. 1992. *Pottery Function: A Use-Alteration Perspective*. Plenum, New York.

Skibo, James B., Eugene B. McCluney, and William Walker. 2002. *The Joyce Well Site on the Frontier of the Casas Grandes World*. University of Utah Press, Salt Lake City.

Snow, Meradeth, Harry Schafer, and David Smith. 2011. The Relationship of the Mimbres to Other Southwestern and Mexican Populations. *Journal of Archaeological Science* 38:3122–33.

Sobolik, Kristin, Laurie Zimmerman, and Brooke Guilfoyl. 1997. Indoor Versus Outdoor Firepit Usage: A Case Study from the Mimbres. *Kiva* 62:283–300.

Speller, Camilla, Brian Kemp, Scott Wyatt, Cara Monroe, William Lipe, Ursula Arndt, and Dongya Yang. 2010. Ancient Mitochondrial DNA Analysis Reveals Complexity of Indigenous North American Turkey Domestication. *Proceedings of the National Academy of Sciences* 107:7:2807–12.

Spielmann, Katherine (editor). 1998. *Migration and Reorganization: The Pueblo IV Period in the American Southwest*. Anthropological Research Papers No. 51. Arizona State University, Tempe.

Spielmann, Katherine. 2002. Feasting, Craft Specialization, and the Ritual Mode of Production in Small-Scale Societies. *American Anthropologist* 104:195–207.

Spielmann, Katherine, and E. A. Angstadt-Leto. 1996. Hunting, Gathering, and Health in the Prehistoric Southwest. In *Evolving Complexity and Environmental Risk in the Prehistoric Southwest*, edited by J. Tainter and B. Tainter, pp. 79–106. Santa Fe Institute, Santa Fe, New Mexico.

Sprehn, Maria S. 2003. Social Complexity and the Specialist Potters of Casas Grandes in Northern Mexico. Ph.D. dissertation, Department of Anthropology, University of New Mexico, Albuquerque.

Stanish, Charles. 2009. The Evolution of Managerial Elites in Intermediate Societies. In *The Evolution of Leadership: Transitions in Decision-Making from Small-Scale to Middle- Range Societies*, edited by K. Vaughn, J. Eerkens, and J. Kanter, pp. 97–119. School of American Research Press, Santa Fe, New Mexico.

Stewart, Joe D., Jane H. Kelley, A. C. MacWilliams, and Paula J. Reimer. 2005. The Viejo Period of Chihuahua Culture in Northwestern Mexico. *Latin American Antiquity* 16:169–92.

Swannack, J. D. 1969. *Big Juniper House of Mesa Verde, Colorado*. Paper No. 7C. National Park Service, Washington, D.C.

Swanson, Eric R., Kirt A. Kempter, Fred W. McDowell, and William C. McIntosh. 2006. Major Ignimbrites and Volcanic Centers of the Copper Canyon Area: A View into the Core of Mexico's Sierra Madre Occidental. *Geosphere* 2:125–41.

Szarka, Heather J. 2006. Exotica and Ritual Power at Casas Grandes and La Tinaja: Two Contemporary Sites in Northwest Chihuahua, Mexico. Master's thesis, Department of Anthropology, University of Oklahoma, Norman.

Taylor, R. E. 1997. Radiocarbon Dating. In *Chronometric Dating in Archaeology*, edited by R. E. Taylor and M. Aitken, pp. 65–96. Plenum, New York.

Thibodeau, Alyson, Leonardo López Lujan, David J. Killick, Frances F. Berdan, and Joaquin Ruiz. 2018. Was Aztec and Mixtec Turquoise Mined in the American Southwest. *Science Advances* 4:1–8.

Thomas, David. 1986. *Refiguring Anthropology: First Principles of Probability and Statistics*. Waveland, Prospect Heights, Ill.

Tomka, Steve, and Marc G. Stevenson. 1993. Understanding Abandonment Processes: Summary and Remaining Concerns. In *Abandonment of Settlements and Regions: Ethnoarchaeological and Archaeological Approaches*, edited by C. Cameron and S. Tomka, pp. 191–95. Cambridge University Press, Cambridge.

Townsend, Richard. 2005. Casas Grandes in the Art of the Ancient Southwest. In *Casas Grandes and the Ceramic Art of the Ancient Southwest*, edited by R. Townsend, pp. 14–65. The Art Institute of Chicago and Yale University Press, Chicago and New Haven.

Tucker, Fiona. 2010. Woven into the Stuff of Other Men's Lives: Treatment of the Dead in Iron Age Atlantic Scotland. Ph.D. dissertation, Department of Archaeology, Geography, and Environmental Sciences, University of Bradford, UK.

Turner, Christy. 1999. The Dentition of Casas Grandes with Suggestions of Epigenetic Relationships Among Mexican and Southwestern U.S. Populations. In *The Casas Grandes World*, edited by C. F. Schaafsma and C. L. Riley, pp. 229–33. University of Utah Press, Salt Lake City.

VanPool, Christine, and Elizabeth Newsome. 2012. The Spirit in the Material: A Case Study of Animism in the American Southwest. *American Antiquity* 77:243–62.

VanPool, Christine, and Todd VanPool. 2007. *Signs of the Casas Grandes Shamans*. University of Utah Press, Salt Lake City.

VanPool, Christine, Todd VanPool, and David Phillips (editors). 2006. *Religion in the Prehispanic Southwest*. AltaMira, New York.

VanPool, Todd, and Robert D. Leonard. 2002. Specialized Ground Stone Production in the Casas Grandes Region of Northern Chihuahua, Mexico. *American Antiquity* 67:710–30.

VanPool, Todd, and Christine VanPool. 2016. Animating Architecture and the Assembly of an Elite City: Birth and Dedication of Nonhuman Persons at Paquimé, Chihuahua, Mexico. *Journal of Anthropological Research*: 3:311–66.

VanPool, Todd, Christine VanPool, Rafael Cruz Antillón, Robert D. Leonard, and Marcel J. Harmon. 2000. Flaked Stone and Social Interaction in the Casas Grandes Region, Chihuahua, Mexico. *Latin American Antiquity* 11:163–74.

Vargas, Victoria D. 1995. *Copper Bell Trade Patterns in the Prehispanic U.S. Southwest and Northern Mexico*. Archaeological Series 187. Arizona State Museum, Tucson.

Varien, Mark. 1999. *Sedentism and Mobility in a Social Context: Mesa Verde and Beyond*. University of Arizona Press, Tucson.

Varien, Mark. 2010. Depopulation of the Northern Southwest: A Macroregional Perspective. In *Leaving Mesa Verde: Peril and Change in the Thirteenth Century Southwest*, edited by T. Kohler, M. Varien, and M. Wright, pp. 1–33. University of Arizona Press, Tucson.

Varien, Mark, and James Potter. 2008. The Social Production of Communities: Structure, Agency, and Identity. In *The Social Construction of Communities: Agency, Structure, and Identity in the Prehispanic Southwest*, edited by M. Varien and J. Potter, pp. 1–20. Altamira, New York.

Vierra, Bradley. 2020. Chipped Stone Artifact Analysis. In *Early Farming and Warfare in Northwest Mexico*, edited by Robert Hard and John Roney, pp. 311–42. University of Utah Press, Salt Lake City.

Walker, William, and Judy Berryman. 2023. Ritual Closure: Rites de Passage and Apotropaic Magic in an Animate World. *Journal of Archaeological Method and Theory* 30:449–94.

Walker, William H., and Gaea McGahee. 2006. Animated Waters: Ritual Technology at Casas Grandes, Chihuahua. In *Precolumbian Water Management: Ideology, Ritual, and Power*, edited by L. Lucero and B. Fash, pp. 189–203. University of Arizona Press, Tucson.

Waller, Kyle. 2017. Bioarchaeological Analysis of Paleodemography and Violence at Paquimé, Chihuahua, Mexico. Ph.D. dissertation, Department of Anthropology, University of Missouri, Columbia.

Waller, Kyle, Adrienne Offenbecker, Jane Kelley, and Anne Katzenberg. 2018. Elites and Human Sacrifice at Paquimé: A Biological Assessment. *Kiva* 84:403–23.

Ward, G. K., and S. R. Wilson. 1978. Procedures for Comparing and Combining Radiocarbon Age Determinations: A Critique. *Archaeometry* 20:19–31.

Ware, John. 2014. *Pueblo Social History: Kinship, Sodality, and Community in the Northern Southwest.* School for Advanced Research Press, Santa Fe, New Mexico.

Weaver, David S. 1981. An Osteological Test of Changes in Subsistence and Settlement Patterns at Casas Grandes, Chihuahua, Mexico. *American Antiquity* 46:361–64.

Welch, Paul. 1998. Outlying Sites Within the Moundville Chiefdom. In *Archaeology of the Moundville Chiefdom*, edited by V. Knight and V. Steponaitis, pp. 133–66. Smithsonian Institution Press, Washington, D.C.

Whalen, Michael E. 1994. *Turquoise Ridge and Late Prehistoric Residential Mobility in the Desert Mogollon Region.* Anthropological Papers No. 118. University of Utah Press, Salt Lake City.

Whalen, Michael E. 1998. Ceramic Vessel Size Estimation from Sherds: An Experiment and a Case Study. *Journal of Field Archaeology* 25:219–27.

Whalen, Michael E. 2013. Wealth, Status, Ritual, and Marine Shell at Casas Grandes, Chihuahua, Mexico. *American Antiquity* 78:624–39.

Whalen, Michael E. 2022. Obtaining Macaws: Breeding Versus Procurement, and the Case of Paquimé, Chihuahua, Mexico. In *Birds of the Sun: Macaws and People in the U.S. Southwest and Mexican Northwest*, edited by C. Schwartz, S. Plog, and P. Gilman, pp. 221–40. Amerind Studies in Anthropology. University of Arizona Press, Tucson.

Whalen, Michael E., Arthur MacWilliams, and Todd Pitezel. 2010. Reconsidering the Size and Structure of Casas Grandes, Chihuahua, Mexico. *American Antiquity* 75:527–51.

Whalen, Michael E., and Paul E. Minnis. 2000. Leadership at Casas Grandes, Chihuahua, Mexico. In *Alternative Leadership Strategies in the Prehispanic Southwest*, edited by B. Mills, pp. 168–79. University of Arizona Press, Tucson.

Whalen, Michael E., and Paul E. Minnis. 2001a. *Casas Grandes and Its Hinterland: Prehistoric Regional Organization in Northwest Mexico.* University of Arizona Press, Tucson.

Whalen, Michael E., and Paul E. Minnis. 2001b. Architecture and Authority in the Casas Grandes Region, Chihuahua, Mexico. *American Antiquity* 66:651–99.

Whalen, Michael E., and Paul E. Minnis. 2009. *The Neighbors of Casas Grandes: Excavating Medio Period Communities of Northwest Chihuahua, Mexico.* University of Arizona Press, Tucson.

Whalen, Michael E., and Paul E. Minnis. 2012. Ceramics and Polity in the Casas Grandes Area, Chihuahua, Mexico. *American Antiquity* 77:403–23.

Whalen, Michael E., and Todd Pitezel. 2015. Settlement Patterns of the Casas Grandes Area. In *Ancient Paquimé and the Casas Grandes World*, edited by P. Minnis and M. Whalen, pp. 103–25. Amerind Studies in Anthropology. University of Arizona Press, Tucson.

Whittaker, John. 1994. *Flintknapping: Making and Understanding Stone Tools.* University of Texas Press, Austin.

Wilcox, David. 1995. A Processual Model of Charles C. Di Peso's Babocomari Site and Related Systems. In *The Gran Chichimeca: Essays on the Archaeology and Ethnohistory of Northern Mesoamerica*, edited by J. Reyman, pp. 281–319. Ashgate, Brookfield, Vt.

Willhite, Brenton. 2016. Status and Stones in the Casas Grandes Region: Analysis of Debitage from the 76 Draw Site (LA 156980). *Kiva* 82:95–116.

Wills, Wirt, and Patricia Crown. 2004. Commensal Politics in the Prehispanic Southwest: An Introductory Review. In *Identity, Feasting, and the Archaeology of the Greater Southwest*, edited by B. Mills, pp. 153–72. University Press of Colorado, Boulder.

Wills, Wirt, and Robert Leonard. 1994. Preface to *The Ancient Southwestern Community*. Edited by W. Wills and R. Leonard, pp. viii–xvi. University of New Mexico Press, Albuquerque.

Wilson, S. R., and G. K. Ward. 1981. Evaluation and Clustering of Radiocarbon Age Determinations: Procedures and Paradigms. *Archaeometry* 23:19–39.

Windes, Thomas. 1987. The Use of Turkeys at Pueblo Alto Based on Eggshell and Faunal Remains. In *Investigations at the Pueblo Alto Complex, Chaco Canyon, New Mexico*, vol. 3, part 2, *Artifactual and Biological Analyses*, edited by F. Mathien and T. Windes, pp. 679–90. National Park Service, Santa Fe, New Mexico.

Yaeger, Jason, and Marcello Canuto. 2000. Introducing an Archaeology of Communities. In *The Archaeology of Communities: A New World Perspective*, edited by M. Canuto and J. Yaeger, pp. 1–15. Routledge, New York.

Index

abandonment: Di Peso's model of Casas Grandes River valley, 36–37, 264, 267; door sealing and, 93, 241; gradual, 265; new interpretations of, 264–66; possible "rebound" of environment after, 243; as redistribution of population, 266; ritual closure and, 115, 118

Adams, E. Charles, 90

agave: cultivation, 46, 85; as important food, 213, 214–15; large-scale baking more an Outer Core than Inner Core phenomenon except at Paquimé, 215, 247; ovens, 48, 212, 247; piedmont slopes as prime land for, 85, 172, 247; tabular knives, 166, 180, 194

agriculture: flood plain, 211; irrigation, 210, 255; upland, 211–12. *See also* agave; maize

Ahumada Polychrome, 71, 80, 81, 129, 131, 134, 135

Alamito site (Site 178), 261

Animas area, 259

antelope, 226, 228

Antelope Wells obsidian source, 163

anthropogenic ecology/environmental change, 210; in animals, 234–35; in plants, 216, 223–24, 236

architecture: adobe construction, 8, 79, 94–96; columns, 109, 110; continuities between Early and Late Medio of, 8; doorways, 91–93; jacal, 68–69, 81–82; pit structures, 308; post collars, 96–97; room alcoves, 87–88, 89; room shape, 87–88; room size, 81–82, 85–87; sealed doorways, 92, 93; storage boxes, 88; styles of used by Di Peso to define phases at Paquimé, 6–7; T-shaped doorways, 91; wall niches, 93, 94; wall thickness, 82–85, 246. *See also* "architecture of power," ball courts; Casas Grandes Architectural Tradition; fire features; Post-Casas Grandes Architectural Tradition; room block mounds; room function; under individual site names

"architecture of power," 10, 86, 87; large rooms with elaborate shapes as, 246; in miniature at Site 242 and Site 298, 85; multistoried room blocks with thick walls as, 227, 246; platform hearths as, 104; ritual architecture as, 247; used to emphasize Paquimé's

legitimacy, 22; wall thickness as, 246

Arthur, John W., 158

Babícora Basin, 259

Babícora Polychrome, 131, 135

ball courts, 29; absence in Inner Core settlements and centralization at Paquimé of, 260; at Alamito site, 261; at Animas sites, 259; I-shaped, 141, 153, 154, 247, 253–54, 256, 259; lacking in Middle Zone, 17; in Outer Core, 259, 260; at Paquimé, 6, 17, 255; possible elaboration of forma of in Late Medio, 153–54, 260; public ritual centered on, 247; at Site 204, 151, 153, 247, 261; at Site 242, 21, 141, 227, 247, 255, 261; sooted sherds and, 153, 248; types of, 253–54, 260

Bartlett, John, 258

Beck, Robin A., Jr., 254

Berryman, Judy, 115

Billman, Brian, 249

bison, 208, 226, 227, 235

Black ceramics: associated with ritual, 146; on Core Zone sites, 121, 127, 128, 129, 138–39, 140; erosion of, 157, 160, 161; jar volumes of, 147

Black-on-red ceramics, 81, 121, 130, 133, 140, 160
Brand, Donald D., 14–15
Buena Fe phase, 9
burials and human remains: disarticulated, 89–91, 118; intramural, 88–91, 111–12; maize starch grains in teeth of, 158, 213; most were not elaborate, even at Paquimé, 209; were often in room corners, 74; at Site 315, 111–12, 118

cacao or yaupon holly, 218–19
Casa Chica, 44
Casas Grandes Architectural Tradition (CGAT), 63; burial pits in room corners characteristic of, 74; ceramic type diversity during, 128–29; did not originate with Paquimé, 125; end of, 113, 118; late remodeling at Paquimé of, 242–43; room size of, 85–87; Type 1 architecture of, 121–22; wall thickness of, 82–85; See also "architecture of power," ball courts; Medio period; room block mounds
Casas Grandes region, 4–5; diet focused on maize with animals and wild plants important in, 236; Late Medio effects on animal and plant populations in, 234–35; occupation extended beyond the abandonment of Paquimé in, 241–44; population of overestimated by Di Peso, 35; possibility of small occupation into the 1500s in, 243; scalar hierarchies in, 239
ceramic function: erosion/pitting, 156–58, 161; residues, 156; sooting, 151–56, 160, 248; very large jars likely for food preparation of communal events, 213, 214
ceramics: assessment of proposed Late Medio I/II distinction,

131–36; distribution in Core Zone of, 128–31; diversity of, 128–29; Early Medio, 129, 130, 131, 132; frequency of imported, 29; jar/bowl ratio of, 160; jar and bowl rim sherd counts of, 140; Late Medio, 129–30, 131–36; type diversity of, 128–29; use of rim sherds to distinguish bowls from jars, 138–39; vessel diameters of, 148–51; volumes of, 141–47; ware summary, 126–27. See also ceramic function; polychrome ceramics; individual type names
Cerro Juanaqueño, 163
Chaco Canyon, 93, 231–32, 269
chile, 213, 214, 216, 217–18, 220, 235
chipped stone: analysis methods, 164; assemblage composition, 167; bipolar flaking, 181–82, 193; cores, 167, 168–70, 193; discard rate compared with ceramics, 166, 193; expedient production and use of, 193, 194; flake characteristics, 170–71, 173–79, 194; flake size, 194; raw materials, 163, 166, 167, 171–73, 193; retouched tools scarce, 194; soft vs. hard hammer reduction, 194. See also projectile points; obsidian
Chupadero Black-on-white, 29, 135
communities: apical organization of seems doubtful, 241; association with places of, 258; are close together in Inner Core, 36; concept of "larger community of interests" for, 259–60; definition of, 18, 257; identity formation and, 257; indicators of complexity in, 10; richness measures of, 246, 249–51. See also Inner Core Zone; Outer Core Zone; individual site names
Convento site, 15, 67, 68–69, 253
copper, 204–6, 248, 250

Core Zone: community richness scores of, 250–51; date frequency histograms for small sites in, 241–42; occupation histories of, 61–62; stone tool use in, 193–96. See also Inner Core Zone; Outer Core Zone
corn beer, 158–59, 161, 213
Corrugated Brown, 81, 130
Crumley, Carole, 239
Cunningham, Jerimy J., 255, 260

Diablo phase, 36–37, 113, 125, 242, 246. See also Terminal Casas Grandes Architectural Tradition (TCGAT)
Di Peso, Charles C.: asserted that bison were the main source of meat at Paquimé, 226; believed existence of Paquimé the result of Mesoamerican stimuli, 6; on end of Paquimé, 112; overestimated population of Paquimé, 35; on Paquimé people as "virtually vegetarians," 213; on platform hearths, 102; room function classification of, 106–8; saw break in architecture from Late Viejo to Early Medio, 67–68; saw massacre as cause of end of Paquimé, 264
Dublán Polychrome, 39–40, 72, 131, 135

Early Medio, 5; architecture, 8–9, 60, 67, 252; ceramics, 39–40, 72, 81, 129, 130, 131, 132, 134–35, 159, 252; chile use, 217–18; dating of, 7, 251; development scenario, 254–55; large roasting oven in, 59, 254; has less disturbance plant taxa than Late Medio, 224; lithic technology, 164–65; obsidian in, 253; ritual paraphernalia less common than in Late Medio, 253; shell, 199–200, 253. See also Site 204; Site 299A; Site 315; Site 565

El Paso Polychrome, 80, 81, 134–35
El Zurdo site, 233

faunal remains: analysts erro-
neously overestimated role
of bison and other species at
Paquimé, 226, 230; important
food species were antelope,
deer, and rabbits at Paquimé,
226; shift from jackrabbits to
cottontails in PCGAT related
to changing brush cover, 229;
species list of, 228
Feinman, Gary, 268
fire features: fire pits, 98, 99;
hearth sizes, 100–102; platform hearths, 98, 99–100,
105; type frequencies of, 101;
served common essential
domestic functions, 104; uses
of, 105; vented hearths, 98, 99

Galeana site, 259
Gamboa, Eduardo, 5–6, 61
Gila Polychrome, 80, 132, 135
gourds, 213, 220
Grasshopper Pueblo, 90, 257
ground stone, 183; bird cage doors
and stoppers, 184, 186, 187, 188,
195; bowls and pestles, 191–93;
diversity differences in small
and large sites of, 195–96;
effigies, 187; food preparation
with, 185, 188; frequencies, 184;
luxury, symbolic, ceremonial,
and architectural functions of,
185–86; manos, 184, 188–89;
metates, 190–91; other implements, 191–93; raw materials
used for, 162, 195

Harmon, Marcel J., 260

Inner Core Zone: alcoves in, 89;
caffeinated drinks in, 218–19;
ceramic densities on mounds
in, 28; ceramic diversity in,
128–29; chipped stone from,
165–82; as a community, 257,
258; community function

indicators for sites in, 10;
community richness scores
for, 250–51; date frequency
histograms for, 240–42;
defined, 245, 257, 258; eroded
ceramics from, 157–58; faunal
remains from, 227–29; fire
features in, 98–100, 103, 104;
fragmented social landscape
beyond, 259; ground stone
from, 183–93; imported
ceramics from, 29; intramural architectural elements
in, 91–97; jar/bowl ratio
in, 140–41; jar diameter in,
150–51; jar volume in, 142–48;
lack of evidence of anthropogenic ecological change
in, 224; lacks ceremonial or
feasting facilities outside of
Paquimé, 256; large ovens
rare in outside of Paquimé,
215; large sites in, 38–41; loss
of sites in, 38; luxury items
and exotica rare outside of
Paquimé, 195, 198–201, 204,
207–8, 209, 248; map of sites
in, 39; mound density in, 25;
mound heights and areas in,
19–24, 32, 33; occupational
histories in, 61–62, 240–45;
organization of, 245; PCGAT
remodeling at small sites
in, 243, 268; Ramos Poly-
chrome in, 249; remodeling
at small sites in, 243, 268;
ritual architecture rare in
outside of Paquimé, 247–48;
room blocks per settlement
in, 26–27, 34; room shape in,
87, 88; room size in, 85–86;
settlement distribution in,
36; settlements in dependent
upon Paquimé, 250, 258,
260, 261; site selection in,
38–40; small sites in, 41–52,
242; sooted sherds from, 153,
154, 160; turkeys from, 236;
Viejo occupation in, 63–67;
wall thickness in, 83–85, 246;

wood from late sites in, 222.
See also Convento site; Los
Reyes No. 2; Paquimé; Site
290; Site 291; Site 299A; Site
315; Site 321; Site 355; Site 565

Joint Casas Grandes Project
(JCGP), 3, 15, 16. See also Di
Peso, Charles C.
Joyce Well site, 202, 259

Late Medio, 36; access to marine
shell reduced and use of
freshwater shell increased in,
200, 252–53; anthropogenic
ecological change in, 224,
234–35, 236; architecture
continuity with Early Viejo
of, 8–9, 252; ball courts/
games of, 154, 253–54; ceramic
erosion in, 157–59; ceramics,
129–30, 131–36; chile use in,
217–18; dating of, 7, 251; development scenario for, 255–56;
end of, 136–37, 262–68;
faunal remains from, 227–28;
fluorescence of CGAT in, 125;
increased ritual activity in,
253, 254; more intense lithic
reduction in, 165; obsidian
use dominated by Paquimé
in, 253; occupation history
of sites in, 61–62, 239–44;
plant use diversity high in,
219; proposed I/II ceramic
division of, 131–36; radiocarbon dates for, 55, 56–60, 79,
80; separation from Early
Medio based upon presence
of Ramos Polychrome, 8,
129–30; use of pine in, 223;
utilitarian ceramics from, 8,
244. See also Casas Grandes
Architectural Tradition
(CGAT); individual site
names
Lekson, Stephen, 5, 15, 99–100
Little Barley, 214, 216, 220, 235
Los Reyes No. 2, 70–72
Loven, Jeremy, 235

luxury items and exotica, 183, 195: concentrated at Paquimé, 209, 248, 258; local, 249; nonlocal, 248; as sacred, animate objects that sanctify and empower the place where they are concentrated, 263. *See also* copper; macaws; shell; turquoise

macaws, 29, 248, 253
maize: cob found in hearth, 215; as most common plant remain, 213; has greater ubiquity in Casas Grandes area than in southern Chihuahua, 225. *See also* corn beer
McConnan Borstad, Courtney, 236
Medio period: early recording from surveys of, 14–16; most utilitarian ceramics used in continued after decline of Paquimé, 244; original definition of, 6–7; proposed starting date in mid-twelfth century for, 69; surface structures in, 69. *See also* Early Medio; Late Medio; Casas Grandes Architectural Tradition (CGAT)
Mendez, Keith, 180
Mesoamerica, 263; ball courts in, 254, 260; crops from, 217, 218; Di Peso conviction that Paquimé owed its existence to stimuli from, 6, 13, 67–68, 207, 251, 252; symbols on Ramos Polychrome derived from, 252, 256
Middle Zone: ball courts absent in, 255; ceramic densities, 28; contrasted with Inner Zone, 17; definition of, 16; few sumptuary or exotica items in, 209; imported ceramics in, 29; map of, 17; mound area and room block size in, 22–26, 31–33, 45; mound groupings in, 30–33; obsidian sources in, 163; as part of Paquimé's "larger community of interests," 259;

population estimate for, 34; Ramos Polychrome common in, 249; room block size and mound height in, 19–21; room count in, 34; sherd density in, 28; smallest site size histogram for, 45
Mimbres area, 233, 265, 267
Mimbres Black-on-white, 14, 29, 68–69, 135
Minnis, Paul E., 269
Mission of San Antonio de Padua, 244
mounds. *See* roomblock mounds
Moundville site, 241

Noguera, Eduardo, 19

obsidian, 163, 172, 195, 249
Outer Core Zone: anthropogenic ecology change in, 224; ball courts and large feasting ovens in, 247, 260; bird cage doors abundant in, 29, 204; ceramics from, 127–29, 131, 146, 249; chipped stone flakes from, 164–65, 167–69, 171, 173–74, 176–79; chipped stone tools from, 180, 182; community richness scores for, 250–51; copper from, 205, 206; definition of, 258–59; eroded ceramics from, 157–58; faunal remains from, 227, 229, 236; fire features in, 98, 100, 101, 103–5; ground stone from, 183–86; imported sherds from, 29; intramural architectural elements in, 88, 91–96; jar/bowl ratio of, 140–41; lithic materials from, 166–67, 170–73; luxury items and exotica rare from, 248; macaw from, 204; minerals and ornaments from, 207; mound area and room block size of, 22–26, 31–33; mound heights of, 19–21; had no frequent face-to-face interaction with Paquimé, but part of "larger community

of interests," 258–61; obsidian from, 163; plant remains from, 19–20, 212, 213, 214, 216, 219–20; population of settlements in, 35; projectile points from, 182; room blocks per settlement, 30; room count of, 26–28, 34; room floor area of, 85–86, 105; shell from, 198, 200; sherd density of, 28; site occupation spans in, 61–62, 239–40, 242, 243; small sites in, 62, 86, 100, 113, 128, 140–41, 153, 158, 168–69, 172, 173–74, 186, 216, 227, 243, 248, 251; sooted sherds from, 153–56; has suitable environment for agave, 247, 262; tabular knives from, 194; vessel diameters of, 150–51; Viejo pit structures in, 64, 65, 66; wall thickness of, 82, 83–85. *See also* Casa Chica; Site 204; Site 231; Site 242; Site 317
Outer Zone, 16–17, 163, 202, 259
ovens: common in Outer Core, 247, 260, 261; Early Medio example at Site 299A, 59, 254; few found within 15 km of Paquimé, 17–18; as indicator of community richness, 250, 254; large, as indicator of community complexity and commensal activities, 10, 224; at Paquimé, 48, 212, 215, 247; at Site 204, 153, 247, 261; at Site 315, 115; at Site 317, 247; very large one at Site 299A, 48–49, 247

Pailes, Matthew, 209, 263, 269
Paquimé: adobe columns and stairways at, 95, 96; architecture an extreme amplification and elaboration of Early Medio, 252; arose out of regional Early Medio cultural tradition, 260, 267; ball courts at, 6, 17, 48, 212, 215, 247, 255; beginning of, 5; ceramic

tradition extended beyond decline of, 242; collection of faunal remains sporadic and limited at, 225; "community of interests" of, 259; community richness score of, 250, 251; concentration of ceremonial and feasting facilities at, 256; corporate mode of organization of, 263; dating with ceramics from, 131–32; defined storage rooms lacking at, 106–8; doorways at, 92, 93; elaborate room shapes at, 87, 246, 250; as an elaborate, short-lived version of preexisting Casas Grandes culture, 9; end of, 5–6, 262, 266, 267; environmental degradation and subsistence stress were factors in abandonment of, 266; eroded ceramics from, 158; fire features at, 98–99, 101–4; ground stone from, 184; jacal-walled structures at, 69–70; lack of evidence of massacres in abandonment of, 266; large amount of obsidian going into, 195; Late Medio rise of, 255–56; limit of daily interaction with estimated at 15 km, 18; monopoly of exotic and imported goods by, 196, 200, 256, 258; as only site with indication of large-scale storage, 248; organized more closely to Southwest Pueblo societies than Mesoamerica, 266, 268; ovens at, 48, 212, 215, 247; peaks in mounds at may represent founding social units at, 257–58; pit ovens at, 212, 215; plant remains from, 212; productive advantage over peers of, 255; projectile points from, 181; pull factors in founding of, 266; radiocarbon dates from, 6; revised concept of community for, 257–58; rise of correlated with addition

of fine-line ceramic painting, 8; rise of new ideology with, 256; ritual architecture at, 6–7, 153, 247, 258; ritual rather than elite leadership at, 263, 264; room block size and height at, 18–19; room floor area of, 86; room function at, 106–8, 112; room size at, 104; shell from, 198, 201–2; sooted vessels from, 153; subterranean rooms at, 112; turkey use at, 234; utilitarian sherds from, 141; Viejo period at, 61, 69–70; wall niches at, 93; wood use at, 221, 236. See also "architecture of power"
Phillips, David, Jr., 5–6, 61
Pierce, Linda, 234
Pitezal, Todd, 186, 190, 253, 258
Plain Brown: body diameters of, 150; as dominant ceramics in Casas Grandes area, 8, 127–28, 130; jar and bowl volumes by site size for, 143, 144; jar/bowl ratio for, 140; surface erosion of, 157; survived end of Paquimé and continued in use in early colonial period, 137, 159, 160, 244, 268
plants: remains of, 211–25; anthropogenic ecology of, 223–24; regional comparison of, 224–25; ubiquity scores of, 214, 220. See also agave; little barley; maize; wood
Playas Red, 81, 112, 133, 134, 135
polychrome ceramics, 8; bowls rare in, 160; diversity at small sites of, 129; Early Medio, 68, 71–72, 129, 131, 132, 252; erosion rare on, 157, 160, 161; high frequency of as measure of community complexity, 10; jar/bowl ratio of, 140; jar volumes of, 146–47; Late Medio, 129–30, 131–33, 134, 137; Medio painting styles, 130; progression at Site 315, 131; residues on, 156, 218–19; as special

use containers, 128. See also individual type names
population: date frequencies used as proxy for, 239–42; issue of estimating settlement, 33–35; Late Medio envisioned to have large, 235; of Medio period overestimated by Di Peso, 35
Post-Casas Grandes Architectural Tradition (PCGAT), 113, 125, 160; continued use of Late Medio ceramic tradition in, 267, 268; crude remodeling of small Inner Core sites in, 243, 251; jar volumes of sites of, 144; lithic technology of, 194; has lower ceramic diversity than CGAT, 128–29, 159, 161; as time when shell was not coming into area, 199. See also Site 242; Site 290; Site 315; Site 321; Site 355
Preucel, Scott, 257
projectile points, 110, 170, 181–83, 194–95
Pueblo Alto, 141, 233
Pueblo Bonito, 93

radiocarbon dates: from Di Peso's work, 6, 61; from human remains, 6; for Ramos Polychrome, 8. See also under individual site names
Ramos Black, 81, 127, 133, 134, 135
Ramos Polychrome: was added to preexisting Early Medio ceramic assemblage, 252; associated with new ideology and Mesoamerican symbolism, 256; defines Early/Late Medio boundary, 8; imprecisely defines Late Medio I and II, 131, 159; as measure of participation in a ritual-based system of community organization, 249; as "signature ware" of Paquimé, 249; at Site 204, 132–33, 134; at Site 290, 46, 121; at Site 315, 135; at Site 565, 80

Ramos site, 205
Red-slipped (Red ware) ceramics, 126; bowl/jar ratio of, 160; on Core Zone sites, 127; jar volumes of, 145–46; pitting of, 157, 161; rim characteristics of, 140; at Site 204, 129; at Site 321, 121; very large jars of, 127, 140, 213–14
Riggs, Charles R., 92–93
Riley, Carroll L., 6
Rinaldo, John B., 138, 188, 192, 193
Rio Gavilán Composanto site, 259
ritual architecture and paraphernalia, 10: at Paquimé, 6–7, 153, 247, 258; at Site 204, 250; at Site 242, 262
ritual closure or termination, 115–18
Robles phase, 37, 244
room block mounds: as basic unit of analysis for Medio period, 18; groupings of, 30–33; peaks in at Paquimé may represent founding social units, 257–58; relation of mound size and ceramic density, 28–29; room block size and height of, 19–22; room block size estimated from mound area, 22–26; room counts estimated from mound area, 26–28, 34; sherd density on, 28–29; small mounds with low ceramic density represent briefly occupied sites, 28
room function: does not sort into clear categories at Paquimé, 106–8, 112; issue of defining store rooms, 106, 107; most rooms in the Core Zone seem to be general purpose, 108–9; special purpose rooms at Inner and Outer Core Zone sites, 109–12

Sand Canyon Pueblo, 141
Sayles, Edwin B., 14, 15
Schaafsma, Curtis F., 6

Searcy, Michael, 186, 190, 209, 253, 258, 263, 269
Senior, Louise, 234
settlement patterns: differences in organization between Inner and Outer Core Zones of, 18; of Inner Core Zone, 36, 239; Medio, 14–18; scalar hierarchy of among Paquimé neighbors, 239; small site problem, 10–11; three zones used to consider, 15–17; Viejo, 13–14
shell: beads, 197, 198; concentrated at Paquimé but scarce at neighboring communities, 202; counts of, 198; freshwater, 199, 200, 201; as materialization of supernatural power, 201–2; species used, 199–200; use in Early Medio, 252–53
Sierra Fresnal obsidian source, 164
Site 204, 7, 13; adobe columns at, 94, 96; adobe stairway at, 95; agave from, 219, 220, 222; architecture at, 8, 9, 68; ball court at, 247; ceramic change at, 129, 130; ceramics from, 8, 68, 132, 133, 134, 141, 147, 150; ceramics from cast doubt on Late Medio I/II subdivision as a regional pattern, 133; column bases at, 110; community richness score of, 250–51; decline in Late Medio of, 244; Early Medio at, 8, 9, 68, 132–33, 223, 224, 240, 252; empty burial pits and scattered human bone at, 89; eroded ceramics from, 158; exemplifies Early Medio site, 252; exotica from, 248; ground stone implements from, 184; Late Medio rooms at, 133; macaw burial at, 248; ovens at, 247; pit house with adobe platform fire pit at, 64–65, 103; plant taxa show increasing disturbance, 224; population of, 35; as possible community center, 261; possi-

ble subperiod division of Late Medio at, 153–54; radiocarbon dates from, 66, 239–40, 241; ritual architecture at, 250; room floor area of, 86; shell from, 198, 200, 252; small pit house at, 66; sooted vessels at, 153, 155, 159; special purpose room at, 109–10; tabular knives from, 180; ubiquity of plant remains at, 219–20; utilitarian sherds from, 141; vented hearth at, 98; Viejo period at, 239–40, 261; wall niche at, 93; wall thickness at, 84; wood remains from, 222, 223, 224
Site 231, 62, 93; adobe platform at, 94; ceramic type diversity of, 129; community richness score for, 250–51; eroded ceramics from, 158; ground stone implements from, 184; radiocarbon dates from, 62; room floor area at, 86; shell from, 198; sooted vessels at, 153; utilitarian sherds from, 141
Site 242, 62; architectural similarities to Paquimé of, 21–22; butterfly-shaped room at, 87; ceramic type diversity at, 129; commensal activity at, 21; community richness score of, 250–51; eroded ceramics from, 158; evidence of corn beer making at, 247; ground stone implements from, 184, 185; high jar/bowl ratio at, 141; lack of shell from, 202; large mammal bones from, 227; platform hearths at, 103; platform mound and I-shaped ball court at, 141, 227, 247, 255, 261; Plain Brown body diameters at, 141; as possible Paquimé outpost/control node/administrative satellite/agent, 85, 102, 156, 161, 227, 262; ritual architecture at, 250, 262; room floor area at, 86; sooted vessels from, 153, 155, 156; trincheras

near, 85; utilitarian sherds from, 141; wall thickness at, 21, 246

Site 290, 46; architectural simplicity of, 104; Brown jar volumes at, 144; ceramic type diversity of, 129; community richness score of, 250, 251; eroded ceramics from, 158; fire features at, 122, 124; ground stone implements from, 184; late occupation at, 121, 123–24; plan of, 47; radiocarbon dates from, 56–59; room floor area of, 86; sooted vessel frequency of, 153; subterranean room at, 112; utilitarian sherd count from, 141; walls and floors of, 122; wall thickness at, 308

Site 291, 45, 53

Site 298, 26: doorways at, 91, 93; room floor area at, 86; S-shaped rooms at, 87; wall thickness at, 84, 85

Site 299A, 46, 48, 59, 247

Site 315, 40–41; adobe columns at, 96; adobe stair at, 95; agave from, 220, 222; Black jar volume at, 147; Brown body diameters at, 150; burials, 308–9; chile seeds from, 218; colonnaded area at, 109; community richness score of, 250–51; corn cob in hearth at, 215; date frequency histogram for, 240–41; doorways at, 91, 92, 93; Early Medio at, 55, 134–35, 217–18, 240; effigies and bird cage stones from, 187; eroded ceramics from, 158; evidence of ritual closure of, 115, 118; faunal remains from, 227–29; fire features at, 98, 103; flotation samples from, 212, 213; ground stone from, 184; late use of, 113–14; pit structure at, 64, 65; plan of, 40; plans of rooms at, 42; polychrome at, 131, 133–34; post-abandonment activities at, 266; post collars

at, 97, 110; projectile points from, 182; radiocarbon dates from, 54–56, 135, 240; roasting pit at, 114, 115; ritual para- phernalia and exotica from, 247, 248; room floor area of, 86; scattered human remains from, 90–91, 94, 118; shell from, 198, 200; sooted vessels from, 153, 155; special purpose rooms at, 109, 110–11; ubiquity of plants from, 219–20; utilitarian sherds from, 141; Viejo period at, 41, 55, 133; wall niches at, 94; wall thickness at, 83, 84, 85, 246; wood remains from, 221–23

Site 317, 62: ceramic type diversity of, 129; community richness score of, 250–51; eroded ceramics from, 158; gourds from, 213; ground stone from, 184; obsidian from, 163; oven at, 247; pit house at, 64, 65; projectile point from, 182; radiocarbon dates from, 62, 65; room floor area of, 86; shell from, 198, 200; sooted vessels from, 153, 156; utilitar- ian sherds from, 141; vessel diameters at, 163

Site 321, 49; Brown jar volumes at, 144; ceramic type diversity of, 129; community richness score of, 250–51; eroded ceramics from, 158; late remodeling at, 120–21; plan of, 50; radiocar- bon dates from, 59, 60; room floor area of, 86; sooted vessels from, 153; stone building at, 49, 50; utilitarian sherds from, 141; wall thickness at, 85

Site 355, 46, 49; Brown jar vol- umes of, 144; ceramic type diversity of, 129; community richness score for, 250, 251; doorways at, 91–92, 93; Early Medio occupation at, 60; eroded ceramics from, 158; faunal remains from, 227–29;

ground stone from, 184; hearth at, 103; late construc- tion/remodeling at, 118–20, 243; Plain Brown jar volumes at, 144; plan of, 51; possi- ble evidence of rebound of mammal populations from hunting pressure in Late Medio at, 235; possible turkey bones from, 233; radiocarbon dates from, 60, 243; room floor area at, 86; shell from, 198, 200; sooted vessels from, 153; stone construction at, 51, 52; utilitarian sherds from, 141; wall thickness at, 85

Site 565, 41, 44; adobe platforms and steps at, 94–95; Area Z at, 72–82; Black jar volume at, 147; Brown pottery diameters at, 150; ceramics from, 80, 81, 141; chile seeds from, 218; community richness score for, 250–51; date frequency histogram for, 240–41; Early Medio at, 67, 78, 80, 81, 240; eroded ceramics from, 158; exotica from, 248; fire pits at, 98, 99; flotation samples from, 212, 213; ground stone from, 184; jacal structures at, 67; pit structure at, 66, 67; plan of, 43, 44; platform hearths at, 103; projectile points from, 182; radiocarbon dates from, 56, 57, 78, 79, 240–41; room descriptions for, 74–79; room floor area at, 86; shell from, 198, 200; sooted vessels from, 153, 155; three occupation episodes at, 79–80; utilitarian sherds from, 141; Viejo period at, 41, 78, 79–81; wall niches at, 94; wall thickness at, 83, 84, 85; wood remains from, 221–23

sotol, 166, 212

St. Johns Polychrome, 135

Tarahumara, 231

Teotihuacán, 241

Terminal Casas Grandes Architectural Tradition (TCGAT), 63, 115, 125. *See also* Diablo phase

Textured Brown ceramics, 127, 145

theobromine, 156, 160

Tinaja site, 10

trincheras, 85, 211–12

Tucker, Fiona, 91

Turkey Creek Pueblo, 106

turkeys: burials of, 233, 234; criteria used to tell if they were eaten, 234; evidence for non-food use of, 234; issues of how intensive turkey husbandry was, 233; possibility of breeding at Paquimé of, 229–30; possibility of capture of wild birds, 231; as source of food in Southwest U.S. after AD 900, 233; use at Paquimé less intensive and shorter duration that in Southwest U. S., 233

turquoise, 207–8

vesicular basalt, 185–88, 249

Viejo period, 5; at Convento site, 64, 67, 68–69; copper from, 206; Di Peso's view of, 12–13; Late surface structures of transitioned to Early Medio architecture, 67–82, 125; at Los Reyes No. 2, 70–72; at Paquimé, 61, 69–70; pit structures of, 63–67, 308; is present on most Medio period sites, 13–14, 29, 61, 240–41; projectile points from, 182; at Site 204, 239–40, 261; at Site 315, 41, 55, 133; at Site 565, 41, 78, 79–81; Southern, 225

Viejo Red-on-brown, 13

Villa Ahumada Polychrome, 80, 131, 135

Villa Ahumada site, 229, 259

Walker, William, 115

Whalen, Michael E., 269

White-Paste Babícora Polychrome, 72, 131, 135

Windes, Thomas, 93

wood: increase of pine in Late Medio indicates depletion of local species, 223, 224; possibility that pine wood was reduced to charcoal before transportation, 223, 236; similarities of flood plain and upland sites in use of, 221–22

About the Authors

Michael E. Whalen (PhD, University of Michigan) is a professor emeritus in the Department of Anthropology at the University of Tulsa. His research interests include complex societies, processes of sociocultural evolution, prehistoric social structure, and ceramic analysis. Before coming to the Casas Grandes area in 1989, he worked in Mesoamerica on the Valley of Mexico Survey Project in central Mexico, on the Valley of Oaxaca Human Ecology Project in Oaxaca, and in several parts of the U.S. Southwest. He has published books, monographs, chapters, and journal articles on Oaxaca, western Texas, southern New Mexico, and northwest Chihuahua. His research has been supported by a series of grants from the National Science Foundation as well as by the National Geographic Society. He has served as a chairman for the Southwest Symposium Biannual Meeting and as editor for the Archaeological Papers of the American Anthropological Association.

Paul E. Minnis (PhD, University of Michigan) is a professor emeritus of anthropology at the University of Oklahoma, now living in Tucson, Arizona, where he is a visiting scholar in the School of Anthropology at the University of Arizona. He conducts research on the pre-Hispanic ethnobotany and archaeology of Northwest Mexico and the U.S. Southwest. Although he has worked throughout the region, his first intensive archaeological research in the area was on the ancient Mimbres tradition centered on southwestern New Mexico, and his primary field research since 1984 has focused on Paquimé and its regional setting in northwestern Chihuahua, Mexico. He has co-directed research projects in this area since 1989, and he has published extensively on ethnobotany. He is the author or editor of fourteen books and numerous articles. He has been the president of the Society of Ethnobiology, treasurer and press editor for the Society for American Archaeology, co-founder of the Southwest Symposium, and co-vice president of the Arizona Archaeological and Historical Society. He has received the E. K. Janaki Amal Medal and the Byron Cummings Award, and he was a Sigma Xi Distinguished Lecturer.